Praise for Linda Crist's *The Bluest Eyes In Texas*

Ravigo Zomana, The Virginia Gayzette

"Crist has done an excellent job of keeping the adventure hopping, as villains come from all different angles, and our lead characters struggle to find balance and safety in their lives. The action is seemingly real and doesn't feel contrived."

Blayne Cooper, Author of *Cobb's Island, Echoes from the Mist, The Last Train Home,* and *Unbreakable*:
"Linda Crist's debut novel is a winner! The novel's easy-to-read style, realistic dialogue, and good pacing make it a pleasure to read. The plot is two-fold and well-crafted. Office intrigue allows for plenty of action and conflict while the women's budding romantic relationship is allowed to progress at a solid, believable pace. The author takes her time, treating the reader to hours of great reading and drawing you into the storyline inch by inch. I'm anxious to see other works from this new author."

Stephanie Solomon, Editor of Telltale Kisses:
"What a *fantastic* book! I can't recommend it highly enough! It's a must-have for any home library."

Galveston 1900: Swept Away

Linda Crist

Yellow Rose Books

Nederland, Texas

ISBN 1-932300-44-9

First Printing 2005

9 8 7 6 5 4 3 2 1

Cover design by Donna Pawlowski

Published by:

Yellow Rose Books
PMB 210, 8691 9th Avenue
Port Arthur, Texas 77642-8025

Find us on the World Wide Web at
http://www.regalcrest.biz

Printed in the United States of America

Acknowledgments

Thank you to:

Liz Brock, for sending me the book, *The Good Old Days – They Were Terrible*.

Blayne Cooper for suggesting the books *Everyday Life in the 1800's*, and the *Sears Roebuck Catalogue*.

Cindy Cresap, for your invaluable insight and suggestions, and your hours of hard work on the first round of edits.

Donna, for the fabulous cover art.

Lucy, Renee, and Rob, the original sources of inspiration.

Phil (The Great Oz), for maintaining the Galveston Café Press charity shop at the Academy.

Stephanie Solomon, for creating the artwork for the products at the Café Press shop.

The many people who sent me photographs and links on Galveston.

A few years ago someone mentioned she would like to see a story about the 1900 hurricane. Thank you, Gloria, for the idea and the inspiration. This one is especially for you and Jodi.

Dedication

To the Posse, the BB's, the Orlando BardCon staff, the Subtext Virtual Season staff, and the Texas Pups—thank you for sharing fun, friendship, and your lives.

To the on-line readers—thanks for riding along on this crazy ongoing adventure in writing.

And as always, to Suzanne, Jay, and Henry, with much love.

Chapter
One

A SHINY BLACK bicycle sped around the corner onto Broadway, and down a low-grade hill. The rider held onto her straw cowboy hat, her long wavy chestnut hair streaming out behind her as she dodged pedestrians and buggies. She bumped precariously over clumps of sandy soil in the middle of the packed dirt street, causing horses at various hitching posts along the way to shy, while others merely whinnied in protest at the disturbance of another busy March morning. The woman steered the vehicle sharply to the right and skidded to a stop in front of the general store. She quickly dismounted and leaned the bicycle against a post before entering the small market.

Her eyes wandered over the tidy interior, as she glanced wistfully at rich slabs of cheese and barrels of bright-colored hard candy and an array of expensive chocolates behind a glass case. She pushed back her hat and let it dangle against her shoulder blades from two rawhide ties as she shook her thick hair into some semblance of order. She hooked her thumbs into a pair of navy blue suspenders and rocked back on her heels, pretending to decide what she wanted.

"Good morning to you, Miss Travis." The shopkeeper nodded at her before turning his attention back to a precisely lined ledger, his pencil scratching across the surface as he calculated sales for the prior month. "Your tab will be due next week." He glanced back at her. "Just a reminder."

"Morning, Mr. Williams." She moved closer to a case of meats and breads. "I get paid this evening. I'll settle up with you on Monday if that's all right."

"That will be fine, Rachel." Mrs. Williams, a short plump woman with graying hair and round spectacles entered from a back storage room, offering her a pleasant smile. "What would you like this fine day?"

Rachel gazed longingly at hearty roast beef and ham and released a quiet sigh. "Quarter pound of the pre-cooked salt pork and a half dozen plain wheat crackers, please." Browsing the offerings was merely a diversion, and they all three knew it. Rachel Travis ordered the same thing, five days a week, come rain or come shine. It was all she could afford.

"Tchh." Mrs. Williams shook her head in kind reproach. She wrapped up the order in a brown bag and winked at the younger woman, then tucked in two dill pickles and several licorice whips, an extra treat at no charge. "Hard-working girl like you needs more than crackers and pork to get you through the day. It's a wonder you don't shrink up and blow away."

"I get two squares a day with my room." Rachel smiled and accepted her dinner. "I get by on that pretty well. This is just a snack to tide me over until supper time." She pulled her hat back up and secured the ties under her chin. "Thank you, ma'am. If you'll add it to my tab, please."

"Have a good day, Miss Travis." The shopkeepers watched the proud woman turn, the sunlight burnishing her hair with bright auburn highlights as she made her way back outside.

She hopped back on the bicycle and dropped her bag into a basket on the back, and then she was off. A cool salty breeze blew in from the Gulf and she inhaled in appreciation, feeling the early morning sun on her tanned face. She would be cursing the sun before day's end, but for now, in the first rays after dawn, the warmth was welcome as it beat through the light-weight blue-checkered cotton of her long-sleeved shirt and the darker navy material of her denim work trousers.

Four blocks from the Port of Galveston, her destination, she heard a loud explosion and felt the front tire rim on her bike begin to rattle. "Dammit!" The rubber outer tire was quickly shredding, along with the inner tube. She took a firm grip on the handlebars, trying to control the metal rim, to no avail. The rim stuck in a rut and the frame twisted sideways, throwing her headfirst over the handlebars. She tucked and rolled, tumbling into tall marsh grass at the side of the road.

"Ouch!" She stood, rubbing her elbow, and glanced down at it. Her shirt was ripped and the elbow was scraped and bleeding. "Damn." She bent over, retrieving her now-crushed straw hat, and hobbled back to the bike. A quick self-assessment revealed that her pride was damaged most of all. The bike tire and tube could be replaced, and the dirt on the frame buffed off. Her elbow would heal. She would, however, be late for work.

"Hey!" Several seagulls swooped down, snatching up what she realized were her crackers, which had spilled out of the dinner bag. She ran over and grabbed the salt pork, pickles, and licorice, blowing sand off them, then stuffed them back inside the torn bag. "Perfectly good waste of money," she muttered under her breath, glaring at the birds, which hovered overhead mocking her, the crackers clutched in their sharp beaks. "Go on! You won't be getting anything else from me." She shooed at the air with a wide sweep of her arm, and watched them fly away toward the water.

It was a long walk, pushing the bicycle the last four blocks.

The Wall Street of the Southwest, Galveston was the second wealthiest city in the country, due to the vast port, which was visited by over one thousand freighters a year. Just a few blocks from port, the cotton mill and the factories added to the pot, providing jobs and income to many of the island's thirty-eight thousand residents. Goods were shipped in and out of the city, between Texas and the Midwest, much of the rest of the country, and even overseas.

As Rachel neared the port, she could see the burly dock manager standing at the end of the pier, hands on hips, waiting for her. *Great. Just great.*

"Travis." His disapproving voice carried across the last half block. "You're fifteen minutes late. Either you work late to make it up, or I take it from your pay this evening. Your choice."

"Sorry I'm late, Mr. Avery. As you can see, I have a flat tire. I'll work the extra minutes tonight." She parked the useless bike against the pier railing. "Where do you need me today? Back on the cotton freighter?"

"Yes. Show some hustle. They need all the hands they can get to load that boat so it can pull out of here at first light tomorrow." He dismissed her with a wave of his hand, stroking his short black beard with the other as he checked her off on his list, the last employee to arrive for the day.

"Yes, sir." She pulled a pair of thick work gloves from her back pocket, donning them as she trotted toward the last boat off the end of the pier, her heavy boots clunking loudly on the wooden planking of the dock. Without a word, she took up a place among a group of workers, nodding a brief greeting at the two men on either side of her. They formed a line, loading large bales of cotton from the Galveston mill onto a freighter, which would then deliver the cargo to ports all along the Gulf coast and up the Eastern seaboard.

The job would last until sunset. Before day's end, the men would be stripped to their bare chests, and Rachel would be down to a sweaty cotton undershirt, which clung to her skin, along with sand and sea salt, forming a fine layer of grime over her arms, neck, and face. She fell into the familiar routine, working alongside her male companions.

She was accepted as one of the boys, and had worked at the port since running away from home at age fifteen, her body changing from that of a girl to a young woman in the eight years that had passed. It was a strong body, lean and carved with muscles, but the body of a woman, nonetheless, a fact not lost on many of her fellow dock workers, especially on days like the one at hand, when she started out with her hair spilling over her shoulders and down her back. By noon it would be braided, or pulled up into a knot against the back of her neck.

Rachel felt the sun growing warmer, and broke from the line long enough to dampen a handkerchief in the water bucket before folding it and tucking it into the brim of her hat, taking a long sip from the dipper while she was there. Working the cotton line wasn't her favorite assignment, but it was honest labor and her wages were fair. She much preferred the days when one of the fishing boats called her aboard, and she could spend the day out on the open water, sharing cigars and whiskey while they trawled for shrimp or moved to deeper seas in search of bigger fish.

At noon she hastily ate her salt pork dinner, then resumed her place in line. Rachel mused that she was glad to be handling the end product outside, under the wide-open sky, rather than inside the sweltering heat of the nearby factory with the mill workers. She had known from an early age that she wasn't meant to be cooped up inside for long. Her skin — indeed, all her senses — craved the sun, the wind, the rain, or whatever Mother Nature had to offer.

When the sun finally set, the dock master carefully counted out their weeks' wages and the workers scurried away. It was Friday and most had families to go home and tend to. Others, like Rachel, had evening plans. True to her promise, she took up a long-handled broom and began sweeping the dock area of bits of cotton and baling material, a task often reserved for whoever arrived late for assignment.

"Rachel." A sandy-haired man stopped on his way to the end of the pier. "Will you be joining us for some draw-poker this evening?" He clapped her on the back with one hand, withdrawing a hand-rolled cigar from his shirt pocket with the other.

"Hello, Billy. You have another one of those?" Steel-colored eyes twinkled at him charmingly.

"For you, of course." He retrieved another and reached across, tucking it into Rachel's own front pocket with a cheeky grin.

"I'll be at the saloon, but I'm tending the bar tonight, so I won't be able to play." Her voice was filled with regret. Rachel loved nothing better than a good game of poker, especially on payday. Unknown to the others, she could and did count cards. She didn't do it every game, but sometimes, when she really needed extra income, she wasn't beneath using her secret skill to her own advantage.

"Well, then, I reckon I'll see you later tonight, if not at supper." Billy tipped his hat to her and moved on, making his way four miles southeast across town to the same boarding house where Rachel lived.

"Thank you kindly for the cigar." She waved at him, then quickly finished her work, dumping the sweepings in a large barrel for burning later. After collecting her wages and apologizing again for her tardiness, she began the long walk home, pushing her bicycle along beside her. The store was already closed, so she wouldn't be able to purchase a new tire and tube until the next morning. Her shoulders slumped. *There goes more money I wasn't planning on spending. Maybe I can manage to play a few hands of poker and make up the difference.*

She reached the boarding house and slipped through the main entry parlor into a long hallway. It was cool and humid inside, a welcome respite from the day's activities. She wearily climbed the stairs and turned, opening the first door to the right, entering her room. She quickly grabbed a change of clothing from an old armoire, along with a towel, and ducked back out, eyeing the community water closet at the far end of the hall. Rachel smiled. The door was open, indicating it was available.

Much later, after a quick bath in the large claw-foot tub, and an even quicker supper of ham and baked beans, she rode to the end of the trolley line, then hitched a ride on the back of a buggy to a small establishment a few miles south of town, which was typically filled to the rafters on Friday and Saturday evenings. It was there that Galveston's finest often co-mingled with the seedier members of society. Wealthy bored men came to spend their money on poker and fine liquor. The less fortunate came to win the spendings of the wealthy, while drinking the cheaper whiskey offered as the house staple.

Although there were many finer drinking establishments in town along the Strand, many men came to partake of one of this particular saloon's less-advertised offerings. It was more than a place to drink and play games. It was also an assignation house, frequented by some of the city's young beautiful ladies of ill repute. Local authorities turned their heads, for the most part.

Rachel entered the saloon, blinking at the already smoke filled room. Laughter rang out, along with the clinking of glass and the shuffle of cards, while a piano player produced raucous music from an upright instrument in one corner, one foot tapping against the wood-planked floor, while the other worked the piano pedals.

"Hi, Lil."

She smiled at one of the prostitutes who lived above the saloon. "How's business?"

"We'll see." The blonde woman moved closer, whispering conspiratorially as Rachel took her place behind the bar, automatically grabbing a rag to swipe down the counter. "See that gentleman over there?" Lillie nodded slightly toward an olive-skinned man who was involved in a poker game with some of the town's high rollers.

"Good prospect?" Rachel immediately disliked the man, finding his straight black hair annoying, and his dark eyes too beady. She didn't trust him, though she didn't know why.

"Maybe." Large blue eyes met Rachel's, and Lillie twisted a purple grosgrain hair ribbon around one finger while she talked. "He's been buying me drinks all evening, and he comes over and talks to me during breaks in the game. He seems to have a lot of notes to spend."

"I hope it works out for you," Rachel lied. She did hope good things came her friend's way. A part of her, however, felt protective of Lillie. And, she acknowledged, possessive. Lillie alone knew Rachel's deepest darkest secret, and often indulged it, when not otherwise occupied. Rachel reached out, tugging a long blonde ringlet affectionately. "Looks like his game is finished."

Lillie looked up, just as the man approached the bar. "Shot of whiskey." His voice was flat, his eyes flicking over Rachel before quickly dismissing her. "And a brandy sour for the lady." The last word was drawn out, whether as a compliment or as a sarcastic slight, Rachel couldn't tell. Her dislike deepened.

"So, sweet thing," the man turned all his attention on Lillie, "perhaps you can give me a tour of this fine establishment." His eyes wandered toward the staircase, his intentions obvious as he casually rested one hand on Lillie's rump. Rachel looked away and clenched her fists, twisting them in the bar rag, lest she start a barroom brawl.

"I believe I might be able to do that." Lillie batted her pale lashes playfully, then picked up the brandy glass. "This way, sir." She made her way around the bar, holding out her arm. The man took it and they disappeared up the stairs. Rachel watched as Lillie's full lavender skirts swirled around the first bend out of sight. *That's my favorite skirt.* She sighed.

Rachel shook her head, clearing it of morose thoughts, then walked around the bar and began working the tables, taking drink orders and filling them quickly and efficiently. It was a full house and more than one patron tucked extra coinage and even a few paper notes into her hands while paying for the libations. In less than an hour she had earned the price of a new tire and tube for her bicycle.

She folded the bills and tucked them into a back pocket of her trousers, carefully buttoning it closed. The coins went into a front pocket of her shirt, which she also buttoned closed against pickpockets. She smiled at her good fortune, glad she'd earned what she needed so quickly. The smile was cut short by an ear-piercing scream from upstairs.

Rachel turned and ran, taking the steps up to the back rooms two at a time. *Lil.* She was almost certain her friend was the one who had screamed. Several men followed behind her, some out of curiosity and some bent on helping a damsel in distress. She was halfway down the hallway when she heard a second scream, definitely coming from Lillie's room.

With no further thought, she flung the door open. Lillie was on the bed, face down, her skirts pushed partway up her bare legs. The man was on top of her, holding her down, his features contorted in rage. Rachel's eyes swept over the scene, realizing Lillie's hands were bound and tied to the ornate brass bedpost. "Get off her!" She bodily grabbed the man, hauling him to his feet by his shirt collar. Before he could react, she cocked a fist and punched him soundly across his face, breaking his nose.

"You wench!" Blood spurted over his shirt as he swiped at his nose with the back of his hand. He kicked her in the shin and she kicked back, making contact with his groin. He grabbed his private parts and sank to his knees, an unintelligible groaning sound escaping his lips.

"Get him out of here." Rachel booted him from behind, sending him sprawling on his belly to the floor and eliciting another groan. "I'll take care of Lil."

Three men grabbed hold of the man and hauled him away, leaving the two women alone.

"Are you injured?" Rachel moved to untie her, working at the knots in a pair of leather suspenders.

"I think so." Lillie rolled over and sat up, rubbing her wrists where the suspenders had bound them, cutting into her skin enough to leave indentions. "Bastard."

"What happened?" Rachel sat down next to her, hesitantly touching a bruised cheek. "You've got a shiner there, Lil."

"Bastard wanted to kiss me, and you know I don't kiss my gentlemen callers. It's simply not done." She rubbed her face. "We'd already — you know — one time. He couldn't even wait for me to get my clothes off, and then he started in trying to force me to kiss him. When I refused, he punched me, and next thing I knew, he was wrestling me down and tying me up. Said he was going to take me in my arse. I think he would have, too, if you hadn't heard me." She wrinkled her nose in disgust.

"Glad I got here in time." Rachel folded her own hands, pressing them between her knees and looking down.

"Me, too." Gentle fingers tilted Rachel's chin up. "It's your lucky night, Miss Rachel. I'm not going back downstairs, and I'm not in the mood to sleep just yet."

Steel-blue eyes studied her almost shyly. "I don't have the money tonight, Lil."

"No charge." Lillie smiled. "Consider it my way of showing my gratitude for your heroic actions. Besides..." she reached inside her half-open bodice, pulling out a wad of notes. "He paid me up front, so I'm settled up for the evening."

"Are you certain?" Rachel pushed disheveled blonde curls back from Lillie's face, smoothing a mussed hair ribbon. "I mean, after what he did, maybe you should just rest."

"Nah." Lillie cuffed her on the arm. "It would take more than that bastard to put me out of commission. Come on. It's been a while anyway. You're a breath of fresh air, Rachel, especially after the steady company of gentlemen for a few weeks. The best medicine for me is to get right back up on that horse and ride. No offense, but you're one of the more gentle horses."

This brought a genuine smile. "Well then." Rachel slowly stood. "Let me go close down my part of the bar tab. It'll be easy enough to tell them you don't want to be alone, and I'm going to sit up with you for a while. They'll leave us alone that way."

"Don't be long." Lillie stretched out on the bed, curling up on her side on the patchwork quilt and propping her head in one hand. She twirled a bodice lace between her fingers and smiled fetchingly at her.

"I won't." Rachel slipped out of the room, hurrying quietly down the stairs.

"RACHEL." LILLIE GENTLY prodded a bare arm.

Rachel was sprawled stomach-down across her, her long hair spilling over both of them. Her head was cradled against Lillie's shoulder and she had one leg tossed across Lil's thighs.

"Sugar, you need to wake up."

Rachel mumbled something unintelligible, and slowly stroked her hand around the curve of Lillie's hip and up her side, cupping her breast while she ground her pelvis against her leg. "Mmm. I've missed you, Lil." She smiled, her eyes still closed, savoring the memory of their tryst the night before.

"I've missed you, too, but you must wake up now." Lillie shoved a little harder. "Sun's already up."

"Eh?" Rachel shot up to a sitting position, groaning and throwing one arm across her eyes. She peeked out again and cursed quietly at the pale gray light filtering through the lace curtains hanging over the window. "Dammit!"

Long legs swung over the feather bed and she scrambled into her drawers, then hopped around the room pulling up her trousers while she tucked in a very rumpled shirt, while Lillie giggled quietly at her. She located her stockings under the bed and tugged them on, followed by her boots. "Can you...?"

Lillie grabbed a brush from the top of her armoire and motioned Rachel to sit down while she ran it through tangled brown waves, trying for some semblance of order. "Stop that!" She swatted a wandering hand away from her bare inner thigh, then grinned affectionately at the blue eyes that batted innocently back at her. "You are going to go to Hell, Miss Travis."

"Guess I'll be in good company, then." Rachel stood as Lillie laid the brush aside. "Thank you, my dear." She took one soft hand in her own and pecked the top of it, the only kiss she was allowed. "For everything." She winked, then turned the doorknob.

"You be careful, Rachel." Lillie untwisted one of her suspenders, playfully snapping it into proper place. "Don't let anyone see you leaving here."

"I'm always careful." Then she was gone, the door clicking softly closed behind her.

The hallway was blessedly empty, and she crept quietly around those boards that she knew creaked. She reached a narrow door and pushed it open, coming out on the fire escape. She scanned the alleyway, and satisfied she had no observers, quickly clamored down the rickety stairs and made the last long leap to the ground. Pausing for a moment, she leaned against the back wall of the saloon and waited for her heartbeat to return to a normal pace.

Being with Lillie was dangerous. She wasn't entirely sure she would be prosecuted, but at best, if they were caught together, she would be ridiculed publicly. More likely, they might both be run off the island. She kicked the sandy ground savagely and began walking in no particular direction, her boots crunching in the hard-packed loam. Home was several miles north, and it wasn't appealing to her at the moment.

After wandering aimlessly for a while, she wound up on the beach south of town, facing the Gulf of Mexico, a place that always soothed her soul. It was just past dawn, the pink-tinged sky stretching to meet a silver-hued ocean at the horizon. A gentle steady breeze blew in off the waves, rustling the tall grasses in the sand dunes that formed natural protection for the island from erosion. Seagulls chattered among themselves, dipping into the water to catch tiny fish. Small sand crabs scurried away from her feet as she walked, and she smiled slightly as they disappeared back into the water where they belonged.

She reached a private fishing dock and ambled to the end, sitting down and removing her boots and socks. Rolling up her trouser legs, she dunked her feet into the cold water and wiggled her toes in pleasure, listening to the roar of the waves as they washed over her feet. She had no idea who owned the house up the beach that the dock went with, but no one had ever complained about her occasional visits there. It was a place she came to when she was feeling out of sorts.

Rachel closed her eyes, ordering her thoughts. She wondered, for the millionth time, why she was so different from any other women she knew. True, she was accepted in Galveston, having lived there for a very long time without causing any real trouble. She had become a fixture, like the docks, the mill, and the grand old homes in the nicer parts of town. She just was, and no one seemed to mind her being there. Most people were polite to her, if not friendly, and she had a handful of people she considered to be friends, more of them male than female.

She knew some of the townspeople whispered about her when they thought she wasn't listening, knew they found her manner of dress odd, and her choice of work even stranger. She was the only woman who labored on the docks, and the only one on the island who chose to wear trousers and men's shirts. No one had ever directly questioned her about her clothing or her choice of work, and as far as she knew, no one suspected just how different she really was.

Lil. She sighed, then flung a piece of lose planking into the water. Rachel knew who and what Lillie was, and never judged her for it. She, of all people, had no right to judge anyone for their sexual behavior. Rachel was at times deeply ashamed of urges she seemed to have no control over. She worked very hard to never let her true nature show, taking extra care not to stare at any of the pretty ladies in town, or to become overly friendly with any of them. As a result, she had little female acquaintance, though some of the town's matrons had tried, unsuccessfully, to take Rachel under their wing, mothering her to the point of becoming smothering if she allowed it.

Lillie had taken Rachel under her wing in a different way. Lillie just somehow knew what she was, and had made the first move, luring Rachel to her room the first time under the guise of giving her a tour of the upstairs portion of the saloon. Rachel had been to that same room off and on over the six years that had passed since that first time, as Lillie's availability and Rachel's resources permitted.

She had no idea why Lillie was willing to allow the things they did together, and had never questioned it. She was simply grateful Lillie was willing, and she insisted on paying, just like everyone else, rarely accepting "charity" as she had the previous night. Lillie seemed to enjoy her attentions as much as she enjoyed Lillie's, and she allowed Rachel to be the aggressor most of the time.

Rachel brought her feet up and hugged her arms around her knees. She didn't understand why she needed to do the things she did with Lillie. She had tried, for a time, to allow some of the young men in Galveston to court her, even going so far as to wear skirts when she wasn't working. More than a few of the eligible bachelors had taken notice, and for a few months, she was wined and dined at some of Galveston's finer establishments. Rachel in a dress, with her hair curled and pinned up, made an elegant picture of femininity.

It didn't last. She had been miserable the entire time, finding the clothing restrictive and the men unattractive. After that, she tried instead to be celibate. She knew her thoughts and the things she wanted to do were sins, mortal ones at that. Raised Catholic, she hadn't been to confession in years. She occasionally attended mass, but always sat in back and slipped away without taking the communion sacrament.   Her soul was too soiled to deserve communion, or to be redeemed by penance.

Celibacy didn't suit her either, and she eventually found herself back at the saloon and in Lillie's bed. She tried after that, to accept things for what they were, and herself for whom she was. If she was going to go to Hell, she might as well enjoy the journey. On mornings like the present one, however, she hated herself and who she was all over again, and she hated having to sneak away from the saloon in shame.

She closed her eyes and tilted her face up toward the sun, which was rising higher in the sky. She enjoyed the sensation of the wind as it whipped through her hair and sniffed delicately, then opened her eyes again, looking down to locate the source of the scent of fresh tobacco. Ah. She spied her cigar. She had transferred it from her torn checkered shirt to the white one the night before, but never got around to smoking it. That could be remedied, later. She drew the cigar out and sniffed it in appreciation, running its length under her nose.

Her nose twitched and she tucked the cigar back into her pocket, instead lifting the collar of her shirt and inhaling the scent of Lillie's Lemon Verbena Toilet Water. Another twitch of her nose singled out another, more personal fragrance of Lillie's, and Rachel blushed at her own thoughts. She wrapped her arms around her legs again and rested her forehead on her upraised knees. "Why did you make me like this?" It was an almost silent whispered prayer, something she rarely did anymore, convinced no one was really listening.

Her thoughts were interrupted as something large and soft brushed against her arm and wrapped around it. "Yah!" Her head popped up and she grabbed the offending object, almost flinging it away. It was a large piece of cream-colored paper and she stopped, noticing some charcoal etchings. "What's this?" She carefully spread it open, studying an etching of the Gulf shoreline, and a dock, and — she tilted her head and scrunched up her forehead — a woman with long dark hair wearing trousers and sitting on the end of the dock. "That's me," she said to no one at all, tracing the drawing with her fingertip while she held the paper down against the dock with her other hand and one knee.

Slowly, she looked around and down the beach, trying to determine where the etching had come from. Another pass located a color amiss among the browns and greens of the dunes, a bit of unnatural blue. Rachel stood, making out a woman's shoe as well, along with what appeared to be the top of a hat. "Ma'am?" She rolled up the drawing. "Is this yours?" She held it up in her fist, over her head.

The shoe moved and another appeared next to it, then the hat began moving upward, disclosing reddish-auburn hair and a pale face. Pale except for her cheeks, which were blushing nicely, clearly visible even from where Rachel stood.

Rachel chuckled and began walking back up the dock to the beach and through the thick loose sand above the packed part closer to the water, until she reached the spot where the shy artist stood, looking down at her feet and shuffling uncertainly from side to side.

"It's very good," Rachel offered.

"Thank you. Both for the compliment and for catching it. The wind blew it out of my hands." Very slowly, the dove-colored bonnet tilted up, and a pair of wide hazel eyes blinked sheepishly. "Please forgive me," she said in a soft melodic voice. "I didn't mean to intrude on your privacy."

"No need to apologize." Rachel held the drawing out to the woman, while taking in her thick red hair, pulled into a twist at the back of her neck. The woman wore a crisp white ruffled blouse, which was tucked into a blue skirt that was fitted at the waist, then flared out, falling to just above her black shoe-tops. Her features were very young. Rachel frowned, as she noted a fading bruise around the woman's left eye, marring an otherwise perfect face with almost translucent pale skin, lightly dusted with freckles across a cute perky nose and high cheekbones. "You're quite an accomplished artist."

"I —I am?" Red lashes blinked uncertainly. "I mean, thank you." The hazel eyes dropped back down.

"You're welcome, Miss...?" Rachel trailed off, holding out her hand in formal greeting.

"Oh." The woman took her hand, and Rachel felt soft skin against her own calloused palm. "I'm Madeline. Madeline Crockett, but you can call me 'Mattie'. Most folks do."

"Pleased to meet you, Mattie." Rachel reluctantly dropped her hand after briefly shaking it. "My name is Rachel Travis."

"Likewise." Mattie blushed again. "I truly am sorry for drawing your portrait without asking permission. I come out here sometimes, especially early in the morning when the light isn't so harsh. It's easier on my eyes for sketching." She gestured toward the sand at her feet, where a pad of paper and a few charcoal pencils rested. "I often draw whatever I see out here. Sometimes the gulls, sometimes the water itself. Today, I drew you."

"Well, Miss Crockett..."

"Mattie."

"Mattie." Rachel smiled charmingly. "You can draw me anytime you want to."

"Maybe I will." Mattie glanced up at the sky. The pink tint was gone, replaced by pale blue patches and fluffy white cumulus clouds. "Oh. It's getting late. I'd better be going. My husband will be up by now and I should get his breakfast. Then I've got to go into town to work at the tailor's on Broadway."

"I know the place." Rachel shaded her eyes with her hand, having left her hat back at the boarding house before she went to the saloon. "Do you work there regularly?"

"All day long, Monday through Saturday." Mattie smiled. "Maybe you could stop by the house for afternoon tea sometime."

Blue eyes grew wide at the unexpected invitation. *Tea? No one ever invites me to do anything besides play poker.* She quickly returned the smile. *There's a first time for everything.* "That would be nice. I'd like that."

"Very well then, Rachel. How does a week from tomorrow sound, around mid-afternoon?" Mattie pointed toward a small cottage a ways down the beach. "That's my house, so you can come by then, if you'd like. We haven't lived here very long. It would be nice to have another woman friend. I work so much, I haven't had much time to get out and socialize with anyone."

"A week from tomorrow would be fine." Rachel stooped down, gathering up Mattie's pencils and sketchpad. She handed them over and found the rolled-up drawing pressed into her empty hand.

"Here. You can keep this, seeing as how it's a picture of you." Mattie blushed again. "I'll see you next Sunday afternoon, Rachel."

"Good-bye." She watched Mattie as she made her way up the beach toward the house. "Thank you for the drawing."

Mattie fluttered a hand in response, then clutched her bonnet to keep it from blowing off as she disappeared among the tall dune grasses. Rachel watched until she reappeared further down, and went inside the house.

Did I just make a new friend? Rachel pondered their exchange. Most of the respectable women on the island her age paid little notice to her, and she found herself feeling invisible sometimes. Mattie had looked directly into her eyes, and smiled at her, and hadn't seemed to notice at all that she was wearing men's clothing. *Maybe not everyone thinks I'm so different after all.*

Heartened, she began the long walk home.

MATTIE CREPT WARILY into the house, stepping quietly across the braided-rag rug in the entryway, in case her husband wasn't yet awake. He had come in very late the night before, and slipped into bed while she pretended to be asleep. Prior to coming to bed, he had tinkered around in the water closet for much longer than usual, cursing a few times for some unknown reason. "Adam?" she called out softly.

No answer. She stepped around the corner and into the kitchen, and nearly jumped out of her skin. "Oh."

"Where's my breakfast?" Adam's gruff voice sounded from behind the latest issue of *National Geographic*. He sat at the head of the table, chair tilted back slightly, his leg crossed over his knee, and his cigar smoke curling up from an ashtray. He didn't bother to look at her as he spoke, rifling idly through the magazine instead.

"There's some fresh-squeezed juice in the ice box." Mattie placed her sketchpad and pencils on the end of the table and hastened to pour up a glass, setting it next to him at arm's length. "Coffee is staying warm on the stove, and I have flapjacks and ham keeping warm in the oven."

"Flapjacks?" His voice gentled and he finally looked up at her turned back. "My favorite."

"I know. That's why I made them." She fetched a plate from the cupboard and opened the oven, releasing the tantalizing scent of the cornmeal cakes and melting butter, along with the rich ham. It wafted through the kitchen, warring with the cigar smoke for dominance. She dished up the meal and placed it in front of him, carefully tucking a cream-colored napkin in his lap before quickly stepping back.

"You been wasting time with those pictures again?" Adam scowled at the pad and tilted his head in scrutiny. A breeze from the open window had flipped open the cover, and a second drawing of Rachel walking along the beach was plainly visible. "Who's that?"

"Oh." Mattie ducked her head into the cupboard, searching for the maple syrup, grateful for the hidden moment to let a rising blush fade. Why she was blushing, she had no idea. "Someone who was walking on the beach. A stranger." *For now,* she added silently.

"You spend too much time out on that beach." He took a sip of coffee and spluttered, spitting it across the table. "Too damned hot!" His face clouded with anger, and she cowered.

"I'm sorry." She grabbed a dishrag and wiped up the coffee. "Here, let me put it in the ice box for a few minutes."

"No. Never mind." Adam swiped his face with his hand.

Mattie really looked at his face for the first time since entering the kitchen, her hazel eyes growing wide. "What happened to your nose? Is it broken?" His entire nose was swollen and red, and the bridge appeared to be slightly crooked.

"None of your business." He laid down the magazine and picked up a fork, savagely stabbing at the ham. "I don't know if it's broken."

"Maybe we should put some ice chips on it." Mattie opened the icebox door again.

"No!" he barked at her. "Just leave me alone and let me eat my breakfast in peace."

Her eyes stung, and a familiar sick sensation twisted in her gut. "As you will. Let me make up a plate for myself and I'll..."

"Get out!" He picked up the magazine and hurled it at her.

Mattie ran from the kitchen and felt a hail of charcoal pencils hit her in the back as she fled. She scrambled across the front room, dodging a low table and two parlor chairs.

"Maybe if you'd pay more attention to being my wife, and less attention to daydreaming on the beach, maybe my mouth wouldn't be burned, and maybe I would have come home earlier last night. Maybe then I wouldn't have a broken nose." He stood in the kitchen doorway, glaring at her as she stopped and stood rooted in place.

She didn't know what to do. If she left, she'd go back down to the beach for a while, and that seemed to be what was making him angry. She couldn't stay because he'd just asked her to leave. Slowly, she eased toward the bedroom door. "Adam. I'm sorry. Please go eat your breakfast. I'll go tend to the wash I need to do tomorrow." She didn't dare mention her job at the tailor's shop. He usually drove her into town. She ducked into the bedroom and closed the door.

Her pulse slowed, and she began to shake. "Oh, dear God." Her knees gave out and she sank down onto the plump down mattress, feeling her entire body shudder. The tears came next. She despised herself, and grabbed a handkerchief from the night table, dabbing angrily at her face. *Why can't I do anything right?*

She waited for a long while, relieved at the silence on the other side of the door. *I need to get to work.* She was late for work often. Luckily, the tailor seemed to genuinely like her, and had never complained. After a brief moment weighing her options, she did indeed get up and move to a hamper in the corner, pulling out assorted soiled items of clothing and stuffing them into a canvas bag which would later be toted into the kitchen and out onto the back porch where she kept the wash tub.

Finally, she heard Adam's heavy boot steps as he walked through the living room. The front door slammed, and her entire body relaxed. A few minutes later, she looked out the window and saw Adam climbing into their lightweight buggy. He flicked a small switch and their two bay mares took off, trotting from in front of the stable past the house, and out onto the road. She had no idea where he was going on a Saturday, and she didn't much care, as long as he stayed gone until she could get to work. Of course now, she reflected, she would have to walk up to the main road and catch the trolley for the five-mile ride to the shop.

The mirror in the water closet revealed puffy red eyes. They would look normal again by the time she reached the tailor's shop. She quickly twisted her hair back into a tighter knot, pinning it up securely with a few long ivory hairpins. Twitching the ruffles on her blouse into place, she made one last self-assessment, then left the room.

Before leaving the house, she went into the kitchen and made sure the fire in the stove was out. The dirty dishes were quickly piled into a dishpan for washing later. She hesitated, debating whether to wash them right away, but that would make her even later than she already was. She covered the pan with a large kitchen towel and placed it in the deep sink. Maybe Adam wouldn't even notice it there. Or maybe he would. She'd just have to get home before he did and take care of them then. She was certain Mr. Vaughan, the tailor, would allow her to leave early. He was generally lenient, no matter what she asked of him.

As she left the room, her eyes fell on the still-open sketchpad, and the drawing of Rachel. She picked it up, studying it carefully. It was nice, she decided, with her new friend's long hair whipping back in the wind, her hands shoved into her pockets. She had seemed to be deep in thought, and Mattie wondered what went on behind those eyes. She closed her own and concentrated, trying to remember. Steel blue. That's what color they were. A pair of kind eyes, along with a warm sunny smile and a raspy Texas twang. She found herself looking forward to tea the following week. Was Adam still going into Houston on business for the weekend? She frowned. *I hope so.*

THE NEXT WEEK flew by in a haze of activity. A few more days were spent loading cotton freighters on the docks until finally, one of the fishing boats requested that Rachel be assigned to work on board for the remainder of the week. She smiled broadly at the news. Life was good.

Friday came, the final day of the fishing assignment, and she arrived at the gulf-side fishing wharf bright and early, parking her now-repaired and shined bicycle and making her way down the dock among a long row of fishing boats until she reached her destination. "Ahoy." She grabbed a thick rope and half-stepped, half swung from the dock onto the boat's deck.

"Ahoy, Rachel." Her friend Billy had also been hired to work on the boat, and together they prepared to untie several lines and shove off. It was a beautiful day, with a hint of a breeze and not a cloud in the sky.

Once they were underway and the sails unfurled, Billy took control of the helm and the rudder, leaving Rachel to set up several fishing poles along the railing. They were fastened firmly into some new-fangled stands that kept them from falling overboard. They didn't have to hold onto them, but could merely walk along, monitoring the lines for signs of activity. She also unrolled a large net and hooked it onto the back of the boat so it could drag along behind. Hopefully they might snare some more fish in that manner.

Satisfied everything was in place, Rachel kicked off her boots and stockings, lit up a cigar, and plopped onto a bench off to one side, where she baited a hook and dropped it into the greenish-brown water. The sea near Galveston was not the beautiful aquamarine she had heard of closer to Florida. Far away as it was, the Mississippi delta was a constant source of sand and all kinds of waste materials, which washed out in all directions from southern Louisiana for hundreds of miles. The waters of her hometown were colored almost a mucky brown at times, as a result.

She loved being out on the water, regardless of its hue, and secretly hoped she might have a boat of her own someday. Hiring out on fishing boats would have to do, for the time being. The current assignment was one of her favorites.

The boat was owned by a long-time acquaintance of hers, David Gentry, a man she had met her very first week in Galveston. He was down below, most likely still asleep. He was a friend of the bottle and had been for years, although he was a harmless drunk. They'd wake him up once they got further out past the island into open water. He had taken her into apprenticeship, and taught her the fine art of deep-sea fishing. It was a lesson well learned, and had kept food in her belly during those early months on the island, when she was still learning her way around.

She'd been such a child back then, she mused, alone and scared. She'd lied about her age for a while. She had to in order to rent a room and find suitable work. Had anyone known she was only fifteen at the time, they might very well have placed her in the orphanage or set her to work at the looms in the cotton mill.

Or worse, one of the bachelors in town might have tried to arrange to marry her. She shuddered at the possibility. It was one of the reasons she had run away from Fort Worth in the first place. She could still hear her father's voice, screaming at her as he towered over her while she sat hunched down in a corner of the bedroom she shared with her two younger sisters.

He'd caught her out in the barn, spooning with Sarah, a girl who had recently moved back to Fort Worth from Europe, France, to be exact. Sarah was an American, but had been away at a fancy French finishing school. Sophisticated and beautiful, she was eighteen, a grown woman, and wise in the ways of the world. The daughter of a wealthy Fort Worth socialite, she'd caught Rachel's eye at the ice cream parlor, and they struck up an immediate, if odd, friendship.

Sarah wore the latest Gibson girl fashions, and kept her long black hair finely coiffed, piled up in soft curls on top of her head. She was slender and refined, with milky-pale skin and she always smelled nice. It was a stark contrast to Rachel's overalls and work boots, which were often liberally covered in cow manure. Even back then her days were spent in hard labor, working her father's farm as he struggled to feed his large family. Rachel was the oldest of seven children. In addition to the sisters she shared a room with, she had three younger brothers and a baby sister. The baby slept in a cradle in her father's room. Her mother had died giving birth to the baby.

Rachel couldn't remember how it had all started. She and Sarah spent time together whenever they could, but due to the disapproval of Sarah's family, much of it was stolen time, either at the ice cream parlor or meeting up in a park near Sarah's home. She couldn't remember for sure, but she believed Sarah had made the first move.

It was common for girls to hold hands when they walked together, but when Sarah took her hand, Rachel remembered subtle playing of their fingers and more than a few inquisitive sideways glances. It had felt strange and wonderful. She had never had a beau, and she gradually realized that her feelings for Sarah were probably not normal friendly affection.

One thing led to another, and after a few months, they ended up in her father's barn. It was innocent enough, and they spent several long rainy afternoons passing the time kissing. It hadn't progressed much further until the afternoon they were caught. That afternoon they had shyly removed their tops. She could still remember what it felt like that first time, as her bare body brushed against Sarah's, sending jolts of pure sensation into her gut. Sarah assured her that she had done the same thing many times in France, and she would show Rachel some things that would make her feel very good.

It never happened. Her father came storming into the barn, and she later suspected one of her siblings had seen them first and told him. She had been way too caught up in what she was feeling to pay attention to the sounds outside, which were muted by the falling rain. All she knew was that one minute she was lying down with Sarah in a cushion of clean hay, and the next she was being hauled into the house as she tried to get her shirt back on, the rain pelting her shameful body.

She never knew what happened to Sarah after that, but she never saw the older girl again. After being yelled at for what seemed like hours, Rachel had been banished to her room until her father could determine what to do with her. She wasn't allowed to leave the house except to do her chores, and was allowed minimal contact with her brothers and sisters.

Finally, after a week, her father offered her two options. That she was given options at all was surprising, but when she heard what her choices were, her heart sank into utter despair. He had talked to a convent over in Dallas. The nuns were willing to take her in and train her for a life in the service of the church. She thought that option was bad enough, until she heard the other. One of her father's widower friends, a man over twice her age, was willing to marry her, and help "cleanse" her of her misguided desires.

She packed up one small carpetbag and left that night, slipping out of the bedroom window while her sisters slept. She'd never looked back. She had stopped in a church long enough to confess her sins with Sarah, and to ask for proper penance for stealing the money from the cookie jar in the kitchen. It wasn't much, but it was stealing nonetheless, and part of her felt badly about that.

After that, she began riding the rails, skipping from one train to another in a long journey south. It had taken some stealth, hiding behind train stations and listening to determine where the various trains were headed. The long ride on the rails in lonely boxcars gave her a lot of time to think. She was never going back to Fort Worth. It was no longer her home. She also knew that her increasing desire to have physical contact with other girls must be shoved down, deep inside. It was wrong and it would only get her in trouble, no matter where she went.

At first she had thought to head to Mexico, but she didn't speak Spanish and decided instead to go see the ocean. She'd never been to the beach. Never been past the farmer's market in Dallas. She'd never seen mountains either, but had heard the closest ones were way out in far West Texas, and she wasn't sure how to get to them. A few days later she rode across the two-mile long railroad bridge from the mainland to Galveston.

Her first stroll on the beach had been glorious. It was unlike any other experience of her life. The salty breeze smelled so good, and the roar of the crashing waves was like music to her young ears. The sun was so warm and the wet sand felt nice and cool under her bare feet.

As she walked in the surf, her trouser legs rolled up, she felt truly free for the first time in her life. No more farm work. No more long hours taking care of her siblings. She would miss them, but there were plenty of them left to take care of the house and the crops. She half-suspected her father had been ready to get rid of her anyway. She was almost an adult, and was an extra mouth to feed that he most likely didn't need. Maybe he had been planning to marry her off anyway, and finding her with Sarah had only hastened a decision he had already made.

That first day in Galveston, she sat on the beach in the early morning light and made some sketchy plans. She would get a job, the best one she could get with her skills. Studying her calloused palms, she ruefully realized that she would probably end up doing some kind of hard labor. It was what she was good at, and she was strong enough to easily lift a fifty-pound grain sack and hoist it over her shoulder. She also needed to find a place to stay. And she needed to keep her nose clean. No more girls and no more stealing.

Two years passed before she met Lillie, and finally learned all the great mysterious lessons Sarah was never able to teach her. With Lillie, she finally felt safe to indulge her curiosity. No one knew what they did together, and most likely, no one cared enough to think about it. Lillie was a whore and Rachel was an oddity. Lillie tried to make her feel good about what they did, and Rachel tried very hard to believe it was right. Deep down inside, she didn't. Lillie's rules applied to Rachel, just like they did to her other customers. Rachel hadn't kissed another woman since that rainy afternoon in the barn with Sarah.

She took whatever Lillie was willing to give, but it sometimes made her feel vaguely dirty. She remembered those soft kisses with Sarah. She missed them badly, and sometimes wished Lillie would make an exception for her. A part of her wondered if kissing would make what they did seem more like love, and less like something cheap and wrong, a purely physical release. It was merely speculation. She would never push for it, for fear Lillie might take away the rest as well. For someone like Rachel, Lillie was the best she could ever hope for, and she wasn't about to risk losing a trust she had worked so hard to gain. She knew that what she shared with Lillie was certainly not love, although they cared for each other deeply as friends.

"Rachel." A strong hand shook her arm and she almost fell off the bench, forgetting where she was. "Rachel!" Billy shook her harder, waving his other hand in front of far-off eyes. "I need some help here, please."

"What?" Her mind came racing back to the present from her musings about the past. "Oh." The fishing pole in the stand next to her was bent almost double, some large fish trying to tug both pole and line into the water. She quickly transferred her cigar to her lips and shoved her own fishing gear aside, jumping to her feet and grabbing hold of the creaking pole, bracing her feet wide against the overpowering strength of the creature she was battling.

Billy also grasped the pole, and they pulled hard, maintaining a fine balance between working the pole and breaking it. The fish on the other end pulled harder and they almost lost their balance. It was a thick pole of flexible wood, with heavy interwoven line, but whatever was on the hook was testing it with all its strength.

After a long slow battle, the fish grew tired and they hauled it on board, dragging it over the railing before cutting the line coming from its mouth. "Will you look at that?" Billy's eyes shone. "Must be a hundred pounds, easy!"

"Yes." Rachel was busy holding the flopping marlin down as it tried to slither across the deck and back toward the water. "Club. Come on. Hurry, will ya?"

"Oh. Sorry." Some of the gleam cleared from Billy's green eyes, and he dug into a large box that was bolted to the deck, retrieving a sizeable club. After a swift blow to its head, the fish grew still.

Rachel finally sat up, gingerly rubbing her aching biceps and forearms. She grinned and took a puff from the remaining stub of her cigar, which still hung delicately between her lips. A perfect smoke ring curled up and around her head before blowing off the bow and out to sea. "Good job, mate. We've already taken the day's catch and we haven't even woken Mr. Gentry up yet."

"What ever shall we do now?" Billy's smile matched Rachel's, and he rolled up his trousers leg, pulling a flask from inside his boot top. He unbuttoned a shirt pocket and produced two more cigars. "Might as well let the old man sleep for a while longer, eh?"

"Yes. " Steel blue eyes danced in merriment. "He probably needs his rest." She plucked a cigar from Billy's fingers and lit it, drawing deeply until the red flame took hold. "May I?" She took the other cigar and lit it off the first one, then handed it back across.

"Thank you, my dear." He located an empty mug and poured a healthy portion of smooth amber whiskey, and traded it for the cigar.

"You are a picture of gallantry and chivalry."

"I do my best, sir." Rachel laughed and clicked her mug against the silver-plated flask. "Cheers."

They enjoyed the cigars in silence, taking in the pleasant breeze and listening to the gentle lap of the waves against the side of the boat. Billy eyed her speculatively, debating a question. Rachel was in a rare good mood. She was always pleasant, but her smiles and laughter were usually reserved for winning poker hands. She was a friend, and he had never thought to take it any further, instinctively knowing attempts at courting her would be rejected. He took a deep breath and another swallow of whiskey. "Rachel, you need to be careful."

The pleasant expression on her face disappeared, along with her good humor. "Careful about what?" Cold blue eyes peered steadily at him, her defenses swiftly in place.

"That man, the one you popped in the face last Friday night..." He twirled the cigar between his fingers and flicked some ash over the railing. "He's been asking about you around town."

"Billy, I think you and I both know I can take care of myself." Her words were measured, giving away nothing. "I've been on my own for a very long time, and been in a fair share of fist fights." She had. Survival on the docks and in the gaming houses depended on it.

"That's not what I mean." He took a deep breath and looked right into her eyes, an unspoken truth passing between them. "He's been asking about you. Where you live. Where you come from. He asked about your clothes."

Rachel closed her eyes and swallowed hard. "And?"

"He said some things — we were at the saloon a few nights ago." Billy studied his feet, unable to look at her while he spoke. "A couple of us, we tried to defend your honor — almost got into a fight. I wanted to re-break his nose, I can tell you that."

"Please, Billy." She reached across, lightly touching his arm. "I don't have much honor and you know it. I smoke. I drink. I gamble. I'm not a society lady and don't pretend to be. You all, the boys at the saloon, you're my friends, but I can hardly imagine you would get into a fight over me being accused of things I openly do on a regular basis. Tell me what he said. Please. It's important." Her mind raced and her blood boiled in anger, thinking of Lillie. *He goes after her, and I'll kill him.*

"He said you were 'unnatural'." The word tasted bitter in his mouth. "We tossed him out on his seat after that."

"Did he say anything else?" An eternity passed before he answered.

"No." He spat onto the deck. "What he said was enough. I thought you should know, in case he's after you for getting him thrown out last weekend."

"Thank you." She squeezed his arm and managed a smile. "I'll be careful, but please, don't worry. I'll be fine."

"You're welcome." He thought to question her further, then decided against it. "If you need any of us to go pound the bastard, don't hesitate to ask."

"I'll keep that in mind." She smiled, a gesture that reached her lips but not her heart, and sat back, trying to calm her suddenly jittery nerves. Lillie was the only female friend she could be completely open with. Now she wondered if it would be in Lillie's best interest if she backed way off. The man could easily get Lil in trouble for prostitution, if he wanted to. She mulled that over, and came to the conclusion that he was most likely after her and not Lillie.

When the whiskey was gone and the cigars smoked down to stubs, they finally woke Mr. Gentry. He took one look at the marlin and declared they should head back to shore and take the afternoon off. As an added bonus, they found other fish, including some tuna and small sand sharks on some of the other lines. Back at the docks they spent an hour cleaning fish, working happily despite the overwhelming fishy smell that was amplified by the baking sun. The large catch meant extra income for Mr. Gentry at the fish market, and some bonus wages for Rachel and Billy.

It was Friday. There was poker to play and more whiskey to consume. Now they would have extra funds to play with. And, Rachel considered, she needed to talk to Lillie anyway. She might as well buy some time with her and make it enjoyable. Her decision justified in her own mind, she set diligently to work. The sooner they finished, the sooner they could get on to more pleasant activities.

LATE SATURDAY AFTERNOON, Mattie folded up a partially-completed shirt and set it on a stack of other garments that were ready for finishing — sewing on buttons, collars, cuffs, lace, ruffles, and other notions. They would have to wait until Monday. She had some shopping to do.

"Good evening, Mr. Vaughan." She stood and donned her navy-blue sailor-style straw hat, placing it carefully over her hair, which was pulled back in soft red curls and twisted at the base of her neck. She straightened the white ribbon trim, fluffing out the bow, then tied the hat under her chin with matching thinner ribbons. The hat complimented a navy and white pinstriped skirt and shirtwaist she had made for herself during spare moments at the shop. Finally, she picked up a small navy pocket book. It held the wages the tailor had counted out for her during the noon hour.

"Have a pleasant evening, and Sunday as well, Mrs. Crockett." The tailor nodded politely, then resumed the tedious task of hemming an ornate wedding gown for one of Galveston's socialites. The wedding was a week out and the dress was behind schedule. Both

Mattie and Mr. Vaughan had taken turns soothing both mother and bride, assuring them that it would be ready a few days before the big event.

Mattie stooped down, picking up a scrap of lace that had fallen to the floor. She waved goodbye again and walked out into the busy street. A hodge-podge of people, some shopping and some getting off work, wandered up and down the board sidewalks, moving in and out of the stores and greeting their friends and neighbors. It was a happy time of the week, Saturday afternoon, payday for most workers in town. Most laborers had Sunday off, giving them even more reason to be light-hearted.

She studied the lace and twisted the plain gold band on her left ring finger, remembering her own wedding, a simple yet elegant affair that had earned a few lines in the El Paso newspaper's society section. Her family, while not wealthy, was definitely not poor. Adam, however, came from privileged stock and a well-known heritage. He was a distant relative of Davy Crockett, who fought and died a hero at the battle of the Alamo. *Adam David Crockett.* She shook her head. *You sure don't live up to your namesake.*

Marriage had not been a choice. It had not even been well thought out. It was expected, though most women didn't marry quite as young as Mattie had. Adam Crockett had paid his first social call to her family when she was thirteen years old. It became obvious that the twenty-eight-year-old Adam had his sights set on the pretty redhead, while Mattie herself was barely out of pinafores, still a school-girl studying upper-form subjects.

At the tender age of fourteen, she sat in her family's formal parlor and listened to Adam ask her father for her hand in marriage. It was settled, just like that, and in one short June afternoon in the largest Catholic church in El Paso, Mattie was propelled from childhood into womanhood. Many of the town's elite had turned out for the affair, along with the formal supper party the groom's family had hosted afterward at one of the downtown hotels.

She had enjoyed the party, although the man who sat next to her, her husband, was for all practical purposes a stranger. They had not spent one moment alone during their brief courtship, as her mother had insisted on a chaperone at all times. Their first private time alone together was on their wedding night.

It had been a nightmare for Mattie. She knew nothing of the physical aspect of marriage. It was not discussed, not even between mother and daughter. She had never been kissed and had no idea what to expect. She truly had thought they were simply going to bed, although she donned a brand new long white lace nightgown, something her mother had insisted she should do. What Adam did to her that night was shocking. And painful. He had brought her pain ever since.

In retrospect, she believed he had never been terribly enamored with her when he came courting, but rather that he needed a wife in order to be socially acceptable. Mattie was attractive, well mannered, and a sharp dresser. She was a fair cook and seamstress, and had always kept her room tidy, and later, her home. They had married just shy of Adam's thirtieth birthday, late for a man to be marrying. He needed her to keep house for him and appear with him at social affairs. Otherwise, he needed her to be quiet, stay busy, obey him, and not ask questions.

She also suspected some money had changed hands prior to their engagement, though whether her father paid off Adam, or Adam paid her father, she could never be sure. Her parents had both explained to her that she was fortunate to have him. Girls of her social standing did not often marry as well as she had. He was a catch and she had landed him, mostly with her fair face, slim figure, and thick shining red hair that fell almost to her waist when it wasn't pinned up. That had always puzzled her. At thirteen, she certainly hadn't set her cap for anyone, nor done anything to try to "land" Adam. She was doing what she was told to do.

You're a lucky young lady, Madeline. Her mother's stern words echoed in her memory. She had gone home for an afternoon visit the week after the wedding, and hesitantly broached the subject of annulling the marriage. She told her mother, in carefully chosen words, that she wasn't happy, and feared they had made a terrible mistake. Blushing, her mother first asked her in cryptic terms if the marriage had been consummated. When Mattie confirmed it had, her mother said an annulment wasn't possible, that her life's path was set, and the family would not tolerate the scandal of divorce. That was when her mother told her she was lucky. She also told her to never bring up the subject again. If things turned out well for Mattie, perhaps Caroline, her younger sister, might also land a wealthy husband.

The first three years of their marriage were spent living in a large house not too far from her parents' home. Adam had worked regularly in downtown El Paso at his father's bank, although she never knew exactly what he did there. One night he came home early, and without so much as a word, began packing up their things. Within a few days they had sold their house, said goodbye to her parents and sister, and made the long train-ride to Houston.

She never knew why they left El Paso, and Adam was unapproachable on the subject. They had spent two months in a boarding house in Houston, then made the move across the bay to Galveston. They had lived in their current house for a little over four months. It wasn't nearly as grand as the house they left behind, which was fine with Mattie. The new home was a lot less work to keep up, and she loved living on the beach, so different from the desert hills and mountains she grew up in.

She still didn't know what Adam did in town, but assumed it had something to do with trade and shipping. He frequently went into Houston on business, and came home late more often than not. That also suited Mattie. If she was lucky, she was asleep by the time he got home. The fewer waking hours she spent with him, the better.

Adam had reluctantly agreed to her taking the job at the tailor's shop, and had only given in when she promised it wouldn't interfere with her running of their household. Being alone in the house for long stretches was depressing. She had no real friends and only a handful of acquaintances. Adam forbade her to socialize without him, other than allowing her to attend mass on Sundays, whether he was in town or not. Working at the tailor's gave her the opportunity to at least meet and talk with a variety of the townspeople, and kept her from climbing the walls in loneliness.

Now she had finally, tentatively, reached out to someone. She fervently hoped Rachel would become a real friend. The tall brunette was the first person who had truly seemed to see her, and not look through her. She was a little curious about Rachel's choice in clothing, and fancied the woman must be a free spirit of sorts, something Mattie herself could only dream of being.

The invitation to tea had been quite impetuous and bold. Not normal for Mattie at all. She laughed silently. If Rachel was indeed a free spirit, perhaps she was wearing off on Mattie already.

Now, what to buy for the tea party? She stepped off the sidewalk and into the street, looking both ways for buggies and Galveston's two automobiles. She was surprised Adam hadn't purchased one of the horseless carriages yet. He had been considering it before they moved, but it hadn't come up since then.

She shrugged and forgot about automobiles, in the excitement of planning her own little party. Adam had left on the train for Houston that morning, and wouldn't be home until Monday afternoon. There would be no worries that he might forbid the party altogether, or worse, come home and embarrass her in some manner in front of her guest.

It was going to be perfect, she just knew it. She had tea, and sugar cubes, and flour. *Cream.* She mentally ticked off items in her head. *I need cream, and some of that confectioner's sugar to make those little teacakes. Yes. That should be very nice.* A smile made its way from ear to ear, wrinkling her nose. She hadn't had a tea party with a girlfriend since she was twelve, although she had hosted social teas for some of Adam's associates and their wives. This was going to be an adventure.

LILLIE CRIED OUT softly and Rachel smiled against her skin, mission accomplished. She kissed a soft inner thigh, then slowly nibbled her way up her stomach, stopping to pay one last round of homage to two enticing breasts. She guiltily enjoyed the salty taste of Lillie's skin, and the sensation of her muscles moving under her touch. Finally, she collapsed down onto the bed, propping her head up on one elbow and watching, waiting for her to catch her breath.

Large violet-blue eyes fluttered open and Lillie sighed in contentment. "My sweet lord, but you've gotten good at that."

"I aim to please, ma'am." She trailed a finger down Lillie's cleavage.

"Well you're the only one, that's for darn sure." Lillie also rolled to her side, facing Rachel and mimicking her posture. "All those old men I entertain, none of them give a fig whether I enjoy myself or not, and they sure as heck don't take care of me first, if they take care of me at all."

"Numbskulls." Rachel snorted. "Don't know what they're missing." She blushed slightly. "I...kinda like doin' that to you." Her eyes lowered in embarrassment.

"Rachel, darlin'," Lillie traced a tanned cheek until she made eye contact. "You have nothing to be ashamed of. Someday, you're going to make someone a very fine lover, I guarantee it."

"How can you say that?" A profound sadness clouded the steel-blue eyes. "You know I'm not ever getting married. I don't care for men — in that way."

"Didn't say you were goin' to marry a man, sugar. I figured someday you'll make a life for yourself with another woman." They had never really talked much about Rachel's future, and Lillie suddenly realized that Rachel probably didn't have much of a social life outside of the saloon. "You're not the only one, Rachel. There's others like you."

"Who?" Rachel's interest suddenly piqued and she shifted closer. "Where?"

"You know the widows Sanders and McKenzie, don't you?" She traced Rachel's thigh, which was curved up between them.

"Yes. Two old ladies — they're at early mass every Sunday." She frowned before the truth dawned. "You don't mean...? Lil, they're a couple of old ladies."

"I most certainly do." Lillie smiled. "They've lived together going on thirty-five years now. No one really knows where they lived before Galveston, and no one ever knew their supposedly dead husbands. They sure haven't ever made any effort to find new husbands, and no one has ever known them to entertain any gentlemen. Fact is, my dear, I know a few men whose advances those sweet ladies have rejected outright. Men that would have been good catches. And I've heard they share a bed, even though they have three bedrooms in their house."

"So there are two other old women like me," Rachel conceded.

"Doesn't bode well if we're the only ones, Lil. Not only are both of them way too old for me, but they're both spoken for."

"Ah, Rachel." Lillie rolled her eyes in frustration. "There has to be more than three of you. I'm certain of it. My point is, you just need to keep your beautiful blue eyes open. There's someone out there for you."

"I don't know." Rachel flopped over onto her back and tossed one arm over her forehead. "It seems like it would be so hard, living like those ladies do. They've had to hide what they are from everyone all these years."

"I'll bet if you asked them, they'd tell you it was worth it." She placed a soft kiss to the upper curve of a breast. "I like spending time with you Rachel, I do." She moved lower, drawing a groan from Rachel's gut. "But someday, darlin', I hope you no longer need my services. You're my friend, and I want to see you happy."

"I...you're...good enough." Lillie's lips and fingers were rapidly making thought and speech optional. "Ah." Lillie moved lower, flicking her tongue across Rachel's stomach and around her navel. "I can't think right now."

"Shhh." Lillie looked up. "I understand." She drifted still lower, paying Rachel back in kind.

Much later, they lay entwined, listening to the muted sounds of the saloon below, the mixture of music and drunken voices drifting up through the open window. Rachel's head was pillowed on Lillie's stomach, the blonde's fingers making gentle patterns against the skin on her muscular back. "That feels nice." She smiled, snuggling up closer. "Lil, what about you?"

"What do you mean, 'what about me'?" She ruffled the long chestnut hair, mussing it affectionately.

"Are you ever going to move on from here?" She broached the subject delicately, not wanting to offend her.

"Maybe someday I will." She smiled. "Find me a wealthy gentleman to take me away from all of this. But I'm not unhappy, Rachel. I know I'm not the most respectable person in town, but I make a lot more doing what I do than I would in the mill, or working in a shop in town. Besides, I'm pretty good at it, from what I've been told."

"Yes, ma'am, that you are." Rachel shifted upward until Lillie was holding her, her head cradled against her shoulder. "And I find you most respectable, Lil. Don't you go listening to any snooty society ladies. They're probably all afraid you're entertaining their husbands."

"I probably am." Lillie laughed heartily, the sound bouncing off the walls of the room. "Speaking of, you said you needed to talk to me about one of my customers, before we came up here. I think we got distracted."

"Oh." A hint of anger flashed in Rachel's eyes. "Yes. Be careful if that bastard I wailed on last weekend comes back around. I think he has it in for me, and I don't want you to get hurt if he does."

"Rachel, has he come after you?" Lillie looked down at the brown head, but Rachel didn't look up at her.

"No." She had looked for him when she first entered the saloon, and had a kept a wary eye out all night, up until she discreetly slipped up to Lillie's room. "But he's been asking about me. At first I thought he might be after you, but I figured he could just turn you into the sheriff for prostitution if that were the case. No." She released a long sigh. "I think I busted more than his nose, and now his pride is out of joint as well."

"You're the one who should be careful." Lillie rubbed broad circles against Rachel's bare back. "Much as I like you coming around here, maybe you better find something else to do on the weekends, or at least not be in here on the evenings you aren't working the bar."

"I can take care of myself, Lil. And I don't know what else I'd do to occupy my time." A thought occurred to her and she abruptly sat partway up. "Lil, what do you take to tea?"

"What?" Lillie's eyebrows shot up at the sudden change of subject. "What are you talking about?"

"I was invited to tea." Rachel smiled hesitantly. "By a society lady, I guess. Leastways, she sure was dressed like one."

"When? By who?" Lillie also sat up, curiosity written all over her face.

"A lady named Mattie. I was walking on the beach and we struck up a conversation." For some reason she felt shy about relaying the part about Mattie's drawing of her. "I've never been to tea, Lil. I don't know what you do at a tea, or what I should bring, or what to talk about. I--"

A hand clamped over her mouth. "Whoa, Nellie. Slow down." Lillie grinned. "First of all, it's pretty simple. You drink tea and talk about all kinds of frivolous things."

"Like what?" Rachel scowled. "I'm not good at 'frivolous' and you know it."

"You most certainly are. Fishing, cards, brands of whiskey, cigars, kinds of boats..." She smiled as the scowl deepened and Rachel opened her mouth to protest. "No, no, no." Her hand covered the full lips again. "Those are just as frivolous as talking about dresses and babies and the *Godey's Ladies Book*. When is this tea, anyway?"

"Argh." Rachel groaned, feeling suddenly way out of her league. "Sunday. '*Godey's Ladies Book*'? Lil, what am I going to do?"

"You are going to go to tea and be your charming self." Lillie removed Rachel's hand from her eyes, peering into the steel blue orbs, which bore a faint hint of terror. "And wear your nicest shirt and trousers, unless you have a dress?" Her voice was teasing, and she received a swat to her behind for it. "Ouch. That hurt, missy." She rubbed her offended backside. "Go pick some of those early spring flowers blooming by the church, and take those along as a hostess gift. Or you could splurge on some little trinket for her house."

"Flowers?" Hope appeared in Rachel's eyes. "I can pick flowers."

"Sure you can." Lillie pulled her into a comforting embrace. "Come on, let's get some sleep. You need to be rested up by Sunday."

Rachel cuddled into the warm arms, inhaling Lillie's familiar comfortable scent. She fell asleep, and dreamed of flowers and a pair of twinkling hazel eyes.

Chapter
Two

THE BICYCLE TIRES sounded unusually loud as they crunched
through the sand and crushed seashells that comprised the beachfront
road. It was pleasantly cool, with a light breeze blowing in off the
Gulf and large cirrus clouds feathered high across the sky. Rachel
stood on the pedals, guiding the vehicle around a curve. The wind felt
good in her loose hair. She had left her hat behind at the boarding
house. A few more strokes and she was in front of Mattie's house,
gliding to a halt and swinging one leg over the saddle, as she leaned
the bicycle against the porch railing.

Before she had time to think, the front door opened and Mattie's
smiling face was greeting her. "Hello, Rachel." She moved out onto
the porch. "Perfect timing. I just took the teacakes out of the oven."

Teacakes? Rachel wasn't sure what they were, but she figured
anything called "cake" couldn't be a bad thing. "Howdy." She had
forsaken her heavy work boots for a lighter pair of dark brown
cowboy boots, and unconsciously buffed first one toe, and then the
other, against the backs of her trouser legs. One disadvantage of the
bicycle was a constant layer of sandy dust on her boots after each ride.
She smiled and started to take the steps up, then turned. "Oh. Almost
forgot." She reached into the back bicycle basket, untying a large
bundle loosely wrapped in newspaper. "For you." She made her way
up and handed over the surprise.

"What on earth?" Mattie carefully unrolled the paper. "Oh. How
pretty." Inside was an assortment of multi-colored wildflowers, their
sweet scent rising pleasantly around her. "Thank you." She smiled
brightly. "Come on inside and have a seat."

"You're welcome." Rachel followed her into the house, careful to
wipe her feet on a round rug inside the doorway. She looked around,
taking in the unfamiliar surroundings. The room was light and airy,
with large bay windows facing the Gulf, and lace curtains draped over
brass rods. Against one wall was a comfortable-looking stuffed sofa,
upholstered in pale yellow flowered brocade. A matching easy chair
and rocking chair sat across from it, with a low oak parlor table
between them. In one corner was a bookcase filled with books, and in
another was a tall whatnot, bearing an assortment of small knick-

knacks. A hall tree was immediately inside the doorway, with a dainty cream-colored parasol and a plain black umbrella hooked over one arm, along with a forest-green woman's cloak and a man's black overcoat.

Her eyes quickly swept over the room as Mattie led her to the sofa. "Have a seat." She handed Rachel a copy of the *Farmer's Almanac*. "I'll go make us up a tray and be right back. And put these in some water." She waved the flowers slightly and smiled, then disappeared into the kitchen.

So. It had been a long time since Rachel had been inside a proper home. This one was more than proper. The furniture was obviously factory-made, and she could only imagine what topics might be covered in all those books. She wanted to get up and look at the trinkets on the whatnot, but her good manners told her to stay seated. She quickly thumbed through the *Farmer's Almanac*, then set it aside. *Ah.* Another magazine caught her eye and she picked it up, slowly perusing sketches of women in fancy dresses and shoes.

A quiet laugh made her look up, and blush. "Didn't figure you for the *Godey's Ladies Book* type," Mattie laughed again, her eyes crinkling at the edges.

"I'm...um...not, actually. Just thought I'd see what the latest fashion was." She grinned sheepishly. "I'm a little out of touch when it comes to things like that."

"Well." Mattie set a crystal vase on a side table and fluffed the flowers, fussing with them until they were arranged to her satisfaction. "Staying in style is more trouble than it's worth, most of the time. Here." She placed a *National Geographic* in Rachel's lap. "My husband truly likes this one. It is fascinating. I'll be right back with our tea."

"Thank you." Rachel watched her leave again, noticing a slight hitch in Mattie's hips as she walked, which caused her skirts to swoosh back and forth around her ankles. She opened the magazine and her eyes grew wide. There were black and white photographs of strange animals inside, many of them unfamiliar to her. One in particular, an animal with large spots and a very long elegant neck, she had never seen before. She recognized some monkeys and an elephant. She had seen some when a traveling circus came through Fort Worth once. She and a couple of her siblings had snuck under the large striped tent and hid under the bleachers to watch the show.

Mattie re-entered the room, placing a silver tray on the table. It was filled with all kinds of good-smelling things—a pot of fragrant steaming tea, a bowl of sugar cubes, a china creamer, and a matching platter of pale yellow cakes, dusted with white powder. "I made too many cakes." She sat down, smoothing her sage green skirt and pushing up the leg of mutton sleeves of a white shirtwaist. Thin pleats and small pearl buttons adorned the front of the shirt, which ended with a high collar at her throat. "I hope you're hungry."

"I am, thank you." Rachel watched Mattie pick up a china saucer, and followed suit, accepting one of the small cakes and a tiny fork.

"One lump or two?" Mattie poured her a cup of tea. "Cream?"

Rachel thought quickly. "Two, with cream please." She had no idea. Hot tea was out of her realm of experience. The boarding house typically served up coffee on most mornings. It often had the consistency of hog swill, and required quite a bit of both cream and sugar to make it palatable. "Thank you." She accepted the tea and sniffed it curiously. It smelled sweet and very different from coffee. Cautiously, she took a sip and smiled. "That's very good."

"It's just tea, silly." Mattie absently patted her on the leg, then picked up her own cup. "Adam doesn't like hot tea, so it's a treat for me. He prefers coffee."

"Adam?" Rachel raised an eyebrow in question, and took another sip of tea.

"My husband." Something in Mattie's face told Rachel not to ask too many questions about Adam. "He's in Houston on business until tomorrow, so it's just us girls this afternoon." The sunny smile returned, erasing the brief clouds in her eyes. "So, Rachel, tell me all about yourself. Are you from Galveston?"

"No," Rachel picked at the edge of her cake with the fork and nibbled tentatively at a flaky bite. The sweetness washed over her taste buds as the powdered substance melted on her tongue. "Oh. That's very good." She swiped at her lips with a napkin, careful not to let the powdered sugar get on her tan trousers. "No, I'm from near Fort Worth—grew up on a farm just outside of town there. I moved here several years ago. Wanted to see the ocean and all." She desperately hoped Mattie didn't push for more details. She wasn't ready to share all the complications that had actually brought her to the island.

"So you packed up and moved here, just like that?" Mattie couldn't imagine being so brave.

"Pretty much, yes. How about you? You said you hadn't been here very long. Where did you live before?"

"I grew up in El Paso. That's where I met and married Adam. We stayed there for a little over three years before he decided to move here, so here we are." She looked down quickly, hoping Rachel wouldn't ask why they moved, since she hadn't a clue.

"You don't look old enough..." they spoke in unison, then stopped, bursting out in shared laughter.

"Go ahead," Mattie giggled.

"I was going to say, you don't look old enough to have been married for over three years." Rachel smiled. "What were you going to say?"

"Well, first of all, Adam and I will have been married four years this June, and I turned eighteen a few weeks ago." She ignored the shocked look on Rachel's face, and continued. "And I was going to say you didn't look old enough to have been on your own for several years."

"I've been here almost eight years. I'll be twenty-three years old at the end of this month." She watched Mattie's own surprise.

"Oh. Sounds like we both became grown-ups at a young age." Mattie waxed melancholy for a moment. "I was expected to marry Adam. He was a catch. Best offer I was ever going to get." She smiled wanly. "His family is wealthy, while mine — we were comfortable, but with Adam, my future is set. My parents were very happy with our marriage."

Were you happy with it? Rachel didn't dare ask, but unmistakable sadness in Mattie's hazel eyes gave her the unspoken answer. "I had to leave home." Rachel trod delicately around the real reason she left. "I'm the oldest of seven. My mother died in childbirth with my youngest sister. After that, I don't think my father was able to properly care for all of us. He was about to send me to a convent or else force me to marry someone I didn't want to marry. I had to leave."

"You ran away?" Mattie's face was incredulous. "Does your family know where you are?"

"I did, and they do know now, though I only keep up with one of my brothers, Jonathon." She took another nibble of cake and washed it down with more tea, trying to wash away a rising lump in her throat. "He's at the University in Austin. When I finally let my family know where I was, he was the only one who wrote me, and still does. I think he wanted to get away as badly as I did, but for different reasons. He hated working the farm and plans to be a doctor. He might even move here when he finishes school. I send him money every month to help him with his room and board."

"That's very sweet of you, but I'm sorry about your family." Mattie's eyes grew misty all of a sudden and she drew a deep breath. "I noticed you ride a bicycle. Is it ever so nice? I've never ridden one before."

"Really?" Rachel flashed a genuine smile, grateful for the new subject. "How would you like to try it out?"

"Oh." Mattie fretted, tugging at her skirt. "I don't have any trousers or any of those bicycle skirts. This long thing, it would probably get caught in the pedals or something."

"Don't need 'em." Rachel leaned closer, drawing Mattie in with her mischievous eyes. "I'll set you up on the crossbar and give you a ride. Would you like to try it?"

It took but a moment to decide. "I'd love to, after we finish our tea, that is."

"It'll be fun, I promise." Rachel accepted a refill, along with a second cake.

"I'm sure it will be." Mattie's smile erased years of sadness from her face. They quickly finished the tea and another round of cakes. Rachel stepped outside to make sure the bicycle's crossbar wasn't covered in dust. She turned as Mattie came outside, tying a bonnet securely under her chin, covering her pinned-up red hair. "That should protect me from the wind." She smiled in eager anticipation. "Now, what do I do first?"

Rachel wheeled the bicycle over until the saddle was on a level with the top porch step. "First thing, it might be easier if you climb on from the middle of the steps."

"Very well." Mattie moved lower while Rachel braced the vehicle, then carefully sat across the bar, facing to one side. "Where's the best place for me to hold on?"

"Just a minute." Rachel mounted the bicycle, keeping one foot on the ground for balance. "Let me work this out." She placed one arm on either side of Mattie, grasping the handlebars. "Hang onto either side of the bar, next to your hips. My arms form a kind of cage here to keep you from falling, see?"

"Oh. Yes." She grabbed on tightly to the crossbar.

"Ready?"

"Yes."

"Here we go!" With a quick shove-off, Rachel brought her other foot up and they began rolling down the driveway out to the road.

"Oh, my." Mattie gasped. "This is wonderful." It felt more daring than riding in the carriage. In the carriage she could feel the wind in her face, but on the bicycle it washed all over her, and she could feel the rough road under the tires. She also felt Rachel's arms brushing lightly against her stomach or back, if she began to tilt one way or the other. Unless Rachel let go of the handles, there was no way she could fall off.

"Like that, eh?" Rachel laughed. "I can go faster."

She sped up, and they flew down the low incline. She took a turn off to the left that led down to the beach. "Hold on, gonna get a little bumpy for a minute." They bounced over a few sand dunes, then swiveled through the looser sand before they reached the packed wet sand near the shoreline. "Smells good, doesn't it?" She inhaled deeply of the salt air.

"Yes." Mattie did the same, drawing in not only the fresh scent of the sea, but also another scent, which she realized was some sort of tonic Rachel wore. It was clean and bold, and not as heavy as Adam's usual fare, and she decided she liked it. It fit Rachel's charismatic personality. She remembered she was wearing her own favorite rosewater, and wondered if Rachel could smell that as well. She looked up curiously, and steel blue eyes locked with hers for the briefest moment, before Rachel's eyes tracked back to the beach in front of them. Mattie looked out toward the water, then back up. Rachel's eyes almost matched the gray-blue depths further out toward the horizon.

"How about going down to the shell beach?" The smooth voice was right next to her ear, and Mattie felt a pleasant internal shiver. She swallowed, unsure of where the sensation came from.

"Shell beach?" She'd never heard of it before.

"Just a couple of miles further down. There's a bend in the beach there, and some sort of dip in the ocean floor a ways out from there. Lots of shells get trapped in the trough and wash up during high tide, then they're left there for easy collection when it goes back out again." She looked down at wide-open hazel eyes. "Lots of pretty ones there, usually."

"I'd love to go down there." Mattie had done very little beach-combing since moving to the island, her forays limited to quick jaunts out in front of her house, or the occasional slightly longer walk on the Sundays that Adam was out of town. She had a few shells on her whatnot, and one nice piece of sea sponge, but most of her treasures were from back home in El Paso — arrowheads and bright colored rocks from the desert.

They rode on in comfortable silence, enjoying the pleasant afternoon and the light spray as the waves broke nearby. Soon, they reached the beginning of the shell beach and Rachel allowed the bicycle to roll to a stop. "Need to get off and walk from here. The tires might crush some of the shells."

Mattie felt a light touch to her lower back, then she slid off the crossbar onto the sand. She watched Rachel bend over, removing her boots and rolling up her trouser legs. She placed the boots and stockings in the basket. "If you want to take your shoes off, there's plenty of room for them back here."

"Oh." Mattie stooped down, unlacing her shoes. She pulled them off, then blushed, turning her back as she raised her skirts high enough to unroll her stockings.

Rachel watched for a moment, then averted her eyes, peering studiously out to sea. She felt a tap on her arm and turned back around. "All set?" She took Mattie's shoes and stockings and dropped them in next to her boots, then hoisted the bicycle up, carrying it at shoulder level.

"Let's go." Mattie hiked her skirts up enough to keep them from dragging in the sand, and followed behind, carefully picking her way, placing her feet in Rachel's footprints. The sand felt nice and cool as it squished up between her toes, and she felt quite decadent. She began to notice various shells and her eyes lit up. "Oh. Look at this one!" She picked up a curled conch shell and held it up for Rachel's inspection.

"That's a nice one." Rachel held out her hand. "Here. Listen."

She placed it against Mattie's ear. "You can hear the ocean in there, even if you take it back inside your house."

"Really?" Her face was filled with child-like wonder, and Rachel realized that Mattie had probably had even less of a childhood than she had. "Will you hold onto it for me?"

"Sure." Rachel took it and made her way over to a long bleached out log. "I'll just prop the bicycle over here. Any shells you want to keep, put 'em in the basket. I'm going to go wading out in the water."

"Thank you." Mattie was off, darting back and forth all over the beach. She occasionally squealed with delight at a few extra-pretty shells.

Rachel watched her in amusement, glad Mattie was having such a good time. She shuffled along the sandy bottom, moving in a manner to send any hidden stingrays swimming away. The water was cold, not yet adequate for swimming, but it felt good. She felt good. She closed her eyes, sorting out a dozen new emotions.

She liked Mattie. It had been a very long time since she had a close female friend, other than Lillie. There seemed to be no judgment in Mattie's eyes, regarding either her clothing or her circumstances. Maybe Mattie was simply naïve, and hadn't been exposed to enough to know that most people thought Rachel was strange. The girl seemed at once worldly-aware when it came to the manners and behavior expected by society, and at the same time, as Rachel watched her skittering over the beach on her treasure-hunt, she seemed very innocent.

Her thoughts strayed to the mysterious Adam. It was clearly an arranged marriage, and there was no joy in Mattie's voice when she spoke of him. She remembered the fading bruise around her friend's eye at their first meeting, and her own eyes darkened for a moment, wondering where it came from. Men could be cruel creatures, she acknowledged. Her own father had been a little too heavy-handed with the lash. She had vivid memories of welts across her backside when she displeased him too much, usually if she failed to get her chores done in a timely manner, or perhaps forgot to do one of them.

After she left home, she learned to defend herself. The rare man that did try to raise a hand to her usually ended up regretting it. It didn't happen very often; usually at the saloon when a customer became drunk and either became abusive to one of the whores, or forgot that Rachel herself wasn't for sale. She sighed. Her friend Billy was about the nicest man she had ever met. It was too bad, she mused, that there weren't more like him around. She suspected Adam was not, and felt bad for her friend.

"My goodness." Mattie's voice interrupted her thoughts. "It's very cold." She stood uncertainly in barely-ankle deep water, her skirts hitched up to her knees in her fists. "I—I've never been out much further than this. I don't know how to swim."

"You should learn." Rachel's eyes were very serious. "You live way too close to the water to not be able to. I could teach you. When the weather gets warmer, if you'd like."

Mattie bit her lower lip in thought, her face turned down to the water washing over her feet. Slowly, she looked up through auburn lashes. "I probably should learn, shouldn't I?"

"Yes." Rachel held out her hand. "Come on. You get used to the cold real quick. We can't swim right now, but you can get a little better feel for the water if you go a little deeper."

Mattie released an abrupt breath. *I've ridden a bicycle for the first time today, walked barefoot in the sand for the first time, and made a new friend. Oh, why not?* She smiled and reached out, taking the warm hand, careful to keep her skirt out of the water with the other. The frigid water was almost shocking to her bare legs and she gasped. "Oh. Very, very cold."

"Give it a minute." Rachel squeezed her hand in reassurance. She watched the tense features relax. "See?"

"You're right." The sand shifted oddly under her feet and she found herself clinging to Rachel's hand for balance, the cold forgotten. "I feel very light."

"Wait 'til you swim in it." Rachel winked at her. "It's even better than riding the bicycle."

They trod gingerly through the low rolling waves, Rachel on the deeper side and Mattie closest to shore. Before they knew it they had wandered quite a ways down from where they left the bicycle. The sun was sinking lower in the late afternoon sky, and the tide was starting to come in. The waves became more aggressive, and Mattie wrapped her arm around Rachel's waist for better support, Rachel's arm draped casually over her shoulders. They talked idly about the town, and Rachel spoke of her job on the docks while Mattie shared gossip from the tailor's shop.

Rachel's head was tilted to the side, taking in Mattie's animated chatter, when a roar caught her attention and her head snapped up toward the open sea. "Uh-oh. Hang on."

Before she knew what was happening, Mattie was swept up in Rachel's arms and she was hoisted up to chest level. "What are you doing?"

"Keeping you from getting an early swimming lesson." She gestured toward the water with her head, and braced herself, as a large wave came rolling toward them. It crashed down, drenching Rachel up to her waist and catching just the dangling hem of Mattie's skirt.

"Oh my." Mattie found herself laughing giddily, in spite of the situation. "You're soaked."

"I'll live." She smiled. "Trousers are lightweight. They dry fast. Guess we better get back to your house." Rachel waded back to shore, not putting Mattie down. "It'll probably be almost dark by the time we get back." They reached higher ground and she released her. A leisurely walk back up the beach brought them back to the bicycle and a much-too-short ride later they were back, standing on Mattie's front porch.

"Thank you for the tea." Rachel kicked at a knot in the wooden steps with the toe of her boot. "I had a very nice time this afternoon."

"It was my pleasure." Mattie smiled. "Thank you for the lovely ride. I'm going to need more shelves for all these new seashells."

Rachel almost offered to build her a set, then stopped herself. "I don't have a place nice enough to return the invitation, unless..."

"Rachel, I don't care where you live." Mattie took her hand and held it for a minute. "I'm happy to have you for a friend."

"Very well." Blue eyes sparkled warmly. "Still, I don't have a stove or anything to cook on, but I will help you learn to swim, if you'd like."

"I'd like that very much." Mattie released her hand. "But I hope we see each other again before it's warm enough to swim. Why don't you stop by the shop next week? If Adam goes out of town next weekend, maybe you could come over again. I should know by mid-week."

"I'll do that." Rachel backed off the porch and got on her bicycle. "Have a nice evening, Mattie."

"You, too." She watched as Rachel rode off. She turned at the end of the road and waved, and Mattie waved back enthusiastically. When she couldn't see the dark head anymore, she turned and went back inside the house. Her thoughts turned toward Adam and she forced them aside. For now, she had a quiet evening alone to look forward to, and a bunch of beautiful shells to arrange on the whatnot.

SOFT GRAY LIGHT filtered through the lace curtains, and Mattie's eyes slowly fluttered open. She stretched lazily, pushing back a lightweight quilt. She felt uncharacteristically happy, and she pondered that for a moment. She was alone, which was always reason enough for celebration, but beyond that, she found herself unaccountably looking forward to the day, and the week ahead as well. Maybe she and Rachel would be able to get together the next weekend.

She had a friend.

Mattie smiled. She had friends growing up — daughters of neighbors, school friends, and daughters of her father's business associates. Most of her childhood companions were carefully hand-selected by her parents. After a first visit, undesirable friends were not encouraged to make a return visit, and certainly weren't invited back. She and her sister were to be raised properly, and that meant only associating with proper friends.

Her mother certainly knew how society worked, and was determined that her two daughters were going to move up a notch from where they were born. The only way to do that was through marriage. Her father left courting matters up to her mother. His only role in the entire process had been to give Adam his blessing to marry her, and walk her down the aisle at the wedding. Unless they did exchange a payment somewhere, she mused. In that case, her father might have been much more involved than she cared to find out. She truly didn't want to know if she was of no more value to her parents than the price of her dowry.

Mattie thought about Caroline. Her sister was fifteen now, and their mother most likely already had her eye on suitable beaus. She and Caroline, "Carrie," wrote every few months. Carrie's letters were newsy and Mattie suspected their mother censored what was written. Mattie's own letters were guarded. That she was miserable was not shared. There was no point. She was much too far away for her family to make any difference in her circumstances.

Rachel was the first friend Mattie had ever made all by herself, without fear that her mother would not allow her to see Rachel anymore. *Oh,* she grinned, *Mother would most definitely disapprove of Rachel. So would Adam, most likely.* She frowned. She would just have to do her best to keep the friendship secret for as long as she could.

With that thought in mind, she got up, washed her face, and got dressed. After a brief breakfast of leftover teacakes and hot tea, she wrapped up the remaining cakes to take to the shop to share with Mr. Vaughan, and his wife and children if they decided to pay a visit. She picked up the bundle and wandered into the parlor, running her fingers lightly over the new shells. She held the conch up to her ear and listened.

Sure enough, she could hear the sound of the ocean, and she smiled, remembering her adventures from the day before. Riding a bicycle had been exhilarating, wading in the water was a little frightening, and if not for Rachel, she might have drowned. *Lucky she's strong enough to pick me up.* That had felt...different, and very safe. She pondered that for a moment. What she remembered was an incredible sense of peace as she was carried back to shore. Peace was something she rarely felt.

What a strange thing to feel. She shook her head and dismissed it as a mystery.

She put the conch back down and bit her lower lip, debating. Would Adam notice the shells and become angry? Maybe. Surely he wouldn't become too enraged over a simple walk on the beach. He didn't have to know she wasn't alone. *Very well, I won't hide them.* She turned to leave and spotted the flowers. Her heart sank. She'd never be able to explain those away. She had never picked wildflowers during the entire time they were married.

She removed them from the vase and took the large etched crystal container into the kitchen, where she rinsed it out and carefully dried it, before placing it in the cabinet. The flowers would go to the shop, too. Mrs. Vaughan would like them, and there was already a vase there they could put them in. She could look at them all week and no one would know where they came from except her.

She took one last look around the kitchen and parlor. No sign of her little party remained, save the shells on the whatnot. Her eyes stung and she blinked away a scattering of unexpected tears. *Drat him.* She grabbed a handkerchief from the armoire in the bedroom, dabbed her eyes, and left for the walk up to the main road, where she could catch the trolley to the tailor shop.

The day passed quickly. The shop was busy, with several customers coming by to place new orders for spring and summer clothing. Both Mattie and Mr. Vaughan were constantly discussing material and style with their clients, then pulling out tape measures and taking the customers into a back room to record size information. Mrs. Vaughan came by at the noon hour and stayed the rest of the day to help out. She complimented Mattie on both the cakes and the flowers, and as they got ready to close for the evening, wrapped up a few cakes to take home and share with their children, two little boys who had been sent to stay with a neighbor.

As Mattie was putting away her sewing basket, Adam pulled up in front of the shop and came in to pick her up. "Hello, Matthew, ma'am," he nodded briefly to Mr. And Mrs. Vaughan.

"A good evening to you, Adam." The tailor stood by the door, prepared to lock up after everyone had cleared the shop.

"I'll see you tomorrow, Mr. Vaughan." Mattie tied her hat under her chin. "Will you be coming in tomorrow as well, Eliza?"

"I don't know yet, Mattie. Most likely I will. You all sure are busy enough for it." She picked up her napkin-wrapped cakes. "Thank you for these lovely cakes, by the way. The boys will certainly enjoy them."

Too late, Mattie caught the tempest in Adam's eyes. "You're welcome," she stammered. "See you tomorrow. Let's go home, dear." She scurried out of the shop before either of them thought to mention the flowers and dig her in any deeper than she knew she already was.

"Cakes?" Adam gave her a hand up into the carriage and tucked a lap robe around her skirts.

"Oh, it was nothing, really." Mattie tried to sound nonchalant. "I had a hankerin' for some hot tea, and wanted some cakes to eat with it. I guess I got carried away and made too many."

"Did you save any for me?" He climbed in and flicked a light switch, then guided the horses down the street.

"No. I'm sorry, dear." She smiled her most charmingly innocent smile. "I didn't know you cared for teacakes, being as you don't like hot tea. If I ever make them again I'll make sure to save you some."

"Hmph," he grunted, his eyes on the road.

"How was your trip to Houston?" She breathed an internal sigh of relief, hoping the topic of cake was finished.

"Not as profitable as I had hoped." His jaw line was tense and Mattie mentally slapped herself for not having looked for the telltale sign before asking the question.

"I'm sorry to hear that." She reached over and quickly patted his arm before just as quickly drawing her hand back into her lap. "Maybe it will turn out better next time. When do you expect to go back?" *There. Easy way to ask that question legitimately.*

"Probably next weekend." He missed her tiny smile as he flicked the switch and the horses broke into a smooth jog.

They turned onto the beach road that led to their house, and traveled the rest of the way in silence. Mattie couldn't help but compare it to the comfortable stretches of silence during the bicycle ride the day before. She suddenly realized that even though she barely knew Rachel, she was much more comfortable riding with her than she was with Adam. She didn't recall worrying too much about what she said to Rachel, or how she said it, or even if they said anything at all. Her shoulders slumped and she looked away from Adam, staring at the high marsh grass on the side of the road as they sped by.

They reached the house and Mattie jumped out of the carriage as Adam pulled up in front of the house before taking the rig and horses back to the stable. "Supper will be ready in about thirty minutes, so take your time." She smiled and quickly made her way inside the house, where she pulled a leftover roast from the icebox, popping it into the oven along with some vegetables she had chopped up the night before.

A thought occurred to her and she went into the bedroom. She looked out the window, and satisfied Adam was still in the stable, she knelt down and dug into the back of a bottom drawer in the armoire, pulling a box from under a set of bed linens. She quickly went into the water closet and emerged a few minutes later, looked back out the window, and put the box back in the drawer, carefully covering it up. She felt beaded sweat on her forehead, and dabbed it away with her sleeve before returning to the kitchen.

Adam returned from the stable and they shared a mostly quiet supper. Mattie told him of the priest's lessons from Sunday's mass, and Adam made idle comments about predictions for a very hot summer. Mattie remembered the promised swimming lessons from Rachel and barely held back a smile at the news.

After supper, they retired to the parlor where Adam caught up on reading the newspaper, while Mattie dove into a most fascinating novel by her favorite writer, H.G. Wells. It was titled *War of the Worlds*. She had devoured *The Time Machine*, and was delighted when the newest book became available for order. Adam summarily dismissed her taste in reading material as "futuristic gibberish."

She was completely lost in her novel when she was suddenly yanked out of the chair by the arm, her book falling to the floor. "What are you doing?"

Adam roughly pulled her to the whatnot. "What are these?" He squeezed her wrist harder and gestured toward the shells on the top shelf.

"Shells." She tried to free her wrist. "Let go. You're hurting me."

He ignored her and twisted her arm slightly. "I know what they are. How did they get there?"

"I went for a walk on the beach and picked them up." She pulled at her arm again, trying to get him to release it.

"You know I don't like you going out when I'm not home. Haven't you been the busy one this weekend, making cakes and going for walks? Did you get any housework done at all?" He quickly twisted her wrist further, then released it.

Mattie cried out, grabbing at her arm. Her wrist was throbbing and she examined it, certain it was sprained. "Does the house look dirty?" She scowled boldly, showing her displeasure. "I didn't do anything wrong. Just went for a walk on the beach is all."

"It's still going out. There could be vagrants walking these beaches. They come into town on the trains." He moved back to the chair and sat down. "Don't do it again." He picked up the paper and disappeared behind it as if nothing had happened, effectively dismissing her.

Mattie's lower lip trembled and she quietly picked up her book and set it on the table, then went in the kitchen to get some ice and a rag. Her eyes blurred as she made up the ice pack, then applied it to her painful wrist. It was starting to swell and the skin was red where Adam had squeezed it. She tiptoed back through the parlor and into the bedroom, where she dressed in her nightgown and curled up on the bed in the dark. She tried very hard not to cry. It never worked.

She sniffled a few times and rearranged the ice to cover more of her wrist. She wondered if she would ever do anything in a manner that would please her husband. Nothing she said or did ever came out right, no matter how hard she tried. Her mother had been the same way, never happy with Mattie, but chose to punish her with words rather than physical force. She couldn't recall either of her parents ever raising a hand to her, although a chastising from her mother was almost as effective as a beating.

She wasn't sure how much time had passed when Adam came into the room and switched on a lamp. She closed her eyes tightly and pretended to be asleep. A hiccup gave her away. She cursed silently, continuing to face the wall, knowing he was watching her back.

"Mattie." Adam sat down on the bed behind her. "I'm sorry if I hurt you."

She remained silent, staring at the paisley flowered wallpaper.

"I need you to do what I tell you to, that's all." He reached out, touching her back. "Do you understand?"

"Yes," she answered softly, still not facing him.

"Here, let me take a look at your arm." He rolled her over onto her back and took the injured limb into his hand, removing the ice pack and studying it. "I'm sorry. It'll be healed up in a day or so."

"I know." She sighed helplessly, as he leaned closer and kissed her. His breath stank, and she realized he had pulled out the whiskey decanter after she'd gone to bed. She held her breath against the stench, and waited.

He kissed her again, and stretched out next to her. "Let me make it up to you, Mattie." He continued to kiss her, and she felt him pushing her nightgown up around her waist, then his hand fumbled with the buttons on her bloomers.

As she felt the bloomers slide off, she had just enough presence of mind to be grateful she'd remembered the pessary. Adam would probably kill her if he ever found out she used them. It was a sin according to the church, but she wasn't ready for children. She wasn't sure if she would ever be ready for them with Adam. It was difficult enough with just the two of them. She was certain the greater sin would be to bring children into her situation.

She closed her eyes and tried to relax, waiting for it to be over.

THE SHOP BELL jingled in greeting as Rachel pushed the front door open. She poked her head in and looked around, spotting the back of a familiar red head bent diligently over a sewing machine. Mattie's hair was twisted up off her pale neck, a few loose strands hanging down over the back of her collar. The quiet whir of the sewing machine spindle and the rhythmic tapping of Mattie's foot on the pedal filled the otherwise quiet shop. "Hello there."

Mattie stopped in surprise right before she would have sewn her finger onto the sleeve of the shirt she was stitching. She'd been so engrossed in her work that she hadn't noticed the doorbell. She turned around and smiled warmly, having already recognized the smooth voice at her back. "Hello, Rachel." She stood and wiped her hands on the front of her apron. "Good to see you."

"You, too." Rachel grinned and stepped all the way inside. "You running the shop alone today?"

"Oh." Mattie looked around, as if she had forgotten she was the only one there. "Oh, no. Mr. Vaughan went to meet Mrs. Vaughan for dinner at the hotel. I told them I'd wait until they return before taking mine. How are you?"

"I'm fine." Steel eyes studied her surroundings. One wall was covered in floor-to-ceiling shelves, which were filled with an overwhelming assortment of bolts of cloth, spools of thread, containers of buttons, and a variety of other sewing goods. The strong scent of unwashed dye assaulted her nose, almost making her sneeze. Three sewing machines lined another wall, and a long worktable filled the space under the front window, which looked out over the street. A curtain marked the rear edge of the room, obscuring whatever might be behind it, and a mannequin stood in one corner, wearing a half-finished lady's gown. In the middle of the room was another table that bore various fashion magazines and catalogues. A hat tree beside the door was adorned with a dozen assorted men's and women's hats. "Nice place. How are you doing?"

"Fine, thank you." Mattie shyly looked down and clasped her hands behind her back. "Adam is going to Houston again this weekend, if you'd like to come over for tea." She tried not to appear as eager as she felt at the prospect.

"I'd love to." Rachel flashed another bright smile. "I brought you something to mend up." She held out the checkered shirt she had torn when she fell off her bicycle. "I never was good at patching up elbows."

"Oh, my." Mattie took the garment and delicately fingered the shredded hole. "I hope your elbow fared better than the shirt." She unconsciously reached out and touched Rachel's arm, giving it a little squeeze.

"Nah. Barely a scratch." It warmed her all over, and Rachel looked down at the smaller hand clasping her arm. And frowned. "Hey." She took Mattie's hand in her own. "What happened to you?" Mattie's wrist was swollen and a bruise circled it. She carefully turned it over, not missing more bruises that were obviously fingerprints.

Mattie felt the blood drain from her face, and tried to hide it with a flustered smile. "It was nothing, really. I'm so clumsy, you see." She gently withdrew her hand. "I tried to pick up a heavy box of books at the house and dropped it. Twisted my arm in the process."

Rachel frowned, her ire rapidly rising. *Bastard.* "You should wrap it up. Sprains heal better if they're bound." She looked around, spotting a scrap basket. She walked over and sorted through it, picking out a few long white strips of cotton shirting material. "I can wrap it for you, if you like. The fellows are always hurting themselves on the docks. I have a lot of experience in this area."

"Very well. Shall I sit down?" Mattie indicated her chair.

"Yes." Rachel grabbed a second one and pulled it up next to Mattie's chair, but facing in the opposite direction. "Give me your hand."

Mattie complied, and watched as Rachel unbuttoned the cuff on her blouse and rolled it halfway up her forearm. She noted the careful attention to the simple act, and that Rachel made sure the rolled sleeve would stay up. Then she began slowly and methodically wrapping her wrist with the cotton strips, alternating over and under her thumb until her wrist was immobilized. "Thank you." Mattie flexed her fingers, which were still moderately serviceable. "I think I can even still work this way."

"I tried to wrap it so that you could." Rachel realized she was still cradling the injured hand in her own, and gently let go of it, placing it back in Mattie's lap. "But you should try not to work so much for a few days, if you can. I can bring the shirt back another time." She started to retrieve the garment where she'd left it on the table, only to feel a gentle touch to her leg.

"No need." Mattie patted the firm thigh. "I think I can manage one small elbow patch. I promise if my arm becomes fatigued I'll put it aside for a few days. It will be nothing compared to all the shirts I need to finish this week."

Rachel considered that, and looked down at her own plain white work shirt. She only had three good serviceable ones to wear to the docks, and found herself washing out one shirt a night in order to always have a clean dry one ready. "How much does it cost, for a shirt like this one?"

"Your shirt is top-quality muslin, correct?" Mattie ran one finger along the shirtsleeve, briefly looking up into proud blue eyes. "Smart woman." She smiled, watching a matching curve grace Rachel's lips. "So many of the workers try to cut corners and save a few bits by ordering lower quality shirts, but they wear out faster. Shirts like yours are generally a dollar a piece, or six for five dollars, but they wear much better over time."

"That's all?" Rachel's eyes grew wide. "That's the same price as the catalogue, but with no shipping charge."

"Mr. Vaughan wants to stay competitive." Mattie got up and brought over a bolt of not-quite-pure, white, sturdy muslin. "He tries to match catalogue prices in the hope that folks will order tailor-made shirts through his shop, rather than getting something from the catalogue that might not fit so well."

"I'd like to order six shirts," Rachel declared, "on one condition."

"What would that be?" Mattie set the bolt of material aside and picked up her tape measure.

"You make them, and you don't make them until your wrist is healed up." She clasped Mattie's arm, holding it loosely in her hand. "And I mean that."

"Very well." Mattie pulled the curtain aside, revealing a small room that contained a step stool, a chair, and a full-length mirror. "Come on then, off with your shirt."

"What?" Blue eyes grew round as saucers.

"I have to measure you if I'm going to make shirts that fit, silly." She gestured toward the room and held up the tape measure. "So come on in here, unless you want people on the street to look in the window and see you in your, um..." she trailed off, unsure of what Rachel had on under the shirt. She was fairly certain it wasn't a chemise like her own.

"Undershirt," Rachel supplied helpfully, watching Mattie blush. *Turn about's fair play*, she laughed to herself.

"Yes," Mattie's voice was flustered. "Undershirt."

Rachel ambled behind the curtain and heard the swoosh as Mattie let it drop behind them. She quickly unbuttoned her shirt and drew it over her head, folding it carefully over the back of the chair. She was glad she'd bathed the night before. She bathed almost every night after working on the docks all day, a practice she wished her fellow dockworkers would all take up. The day was warm and she was also glad she'd splashed on her bay rum tonic that morning, as the scent came wafting up from her sun-kissed skin. Her arms, neck, and face were a dark golden brown from working so often in her undershirt.

"Ready." She turned, facing Mattie, wearing her denim work trousers and ribbed cotton short-sleeved undershirt. "Should I leave these down as well?" She tugged at her limp suspenders.

"Yes." Mattie moved closer, helping her without really thinking about it, unconsciously inhaling the bay rum scent in idle pleasure, remembering it from their outing on Sunday afternoon. She decided she liked it much better than Adam's tonic.

She began measuring Rachel's arms, making idle comments as she went. Rachel was a curious mixture of well-developed muscles and soft feminine skin. She understood now why Rachel had so easily lifted and carried her out of the water — her biceps fairly bulged against the edges of the undershirt sleeves. "You're going to love tailor-made shirts." She paused and wrote down some figures on a pad that rested on the footstool. "I'd guess you've never had a catalogue-boughten one that fit you perfectly all over, am I correct?"

"Yes." She felt the tape measure stretched across the back of her shoulders. "That's true. If they fit through the shoulders, the sleeves are usually too long, and if the sleeves are the correct length, I tend to rip them out through the shoulders."

"Well, then," Mattie moved around in front of her, indicating she should raise her arms up a bit, "I'm going to make you a set that will fit all over, just right." She took her bust measurement, and noticed Rachel's nipples harden under the cotton undershirt as the tape brushed over them. She blushed herself, and dared not look up. It puzzled her, and she briefly glanced at the curtain, wondering if there were a breeze blowing in, making Rachel cold, although she herself was not cold at all. "There. All done." Mattie patted her gently on the hip.

"Finished?" Rachel lowered her arms as Mattie turned to write down the final figures. She was anxious to get her shirt back on, recognizing her reaction to Mattie's measurement of her bust line for exactly what it was. *Dammit, I've got to cut that out right now. She's my friend and she's married.* She could still see the results of Mattie's touch in the long mirror, and hastily donned her shirt, buttoning it up as quickly as she could.

She pondered Mattie's husband and the ugly bruises on her wrist. She thought about the fading bruise she had seen on her face the morning they met, and Mattie's listless voice whenever she talked about — *Adam. Yes, that was his name.* She despised him without having met him, and turned as she tucked in her shirt and pulled the suspenders back up. She followed her out into the shop and waited while her work order was placed in a drawer on top of a pile of orders. She nodded her head imperceptibly, a decision made, the consequences be damned. "Mattie, I need to say something, and I hope I'm not out of line."

Troubled hazel eyes met blue and Mattie moved closer, feeling Rachel pick up her injured arm, holding it as if it were a piece of fine china. "What is it?"

"I know we just met, but I hope you know you can trust me, and I'm your friend." She reached out and stroked Mattie's cheek once, allowing her fingers to linger there, feeling warm skin pressing back against her fingertips. "I'm going to tell you where I live. If you ever need a place to go, for any reason, to talk, or for — for any reason at all, even if I'm not there, consider my home — my room — to be yours, if you need it." The words came tumbling out and she waited, hoping she hadn't scared her new friend away.

Their eyes locked in silent understanding. Rachel knew her secret. Mattie had but a moment to decide whether to trust this person she barely knew, or throw away something she felt might be very precious. She took a deep breath and closed her eyes. Her heart told her that Rachel was a good and decent person. Her heart also told her that their friendship was already much deeper than perhaps she was willing to admit. "Thank you." She patted Rachel's hand, which still rested against her face. "I appreciate that."

Rachel picked up a pencil and a scrap of paper, and scribbled down her address before laying the paper down on Mattie's sewing machine. "Well." She suddenly felt shy. "Guess I better get back to the docks. The noon hour is about up, and you're probably starving by now."

"Oh. Yes. I quite forgot about dinner." Mattie glanced at the address, already committing it to memory, knowing she dared not take the piece of paper home with her. She picked it up and slipped it into the drawer where she kept a few personal items, and closed it with a click. "Rachel."

The brunette paused at the door, raising one brow as Mattie

moved directly into her space. Before she could blink, she felt a feather-light kiss to her cheek. Mattie drew back, her eyes shining in sincere gratitude. "Thank you. Will I see you Sunday?"

"I look forward to it." She ruffled the red head, then slipped out the door and onto the sidewalk. Standing with hands on hips, she looked up at the sky, then picked up her bicycle and wheeled it out into the street. She stopped and looked back at the closed door of the tailor shop. Shaking her head, she reached up, touching her face where Mattie had kissed her, a hundred confused emotions racing through her brain. With a heavy sigh, she pushed off, pedaling her way back to the docks.

RACHEL DRIED HER long hair. It felt good to be clean, and even better that it was Friday, and she had two days of rest to look forward to. She was scheduled to work the bar at the saloon that evening, but had tentative plans to meet up with some of the boys from the dock for a poker game on Saturday evening.

Her wages were carefully tucked into a small box she kept in an armoire drawer. It was one week from the end of the month, and she needed to stretch her earnings, as rent would come from the following week's wages. She ruefully realized that she would probably be counting cards the next evening, and firmly hoped one of the wealthy Galveston businessmen would join them. She felt less guilty winning their funds than those of her fellow workers.

Clad in a clean undershirt and navy blue trousers, she sorted through her meager selection of shirts, trying to decide what to wear down to supper and the saloon. It was a little warmer outside than it had been since early autumn, a hint of the rapidly approaching summer. She considered that and reached back, braiding her hair against the heat. She could do it by feel alone, but its thickness and length made it a chore.

A quiet tapping at the door caught her in mid-twist, and she held her spot, slipping across the room and opening the door with her free hand. It took a moment for her guest's identity to register. "Oh, hello." A delighted smile lit up her face. "Um, come on in."

"Thank you." Mattie entered the room. "I hope I'm not intruding. I finished this up yesterday, and since you told me where you live..." Her eyes shone with the warmth of their budding friendship. She swallowed and held out Rachel's mended shirt. "Anyway, I thought you might need it before Sunday. I took the liberty of washing it for you. I hope you don't mind."

"No, no. Not at all. Thank you. I was just trying to figure out what to wear tonight, and this one matches my trousers just right." Rachel took the shirt and draped it over the end of the bedpost. "Nice work." Mattie had not just mended the elbow, but had covered both elbows in soft pale blue patches of material that contrasted nicely with the checkered cloth.

"I thought the patches looked better than just stitching up the tear." She watched Rachel fumble with her braid, almost losing her place. "You want me to finish that up for you?"

Bad idea. Very bad idea. "That would be fine," she heard herself say. She sat on the edge of the bed and Mattie slid in behind her. She felt nimble fingers take the braid, and the gentle tugging of Mattie's hands as she worked at the nape of her neck.

"So this is where you live." Hazel eyes slowly swept the room. It was simple and almost bare. There was nothing on the walls save faded gray wallpaper. The double bed on a plain iron frame was tucked into the corner, an unadorned cream-colored quilt covering it, with two white pillows propped up at the head. A lone armoire rested against the far wall, one door open to reveal a small selection of clothing hanging on a single bar. A pair of work boots, pair of cowboy boots, and one pair of dressier shoes were lined up neatly in a row under the armoire. Two straight-backed chairs sat in another corner. Between the chairs and a nightstand was a window.

The window was propped open as wide as could be, and a patch of mosquito netting was tacked to an outer frame. It overlooked an alleyway, and the sounds of children playing below drifted up. Community clotheslines were strung between buildings, and Mattie noted that one of Rachel's work shirts was hanging on the line just outside the window.

"Yep. This is my humble abode." Rachel looked around herself, truly seeing her meager room for the first time. "Pretty different from what you're used to, I'd wager."

"I like it," Mattie answered honestly. "It fits you."

"You saying I'm plain and simple?" Rachel laughed quietly, ribbing her friend. She wasn't offended in the least.

"No. What I mean is, I don't see you as a person who lives their life indoors very much. You seem like you enjoy being outdoors as much as possible." She knew it sounded strange. Her assessment was based upon instinct, more than anything. She didn't really know Rachel that well, and yet she felt as if they had been friends for a very long time.

"Oh." Rachel considered that. "That would be true. I feel at my best when I'm outdoors. This room is where I change clothes and sleep, for the most part."

Mattie came to the end of the damp braid and reached for a tie on the nightstand. "And read, too, apparently." Her eyes fell on a book, and her brows scrunched together as she took in the title. An errant giggle escaped and she patted Rachel's arm. "*McGuffey's First Reader?*" She traced the intricate pen-and-ink drawing that decorated the book cover. "I have a great number of books you're welcome to borrow, if

you're looking for something a bit more interesting." She picked the
book up, spying the second and third readers, and a dictionary
underneath it, suddenly understanding her *faux pas*. "Oh."

"I know. I saw your books." Rachel felt the heat rising up her
neck and into her cheeks, and knew Mattie could probably see the
blush at the back of her neck. "I can't read." The words were an almost
inaudible mumble. "Leastwise, not very well."

Mattie felt horrible for making fun of her. "Oh, Rachel, I'm sorry.
I did not mean to embarrass you." She tied off the braid. "Done." She
tugged playfully on the long tail, hoping to lighten the situation.

Rachel turned. "Don't worry." She looked down, twisting her
hands in her lap. "I'm trying to teach myself. Kinda difficult, though.
Since I can't read, looking words up in the dictionary is almost
pointless. I can find them based on the spelling, but can't always
understand the definitions or how to pronounce them."

"How do you get by?" Mattie had been reading for as long as she
could remember, and wondered what it must be like to be unable to.

"I know my numbers, so I don't get cheated when I buy things."
Rachel looked up, her eyes moist with tears she refused to shed. "I'm
the oldest of a farm family, remember? My father needed all the help
he could get with chores. Then all my brothers and sisters came along,
and when I wasn't mucking out stalls or planting crops, I was
diapering their little tushies and making sure they were all dressed.
My parents never got around to sending me to school. All my brothers
and sisters went, but every time I thought it was my turn, they needed
my help with yet another newborn child. Finally, I was simply too
old, and I'll admit, too proud, to try to start school from the beginning,
when I was years behind the other children my age."

"I can help you, if you'd like." Mattie reached out, touching
Rachel's leg. "Learn to read, that is."

"Really?" The blue eyes lost some of their sadness. "I'd like that
very much. I can't even read letters. Have to have Billy read 'em to
me."

"Where are you in the reader?" Mattie picked it up and flipped
through the pages.

"I've gone all the way through that one, but I'm not certain I'm
getting all the words correctly." She picked up the second reader.
"I've gone through this one, too, and I'm working my way through the
third one."

"Maybe we should start from the beginning." Mattie reached up
and pulled two hairpins from the knot at the back of her head,
releasing several tendrils of hair, which fell into her eyes. She made
an incoherent sound of frustration and tugged the remaining pins
from her hair, the long locks spilling over her shoulders before she
swept them aside and down her back.

Rachel watched in fascination as the low light from the window danced off the red strands, creating gold and copper highlights. She decided Mattie had the most beautiful hair she had ever seen, and she barely restrained herself from reaching out and touching the shiny red waves. She gulped silently. "The beginning might be a good place."

"Here, your turn." Mattie scooted around, turning her back to the taller woman. "Will you please braid mine while I mark some spots in the book with my hairpins?"

Very, very bad idea. "All right." Mattie's hair felt like silken strands against her calloused hands, and she took her time, enjoying the sensation, along with the fresh clean smell that rose up from the long locks.

Mattie perused the book, clipping a few pages. She studied some of the words and picked up the dictionary, marking more pages there. "In the reader, I want you to start at the first hairpin and go to the last one. Then I'd like for you to study the words in the dictionary that I've placed pins directly next to. They're some of the harder words in the reader."

"I can do that." Rachel finished the braid and secured it with a length of green hair ribbon that Mattie fished from her skirt pocket. It matched the green of her skirt. "Is that how we'll spend our time on Sunday? With reading lessons?"

"I think we can spend part of the time walking out on the beach as well, unless you want it to be all work and no play." Mattie turned and winked at her. "And I might be able to whip up some more tea and teacakes."

"No. Play is good as well. So are the cakes." Their eyes met again, much as they had in the tailor's shop. There was a depth of understanding between them that neither woman was willing to voice just yet, a connection of hearts that had yet to be defined.

"Hey, how's your arm?" Rachel changed the subject, taking Mattie's hand and studying it perhaps a bit too diligently. The bandage had been removed and the bruises had started to fade, along with the swelling.

"Much better, thanks to you." Mattie felt long fingers gently probing her hand, and she looked up again, just in time to catch a peculiar glance. "It doesn't hurt at all."

"Glad to hear it." Rachel closed her eyes for a moment, afraid of what Mattie might see there. She allowed herself to fully acknowledge feelings she knew she could never act on. That she had a friend she enjoyed spending time with was a precious thing. It was a bit like torture to know her own emotions were rapidly growing deeper, but the friendship itself was worth any pain she might have to endure. She made a firm decision to allow the feelings, but never to let Mattie see them, if she could help it.

She opened her eyes to see troubled hazel ones looking back at her. "Does your head hurt?" Mattie touched her forehead, not helping matters at all. "I could get you a headache powder if you need it. You seem like you're in pain."

"I'm sorry." Rachel smiled for Mattie's benefit. "It's nothing, really, but thank you."

"Well." Mattie stood up. "I should best be getting home. I've got some chores of my own to finish, and of course work at the shop tomorrow, and I'm guessing you have things to do as well."

"True." Rachel also stood. "I'll walk you downstairs. I need to go grab a bite to eat before I go to my other job."

"Two jobs?" Mattie's head tilted in question.

"I'm afraid so." Rachel fervently hoped she wouldn't be questioned any further, and wished she hadn't commented on her second job. Working in a house of ill repute, even as a bartender, was surely frowned upon in the circles Mattie must run in. "Keeping both myself and Jonathon in food and clothing is a lot of work." She smiled.

Oh, Rachel. Forgetting to ask about the second job, Mattie suddenly wondered what it must be like to support a brother who was attending university, when Rachel herself was struggling to attain a basic skill such as reading. "You must know how to write some," she frowned. "You wrote down your address for me, and you said you send him money every month."

"I know how to write my address and his address, and not much else, unfortunately." She dug a scrap of paper from her pocket and held it out for Mattie's perusal. It contained two carefully printed addresses. "I carry this with me all the time. I've got them memorized, but sometimes I double-check before posting the money. I'd hate to send it to the wrong place by mistake."

"Then we've just added another class to your lessons." Mattie squeezed her arm. "Penmanship. I think I have an old slate and slate pencil around somewhere."

"You don't know how much it means to me." Rachel stammered over her words. "I'd like, someday, to do something besides dock work. I figure I won't always be able to lift the weight I can now, but without being able to read, my choices are pretty limited unless I want to do something truly tedious indoors."

"I'm happy to help." Mattie followed her out the door and down the stairs. They traversed the lower hallway and went through the boarding house parlor and outside to the front porch. "Good evening, Rachel." Mattie impulsively snagged her around the neck, giving her a quick hug.

"I'll see you Sunday afternoon, then?" Rachel felt the annoying shyness again.

"Come over earlier." Mattie fluttered one hand as she spoke. "Directly after mass, if you'd like. I can make us up some dinner before we get to your lessons."

"That would be very nice. I'll be there for dinner, then." She watched Mattie leave, waving as she disappeared out of sight around the corner.

THE SALOON WAS busier than usual. Rachel suspected it was partly to do with payday, and partly to do with the electric ceiling fans that circulated the ocean breeze coming in through the windows. It was a rather pleasant escape on summer evenings, in comparison to the eating and drinking establishments on the island that did not have the modern fans. Mr. Bullock, the owner of the partially illicit business, knew the extra patrons his comfortable joint drew in more than paid for it.

She was busy pouring mugs of strong brew when her nemesis entered the room, the wooden slatted doors swinging behind him. His dark beady eyes surveyed the room and fell on her, his lips twisting into a mocking sneer. "Hey."

She resisted the urge to leap over the bar, quickly shuffling around it instead. "You're..." A strong arm gripped her wrist and she spun, barely stopping herself from punching her captor, who turned out to be Mr. Bullock.

"...more than welcome here, sir." Mr. Bullock finished her sentence for her. "Please take a seat at the table of your choice, and Rachel will bring you a drink on the house."

"But..." Rachel trailed off at the admonition in her boss's eyes.

"Thank you, kind sir." The man flicked a bit of dust from his lapel, pointedly aiming it at Rachel. "I believe I'll take the one next to the front window. Say, is that little blonde whore available this evening?"

Rachel's blood boiled. "She's most certainly not..."

Mr. Bullock squeezed her wrist harder, effectively silencing her. "She's with a client at present, but I'll make sure you get some time with her later, if that would be your preference."

"It would be." The man's dark eyes bored through Rachel, daring her to make a move. "Your hospitality is most greatly appreciated. Bring me a whisky, straight up, would you?" He moved away from them, joining a lively card game at the front table.

"Mr. Bullock," Rachel wrenched her arm free, "that man is a skunk. Last week he..."

"...came very close to turning me and everyone who works here into the sheriff." His gaze was less than kind.

"Oh, for Pete's sake, Mr. Bullock!" Rachel released a frustrated breath. "The sheriff damned well knows what goes on here. Hell's bells, some of his deputies have come in here when they're off-duty. Empty threat at best."

"The sheriff looks the other way because he doesn't get any

complaints. All it would take is a few from the right people, and he'd shut us down and possibly send me and the girls to jail. I wasn't here last week to supervise, so I took full responsibility for your actions when he came to me to complain. I appreciate your desire to keep my girls safe, Rachel, but the fact is, he paid for his time with Lillie, and that means he gets to decide how that time is spent."

"Even if he wants to do perverted things with her?" Rachel's eyes snapped in fury. "Even if it means she gets beaten up?"

"He only hit her once, and his tastes are a private matter, don't you think?" Mr. Bullock looked away, unable to meet her gaze. "Mr. Crockett spends twice as much in here as the average patron. He's a high roller, both here and up in Houston. Fact is, my profits have gone up considerably since he arrived in town a while back. He's been recommending my saloon to his associates in Houston, and some of them have taken to traveling down here on occasion."

"Mr. Crockett?" Rachel's head spun. *No. It can't be.* "Did you say his name is Crockett? Adam Crockett?"

"Yes." The saloon owner eyed her curiously, crossing his arms over his large round belly, his gray moustache twitching in annoyance. "I believe that's his name. Why do you ask?"

"Just curious." She felt almost faint, as her glance strayed over to the dark-haired man who was already dealing cards, a cigar hanging loosely from his lips. *I thought he was supposed to be in Houston on business.* Her eyes narrowed as she reminded herself that murder was a hanging offense. "I'll go get his drink."

"Good girl." Mr. Bullock patted her on the arm before turning to mingle with the large crowd of guests spread out at several tables.

She found her way back to the bar, still trying to grasp the situation. *Mattie's husband.* It had to be. She added it up in her head, realizing that it made perfect sense. *He hit Lil and he doesn't even know her. Why wouldn't he knock his wife around? He tells Mattie he's on a business trip when he's actually out gambling. He plans to spend tonight here, so she'll never know any different.*

She retrieved a glass, bending down ostensibly to find a fresh bottle of whiskey. As she knelt behind the bar, she spit into the glass. Twice. With a satisfied grin, she located their most expensive whiskey and poured it up with an expert hand. She delivered the drink, her eyes impassive as he pointedly dismissed her.

Biding her time back at the bar, she kept a close watch, part of the time studying Adam, and part of the time waiting for Lillie's client to come down the stairs. At last he did, a regular Rachel recognized and often tried to pretend didn't share her friend's affections. As soon as he left, she snuck up the staircase to Lillie's room, knocking lightly at the red-painted wooden door.

"Come in." Lillie was lounging on the bed, clad only in her white chemise. "Darlin'." Her eyes lit up and she smoothed her blonde curls as she rose from the mattress. "What a pleasant surprise. I'd be more than happy to spend some time with you."

"Get dressed." Rachel scurried around the room, gathering up Lillie's scattered clothing.

"Is this some new game, Rachel?" Lillie moved in behind her, nibbling at her neck. "I can certainly play along, although usually you want me to get undressed. Seems to me you're doing things a little backwards."

"No." Rachel turned, practically dressing Lillie herself. "That gentleman from last week is back, and he wants to be with you tonight." She watched the bubbly face suddenly drain to white. "I want you to sneak down the back stairs and go hide out at my place. I'll cover for you with Mr. Bullock."

"Oh, my goodness." Lillie quickly took over the job of dressing herself, making a haphazard stab at buttoning up her shoes, her hands shaking as she grasped the buttonhook.

Rachel took over, finishing the job for her. "I'll pay you for your time, Lil." She pecked the blonde on the forehead as she stood. "I need someone to talk to anyway. Stay with me tonight?"

"I think that would be best, yes." Lillie grabbed a small pocketbook and hastened out the door and down the hallway. Rachel helped her down the fire escape, catching her on the long final drop to the sandy street, and managed a tremulous smile for her friend. "How long until you can come back to the boarding house?"

"Probably a couple of hours." Rachel looked up at the stars regretfully. "It'll look better if I finish out my shift before I leave. Just get some rest until I come home."

"I'll surely try." Lillie clung to her for a moment, willing her own nerves to calm down. "Be careful, Rachel. That man is nothing but trouble."

"I know." Rachel held out her arm, flagging down a buggy. "Believe me, I know. You be careful." She turned to the buggy driver, an elderly gentleman. His mild-mannered appearance reassured her. "Will you please give my friend here a ride to the trolley?"

"Certainly." The man slid to one side and held up a lap robe.

Rachel helped Lillie into the buggy, tucking in the robe and patting her on the leg before they sped away.

Back inside, no one seemed to have missed her. She pulled Mr. Bullock aside, delicately explaining that Lillie's time of the month had arrived. A deep blush and a clearing of his throat told her that was all he needed to hear, and she watched as he made his way across the room, apparently explaining away the situation to Adam Crockett. The dark-haired man nodded a few times, then turned to stare at her as Mr. Bullock made the rounds of the tables again. Adam studied her with cold eyes before turning back to his game.

At last, the evening came to an end, and the various card games began to break up. Rachel was wiping down the bar when an iron grip circled her arm. She spun around to face Adam, resisting the urge to elbow him in the gut as she turned. "Can I help you?"

"I could demand you take her place, you know?" He smirked at her, waiting.

"Do you truly want to be alone with me?" One eyebrow edged up, steel eyes narrowing as she moved closer, using her height to her advantage, topping him by a few inches. Danger rolled off her and she watched the fear rise in his eyes.

He backed up, licking his lips nervously. "I'm watching you, Travis." She stepped forward again, and he took another step backward.

"Seems to me like all you're doing is turning tail and running." An evil smile tugged at her lips, and she noted his nose was still swollen.

A fine sheen of sweat broke out on his forehead. "You're unnatural."

You have no idea. Her thoughts strayed to Mattie, and she wished with all her heart she had met her before she married Adam. "And you're a coward who can only beat up on defenseless women." She backed him into a corner until he could feel her hot breath in his face. "Go on, why don't you take a shot at someone your own size?"

"I am not your equal, you sinful whore." He spat in her face.

She calmly wiped it away. "You've got that right. I'm a better man than you'll ever be." She felt the rage, knowing she couldn't do what she really wanted to do, which was pummel him within an inch of his life. Her own words shocked her. It was the closest she had ever come to admitting what she was, and she tucked it away to ponder later. "You, sir, are no gentleman."

"And you are no lady." He eased away.

"I never claimed to be." She clenched her fists at her sides, wishing he would make a move so she would have an excuse to defend herself.

"We'll finish this some other time." He straightened his collar, his nervous swallows not lost on Rachel. "Right now, I have a train to catch."

Ah. So he was leaving town. *Good.* "Go on." She got in his face again. "Get out of here."

He stood in the balance, torn between wanting to get into it with her, and knowing the last train to Houston was leaving at midnight. The train won, and he stalked away, looking at her with murderous intent one last time before he left the room.

Her knees felt weak, and she went about her clean-up tasks blankly, her mind racing with new knowledge. Should she tell Mattie her husband was a gambler and that he was frequenting a whorehouse? Would it accomplish anything if she did? No. Probably not. All it would do is make her feel even worse about her situation than she already seemed to.

She needs a friend. Rachel forced her own feelings aside. *I can be that for her.*

Later, in Lillie's arms, her need was greater than it had ever been before. Lillie held on, as Rachel trembled against her. Their times together were generally playful, light, and fun. It was a refreshing difference from Lillie's usual patrons, who typically got right down to business and were done when their own needs were satisfied.

Tonight, there was no satisfying Rachel. It wasn't a bad thing— not like the men. She was much more intense, and seemed to have a need to hold onto Lillie, her attentions much more tender and gentle than normal. It dawned on Lillie that Rachel was not simply engaging in physical pleasure with her. There was honest raw emotion behind Rachel's actions.

"Hold on, sugar." Lillie rocked the taller woman in her arms. "I don't know what's going through that pretty head of yours, but I'm your friend. Don't forget that."

Rachel broke away, sitting up on the edge of the bed, cradling her face in her hands. She raked her fingers back through her hair, then got up, leaning against the wall next to the window, gazing sightlessly into the night. "I think I'm in trouble, Lil."

Lillie studied the lanky naked silhouette, appreciating Rachel's form, not for the first time. "Come on back to bed, sugar." She patted the soft mattress. "You come tell Lillie all about it."

Rachel hesitated before accepting the offer, but the words wouldn't come. Before she knew what was happening, they were making love again. Their exchange went on until early morning, when Rachel finally fell asleep in Lillie's exhausted but sated arms. She kissed the dark head in puzzlement, then joined her. There would be time enough to talk about whatever was going on later, in the harsh light of day.

Chapter
Three

THE HOUSE WAS silent. Mattie turned the front door knob and stepped into the parlor. Her footsteps sounded unusually loud on the polished wood floors. There wasn't anything different about her home from any other Friday evening. Adam was gone, and that should have been enough to make her glad of the blessed silence.

Instead, she felt inexplicably lonely. She had felt lonely before in that house, even standing in the middle of a crowded room when entertaining Adam's business associates. His colleagues were polite acquaintances, but nothing more. Not even among the men's wives did she have any friends. She half-suspected they went away and gossiped about her and their humble home. She didn't particularly care, unless Adam felt that as well and blamed her for it, somehow.

Now that she was beginning to understand what true friendship was, she realized that she had been lonely most of her life. She just hadn't known it. Beyond that, she found herself loath to be in Adam's company anymore than she had to be. That he didn't respect her, much less love her, was becoming painfully evident.

Her solitary silence made her mind turn toward things that were difficult to acknowledge. Rachel was always kind to her, and interested in her, and seemed to care about her well-being. Her own husband, however...

"How on Earth did I end up with you, Adam Crockett?" She spied a small oval-framed photo of her husband on the bookshelves, and studied it as if for the first time. His almost-black hair was straight and neatly trimmed, and he had a tidy moustache. His eyes were dark and brooding. He wasn't a large man, only a few inches taller than Mattie's own 5'6" height. From outward appearance alone, he certainly wasn't unpleasant to look at, at any rate. *Unless you know him.*

Next to the photo was a framed copy of their wedding invitation. Madeleine Elizabeth Burnet was to wed Adam David Crockett. She snorted softly. "We're married, but I don't think we count as a family." Family members were supposed to love and support each other, weren't they? "We certainly don't do that."

She set the invitation aside and picked up the third and last photo, one of her in her wedding gown. They had rolled her hair in pin curls the night before, creating a mass of springy ringlets. Part of it was wound in a bun at the back of her head while the rest spilled down her back. On her head was a simple wreath of small white flowers. Her dress was beautiful, of cream-colored brushed silk, but much too grown-up for the extremely youthful girl wearing it. The high neck, fitted sleeves, and bodice seemed harsh and too form-fitting for what was, at the time, her still-growing body. It had buttoned up the front with almost a hundred tiny pearl buttons, and lace adorned it in front and at the cuffs.

The girl in the photo was all wide-eyed innocence. Or perhaps terrified. She remembered putting on that dress and posing for the picture, the morning of her wedding. "Fourteen years old. What were my parents thinking?" If she'd known what the future held, she would have gone running for the Mexican border.

Up until the wedding, Adam had always been formal and polite with her. He had no choice, given that they had always been accompanied by a chaperone, most often her mother, or a part-time nanny who had cared for her and Caroline since they were infants. She tried to remember if there had been any clue of the kind of person he would turn out to be.

She still remembered the first time he hit her. It was a little over a week after their wedding. Adam had been at his job at the bank when she decided to go calling on one of her school friends, Ida Ramsey. She had been longing for some simple girl talk. Time flew by and before she realized it, it was past time for Adam to return from work.

Thinking little of it, she had taken her time going back home, stopping at the market for a few things and even going by the post office to check for mail. He was livid when she got home and chastised her severely, not only for not leaving a note, but also for not having his supper ready when he got home. She raised her voice and it happened so fast, it made her head spin. He'd just done it—drew back his arm and back-handed her across the face, giving her a nosebleed.

They had both been shocked, and she had retreated to the back porch to get away from him. It took him an hour to come and apologize to her. That was when he mandated she should not go out by herself anymore. She never truly raised her voice to him again, but it didn't matter. He had hit, shoved, and otherwise attacked her physically more times since then than she could count. It had gotten worse since they moved to Galveston, and she had no idea why. She had almost given up on ever being able to please him.

He was always gruff with her, unless they were in bed. Even that—there was no love there, only Adam's physical pleasure. She had read a few books. It was supposed to be lovely. She couldn't imagine how.

Her mind wandered to a locked drawer in a narrow oak writing desk that sat against the wall in their bedroom. She had assumed it held important papers Adam kept locked up against thieves. Now she wondered. Before she knew it, she was at the desk, tugging experimentally at the tiny brass drawer handle. It didn't budge.

Now where would he keep the key? She rolled back the desk top and sifted through some papers, digging into a few pigeonholes and searching through some small drawers underneath them. To one side were an inkwell, an abacus, and a small crock that held several pens. She picked up the crock and removed the pens before turning it upside down. Out fell a shiny brass key. *Idiot. If I found it, surely thieves would.*

With no further thought, she unlocked the drawer and opened it. And sat down in the rolling desk chair in shock. On top of some papers were several photographs of partially clad women, most with bared breasts and a few who were almost completely nude. She studied the photographs slowly, not recognizing any of the women. Beneath the photographs was a strange magazine, poorly bound and type-set. She picked it up curiously and thumbed through it. It had no illustration, but appeared to contain stories of an explicit nature. *My goodness.*

She placed the pictures and magazine on the desk top and riffled through some loose papers, most of which appeared to be bank statements. Mixed in she saw several bills from hotels in Houston, presumably the ones where Adam stayed when he was on business. Among the bills were several blank shipping forms. As she neared the bottom, she found some smaller printed notices regarding several gambling tournaments. Upon closer inspection, she realized that all of them had taken place in Houston on the weekends he went there.

She was tempted to put them in chronological order, but was afraid Adam would know she had been in the drawer if anything was out of place. A few moments' reading showed her enough to know that the tournaments had occurred at least once a month since they had lived in Galveston. She wondered how he found time or energy to conduct business during the day in Houston, then attend the tournaments at night.

In the bottom of the drawer were a few brown envelopes, which she opened one by one. The first one contained some notices of debts, which appeared to be owed to some of the gambling houses that hosted the tournaments. The contents of the last envelope took her breath away, and she had to review it twice before her heart stopped racing.

It contained court documents from El Paso, and several letters to Adam from his father. From what she could gather, Adam had been accused of — or possibly caught — pilfering money from the bank where he worked. It appeared that bank examiners had brought him up on formal charges, which had been dismissed. Another set of court documents seemed to be regarding separate charges brought against Adam by some casinos just outside El Paso. His father had ordered Adam to leave El Paso, and had given him a thousand dollars cash to use for moving and setting himself up somewhere else.

A thousand dollars. She almost couldn't fathom it, and wondered how much was left, and if it was kept in the bank in town. She realized that she had no idea what kind of work Adam did since they had moved to the island, and quickly found herself rummaging through the other drawers. There was not a single scrap of paper related to any form of employment. She realized that didn't necessarily mean he wasn't working, but she couldn't help but wonder.

Adam? Her chest was tight with apprehension. *What have you been doing since we got here?* If he had indeed stolen money from his own father's bank, she could only imagine what he might be doing since being forced to make it on his own. It all made sense, because they hadn't received a single letter from anyone in Adam's family since they had moved. She realized her own father hadn't written, either, only her mother and sister.

The house felt even lonelier, and she desperately wished for someone to talk to. She sensed that Rachel was someone she could trust. It was too much new information to absorb all at once—the risqué photos, the magazine, the gambling notices, and the knowledge of why they had left El Paso and her family. Rachel was her friend. Surely she would be willing to listen and perhaps offer some advice.

She felt a headache at the edges of her temples, and decided a light supper, a headache powder, and an early bedtime were in order. She carefully placed the contents back in the drawer in the order she had removed them, locked it, and put the key back in the crock. She would lose herself in her work the next day, and pray for Sunday to arrive quickly.

THE SUN ROSE much too early, throwing a large block of pale light across the faded wooden floor. Rachel had forgotten to draw the curtains before going back to bed, and the sounds of the awakening island drifted through the open window. Along with the high calls of seagulls and the gentle clopping of horses' hooves, the smells of morning also floated around her, tickling her nose with the scent of the ocean breeze and bacon frying.

Mingled with those familiar aromas was the fragrance of Lillie's toilet water and the mild chamomile soap she used to wash her hair. They were tangled in the sheets, their arms and legs entwined, skin pressed against skin. She smiled, her eyes still closed, and gave an experimental nibble to the salty collarbone under her cheek.

"My lord, Rachel." Lillie's tired voice rasped, right next to her ear. "I'm afraid I'm going to have to charge you extra if you want to go at it again. You 'bout wore me out last night. And this morning." She rolled to her side, propping her head on an upraised hand and effectively tossing Rachel onto her back. Luminous blue eyes twinkled back at her. "Although you certainly seem to be in a much better humor than you were when you finally fell asleep. You had me worried. I've never seen you like that."

"Oh." Rachel flung her arm across her eyes and groaned. "That. Yes. Remember my tea last week?"

"Why, certainly." Lillie scooted closer, ready for any morsel of gossip Rachel might throw her way. "How was it? Did you have a good time?"

"I have a friend, Lil. A real friend that likes me for me." She lowered her arm. "Not that you're not my friend, but..."

"No need to explain, sugar." Lillie patted a long leg encouragingly. "I understand. That's wonderful."

"Well. Yes and no." Rachel stretched and sat partway up, leaning back against a soft propped-up pillow. "She's a very nice person. Had a very hard life. A couple of things have happened that could make being her friend extremely complicated, though."

"Such as?" Lillie shifted, all ears. "Ouch!" She reached beneath her pillow where she had slipped an arm, withdrawing a hairpin that had poked her fingertip. She studied it closely. It wasn't hers. "Well, I should say so, you sly devil." She held up the telltale pin, waving it teasingly in front of Rachel's face.

High cheekbones blushed dark red. "That's not what you think." She rolled over and picked up the reader from the night table. "She's going to help me learn to read, Lil. She used the hairpins to mark some places in the book for me. See?" She held out the book for inspection.

"Uh-huh." Lillie grinned mischievously. "But she has been in your room already."

"Come on." Rachel frowned, bordering on angry. "Mattie's married, for goodness' sake."

"Oh." Lillie backed off, looking down and smoothing the sheets. "But you have feelings for her, don't you?"

"Didn't say that." Full lips puckered into a pout.

"Didn't have to." Lillie curled closer, stroking Rachel's arm. "It's written all over your face when you talk about her."

Rachel groaned again and sunk back into the plump mattress. "I did not need to hear you say that. I'm doing my best to simply be a friend. She truly needs one."

"Are your feelings one of the complications?" She brushed back tangled chestnut locks from Rachel's face, admiring the auburn highlights created by the incoming sunlight.

"Yes." Rachel covered her eyes with her hand and peeked through her fingers. "That and the fact that her husband is that cad who punched you last weekend."

"You can't be serious." Lillie moved closer, peering at the troubled face. "You are serious, aren't you?"

"Unfortunately, yes." She got up, walking around the room and pulling on clothing as she spoke, briefly hopping on one foot while she tugged on her stockings. "I don't know how much she knows about her own husband. I don't know what to do. If I tell her he's been calling on ladies at the saloon, it does no real good. If I don't tell her and she finds out later I know about it, it might hurt her feelings or make her lose trust in me."

"You seem to have developed strong feelings for this woman in a very short period of time," Lillie commented softly. "Are you in love with her?"

"No!" Rachel pulled up her trousers with a vicious motion. "Of course not! I have the same kind of feelings for her that I have for you, is all. It's embarrassing, but I'm certainly not in love." She buttoned her suspenders to the tabs at her waistline, her fingers trembling. "Am I?" Frightened eyes begged for some reassurance.

She didn't get any.

"Darlin'," Lillie patted the mattress and crooked a finger in invitation. "Come here. I need to say something you may not want to hear."

Rachel moved warily back to the bed, and sighed quietly as she felt Lillie's arms close around her, pulling her head down to her shoulder and stroking her hair as she spoke.

"You weren't with me last night." Lillie covered Rachel's mouth as it opened in protest. "Shhh. You hear me out, sugar. I'm not offended. Happens all the time. You must remember who I am and what I do. You were with someone else, Rachel, whether you had another face in your mind at the time or not. It was different. You were with me as someone would be with someone they are in love with. I think I should know the difference."

"But—" The hand clamped over her mouth again. She let out a frustrated breath and closed her eyes, listening and enjoying the sensation of Lillie's fingers combing through her hair.

"I have always hoped one day you would find someone to truly love." She kissed the dark head. "Even if it means things between us must change. I am ever so sorry that you appear to be giving your heart over to someone who may not be available to you."

"Is not available to me," Rachel mumbled against soft skin. "And I still am not convinced that I am in love." She sat up, feeling a stubborn self-protective streak rise. "She is a friend, and she needs me to be the same to her. I don't think she has many people in her life she can count on. Certainly not that skunk of a husband she was practically forced to marry, from what she's told me."

"Does she love him?" Lillie sat up, gathering her own clothing and standing in the middle of the room, bathed in a pool of sunlight and dust particles. She looked down at her naked body and delicately closed the curtains.

"I don't know." Rachel drew up her knee and wrapped clasped fingers around it. "I don't think so."

"Then there's hope." Lillie finished dressing and ruffled the wavy head.

"Lillie." Rachel's voice rose in utter frustration. "I am not in love with her, and there could not be any hope, even if I were to be in love with her. She's married. I am trying very hard to remember that, and you are not helping things."

"Rachel." Lillie sat back down on the edge of the bed. "Does he hit her like he hit me?" Her voice was very gentle.

"I think so, yes," her words choked out, her chest heavy with emotion. "And it just about kills me every time I think about it."

"Do you honestly believe she is better off married to a man like that than she would be if she left him?" She was treading on dangerous ground, and she knew it. Divorce was a dirty little word that wasn't often spoken, much less put into action by most women, even in the most dire of circumstances.   "These things only escalate, Rachel. I've seen it."

"I don't believe that's my choice to make," she replied bitterly.

"Maybe not, but Mattie may not realize she has any choices." Lillie patted her leg. "A true friend might help her see what she may not be able to see for herself." She stood, picking up her pocket book. "Just something for you to think about." Moving to the door, she paused. "When do you see her again?"

"Tomorrow," Rachel mumbled listlessly.

"Come by and see me this week, sugar." She opened the door. "Let me know how you're doing."

"Will do." Rachel stood and sidled up to her, giving her a hug. "Thank you. Let me walk you out. I need to grab some breakfast and then I think a long walk on the beach might be a good idea."

"I think so too."

They stepped into the hallway, closing the door behind them.

RACHEL TURNED HER face upward toward the early morning sun, closing her eyes and allowing the warmth to wash over her like an old, familiar friend. She wondered how she had made it through the first fifteen years of her life with no ocean nearby, no seagulls, no sugar-fine sand dunes, and no bright, rosy, unobscured sunrises — nothing between her and the sun but miles of infinite, rolling waves. Of course, she hadn't watched the sunrise on this particular morning, but there had been many mornings when she slipped out of bed in the pre-dawn hours and somehow found herself on the beach, waiting to be the first one to greet the bright pulsing orb as it burst over the horizon.

She had helped Lillie sneak out the back door of the boarding house. It would have done no good for her to be caught there, whether she had been with Rachel or one of the men who lived in the long wooden-planked building. The owner did not approve of prostitution, and more than one renter had been quietly asked to leave when caught bringing ladies of the evening on premises.

Once Lillie was safely on her way home, Rachel had quickly downed a plate of bacon, eggs, biscuits, and gravy, and several cups of bitter coffee, trying to clear her head of her troubled thoughts. It did no good, so she went ahead with her plans for a stroll on the beach. The walk itself had soothed her nerves somewhat, although she chose a different area than her usual spot just down from Mattie's house. For some reason, she didn't want her new friend to come out and see her there, and it was still a little too early for Mattie to have already left for work.

She examined her feelings for the redhead and got distracted for a moment thinking about the hair itself. It was a rich, bright red that caught the sun and shimmered with coppery highlights all along its length. She hadn't realized how long it was until Mattie asked her to braid it. It fell to her waist in thick heavy waves that begged to be touched, and it was so soft, and it smelled so good.

Rachel groaned in frustration and buried her face in her hands, scrubbing her eyes and banging her forehead quietly against her upraised knees. "I have got to stop thinking like that." A pale brown sand crab crept along the wet beach directly in front of her, stopping to examine her bare toes. "Well, I do," she insisted, peering down at the small creature and watching carefully in the event it decided to use its pinchers as part of the examination. Finding nothing interesting or tasty, the crab skittered on its way, searching for some morsel of breakfast.

She watched as it took a detour back into the water. "Life is so simple for you, isn't it?" she called after the crab as it disappeared from sight. A part of her wished she could also just dive into the waves and hide. It would be so much easier than digging down to find reserves of strength she might need for an unknown period of time. A very long time, she feared, if she wanted to be Mattie's friend. "I don't know if I can do this."

Rachel rarely felt lonely. Truth be told, she was almost always around other people, either working at the docks, dining at the boarding house, and especially when she was at the saloon, whether working or joining one of the card games. About the only times she was alone were by choice, either to sleep, or times like the present, when she needed time to think. She had never felt lonelier.

She had many friends — Lillie, Billy of course, as well as other co-workers and fellow boarders she was friendly with. But of all of them, Lillie was the only one she felt close to, and their relationship was certainly not a normal one by society's standards. She thought about the widows Sanders and McKenzie, and wondered how they had met, and where they had found the courage to both live together and hide the nature of their relationship from other people. She wondered if it was worth it, and if they ever felt alone in the world, as she did.

"Probably not," she muttered at a busy sand piper. The tiny bird paused in its fluttered wanderings, tilting its head and studying her with curious black eyes. "At least they have each other." The bird hopped across the sand toward a few others of its kind. "You probably have kinfolk, too." She envied the bird scampering around the sand with the other sand pipers. "I don't have anyone but Lil, and I have to pay her to get what I need from her." She suddenly felt very pathetic and just a little bit ashamed. She knew Lillie was her friend, and that was a part of their relationship she didn't have to purchase.

Her thoughts turned back to Mattie, and how best to support her. Mattie knew she knew about her husband hitting her, yet she hadn't distanced herself, despite the mutual shared, unspoken secret. In fact, Mattie had gone out of her way to seek Rachel out and deliver her mended shirt. Perhaps it would be best to tell Mattie about Adam. If there was one thing Rachel had learned all too painfully well during her short life, it was that the truth always seemed to come out, eventually.

She nodded to herself, knowing it was probably the right thing to do. How to broach the subject would be the difficult part. "And how on Earth am I going to get her thinking about the possibility that she can leave him, and what the heck choices does she have?"

She stood and stretched, retrieving her boots and wiggling her toes in the pleasantly cool, wet sand, walking closer to the water until the edge of the waves washed over her feet as they rushed up onto the shore. Mattie probably earned less at the tailor's shop than Rachel did on the docks, and Rachel was living as best she could, which was admittedly meagerly. "Except Mattie isn't supporting her brother through university." Rachel was also slowly building a nest egg for herself, and had been considering opening a bank account with the funds she had managed to sock away.

Mattie had a nice house, and fine clothing, and every comfort one could hope for, in Rachel's eyes. Every comfort except, perhaps, to feel safe in her own home. What kind of choices could she get Mattie to think about in light of all the conveniences she already had? *Like she'd want to come get herself a room at the boarding house,* she snorted softly.

The people living in the boarding house lived there either because it was convenient, or because they couldn't afford the finer things in life. Rachel herself was working toward having those things — a home, and horses, maybe even one of those new-fangled automobiles and perhaps a phonograph. She could dream, couldn't she?

No, she couldn't picture Mattie leaving Adam without leaving Galveston itself. The scandal might be too much. She found herself selfishly wanting Mattie to stay on the island. *Or maybe I could go somewhere with her.* It wasn't like she was tied to Galveston. A part of her absurdly wanted to somehow find a way to take care of Mattie herself, to provide her with everything she could ever want, including security.

She remembered Mattie's pensive, drawn features when she spoke of her husband. She mulled that over, mentally comparing it to the bright sunny smile and child-like laughter she had exhibited while playing on the beach the prior Sunday. She wondered what life must be like for Mattie, inside that house, when Adam was home. Did he talk to her at all, just about everyday things? Was he pleasant most of the time, and just sometimes lost his temper? Did he comprehend at all what a delightful and kind person his wife was, or how lucky he was to be married to her? Her blood boiled, as she pushed aside thoughts of their physical relationship. The thought that he could both strike her and touch her in love with the same hands was inconceivable, and made her slightly sick to her stomach.

"I can't think about that." She kicked a large shell down the beach, strode up to it, and kicked it again. She continued to mutter angrily under her breath, and when she reached the shell again, she bent over, picked it up, and heaved it savagely into the waves. She flung a piece of driftwood after it, for good measure, then plopped down in the sand again, crossed her legs, and buried her face in her hands in utter frustration. "What am I going to do?"

She looked up at gathering clouds, collecting her thoughts. "Help me?" she whispered softly. "I know I don't deserve your help, but she does." Her throat worked painfully, as she tried to swallow a lump. "Even if it means I get nothing in return, help me figure out how to help her."

Somewhere past the horizon, where she couldn't see, the waves churned, and the echo of distant thunder made its way back to her ears. By the time she completed the long walk home, the clouds were weeping as a spring storm rolled over the island. For a while, she paced restlessly in front of her solitary window, watching the rain fall, before finally settling down to go over her reading lesson.

SUNDAY DAWNED IN a gray overcast mix of clouds, rain, and thunder. Rachel rolled out of bed and stretched, moving to the window and yawning until her jaw popped. She ran her fingers through her hair and stretched again, feeling her muscles slowly come to life. Her hair and — she drew her fingers up and sniffed — her hands stank of cigar smoke, and her throat felt scratchy. Still, she smiled. It had been worth it, her Saturday night poker game a complete success, and she was twenty dollars wealthier than she'd been the night before. It was an unbelievable sum to win in one evening, and she had pulled it off beautifully.

With a quick bath and breakfast, she was out the front door, her book carefully tucked inside an old leather satchel. The showers blew sideways, drenching her clothing. Her boots were covered in sandy muck and her hair was plastered against her head. She caught the trolley, spending some of her hard-earned funds, finding herself quite alone on the rattling car.

"You must have something very important to attend to, to be out in this mess, young lady." The driver, an older gentleman she recognized from around town, tipped his hat as she hopped down from the trolley steps, wrinkling her nose as she barely avoided landing in a cesspool.

"Yes." She smiled, retrieving her satchel. "Yes, I sure do." She watched him drive away, then turned, face into the wind, toward Mattie's house. She was almost oblivious to the weather, her heart soaring at the thought of seeing Mattie, even if they did have some rather grave matters to discuss.

If we discuss them.

She detoured toward the beach for the rest of the short walk. The waves were wild and at least twice as high as usual, the sea awash in fierce-looking whitecaps. No boats were out, and the sea fowl were nowhere to be seen, most likely holed up further inland. The water washed up far onto shore in swirling hissing foam. She trudged along through the rain-flattened dunes. Her boots were a mess, and as tightly sealed as the boots were, she could feel her stockings squishing around her toes.

She topped a low rise and Mattie's clapboard house came into view. She took it in, truly seeing it for the first time. It was painted a fresh pearly gray and had white and blue shutters and trim. The roof was formed of even machine-made shingles, and a cheerful white picket fence bordered the part of the yard that faced the water. Behind the house was a well-built barn, which looked big enough to hold half a dozen animals. The barn was painted in the same pale gray as the house, the barn door painted to match the blue and white trim of the house. A crushed-shell driveway curved up beside the house and back to the barn door, then around the other side of the house and out toward the road that led to town.

Rachel stopped for a minute, just taking it all in. It looked like a much happier place than she knew it to be. A clothesline ran between two posts in the side yard, and several palm trees ringed the house.

The yard was typical of the island — a mix of tough thick marshy grass and weeds, although a small rock, shell, and driftwood garden graced what was once a flowerbed next to the front porch.

Just as she began walking again, the front door flew open and Mattie stepped out, hands on hips as she stood under the shelter of the covered porch. "Rachel?" She moved closer to the edge. "I can't believe you came all the way out here in this weather. Hurry up! Get in here so we can get you dried off. Don't you own a Mackintosh?"

"I own an oil slicker, which I left on Mr. Gentry's boat, along with my rubber boots." Rachel flashed a cheerful grin and closed the distance, removing her muddy boots at the bottom step before ducking under cover. "Figured the company would be worth it." She pushed back rain-drenched hair from her eyes, unsure if she was too wet to go inside.

"Well, come on in." Mattie shooed her into the parlor with a gentle push. "Stay put." She disappeared into the bedroom and returned with a large towel, which Rachel mutely took and began to dry off. "We can hang your clothes up by the fireplace. I lit it earlier. There was a bit of a chill in the air when I woke up this morning. Come on. You can undress in the bedroom." She stopped, measuring the long frame with an educated eye. "I can probably find a pair of Adam's trousers and a shirt that will fit you. Maybe. I think you may actually be a few inches taller than him."

Rachel felt panic rise up in her gut at the thought of wearing Adam's clothing. "No, no. I think my undershirt and drawers are dry enough, if you don't mind me wearing just those until my clothes are dry. If you have a sheet or a quilt or something."

"Very well." Puzzled red brows drew together. "I have a sheet, but truly, I just did laundry a day or so ago. Adam has plenty of clean shirts to spare."

"No. A sheet will be fine." She followed Mattie into the bedroom, trying to study it without staring at anything too much. A plump featherbed on a curved wrought-iron frame was against one wall, the bed covered in a patchwork wedding-ring pattern quilt. Twin oak night tables sat on either side of the bed, each one bearing a cut-glass lamp. A large armoire was on one side of the room and a matching dressing table sat across from it. Against the fourth wall was a low writing desk, beneath a window that looked out toward the barn. Light sheer curtains framed the window, which was closed against the rain. An oval braided rag rug covered the floor at the foot of the bed.

Mattie knelt down next to the armoire and opened a lower drawer, retrieving a sheet. She stood and smoothed down her pale blue skirt. "Here." She held out the sheet. "I'll leave you to undress. Bring your shirt and trousers out when you're ready and I'll hang them up to dry." She shook her head in mild amusement and left the room.

Rachel looked around again, drawing in the scent of fresh clean

linens and the soap Mattie must have used to bathe with, along with
the strong smell of the rain and ocean which hung over everything.
She moved closer to the dressing table and peered into the mirror,
avoiding looking at the bed or thinking of what might go on there.
"Well, I am a sight, aren't I?" She looked like a drowned thing, her
thick hair drenched and completely straight, hanging down her back
and sticking to the sides of her face. "Shoulda put it up and worn a
hat."

She shrugged out of her stockings, shirt, and trousers, and turned
a complete circle in the mirror, making sure she was indeed decent in
only her underclothing. The plain white muslin drawers, her only nod
to feminine clothing, came down to just below her knees, and her
ribbed short-sleeved undershirt bore a three-button placket in front.
Her lower legs were markedly paler than her tanned arms and face,
the result of working on the docks in long trousers and shirtsleeves.
She looked very much like the working-class person she was, and she
found herself feeling ashamed of that fact for the first time in her life.

Her eyes fell on her leather satchel, which she had set down on the
desk. "That's going to change," she scolded herself in the mirror.
"You're going to learn to read, and then you're going to go make
something of yourself." She looked at her eyes and nose, re-
memorizing what they looked like. She didn't spend much time
dwelling on her appearance, but now she sat down on the padded
bench in front of the dressing table, taking a long look at herself. She
wondered if people, in general, found her attractive.

A rustling of skirts behind her made her turn around, to find
Mattie standing in the doorway watching her. "Oh." Rachel blushed.
"I was just thinking about combing out my hair." She stood, picking
up her wet clothing. "Didn't bring a comb or brush with me."

"You can use one of mine." Mattie nodded toward the table top,
and an ivory-backed hairbrush and matching comb. "I can help you
comb it out. Come on out and sit by the fire." She picked up the sheet
and turned on her heels, pausing in the doorway, where she turned
back to Rachel, who stood rooted in place. "Well, come on." She
crooked a finger and smiled.

Rachel's feet moved and she followed, finding herself drawn
down onto a stool in front of the fire. She felt soft light cotton settle
around her shoulders, as Mattie draped her with the sheet, and
pressed a warm cup of tea into her hands. "Thank you." She inhaled
the sweet steaming tea and looked up in surprised gratitude, watching
as Mattie hung her clothes on short pegs nailed into the mantle.

Mattie went back into the bedroom and came out with the satchel
and her comb. "Is your book in here?" She placed the satchel at Rachel's
feet, watching her nod affirmatively. "I'll start combing out your hair.
Why don't you start reading for me? I can see the pages over your
shoulder. The sooner we finish lessons, the sooner we can play."

"True." But Rachel simply sat there, not moving to pick up her book, absorbing something new and different.

"Rachel?" Mattie paused in her attention to her hair. "Is something wrong?"

"No." She shifted, her eyes shining warmly at Mattie. "It's just...I was sitting here, trying to remember the last time anyone took care of me when I came in from the rain. I can't." She shook her head, at a loss for the right words. "I'm sure, when I was a very little girl— anyway, it was always my job to take care of the others." She sipped her tea and looked back up. "Thank you. It's nice."

"It's nothing." Mattie blushed.

"No. It means a lot." Rachel's hand came up, capturing Mattie's wrist in mid-motion, squeezing it before she released it. "Nice to know someone cares." She turned back around to give Mattie access to her hair, soaking in something that was different from physical lust. This was warm and more subdued.

Mattie worked at the thick wavy locks, combing them into order and working out wind- and rain-induced snarls before she braided the mass of hair. "Here, hold on to this." She handed the end of the braid to Rachel and picked up a small box from a table across the room. "Here." She offered the box, taking the braid back so Rachel would have both hands free. "For you."

Puzzled features tilted toward her in question, then Rachel slowly removed a red ribbon tie and slipped the cover from the small white box. Nestled inside was a hair clip, a section of braided leather that had been died a deep dark blue, and fastened to a shiny metal clasp. "What's this for?"

"You said your birthday was at the end of the month." Mattie smiled. "You didn't tell me exactly which day, but being as next week is the last week of March, I figured it must be soon."

"It—it's the 29th—Thursday next." She turned the hair clasp over and over, as if she couldn't believe it was real. "Thank you," she finally said, feeling a little disjointed.

"Happy birthday," Mattie replied brightly. "Can I use it to hold your braid fast?"

"Oh." Rachel reluctantly let go of the clasp. "Sure. Here you go."

Mattie clipped the clasp on the end of the braid and flipped it over Rachel's shoulder where she could see it. Steel eyes trailed downward, lost in thought as long fingers absently traced the twisted leather. Mattie pulled up a second stool and sat down directly across from her, touching Rachel on the knee and waiting for her to look up. "Don't tell me you've never received a birthday gift before."

Rachel looked back down at the gift, then back up. "Not that I remember, no."

"Would it be too much if I told you I made you a cake as well?" She smoothed back damp bangs, fluffing them playfully.

"I-I don't know what to say." Rachel's voice was very soft. "You spoil me."

"Listen, Rachel." Mattie drew her knees up, wrapping her arms around them, her weight resting on the tips of her toes. "I haven't seen my family in several months. I haven't made any friends here, not really. Adam...he...anyway, I miss my sister Carrie terribly. She's about the only person I was ever able to talk to. Last Sunday, it was the best day I've had since we moved here. When I saw the rain this morning, I felt so lonely, because I was certain you wouldn't come. I enjoy spending time with you. I think we can be good friends, at least I'd like for us to be."

Rachel's eyes stung and she blinked a few times until it passed. "I'd like that too." She smiled. "You made me a cake? Really?"

"Yes." Mattie stood up, pushing Rachel back down as she started to follow. "First, though, I made us some little crab-cake sandwiches for dinner. I'll bring them out here so you can keep drying by the fire."

Thoughtful eyes watched, as Mattie disappeared into the kitchen. The day was turning out to be full of surprises, and it wasn't even noon yet.

THEY SHARED SMALL-TALK over sandwiches and cake, then moved on to the reading lesson. To her relief and surprise, Rachel discovered she was much more proficient at sounding out and retaining words than she had originally believed. They were seated next to each other on Mattie's sofa. She was still wrapped in the sheet, but it had slipped down around her waist, leaving her arms free to turn pages in the reader. Mattie had a tendency to either pat her on the leg or touch her on the arm or shoulder each time she completed a lesson successfully, and she pressed against Rachel each time she leaned over to provide correction. It was nice, and distracting as all get out, but she allowed herself to enjoy the innocent contact.

"You're reading complete sentences," Mattie praised her again, the corners of her eyes crinkling in a smile. "The way you were talking, I thought we were going to have to start with the most basic lessons." She flipped to the last two pages of the reader. "Read those for me."

Rachel complied, her words hesitant but accurate. When she finished, she felt yet another squeeze to her arm. "Does that mean I read it all correctly?" She looked down at Mattie's curled fingers.

"Oh." Mattie blushed slightly, a faint hint of pink on her cheeks beneath a light dusting of freckles. "Yes." She trailed her hand down before removing it. "I think we can bypass the first reader and move to the second one. Why don't you read the first five lessons in the second reader this week, one each evening, and we can go over those next Sunday."

"That would be fine." Rachel was pleased that next Sunday seemed to be a given, without question.

"You've got muscular arms, did you know that?" Mattie squeezed her arm again, this time with a more studious attitude.

"Good thing," Rachel snorted softly. "Lifting bales of cotton and crates of dry goods would be awfully difficult otherwise."

"Well, I would suppose so." Hazel eyes moved from her arm to the waistband of her drawers, which bore a white on white stitching of tiny flowers and stars. "I would never have guessed you had these on underneath." One finger reached out, quickly touching a stitched flower before she pulled back.

Rachel's throat went dry and she glanced at her, trying to read her thoughts. Mattie's face bore an open honest quizzical expression, with no trace of any other intent, romantic or otherwise. She swallowed and took a sip of tea before answering. "Didn't realize you thought about me in my drawers." It was a dangerous bit of a tease and she watched the charming blush creep up Mattie's neck again.

"Oh. I-I..." Mattie stammered. Truth be told, she hadn't thought about Rachel's drawers at all, until she saw them. She did wonder, just a little, why Rachel always wore men's clothing. She understood the need for trousers on the docks, but a part of her was curious as to what went on inside her beautiful head. "I apologize. I didn't mean to insult you." She sighed in frustration. "They just seem out of contrast with the rest of your attire."

"It's all right." Rachel laughed softly. "You're not the first person to ask me about my clothes. I've always worn men's and boy's clothing. When I was growing up, it was necessary for the work I did around the farm. It's what I'm comfortable with. And I ride my bicycle so often, a skirt would get in the way. But the plain women's drawers fit fine under my trousers, and they're shaped better for me than men's drawers are. Although you'll never catch me wearing a corset. Can't breathe in them."

"What about when you go out in the evenings?" Mattie suddenly realized she had no idea how Rachel spent her time when she wasn't working, and she remembered mention of a second job.

It was a perfect opening. Rachel shored up her courage, testing the water. "About the only place I go, other than to the docks or to the store, is to a little place out on the far end of the island. It-it's a saloon. I sometimes tend bar there." She paused, reading no judgment in the hazel eyes. She looked down at her hands clasped in her lap, and continued. If they were to truly be friends, Mattie deserved to at least know this much about her. "I play poker almost every Saturday night. For money. I gamble. And I usually drink whiskey and smoke cigars during the games." She couldn't make herself look up, but moved doggedly forward nonetheless, determined to at least gage her reaction to gambling and drinking. "I don't suppose I'm the type of person you would normally choose to associate with."

Mattie stood and walked to the bookcase, her back turned as she looked at the three framed photographs. "No. Not as a general rule." She slowly turned around. "My husband, he drinks. Quite a lot, actually. He's...worse when he does that. And, I just discovered that he gambles. At least I think he still does. I know he used to, although I didn't know about it until Friday evening. I found some things in a desk drawer. They were kind of shocking, but it answered a lot of questions I've had about my life with Adam, and who he is. He scares me when he drinks. I don't like it."

So, this is it. Rachel looked down, waiting to be dismissed from Mattie's house. Instead, she felt a gentle hand on her knee and didn't have to look up, for Mattie was kneeling in front of her at eye level.

"You said you're not the type of person I would choose to associate with. Rachel, I've never had a choice at all as to whom I associate with. My choices have always been made for me. In almost everything I've done. You've been nothing but kind to me. What you've told me is a bit surprising, but I think, as long as you don't come into my house smelling of whiskey, I think I can deal with that part of your life."

"I would never come to your house drunk." She held her indignant emotions in check, glad for acceptance in whatever form she could get it. "I can't remember the last time I got drunk. I usually only have one or two drinks at most during a poker game."

"No, no." Mattie realized she'd offended her. "I'm sorry. That's not what I meant. If you took only one sip, and I smelled it, it would make me feel—brings up some unpleasant memories, is all."

Rachel watched her own hand reach out, tilting up Mattie's chin, which was quivering. "How bad is it, Mattie?"

There was no need for explanation. She knew what Rachel was asking. Mattie blinked away a scattering of unexpected tears. She stood up abruptly and fled to the window, looking out at the steadily falling rain. "It's bad." She drew a shaky breath and it all came tumbling out. "I don't know why he married me. I can't seem to ever do anything to please him. He barely speaks to me, except to tell me what I've done wrong. He's gone all day and most weekends. When he is on the island, he stays out late. Sometimes he doesn't come home at all. What's sad is I don't mind. I sometimes wish he'd never come back again, then I feel so guilty, because it's like wishing him dead, and I fear I'll go to Hell for thinking like that."

Her back was turned and her shoulders slumped, her body shivering just the slightest bit. Before she knew what was happening, Rachel was behind her and then Mattie turned, and Rachel found herself holding on to her, stroking her hair as she talked.

"You know you've only answered part of my question, don't you?"

She felt Mattie trembling against her. "How many times has he hurt you?"

"I lost count a long time ago." She couldn't look up, so she buried her face into Rachel's neck, absorbing the warmth. She couldn't recall anyone holding her in comfort since she was a little girl, when sometimes her nanny might give her a hug if she skinned a knee. "Every morning, I wake up and wonder if he's going to hit me that day. Or push me down or throw something at me." Rachel grew still, and Mattie felt her quit breathing for a long moment. "Every night, if I made it through the day without displeasing him, I say a little prayer of thanks to God for sparing me that day."

"Bastard." A low hissed curse that escaped her lips without thought. "You've done nothing to deserve what he does to you."

"Whether I have or not, does it matter?" Mattie looked up, swiping her hand across her own face. "My mother told me I've made my bed and now I have to lie in it. Only I didn't make this bed. She did." Anger replaced tears. "Now I have to live with him, for the rest of my life."

Rachel wanted to say so much, but sensed the timing was wrong. That Mattie had opened up to her as much as she had was astonishing, and she chose not to prod or make any outlandish suggestions about leaving Adam, just yet. Instead, she kissed the top of Mattie's head, and drew her back over to the sofa. "I'm so sorry, Mattie." It was Rachel's turn to kneel, as she reached out, brushing more tears from Mattie's face. "Sit. Let me get you some more tea."

She found her way into the kitchen and spied the teapot, staying warm on the stove. Quickly, she poured up a fresh cup and added two lumps of sugar and a dash of cream, just as she'd seen Mattie make for herself. As an afterthought, she sliced a small piece of cake and placed it on a saucer, and brought it back into the parlor.

Grateful hands reached out, taking the offering. Rachel watched Mattie's hands shake, and racked her brain for a distraction. She remembered a humorous story from the poker game. It was slightly risqué, but worth taking a chance, if she could get Mattie to smile. "Would you like to hear a funny story?"

"I suppose." Mattie was relieved for the diversion, feeling slightly embarrassed at her emotional outburst.

"One of the men I played poker with last night. He was in New York last month and saw a play. It's called 'Sappho' and it's causing quite a stir among folks. It's the most brash show to come out of Europe in a while." She shifted to the sofa, getting into the story. "Seems at the end, the man picks up the woman and takes her up some stairs, as if he's carrying her to bed. The society ladies of New York are in an uproar."

Mattie's face revealed nothing, so she continued. "Then he tells us about a book called 'Sister Carrie' that's come out at about the same time as this play. The book is about a lady of the evening. Anyway, it's been removed from publication. Between the play and the book, the man said the church leaders up in New York are convinced the country is slipping into moral decay, and that women are going to become crazed and behave wildly. Can you believe it?"

"Not hardly." Mattie didn't laugh, but grew introspective instead. "It would take a lot more than a play or a book for me to enjoy..." She stopped, realizing what she was about to say, and blushed furiously. She peered shyly at Rachel, who only looked back at her in concern.

"I'm sorry, Mattie." Rachel mentally kicked herself. "That story was inappropriate. I shouldn't have told it."

"No." Mattie briefly smiled in reassurance. "My response is what was inappropriate. You're not married. I don't know if I could even explain what I was going to say, and it might embarrass you."

"I..." *How much do I tell her?* Rachel realized Mattie seemed perfectly accepting of her, so far, despite admissions of gambling, drinking, and smoking, and the woman had heard her swear. "I probably know more about the subject than you think I do. I've been with someone. Even though I've never been married."

"Oh." Mattie turned that over in her head. She had never spoken of intimate relations with anyone except her mother, and even then it was in the most cryptic of terms during their conversation after she married Adam. There had been one other clandestine conversation with an older woman of the church in El Paso, who had explained to her what a pessary was and how to use it. Other than that, she had talked about it with no one. It was taboo — something one simply didn't discuss in polite company. Yet she wanted so desperately to talk to someone, and Rachel had admitted to non-chastity. She thought about that. If anyone seemed safe to talk to, it was Rachel.

Mattie was quiet for so long, Rachel was certain she had finally crossed one too many lines during the short time they had known each other. "I'm not a whore, Mattie. I've only been with one person."

"Once was enough, I'll wager." Mattie's voice took on a surprisingly bitter tone.

"I didn't say that." Rachel stepped further out on a limb, guessing at Mattie's meaning. "Some women do find it enjoyable."

"I don't see how." Mattie's face grew even redder and she looked down. "I just assumed only men found it pleasurable, despite what some of those romance novels suggest. My husband obviously does. Even more so than I thought he did. Can — can I show you something? It's not very nice. You might be offended by it."

"I doubt that." Rachel's lips twisted into a quirky half-smile. "I see and hear a lot of ribald things at the saloon."

"Well, then." Mattie got up and went into the bedroom, unlocking the desk drawer and retrieving the photographs of the women. She thought about the rest and left it. For some reason, the thought that her husband was a thief was more embarrassing than the thought that he might enjoy looking at pictures of naked women. She made her way back into the parlor and held out the photographs. "Adam had these hidden in a locked desk drawer. I don't know any of those women, and I don't know where he took their photographs."

Rachel slowly sifted through the half dozen pictures. She had seen some of the same photographs passed around the saloon, and recognized them as items that could be ordered through the mail. "He didn't take these. He bought them."

"You know those women?" Mattie's voice was incredulous.

"No." Rachel handed them back, glad beyond belief that she truly didn't. "I've seen some of the same photos at the saloon. They're illegal, but they can be purchased through catalogues, I believe."

"Oh." Mattie sat down, placing the photographs aside on the low table. "What sort of women would pose for them?"

"Prostitutes," Rachel offered. "They—some of them do what they have to do to survive, Mattie. They can make a nice bit of money posing for those."

"Prostitutes? Do you think Adam...?" She couldn't quite bring herself to ask, but saw something telling in Rachel's eyes, and already knew the answer.

"Yes," Rachel answered softly. "I've—met Adam, Mattie. I didn't realize he was your husband until Friday evening. I've been trying and trying to figure out a way to tell you about it."

"He sees whores?" Mattie was dumbstruck. "At the saloon where you serve drinks?"

"Yes." Rachel slid back on the sofa, as far as she could, waiting to be banished from the house and Mattie's life, forever.

Mattie stood up slowly, and walked back to the window. Rachel heard the loud sigh from across the room and watched as Mattie moved to the bookshelves, picking up a frame. She couldn't see the picture from where she sat. The silence was deafening, the only noise breaking it was the gentle patter of rain hitting the shingles overhead, and the ocean's dull roar from outside. She was very close to just getting up and leaving, thinking Mattie was too angry or too hurt to speak. One arm was braced on the sofa cushion, but a single word stopped her.

"Good."

She sank back down onto the plump cushion in mute shock. "Did you say...?"

"Good," Mattie repeated, this time more loudly. She turned around, her face a mixture of pain and confused relief. "I suspect that's why he leaves me alone most of the time. We don't love each other, you know. We never have. I think he married me for money. I certainly don't enjoy being with him in that way. The less he needs that from me, the better."

It was the last thing Rachel had expected to hear. "You aren't angry?"

"Of course I am!" Mattie spat out. "I'm angry that I'm married to a man who doesn't love me, who is a liar, a gambler, and a thief, and who sees fit to commit adultery while he's married to me. Who, who I live in fear of every day of my life. Most of all, I'm simply angry I'm married to him at all. It's the biggest mistake of my life, and there's nothing I can do about it but live with it. So, yes, I'm angry!" She fumed, pacing back and forth and muttering under her breath.

Rachel watched in silence. She wasn't about to ask what Mattie meant by calling Adam a thief, and she certainly didn't want to risk this being their last get-together. She sensed that there would be plenty of opportunities to get Mattie to think about her options at a later date. "I'm sorry, Mattie." It was all she could bring herself to say.

"I am, too." Mattie's demeanor softened, and she sat back down, clasping one of Rachel's hands between her own. She peered up shyly through red eyelashes. "I'm surprised you aren't mortified at everything I've said."

"Mortified?" Rachel stroked her friend's soft hair with her free hand. "I could say the same thing to you, don't you think? I believe I'm the sinner here, and I can't believe you still want anything to do with me."

"You're my friend," Mattie stated simply, then drew a surprised Rachel into a hug. "I don't care about all your sins, Rachel. I...when I saw you on the beach that first time, you looked kind of sad. I felt something, a kinship with you, because I know what it's like to feel sad and lonely. Yet you're so strong. You always seem to keep your sunny side up, which is what I try to do, at least most of the time." She pulled back, continuing to hold on to Rachel's hand. "You haven't let all the bad things in your life turn you into a bad person, and I want to be the same way."

Rachel tilted her head, studying Mattie's face intently. She was speechless at the complete acceptance. There was no judgment in the hazel eyes, only warmth that reached out and wrapped itself around her heart. She knew her feelings for Mattie ran deeper than they should, but one look at the friendship she was being offered was worth it. She wanted Mattie in her life more than she had ever wanted anything, and she was willing to have her on any terms Mattie was willing to offer. "You? A bad person?" she finally managed to squeak out. "You're the kindest person I've ever met."

"And you're the same to me." Mattie hugged her again. "I've never found anyone I could talk to the way I can talk to you. I don't know why. Maybe it's because we've both had some tough times, eh?"

"Maybe." Rachel looked past her, toward the gray rain and ocean outside. "So." She gathered in her emotions. It was enough for one day. More than enough. "We can't go for a walk on the beach, and it's growing late. Maybe I should go on home."

"But it's still raining, and your clothes are just now getting dry," Mattie protested.

"I'll be fine." Rachel stood and moved to the hearth, feeling her almost-dry shirt and trousers. "At least I'll be dry starting out. I can change when I get home." She removed her clothing from the mantle and retired to the bedroom to dress, then collected her book and placed it back in the satchel.

Mattie pressed a package into her hand, explaining that it was leftover cake and sandwiches she could eat for supper, then walked her to the front door. They stopped, looking at each other awkwardly for a moment. Rachel finally smiled and pulled Mattie to her in a hug, brushing her lips against a freckled cheek as they parted. "Thank you, Mattie. For the birthday gift and cake."

"You're welcome." She walked out onto the porch, watching as Rachel ducked out into the rain and started the trek toward the trolley stop on the main road. "Stay warm and dry." She waved.

Rachel waved back. "I will." *Warm, at any rate,* she added silently, which proved to be true. Despite the driving rain, which soaked her clothing all over again, inside she basked in the warmth of true friendship.

Chapter
Four

TWO WEEKS PASSED without incident. Mattie comported herself with Adam as if nothing were different, but inside, she knew it was. She found herself studying him at odd moments, looking over a book, pretending to read the text while she was actually trying to read her husband. He was a stranger. He always had been, she realized. The information she had gained from Rachel, along with the documents and photographs in the desk drawer, had forever changed the way she would look at him.

She hinted at a desire to go home to see her family, mostly to see what he would say. He grew even more abrupt and cold than usual, and stated he was much too busy with his work to plan such a long journey any time in the foreseeable future. When she asked if she could travel home without him, she watched his jaw line twitch, the anger readily evident, and steeled herself for a blow that never came. Instead, he told her it was too dangerous, and there was to be no further discussion of the matter.

She spent one Sunday with Rachel, going over their second reading lesson. They talked little of serious things on that day, choosing instead to concentrate on the lesson and a long walk on the beach, which ended with wading in the shallow surf. There was a lot of easy laughter and light conversation between them—nothing important, but she reflected it was nice to have a friend she could talk to and simply have fun with. Lord knew she hadn't had a whole lot of fun in her lifetime, and Rachel brought out the little child in Mattie. It felt wonderful, digging in the sand, running barefoot on the beach, picking up shells, and tossing breadcrumbs to the seagulls.

At the end of the weekend, Rachel declared the water was almost warm enough to start swimming lessons. Unfortunately, Adam chose to spend the following weekend on the island. While he was gone from home most of the day on both Saturday and Sunday, the possibility he could return at any moment precluded Mattie and Rachel's usual Sunday afternoon visit.

Now it was Tuesday, and she found herself anxious to see Rachel again. Rachel had been out on a fishing boat most of the time, so even a quick run by the tailor shop during the noon hour was impossible.

Adam had picked Mattie up every evening from the shop, so there was no time to sneak away and visit Rachel at the boarding house.

She missed her with an ache like nothing she had experienced before.

Mattie busied herself at the shop, working on Rachel's shirt order, along with the rest of the orders she had to fill. They were very busy, and there were still more wedding clothes to sew for several customers, all of whom had planned traditional June weddings.

On Tuesday evening, she decided to tell Adam she needed to get to the shop early to finish an order. The ruse went over like a charm, and at dawn on Wednesday, Adam dropped her off at the tailor shop. She waved at him and let herself in, then waited until he was gone, watching out the window through the curtains. Even after he was out of sight, she waited another quarter hour just to be safe, then sharpened a tablet pencil with a small pocket knife before composing a note to Mr. Vaughan, telling him she had been in, but had an errand to run and would be back later.

She took off for the port, moving from the Broadway to the side street, lest Adam come driving back through town for some reason and see her. It was about a half mile away, a short pleasant walk in the early morning breeze. The sun was rising at her back, painting the water in vivid golden and rose-hued ripples, and she thought about buying some of the pastels she had seen in the general store and capturing the scene in color rather than in charcoal or pencil.

As she approached the pier, she realized she had no idea how to find Rachel, or even where to look. She walked across the short bridge that led to the longer row of docks, which was lined with boats of all kinds. Her shoes clicked lightly on the weathered wood and the bridge swayed slightly with her motion. At the end of the bridge stood a large, muscular man with dark hair and beard, his chest already bare in the warm morning air. He held a clipboard, which he was reviewing intently.

"Excuse me, sir." Mattie stopped a few feet short of him, peering up from under her cream-colored straw hat. "Might you tell me if Rachel Travis is working today, and where I might find her?"

"You have business with her?" The man eyed her skeptically, her long skirt and fine clothing completely out of place for her surroundings.

"I—she—I've been trying to reach her regarding an order she placed at the tailor's shop in town." Mattie shifted her weight uneasily, from one foot to the other. "If I might speak with her very briefly, please?"

"Very well." He pointed to his left. "Next to last fishing boat near the end down that way. Better hurry. They're about to pull out for the day."

"Thank you, sir." Mattie scurried along the rough walkway,

picking up her skirts and moving as fast as she could without actually running. She reached the appointed boat and slowed down, taking in the sight of her friend.

Rachel was halfway up the mast, working some knots out of thick rope, her back turned. She was standing on iron rungs and tied off to the pole with more heavy rope. She wore light tan trousers, clunky black work boots, and a short-sleeved undershirt. Her long-sleeved shirt was tied around her waist and she was covered in sweat, her hair in a long braid down her back. A bare trickle of smoke curled up over her head, indicating she was smoking a cigar.

Mattie laughed quietly and moved to the edge of the boat, still standing on the dock. She cleared her throat, unsure of how to address Rachel in front of the older gentleman who was at the front of the boat, and a younger man who was off to the side, working with something in a bucket. "Excuse me, Miss Travis?" Her voice sounded strange to her own ears.

Rachel's arms stopped in mid-motion, and she turned, looking over her shoulder. "Mattie?" she stammered through lips that clenched carefully around her cigar. She quickly untied herself and shimmied down the mast, her biceps bulging nicely with her efforts. When she hit the deck, she trotted over and stood across from Mattie. "Oh." She removed the cigar and dropped it to the deck, crushing it out with her foot. " 'Scuse my manners." She grinned broadly. "How are you?"

"I'm fine, thank you. And you?" Mattie tilted her head up, moving so that Rachel's head blocked the sun from shining into her eyes. She watched a frown replace a smile. "Rachel?"

Rachel jumped the railing and landed precisely in front of Mattie, while long fingers reached out, brushing against Mattie's cheek. She felt the fingers brush a bit harder and she reached up, closing her hand over them. "What's wrong?"

"Oh." Rachel appeared conflicted. "You have a bit of a dark smudge on your cheek. I thought it was—that is I..." She looked down, kicking the toe of her boot lightly against a lose board in embarrassment.

"You thought what?" Mattie reached up with her free hand, rubbing the spot and looking at her fingers, realizing the smudge was probably from the pencil she had used to write her note to Mr. Vaughan. "It's pencil, Rachel, not a bruise."

Pained eyes peered uncertainly at her. "Sorry. I shouldn't be so quick to assume."

"I'm glad you care. You could easily have been right," she whispered softly, then squeezed the hand she still held, and released it. "Anyway, I came down here to tell you that your shirt order will be ready for final fitting on Friday, if you can manage to come by and try them on for any last-minute alterations."

"I might not be able to Friday, but you work Saturdays, correct?" Rachel gestured around the boat. "Shrimping has been very good, and we may be out for the rest of the week. Mr. Gentry has been able to sell a load every evening on the docks when we return, and the more we catch, the more wages Billy and I make."

"Saturday would be fine." Mattie idly looked around the tidy boat. She noticed surreptitious glances from both Mr. Gentry and Billy, Billy's eyes lingering on her a bit longer than necessary. "I'm glad for your good fortune. Adam should be going to Houston this weekend, if you'd like to come visit."

"I'd love to," Rachel interrupted. "I've missed you, Mattie."

"I've missed you too." She glanced at the sun and the sky, which was blue, all traces of dawn gone. "Well, I suppose I should get back to the shop, and let you finish whatever it is you're doing to get ready to fish."

"I'll see you Saturday afternoon, then." Rachel resisted the urge to give Mattie a hug. She felt somewhat shy for some reason, and chalked it up to their ten-day separation.

"I look forward to it." Mattie smiled and turned, making her way back down the dock.

Rachel grasped the railing and vaulted back onto the deck. Billy moved to her side, watching Mattie go. "Lovely young lady."

"Yes, she is," she drawled slowly, amused at Billy's obvious interest. "That was my tailor, Mrs. Madeleine Crockett."

"She's married?" Billy's voice was more than a little disappointed.

"Yes." Rachel snickered, and went back to the mast and began her climb up.

Billy started to walk back across the deck, to begin work with some shrimping nets, but stopped in mid-stride, looking up at Rachel incredulously. "You have a tailor?"

"I do now." She grinned mysteriously, giving him a playful wink. "Come on, Billy, can't a girl want to improve her appearance? I figured some hand-made clothing might help things along."

"I suppose." He scratched his head. Rachel was always dressed neatly, shirt tucked in, shoes buffed, and hair either braided or pinned up, but she had never before seemed the sort to care much about her looks. He shrugged and started unrolling the nets.

THE FOLKSY MELODIES of a fiddle, harmonica, and dulcimer rose up around a happy throng of revelers, who were busy dancing and drinking mugs of homemade wine. They were gathered around several crackling bonfires on the beach near the far southeast end of the island. Rachel sipped at a large mug of something fruity, and tended a fire where a clambake was well underway.

She had been unable to make her appointment for her shirt fitting, due to being needed for an unexpected Saturday morning fishing trip on Mr. Gentry's boat. Billy had written an apologetic note for her, which she slid under the tailor shop door at dawn on Saturday morning. Now it was Saturday evening, just after sunset, and the air was starting to cool down after a rather warm mid-April day.

She looked around. It was not the island's finest, by any stretch, but they were her friends. These were the dockworkers and factory laborers, who toiled by the sweat of their backs during the day, providing goods and services consumed by everyone in Galveston and around the world. It was comfortable. No high rollers were to be found among them — no one who expected special treatment or service. She suspected the saloon was only half-full of its usual patrons. Those that would be there would have plenty of funds to spread around, so she had no fear that Lillie or the other ladies would suffer for lack of clients, even with half the poker players missing.

The clambakes were held a few times each season, and this one was a celebration of a week of abundant fishing, and extra wages for everyone involved in Galveston's fishing industry.   As an afterthought, in her note, she had Billy invite Mattie to the clambake, and give her directions as to what part of the beach the party was to be held. He had looked at her in silent question and she had stubbornly crossed her arms, stating that Mattie was, after all, a tailor, and qualified as a laborer. That they never invited workers outside the docks and factories was not mentioned between them, and the look became less questioning and more knowing, and she ducked her head, hiding a blush she felt burning beneath her skin.

She was certain Billy could read her affections for Mattie. Other than Lillie, he knew her best of her friends on the island, and if Lillie suspected how she felt, Billy probably did as well. He had once questioned her relationship with Lillie, and she had vaguely brushed it aside with the explanation that they were merely good friends. He never asked again, but she knew he knew that people like her didn't become friends with people like Lillie merely for the conversation. Plus, she was way too protective of Lillie.

Now, she poked a stick into the fire, digging out another round of clams that were buried in the ash. Their steamy fragrance rose through the air and made her stomach growl in anticipation. Over the fire, a pot of boiling crabs and shrimp bubbled in an enticing spicy mixture. She peered into it as well, stirring it occasionally. Billy stood beside her, holding out platters as she dished up the clams, which he then passed around to the waiting celebrants.

She shoved more raw clams into the ash, picking out some oysters as well. Some she placed in the ash with the clams, and some she kept aside to eat raw. A gentle breeze stirred her hair, which she had unbraided to hang lose down her back. Her trouser legs were rolled up and she was enjoying the cool wet sand against the soles of her bare feet. Satisfied the cooking was going well, she stepped away from the fire and the group, moving closer to the water.

It was wild out there, dark waves rolling under a rising half moon and a glittering array of stars. It was a clear night, with no clouds to obscure her view. The water churned, its surface reflecting the light, marred only by white caps that broke over a sandbar partway out to sea. In daylight, she had often swum out to the sandbar, where she could stand in waist-high water, an odd sensation given it was so far from shore. She smiled and decided to set a swim to the sandbar as a goal for Mattie to attain.

Just as she thought of her friend, movement in her peripheral vision caught her attention, and she turned to spot a familiar figure making its way toward her from far down the shoreline. She waved and Mattie waved back in kind. Rachel broke into a steady trot down the packed sand, meeting her well away from the party. "Hello, Mattie. I'm glad you decided to join us."

Mattie smiled at her and looked back up the sand dunes above them toward the hidden road. "Thank you for the invitation. The directions were very good. The gentleman who gave me a ride had no trouble finding it." She looked over Rachel's shoulder toward the campfires, the music drifting toward her. "Oh, my. What a big party. Are you sure I'm welcome here? I—I've never been to a party on the beach. Back home, and here, almost all parties involved tea and cakes, and the closest we came to being outdoors was sitting on my mother's screened-in porch."

"You were invited as my guest." Rachel held out her arm and felt a warm hand wrap around it. "It may be a bit rougher of a crowd than you're used to, but they are all good people."

"Well, of course they are," Mattie tisked at her. "They are your friends, aren't they?" Hazel eyes twinkled in the moonlight. "Whatever is cooking smells lovely."

"We're baking clams and oysters, and boiling crabs and shrimp. Part of our take from the catch this week." Rachel guided her to the nearest fire, pulling a large driftwood log closer and motioning Mattie to take a seat. "Would you like a mug of wine?"

"Yes, thank you." While Rachel retrieved her drink, Mattie looked around the area. It was indeed a rough crowd. Many of the men bore untrimmed beards and most of the people wore simple, well-worn clothing, with patches at elbows and knees the rule rather than the exception. She noted that everyone seemed healthy and trim, and she assumed the work they did kept them in good condition. Many were standing in a circle around the musicians, clapping their hands while others danced to a lively jig. It seemed that no one was barred from the gathering, as wives and children were mixed in among the workers. She knew these people had little in the way of money or material possessions, yet all of them appeared happy, as if they hadn't a care in the world.

She envied them.

Rachel returned with not only her drink, but a plate generously heaped with an assortment of steaming seafood. A large slice of buttered cornbread graced one side of the plate, while a thick wedge of apple pie balanced it on the other side. "Do you mind sharing with me?" Rachel sat down and produced two forks. "I tried to get enough for two, but we're running low on plates."

"That would be fine." Mattie studied the plate with some trepidation. She was familiar with shrimp and crabs, but the clams and oysters were a mystery. "How do I eat those?"

"Oh." Rachel picked up a clam, breaking the shell open. "You pick out the meat inside with your fork, and here is how I prefer to eat the oysters." She chose a raw oyster, cracking the shell against the log with a rock. She slurped it down and followed it by sucking on a slice of orange. "Not everyone likes them raw. I brought cooked ones too, just in case."

Mattie felt brave, and picked up a raw oyster. "I'll do it the way you just did. If — if you can help me get it open, that is." She watched Rachel grin, then heard the crack of the shell and gasped in surprise as she held the half-shell up to Mattie's lips. She sucked the slimy oyster flesh into her mouth. It was salty and had the oddest texture, but she decided she liked it, especially the orange slice afterward. "That was good. Can I have another one, please?"

Rachel laughed softly and complied. They became lost in conversation, sharing their meal, exchanging bites of seafood and dessert, oblivious to the curiously watching eyes all around them. Most of the people didn't know who Mattie was, save the few men who had given the tailor shop some business. Her fine skirt and shirtwaist were out of place, yet Rachel obviously knew her well. After a while, attention was turned back to the music and the food, and the women were left to talk in relative privacy.

"I can't believe you came." Rachel offered her a bite of apple pie, watching as full, soft lips nibbled at the sweet treat. She swallowed. Their separation had made it abundantly clear to Rachel that Lillie was correct, that she did have very strong feelings for Mattie, although she couldn't characterize them as love. She'd never been in love, and wasn't sure what it was supposed to feel like. It mattered not. The golden band on Mattie's ring finger precluded anything more than friendship.

"I can't believe you invited me." Red eyelashes blinked shyly. "It means a great deal to me, Rachel. I — I get lonely sometimes, especially on Saturday evenings when I see all the people in town going home to their families. Still, going home to my empty house is better than..." She shook her head sadly, not completing her sentence. "What a lovely evening. I've never been walking on the beach at night."

"That can be remedied." Rachel finished off the last bite of pie and stood, giving Mattie a hand up. Without a word, she led her down to the waterline and they started walking even further south. "Watch the path of the moonlight."

Mattie followed her gaze and laughed in delight. "It's following us. How does it do that?"

"I don't know. It's a mystery." Rachel was still holding Mattie's hand. It was a new and delicious sensation, and she had a hard time concentrating on conversation. "I used to try to outrun it, but couldn't. No matter how far up or down the beach you walk, the moon path follows you."

They walked further and passed a young couple half-hidden behind the sand dunes. The man held the woman's face in his hands, and he was kissing her passionately. They were unaware of Mattie and Rachel's presence, and Mattie found herself watching them, in spite of her better manners. It made her gut twist with the strangest sensation, and she finally averted her eyes in embarrassment.

Rachel only watched the couple briefly, spending most of her time watching Mattie's reaction. It was an interesting combination of desire and wide-eyed innocence, and it lasted but a brief moment before her face grew serious again. She felt Mattie's hand slide out of hers and travel up her arm until it settled into the crook of her elbow. Her own middle fluttered and she drew in a deep breath, then clasped her other hand over Mattie's. "Sorry," she finally spoke. "I didn't know you'd see something like that out here."

"It's fine." Mattie couldn't bring herself to look up. "It was beautiful. Just like some of the novels I've read. I always wondered if people in real life could feel that way, and now I have my answer." Her voice was sad, and she felt as if she'd lost something before she ever really had it. Adam's face had never born the slightest hint of the adoration she had seen on the young man's face. "Have you ever been in love, Rachel?"

The question caught her off guard and she almost stumbled, feeling Mattie's surprisingly strong hand clasping her arm, steadying her. She looked down at the top of the red head, which shimmered in the moonlight. "I — I don't know," she answered honestly.

"I've never been." Mattie looked up at her earnestly. "I fear I've lost out on the chance for that kind of happiness. I suppose it's not meant to be, at least not for everyone. I think love is an ideal that only a lucky few ever get to truly experience."

Oh, Mattie. Rachel's heart ached and she drew Mattie over to another log and sat down, facing the water. It was so damned unfair that someone as young and beautiful as Mattie felt her fate was already sealed. "Mattie, you're bright and beautiful. You — you could have anything you want."

"I don't think so." Mattie's eyes were full of hope. She wanted to be convinced that she was wrong. "My parents didn't include love in the equation when they were selling me off to Adam. No one ever asked me how I felt about him. Truly, I felt nothing, except terror."

"It shouldn't be that way." Rachel kissed the top of her head and drew her close to her side, draping one arm around her. "If you want to be loved, you should have that in your life."

"That's very sweet. I wish I'd had you looking out for me when I was fourteen. I might have found the courage to speak up for what I wanted. Or didn't want." Mattie rested her head on the comforting shoulder and they stared wordlessly out at the Gulf of Mexico, watching the endless waves as they rolled ashore with hissing speed. Her eyes were transfixed on the water, but the rest of her senses took in more—Rachel's scent, the bay rum mixed with campfire smoke and ocean air. A strong heartbeat pounded against her ear and Rachel's chest rose and fell in long steady breaths. After a time, Rachel's hand came up, idly stroking Mattie's hair, a pleasant sensation Mattie reveled in, closing her eyes at the deluge of emotion that washed over her.

She wasn't sure who looked up first, but she found herself gazing into a pair of steel eyes that looked back at her with both concern and affection. Without thinking, she leaned forward, kissing Rachel, first on the right cheek and then the left, before she lightly brushed her lips across Rachel's, just once. She closed her eyes and rested her head back on the friendly shoulder, and felt a tremor run through the strong body that held her. "Are you cold?" She asked, without opening her eyes. She wrapped her own arm around Rachel's waist in an effort to help her get warm.

"No. No, not at all." Rachel stopped breathing for a very long moment. *It means nothing. Nothing.* Her body and heart told her differently, but she kept repeating the word to herself, over and over. Many of the young women in town greeted one another with a kiss, sometimes on the cheek and sometimes with a brief peck on the lips. None of them had ever greeted her that way, but still, it was common. She wasn't sure how common it was alone on the beach in the dark, but she couldn't afford to dwell on it, for fear it would only make her insane.

After a very long while, they walked back to the campfires, hand in hand, in companionable silence, and took a seat among the revelers, who were gathered around the musicians. Mattie clapped her hands and tapped her feet in time to the music, and exchanged pleasantries with several of the workers, who came up and shyly introduced themselves to her. Rachel heard neither music nor conversation. Her head was spinning, as she felt a lingering tingle on her lips, and an ache in her heart she feared would never be soothed.

SUNDAY DAWNED WARM and sunny, a promising day for swimming instruction. Rachel's mind was still jumbled, her body at war with logic. Sitting on the beach with Mattie had felt right— comfortable. Good sense told her what her heart wanted could never be.

She wanted to be with Mattie, just as the widows Sanders and MacKenzie were together. With a single chaste kiss, Mattie had awakened feelings and dreams in Rachel that she had never before imagined. She closed her eyes, her mind adrift, remembering the brief pressure of soft lips against her own. It was the single sweetest moment of her life. She wanted more.

Mattie wanted love and romance and all the things she would never get from Adam. That much was obvious. Whether Mattie felt anything at all for Rachel beyond friendship was a great mystery. Rachel's heart sank, realizing that more than likely, Mattie had no comprehension that two women could share romantic love, and that even if Mattie did have those kinds of feelings for her, she probably didn't recognize them for what they were.

Rachel thought about the widows Sanders and MacKenzie. She knew they were at mass every Sunday at Ursuline Convent, or at least they were every time Rachel attended services. It had been a while. She had little need for organized religion. On this Sunday, however, she had a different kind of need. She groaned and rolled out of bed, and made a quick trip to the water closet to wash her face and braid her hair. Back in her room, she chose her nicest pair of trousers and shirt, along with a cream-colored straw cowboy hat and a fine braided leather pair of suspenders.

Once she was satisfied she was presentable for services, she gathered her things for her visit with Mattie afterward. As an afterthought, she included her harmonica. She didn't play it often, but sometimes she enjoyed sitting on the beach and working out some of the jigs she had heard played in the saloon.

She caught the trolley to the convent and slipped into the back pew just as the service was beginning. The next hour was torture, as she listened to Latin words she didn't understand, and pretended to sing from a hymnal she had difficulty following. Reading words was becoming much easier. Reading music was a different story altogether. The entire time, she watched the two widow ladies, who sat halfway up on the inner aisle.

At last the priest recited a closing prayer, and blessed them all to go on their way. Rachel waited outside, sitting on a bench under a tree in the churchyard, as she watched for the two ladies. As they emerged from the doorway, she stood, slipping her hands in her pockets and slowly walking toward them, stopping at the bottom of the steps while they took time to greet the priest. Finally, they shook hands with him and came down the steps.

"Howdy." Rachel approached them shyly. "I don't believe we've ever been formally introduced, but I'm..."

"Rachel Travis." The taller of the couple reached out to shake hands, and after a surprised moment, Rachel took it. "I know who you are. Seen you around town some. Don't recall who told me your name." Her dark eyes twinkled in the morning sunlight. "I'm Evangeline Sanders, and this is Rebecca MacKenzie, but you can call us Angel and Betsy."

"I..." Rachel's tongue felt too large for her mouth. "Pleased to meet you," she finally stammered.

"Pleased to meet you too, Rachel," Betsy took her hand in turn. She was quite a bit shorter than Rachel, and looked up at her, smiling warmly. "Angel has admired your attire from afar on more than one occasion."

"Aw, Betsy." A pink blush crept across Angel's deeply lined-face.

"Well, it's true." Betsy playfully slapped Angel lightly on the arm. "Angel wishes she could dress like you, but the mill bosses would frown on it if she switched to trousers after wearing dresses all these years."

"I may switch yet," Angel huffed in mock indignation. "The times they are a-changing."

"Maybe we should buy you some, then," Betsy laughed lightly. "But we're being rude. What is it you need, Rachel? You just stop over to say hello after all this time?"

"N-No." She looked down, shrugging her shoulders up a bit, trying to decide what to say. "Could we go somewhere and talk for a while?"

"Certainly, child." Betsy took her arm as they began walking, Rachel knew not where. "It's early yet for lunch, but perhaps you'd like to join us on our front porch for some lemonade."

"That would be mighty fine." Rachel walked along with them, turning after a few blocks onto one of the prettier streets in town. It was lined on both sides with large old Victorian homes, most of them three stories high, all of them with large yards and tall shade trees. Halfway down, they turned up the sidewalk of Angel and Betsy's house.

"Y'all take a seat while I get us some cookies and our drinks." Betsy shooed them toward some wicker chairs off to one side of the long porch.

Rachel sat down, folding her hands in her lap as she looked around, taking in the serenity of the place. Pretty floral curtains hung in open windows, and planters of flowers lined the bed below the porch. A white picket fence enclosed the yard, and a tiny birdhouse hung from one of the trees. "I..." She stopped. How was she going to first accuse the ladies of being like her, and then ask for help? "Can I trust you?" she heard herself saying. "With a secret, I mean."

Angel studied her, her eyes roaming over the manly clothing, her tanned skin, and her cowboy boots. The breeze brought a hint of a fragrance generally worn by men. "Bay rum," Angel remarked slowly. "Wear that myself from time to time."

"You do?" Rachel looked up, trying to read the guarded expression on Angel's face.

"Yes." Angel leaned forward, her weight resting casually on the arms of the chair. "What's your secret?"

"A friend of mine said y'all might be like me." Blue eyes darted down in shame.

" 'Like you'? 'Like you' in what way?" It was a dangerous dance, but after years of caution, Angel wasn't about to start being careless. She sat back, waiting for Rachel to say it first.

"I don't care much for men." Rachel felt very small, her heart pounding in her chest and her skin prickling as she spoke. "Other than as friends." She fixed her gaze on a knot in the painted wood of the porch. "I like women." She swallowed hard. "One I like more than a friend."

"I see." Angel relaxed slightly. "Is she the one who thought we might be like you?"

"No. Another lady — one I've been more than friends with — it's a bit complicated." She searched around for another knot.

"Sounds like it is." Angel couldn't hide a slightly amused tone in her voice. "So you're 'more than friends' with two women?"

"No. Not anymore." Rachel still couldn't meet her gaze. "The one I used to be with, she told me there were other women like me. That I wasn't alone."

"You're not alone," a soft voice answered from the doorway.

Rachel's head snapped up, finding deep compassion in Betsy's eyes as she joined them, setting a tray down on a small whicker table in the middle of the chairs. "How long have you been holding all this inside, Rachel?" Betsy touched her gently on the arm, as she offered her a glass of lemonade.

"Seems like most of my life." She sipped at the drink, wetting a very dry mouth. "Thank you."

"What made you seek us out now?" Angel bit into a sugar cookie.

"I — I think I'm falling for someone." She closed her eyes, diving into her story. "I've spent a great deal of time with a prostitute. I'd rather not say whom. She's a fine lady, very kind to me, and a good friend."

"You've fallen in love with a prostitute?" Angel clucked her tongue slightly. "That's asking for trouble, I'd imagine."

"No. She's not the one." Rachel sighed unhappily. "The one I need to talk about, she's married."

"Oh." Betsy's voice was full of sympathy. "That's even more trouble. Does she feel the same way about you?"

"I don't know." Rachel drained her glass and gratefully accepted a refill. "Thank you. She might. Her husband, he hits her sometimes. I think it's pretty bad. I've spent a lot of time with her. She's not like any other lady I've ever known. She's kind and gentle, and she accepts me just like I am. We—we enjoy each other's company. She...she's become the most important person in the world, to me."

"You're in love with her." Betsy stated the obvious, given the glow on Rachel's face. "You've got a difficult road ahead of you. I imagine you know that."

"I'll be her friend forever," Rachel answered, her eyes snapping fiercely. "I just want her to be safe and happy."

"I was engaged to be married when I met Angel." Betsy nodded as Rachel slowly looked at first her, and then Angel, guarded hope on her face. "I said the road would be difficult, not impossible."

"Keep being her friend. It sounds like she needs one." Angel jumped in. "If she returns your affections, I imagine you'll find out all in good time. As for her husband, if he beats her as you say, she needs to get away from him, regardless."

"I wish I could make her understand that." Rachel's face clouded in anger. "I'm so afraid sometimes. Afraid he'll hurt her badly. Or worse. I don't think I could take it if anything happened to her."

"Rachel." Betsy scooted closer, touching her on the knee. "What Angel said—listen to her. Be her friend. Be there for her. As for yourself, we're here for you. If you ever need anything from us, don't you hesitate to ask."

"First time we've ever talked about this with anyone," Angel stated simply, a touch of wonder in her voice. "Been together going on thirty years now, and never met another soul who shared this particular burden with us."

"Is it?" Her heart ached, wanting something to hold on to. "Is it worth it? The burden?"

"Love is a rare gift," Betsy answered quietly, her eyes glowing. "It's been worth every step we've had to take to protect ourselves. Every deception. Every little white lie. Everything we had to give up to be together. Yes. Don't you ever doubt that. Love is worth it, Rachel. If you find it, you grab onto it and hold on for all you're worth."

"I get so confused." Blue eyes searched their faces for answers. "The church, and the way I was raised. Sometimes I feel guilty for being the way I am, yet I can't seem to help it. I tried—"

"Love is never a sin," Angel cut her off emphatically. "The laws of the church were made by frightened men, trying to control something they didn't understand. The laws of the heart are an altogether different matter. Listen to your heart, and you can't go wrong."

"I'll try to remember that." Rachel pulled a pocket watch out. "Speaking of, I'm due to meet my lady friend, so I'd best be excusing myself." She stood, and found herself unexpectedly drawn into a three-way hug.

"Don't be a stranger." Angel clapped her on the shoulder.

"Yes, do come back around any time." Betsy kissed her lightly on the cheek.

"Thank you." The words sounded so small in comparison to what she'd gained in thirty short minutes. "I can't begin to tell you how grateful I am." She hugged them again, and forced herself to leave the safe haven of their porch. She stopped at the end of the sidewalk and waved before turning and heading for the trolley stop a few blocks away.

She had a lot to think about.

THE TROLLEY RIDE flew by, and soon she was on Mattie's front porch, rapping on the door. The sun was almost directly overhead and there were no clouds at all. The weather was more typical of June than April, and Rachel made a mental note to go visit Mr. Cline, the chief of the local weather station. He would know if it was supposed to be an extraordinarily hot summer.

At last, a very timid-looking Mattie answered the door, only her braided head poking around the sturdy oak doorframe. "I've never worn a bathing suit before." She motioned Rachel inside. "Does it look simply hideous?"

Rachel stepped inside, blinking as her eyes adjusted to the lower light. She had to smile. Mattie was wearing a typical ladies' bathing suit, a navy blue sailor-style top with elbow-length sleeves and large white collar, complete with pale blue bow tie in the middle. Along with it she wore the matching split skirt, which bore a triple row of thin white trim around the hemline. It came to her knees, revealing nicely muscled calves. "It looks very nice," she answered honestly.

"Here." Mattie waved around a pair of navy blue stockings. "I haven't put these on yet."

"No." Rachel playfully grabbed the stockings. "Don't."

Mattie blew a puff of air skyward, ruffling her own bangs. "But all the pictures in the catalogues —"

"— show women sitting lady-like on the beach, or wading in ankle-deep water." Rachel tweaked a pert tilted nose. "We, however, are going swimming, and these will only make it more difficult for you. Best to have your feet and toes free."

"You're certain?" Mattie was unconvinced.

"Cross my heart." Rachel set the stockings aside and sniffed the air appreciatively. "Something smells delicious."

"I made some fresh bread this morning, and baked a ham." She retrieved a picnic basket from beside the door. "I thought sandwiches on the beach might be nice. And I made some oatmeal cookies for dessert."

"It's too much." Rachel ducked her head in embarrassment.

"No it's not. You treated me to a very nice party yesterday evening." Mattie smiled. "Now go change into your bathing suit, and let's go down to the beach."

"I'm already in my bathing suit." Blue eyes twinkled.

"You're in a long-sleeved shirt and trousers," Mattie protested.

"And underneath I have on a pair of men's swimming trunks and top, and that's what I plan to swim in." Rachel crossed her arms but maintained her smile. "I would look ridiculous in a bathing suit."

"I think you would look very nice." Mattie handed her a checkered picnic blanket, and tucked her hand into the crook of Rachel's free elbow. "But I'm sure you'll look just as lovely in the trunks." She squeezed a forearm affectionately. "Let's go. I'm anxious to have my first swimming lesson."

They set out for a stretch of beach further south of Mattie's house. Rachel had selected the spot earlier in the week, a small cove with relatively shallow water that was much calmer than the straighter section of beach where Mattie lived. They tucked the basket, blanket, another bag, and Mattie's sketchpad behind a large dead log, and Mattie cautiously tiptoed down the beach and stepped into the water.

"It's not so bad," she called back behind her. Her skin quickly adjusted to the cool temperature, a strange contrast with the rather warm air. She bravely waded in as far as her knees and stopped to turn, watching Rachel remove her trousers and shirt, impatiently flipping her long braid down her back. The dark form-fitting trunks came to just above her knees and the top had short sleeves that hugged her upper arms.

Mattie studied her now, with guarded interest. She had seen Rachel's upper body in her undershirt, and had even seen her in her bloomers the weekend it rained, but the trunks left very little of her body shape to the imagination. Mattie decided she was very attractive, with nice curves and planes, and a fluid way of moving that was decidedly feminine, despite the more masculine exterior Rachel maintained. She had tried to sketch Rachel from memory several times, and had secretly brought the sketchpad in hope that later, after dinner and lessons, she might persuade her to pose for a live sitting.

Rachel smiled as she approached the water, the bow of her upper lip full, and her teeth even and white. Her eyes sparkled in the sunlight and the auburn highlights in her hair were readily evident. Her face was very tanned, as were her arms, very different from Mattie's own fashionably pale features. Rachel had very nice soft skin, a surprise given the amount of time the taller woman spent in the sun each day. There was no evidence of the leathery texture so many of the older sailors on the island bore as a badge of honor.

"Are you ready?" Rachel moved to her side, giving her a playful splash with a flip of her hand. "Nice day for it."

"Yes." Mattie splashed back. "And yes, it is."

With a few more splashes, they were in an all-out war, Mattie running through the knee-high water, shrieking with laughter while Rachel chased behind, joining in with her own low chuckle. As she ran, she continually batted the waves up with her hands and feet until Mattie was soaked, although she had yet to dunk her head under the water. At last Rachel stretched out and leaped, almost, but not quite, tackling her. It was more of a rough embrace in which they ended up sitting down in water up to their chins, their arms wrapped around each other. Rachel supported her against the unfamiliar sensation as the mild waves rocked them gently back and forth while they sat on their haunches, their toes digging into the sandy bottom for balance.

"How does it feel?" Rachel slicked her own bangs back off her forehead.

It felt nice, and very warm, although Mattie knew that wasn't the question being asked. "It's very different. I feel so light."

"You aren't as heavy in the water." Rachel demonstrated, moving away from her and stretching out, floating on her back. "I don't know why, or how to explain it, but the water holds up your weight. That's why we can swim and float."

"Oh." Mattie eyed her cautiously. She tried to mimic the pose, stretching out her arms, but not quite finding the courage to come off her feet.

"Here." Rachel stood back up and moved in, placing one hand on the small of Mattie's back and the other against her belly. "Let go. I won't let you sink, I promise."

Mattie's eyes locked with Rachel's for the briefest moment, then she slowly leaned back, feeling the strong hand at her back. Gaining courage, she leaned further and allowed her feet to float up, and suddenly she was stretched back in the water, with both of Rachel's arms supporting her from beneath. "Oh." Her own breathing and voice sounded loud in her water-covered ears. "That feels lovely. Like floating on a cloud."

"Floating on the waves," Rachel corrected her. "Relax. Your arms and legs are still very rigid." She watched her comply, and nodded in silent approval. "I'll stay right here. I want you to get used to floating for a bit, then we'll move on to something a bit more challenging."

Mattie closed her eyes, absorbing the sensation of the cool water, the rolling waves, the warm sun on her face, and Rachel's strong arms holding her up. She could feel Rachel's body heat, warming the water around them, and this close, felt the quiet rise and fall of her breathing. It was the first time she had been acutely aware of someone else's physical presence, at least in a way that was so pleasant.

She decided it must be because she was so comfortable with Rachel.

"Are you asleep?" Rachel laughed softly, nudging her in the ribs.

"No." Red lashes fluttered open. "I'm sorry. But it's so very comfortable, I could fall asleep, I think."

"If you're that comfortable, it's time for the next lesson." Rachel slowly released her, not completely letting go until she was certain Mattie's feet were planted firmly on the ocean floor. She turned so they were face to face. "Watch." She held her nose, took a deep breath, and dunked completely under the water, then came back up, tossing her head back to rearrange her braid. "Now, your turn." She grinned.

"Oh, my." Mattie's eyes grew very round, but she took an even deeper breath, pinched her nose between her finger and thumb, and with puffed-out cheeks, disappeared from view. She came back up abruptly, not opening her eyes until she felt a gentle tap to her shoulder.

"You can open your eyes now, you survived." Rachel stood back, crossing her arms over her chest in amusement. Mattie was not only pretty and charming, she was turning out to be absolutely adorable as well.

"Oh, my," Mattie repeated. "That was very different. I've dunked in the bathtub before, but I always felt the sides of the tub around me. That felt queer, surrounded by water and only feeling the sand under my feet."

"Now without holding your nose." Rachel smiled. "Like this. You take a deep breath, then when you go under, you can either do nothing at all, or you can blow little bubbles of air out your nose. I recommend the bubbles. It's much more pleasant than feeling water go up your nose." She demonstrated again and surfaced.

"My turn?" Mattie's voice wavered uncertainly. She took several breaths, then went under. She was fine until she forgot to blow out, and started to draw water in instead. She erupted from the water, coughing and spluttering, her nose and throat burning as she tried to gulp in air.

Rachel thumped her on the back. "That happens a lot the first few times. You'll get used to how it works, eventually. Come on, try again." She smiled encouragement, and Mattie complied.

This time she did it correctly. Rachel continued to praise her, and they spent the better part of the next hour alternating between floating on their backs and ducking under the water. Finally, they progressed to belly floating, face down in the water. After a while, Rachel could tell Mattie was starting to tire. The younger woman was floating on her back, but her skin felt cool to the touch. Rachel laughed and grabbed her arms, pulling her through the water while Mattie remained on her back.

"Rachel," she fussed. "What on earth are you doing?"

"Giving you a ride back to shore." She steered toward the log where their things were stashed. "I'm hungry. That's enough swimming lessons for one day."

"Oh, good." Mattie righted herself, and together they high-stepped through the water toward shore. "I'm hungry, too. Besides, I think we have some other lessons to go over, if I recall. Didn't you progress to the third reader?"

"Yes, I did." Rachel beamed proudly. "I think I like this trading we're doing."

"Trading?" Mattie peered up at her quizzically.

"Yep." They reached the log and Rachel spread the blanket out on the sand in front of it. "Swimming lessons for reading lessons."

"Me, too." Mattie retrieved the picnic basket and opened it up. "Here, teacher," she teased, handing across a sandwich. "You've earned it today."

"Thank you." Rachel laughed, plopping down on the blanket and crossing her legs. They ate slowly, sharing little stories and talking about the week past. It had indeed turned out to be a wonderful day.

THE SUN SANK LOWER, casting long rays of pale warm light cross their blanket, over the brown sand, and out toward the sea, gilding the waves as they rolled ashore from the east. Rachel sat on the edge of the blanket with a towel wrapped around her lower body, her long wet hair combed out and re-braided, enjoying the heat of the sun against her skin. They had gone over reading lessons, swam some more, and eaten the remainder of the sandwiches for supper. Now she was facing the water, playing her harmonica, producing a combination of lively jigs and a few slower tunes she called "cowboy campfire music."

Mattie rested against the log, her sketchpad spread across her outstretched legs, drawing Rachel in profile. She smiled, using her thumb to smudge in some shadows under her cheekbones and below her chin. Rachel had her long legs crossed, and was still wearing her swim trunks and top, and her feet were bare, as was her head. She had shunned a wide-brimmed hat, claiming she wore them all week long at work, even though she hated them.

Mattie did don a sensible straw hat, and even opened up a ruffled parasol, its handle stuck into a crack in the log, providing extra shade. Ladies didn't let their skin get tanned, and she had been raised to be a lady. Rachel didn't seem to care much about being a lady, but for some reason that didn't bother Mattie at all. She liked Rachel's dark golden skin, which made her gray-blue eyes appear even paler than they really were.

It was her fourth drawing of the afternoon, and she was pleased that Rachel seemed willing to sit and pose for as long as she wanted her to. Her first sketch was of Rachel stretched out on her back, cat-napping after dinner. The second was a more active drawing of Rachel swimming in the shallow cove, while the third was a simple pose of the tall woman, standing in the sand dunes, hands on hips, her hair lose and whipping back behind her. Mattie paused and flipped back through the pages, studying the prior sketches. She decided she liked the fourth one best. Rachel looked quite pensive as she stared out toward the Gulf, playing her melancholy cowboy tunes, occasionally closing her eyes, working out the music to her own hearing.

She thought about her art book back at the house, a book she had ordered from Paris through a catalogue. It was for novice artists, and provided instruction on how to draw a number of animals, as well as people. It included a section on the human body, and nude sketches, and emphasized that in order to draw the clothed body, it was important to know how to draw a nude body first. *Well*, she mused. She didn't have any nude bodies to work with, other than her own in the mirror, and couldn't quite bring herself to draw her own naked form.

She remembered Rachel's nicely-muscled upper back, at least what she had seen and felt through her thin undershirt, from measuring her for her work shirts. The shirts were back at the house, and they still needed to fit them for any minor alterations. She'd brought them home from the shop, on the off chance they had time for Rachel to try them on before she went home after their reading and swimming lessons.

At last, she finished her sketch, and held it up for Rachel's inspection. Rachel put down the harmonica and scooted across the blanket, peering down at the drawing. "Don't know why you'd want to draw me." She shook her head, feeling the color rise in her cheeks. "Surely you can find something more interesting."

"Maybe." Mattie poked her in the ribs and laughed. "Maybe not. But you're about the only person I know who would sit all afternoon and let me draw them." She closed up the pad and tucked it back in her bag. "Thank you. I love to draw but I'm still trying to get the human form down. I don't get much opportunity to practice."

"Any time you need a model, you just let me know." Rachel stood, brushing sand off her legs, and they began packing up their things. "You have time for me to try on the shirts when we get back to your house?"

"Yes." Mattie looked up at her, gathering the picnic blanket over one arm and slinging her bag over her shoulder.

Rachel took the heavier satchel and picnic basket, and a tiny smile played at her lips as she felt Mattie's hand slip around her arm, as if it were the most natural thing in the world. "You're sure about the shirts?" She looked down, a question in her eyes. "I'd hate to be there if..."

"Adam isn't due back until tomorrow afternoon," Mattie cut in, guessing at her question. "We have plenty of time."

"Oh. Very well then." Rachel stepped carefully over a dead jellyfish, steering Mattie well clear of its venomous tentacles. "Might as well try them on now and maybe I can pick them up sometime next week."

They arrived back at the house and entered it, setting their burdens down just inside the doorway. Mattie moved around the house, switching on lamps, and putting the leftover food in the icebox. She motioned Rachel into the bedroom and pulled the shirts out from behind a changing screen where she had hung them. "Here. You can just..." She turned around and stopped in mid-sentence.

Rachel was facing away from her, but had already pulled the swimming top off, exposing what was indeed a very nicely muscled back for Mattie's view. *Oh, my. So much for the changing screen.* Mattie swallowed, unable to place the emotions she felt. Rachel was beautiful, the long braid hanging down her broad back to a tapered waistline. Without the longer swimming top, her shape was completely revealed in the form-fitting trunks. Rachel had a very nice body, Mattie decided, and then realized she hadn't seen very many bodies in quite this state of undress.

"Here." She handed one of the shirts over Rachel's shoulder and stepped back.

"Thank you." Rachel pulled the sleeves over her arms and hitched her shoulders up, drawing it up and buttoning it in front, then fastening the cuffs. "How does it look?"

Mattie moved closer, picking up a pincushion from the desktop. "Looks like I might need to take the sleeves up just a tad." She tugged at a cuff that came a little too far down over Rachel's hand. "Hold on. Let me..." She placed a few pins between her teeth and gathered the sleeve in her hands and folded it up a little, pinning it so that it was the correct length. "There." She moved in front of Rachel and fussed with the collar until it settled into place properly, then stood back. "Turn around in a circle for me."

Rachel complied and ended up facing her again, fidgeting a bit nervously with the button placket. "Anything else?" Her eyes twinkled faintly and her cheeks were flushed, though whether from sunburn or not, Mattie couldn't tell.

"No. I believe that's it." She gathered up the other shirts. "No need to try the others. I made a pattern that I used for all of them, so they should all need the same alterations in the sleeves." She watched Rachel turn away from her and begin to unbutton the shirt, and without the more intense eye contact, gathered her courage. "Would you..." Her voice shook a little bit, and she stopped, drawing a breath to steady it. "Would you let me draw you, sitting on the edge of the bed, with your back bare?"

Rachel paused, feeling a sudden rush of blood at her temples as her heart pounded double-time. Without speaking, she sat down on the feather mattress and let the shirt fall the rest of the way down, pooling at her waist and elbows. "Like this?" she almost whispered, turning her head back over her shoulder, but keeping her eyes downcast.

"Yes." Mattie licked her lips. "Just like that. Let me go get my pad and pencil. I'll be right back." She scampered into the parlor and returned out of breath, drawing the desk chair out and sitting down at an angle where the lamplight best reflected off Rachel's back muscles. "Can you turn your head again, like you did a minute ago, so that your face is in profile?"

Rachel did so, hoping the heat she felt under her skin wasn't showing. "You want the braid down my back or in front?"

"Um." Mattie placed the sketchpad aside and stood, moving in behind her. "Could I take it down?"

"If you'd like." Rachel felt the tugging sensation and a pleasant tingle at her scalp as Mattie combed the braid out, her touch sending more chills across Rachel's skin.

Mattie frowned as she realized her own hands were shaking. She had no idea why, nor did she have any explanation for why she was finding it difficult to breathe, or why butterflies were fluttering about in her stomach. She finished, gently arranging Rachel's hair so that part of it fell down her back, but most of it was over her shoulder in front, leaving most of her bare back still painted in the yellow lamp light. As for her own hair, she reached up, pushing damp bangs away from a suddenly-sweaty forehead.

Rachel heard the light patter of Mattie's feet as she moved across the room and sat down, then the faint scratching of a pencil against the rough sketch paper. She swallowed several times. True, she had already felt Mattie watching her for most of the afternoon, but had managed to find other things to distract herself, either swimming in the water, looking up at the fluffy clouds in the sky, or concentrating on playing her harmonica. Now, in the intimacy of Mattie's bedroom, sitting partially exposed, there was very little to focus on other than her own uneven breathing, the sudden dryness of her mouth, and the pulsing of her own blood, which pounded in her ears.

Why she had agreed to this sitting, she had no easy answer. It went against her decision to push her feelings for Mattie aside. She felt Mattie's eyes on her back, almost like a light caress, and closed her own eyes, trying to sort out a myriad of emotions. Mattie had asked, and that was the simple answer as to why she was sitting there half naked before a woman she would like to be completely naked with. She thought about that, and realized there was almost nothing Mattie could ask of her, that she would refuse.

Mattie tried to hurry, and at the same time, wanted to take advantage of what might be her only opportunity to at least study the naked human form from the back. She sketched the outline of Rachel's frame, then filled in the shoulders, the indention of her spine down her back, and the nicely-toned muscles that spread out from there, over her shoulder blades and around her sides out of sight. She finished by adding the wavy thick chestnut mane of hair, wishing again that she had the pastels to work with instead of having only pencil to shade in her lovely hair color.

At last, she finished, and reluctantly placed the pad on the desk top. To ask for a second pose would be rude, she decided, and hoped she hadn't already pushed for more than was polite. "I'm finished, if you want to get dressed."

"Oh." Rachel pulled the shirt off, adding it to the pile of not-quite-finished ones on the bed, and knelt down next to the bed, rummaging through her satchel for her clean change of clothing. She heard Mattie retreat into the parlor, and stood, releasing a long-held breath, feeling her heartbeat slow to something resembling normal. She finished dressing and moved to the doorway, spotting Mattie sitting on the sofa.

"I guess I should be getting back home. Hitching a ride might be difficult this late, and the trolley will have stopped running by now. I should have ridden my bicycle over." She watched Mattie's face fall and without further thought, dropped her bag and moved fluidly across the room to sit down next to her. "What's wrong?"

"Nothing." Mattie looked up at her, pain evident in her eyes. "I always feel a little sad on Sunday evenings. I usually enjoy the weekends Adam is gone. I know that sounds horrid."

"No." Rachel reached across, stroking her cheek. "It's all right, Mattie. Don't feel badly."

Mattie clasped her hand, holding it against her face as Rachel continued the comforting touches. "But now, I'm more sad, because I've come to enjoy our Sundays together. I—I've never felt as close to anyone as I do to you. Does that sound strange?"

"No." Rachel looked down, unable to meet her gaze. "I feel the same way about you."

"Did you know...?" Mattie laughed softly. "Last night, at your clam bake, I—I've never kissed anyone else on the lips, besides Adam."

Uncertain eyes looked back up, studying hazel ones. "Me neither, not since..." *Sarah,* she finished silently. "Not since a very long time ago."

"Was it the person that you were with?" Mattie blushed, not believing she had dared ask the question, and uncertain of where it had come from. "Do you miss him, very much?"

"It—it's complicated, Mattie." She tried to smile, without much success. "I used to, but not so much anymore. As I said, it's been a long time."

"I'm sorry. I didn't mean to intrude on your privacy." Mattie allowed Rachel's hand to fall away from her face, only to find it resting on her leg.

"I don't mind." She squeezed Mattie's leg. "I've never talked to anyone before, about that time, is all."

"Because it hurts too much?" Mattie's voice was full of sympathy. Her romance novels told tales of the pain of unrequited love, and while she had never felt it herself, she wondered if that was what Rachel had been through, a love lost.

"Yes." Rachel released a long breath. That, at least, was the truth, though not for the reasons Mattie probably suspected. The shame of being forced to run away from home because of who she was, that was something she had never shared with anyone, at least not in full. It was painful. She and Lillie had talked enough for Lillie to know there was someone in Rachel's past, but that was as far as the conversation had gone.

"Do you feel very lonely, without him?" Mattie's hand covered Rachel's. She was dying to ask more, wondering why Rachel had had relations with someone she wasn't married to, wondering if maybe she had been betrothed to someone, and perhaps he had died before the wedding. Maybe that was why Rachel lived the life she lived, because of a broken heart. She wanted to ask, but sensed that perhaps it wasn't an appropriate subject.

"Not anymore." Rachel smiled. *Not since I met you, Mattie.* Her heart was longing to say the words, but she couldn't bring herself to. "Time has a way of healing things."

"I'm glad." Mattie stood, drawing Rachel up with her. "I should let you go home. I hate for you to be out in the dark, trying to hitch a ride. I wish I had the horses and carriage here, but Adam always boards them near the train station when he goes to Houston."

"I should be able to find a ride if I walk up as far as the Strand." Rachel tugged at a lock of Mattie's hair. "Don't worry about me. There is always someone out and about on the roads, no matter what time of day or night it is."

Mattie escorted her to the doorway and they stood in awkward silence until Mattie moved closer in her cheek-pecking ritual. She started to move away, feeling Rachel's chest rise and fall, and her tickling breath against her cheek, sweet with the scent of lemonade. Instead of moving back, she moved closer, once again lightly brushing her lips across Rachel's.

She pulled back, feeling Rachel's forehead pressed against hers, and a gentle hand at the small of her back, while another hand came up, cradling her face. Then Rachel kissed her again, a series of light pecks that made Mattie's toes curl, and her blood race. It was the same sensations she had felt while sketching Rachel in the bedroom, only the feelings were intensified.

Rachel started to pull back, and felt Mattie's arms wrap around her in a hug, the red head tucked tightly against her, Mattie's face buried into her shoulder. "I'm sorry, Mattie, I didn't mean to..."

"No." Mattie looked up, pushing stray strands of hair from Rachel's eyes. "No need to apologize. That was nice." To prove her point, Mattie delivered one last kiss to a very startled Rachel, while gently shoving her out the door. "Come by the shop late in the week, and I should have your shirts finished."

"Eh?" Rachel was dazed. "Oh. Yes. Shirts. I will. Thank you for the picnic, Mattie."

"And thank you for the swimming lessons. I should know by Thursday if we can have more lessons next Sunday." She waved at Rachel, smiling, trying to hide a deluge of emotion. When Rachel had blended into the darkness, Mattie closed the door, leaning against the frame to catch her breath. She had a lot to think about.

Outside, Rachel trotted up to the road, her mind taking off in a hundred different directions. "Shirts?" she mumbled, looking up at the unanswering stars. "How can she think about shirts at a time like this?"

IT HAD BEEN a long hard week on the docks, working under the incessant sun, which beat down without mercy on the miserable laborers. To make matters worse, it had rained on and off, just enough for water to pool in low-lying areas of the island. The pools were natural breeding grounds for mosquitoes, which swarmed any warm-blooded creature unfortunate enough to be outdoors, stinging away at unprotected skin. Fortunately, they didn't swarm near the Gulf, so the only time Rachel had to dodge the blood-sucking creatures was in her travels to and from work. She had become proficiently fast at out-pedaling them, for the most part. Still, her forearms, neck, and face were peppered with maddeningly itchy bites.

Her arm and back muscles ached, much more than they usually did on Friday evening. Lying in the tub, she felt as if she'd lost a barrelful of sweat during the day. She was surrounded by lukewarm water, and was drinking greedily from a large mug of cooler water, and still her body felt parched, both inside and out. Wearily, she finished scrubbing the sticky grime from her body and sat up, pulling the stopper and grabbing her towel from the hook on the wall.

This night, she indulged in something she saved only for rare occasions, a liberal dusting of toilet powder from an expensive canister — expensive by Rachel's standards, at fifty cents for four ounces. It had a slightly floral scent, not her fragrance of choice, but on truly humid days, it helped absorb a lingering dewiness to her skin that no towel would remove. It also helped mask the bites. She peered in the mirror and chuckled, thinking that she resembled one of Mattie's teacakes, with the white powder sprinkled over her tanned skin.

She tugged on her lightest pair of trousers and a sleeveless undershirt, and went to her room to finish dressing. She was scheduled to work the entire evening at the saloon, and realized regretfully that she would probably have made more joining a poker game than the few dollars she would earn tending the bar. The boarding house was serving up cold sandwiches and fresh oranges for supper, and she procured one of each on her way out the door.

At the end of the trolley line, she hopped off, and stood in a miserable swarm of mosquitoes before she finally flagged down a ride to the saloon. Sitting on the back of a flat-bed wagon, facing backward, her legs dangling down behind the wheels, she ate her supper in silence, staring out at the high marsh grass and the remaining rays of sunlight that spread out over the island, painting it in deep shadows. With one hand she ate, while the other constantly batted away the pesky mosquitoes. To add to her misery, each jolt of the wagon wheels in the ruts of the road reminded her acutely of her tired, aching muscles, and she was grateful when the driver dropped her off only a quarter mile from the saloon.

She thanked her ride and set out for the remainder of the walk to the saloon. Inside, the ceiling fans were whirring at full speed, and she looked up thankfully at the one directly over the bar area. She poured herself up a tall mug of water and began stacking clean mugs and glasses on the shelves behind the bar, removing them from a small cart the dishwasher had left at the end of the bar. Afterward, she went out back to the storage shed and rolled a fresh keg of ale into the main room, hoisting it up on its stand, feeling her back muscles groan in protest at lifting yet more heavy weight after the countless bales of cotton she had loaded earlier in the day.

Work-weary patrons were already starting to wander in, and a look out the window revealed that the sun had set. Hopefully with the darkness would come a blessed coolness. It was much too warm to be late April. The wilted shirt collars and damp heads of the men gathering around the tables were more characteristic of July. She spun around, as someone tapped her on the back, and grinned broadly. "Hello, Lil." She gave the blonde a big hug.

"Hello yourself, stranger. We missed you last weekend. Hear y'all had a regular shindig down on the beach." Lillie affectionately mussed her hair. "Hear you kept constant company with your little red-headed lady friend."

Rachel felt a blush rise up her neck and into her face. She looked down and grabbed a rag from a rack, and began swiping down the bar. "Just went to a clambake is all. Mattie didn't have anything else to do. Her husband was out of town."

"Oh, yes, sugar. I'm sure every society lady on the island was green with envy, wanting to keep company with the likes of folks like us." Lillie trailed one fingernail across a very pink cheek. "You were the reason she went to the party. I think you know that."

"Maybe." Rachel wondered how much she should share with Lillie. She decided to say nothing, at least for the time being. Her own emotions were all confused, and she wasn't sure if she could talk about them with someone else until she sorted them out for herself, first. *Am I falling in love?* Something was going on inside, that much was certain. She shook her head and tried to push the baffling thoughts aside for later. "Kind of a rough crowd for Mattie, but I think she had a good time."

"Of course she did. She was with you, you charming devil."

Rachel said nothing, but her forehead scrunched into a frown and she renewed her efforts to clean the already well-polished bar.

"Hey. Rachel. I'm just teasing you, sugar. You know that, don't you?" She grabbed Rachel's wrist, forcing her to be still. "You're going to scrub a hole clean through if you don't stop."

"I'm sorry, Lil." Troubled eyes searched Lillie's face. "It's not your fault. I'm just distracted."

"You've gone and fallen head over heels, haven't you?" Lillie's heart ached for her. "Have you talked to her about leaving that no-account husband of hers?"

"No. But we've talked about so many things, Lil. I feel like she knows me almost better than anyone, 'cepting maybe you. There are some things I just can't bring myself to tell her, but she and I have become very close friends these past few weeks. She's one of the kindest, most decent people I've ever known. I-I'd be happy having her as a friend for the rest of my life. As for the rest..."

"Do you think she returns your affections?" The question hung in the air for so long, she was about to move on to another, thinking it was too difficult for Rachel to talk about.

"Don't know, for certain." Rachel folded the rag over and hung it back up. "I think maybe she does. Sad thing is, she hasn't a clue, though. She's making me crazy, Lil. Touching me all the time, hugging me, even kissing me, for goodness' sake. On the lips a few times, no less."

"Talk to her, Rachel." Lillie patted her on the arm. "You're a smart girl. You'll find a way, I'm certain of it." She looked across the room, which was starting to fill up. Several card games were already underway, and the pianist was just making his way to the piano to add to the festive atmosphere. "Well, sugar, I need to go work the room, see if I can catch me a high roller." She winked at Rachel and moved away, hitching her skirts into place and smiling brightly at a table full of single young bachelors.

Rachel merely shook her head and turned to the end of the bar, where several loners were seated on bar stools, watching the crowd and waiting to order drinks. She filled several requests in quick succession, then began making her way from table to table, starting at the far end of the room. She returned to the bar after every few tables to load up trays of drinks, and within thirty minutes, had served the first round to the decidedly loud room. The shuffling of cards, the clinking of ale mugs, and the dull roar of male voices and laughter vibrated throughout the room, and over it all the piano player's melodies rose up through the air, bringing some much-needed cheer at the end of a hard week for the island's laborers.

She tapped her foot idly in time to the lively music, and tried to commit a few new tunes to memory. She admitted to herself that she wanted to play them for Mattie, who had been delighted with her meager abilities on the harmonica, judging from her smile and her comments regarding various songs. She had picked up her shirts on Thursday and sat in the shop chatting with Mattie during the noon hour. Mr. and Mrs. Vaughan had joined them for the last half of the hour, and after a brief bit of awkwardness, she had relaxed, realizing that her presence was welcome. When she left to go back to the docks, Mattie had followed her out and told her Adam would be going out of town, and to come over on Sunday as planned.

Speak of the devil. Her mood turned foul as soon as Adam stepped through the door, surveying the room as if he owned it. His eyes flicked over her and just as quickly dismissed her. *Just as well.* Her eyes lingered on his back as he turned away from her and found a seat at a table full of some of the less-sophisticated poker players. She felt her anger rise. The only reason a seasoned player like Adam would join such a game was to clean up the table, taking advantage of some of the younger men who were novices, and stealing away their hard-earned wages. *Bastard.*

She forced her focus elsewhere, and briefly scanned the room for Lillie, who was engaged in animated conversation with one of the town's bankers. She was seated on his lap, and he had his arm wrapped loosely around her waist. From the relaxed look on his face, he was well on his way to being inebriated. He was one of Lillie's regulars, a docile sort who would treat her well and pay her even better. *Good.* Rachel looked back toward Adam. Lillie would be unavailable for the remainder of the evening. *One less thing for me to worry about.*

She went on about her duties, occasionally watching Adam, but keeping busy most of the time. The room was bursting at the seams, as almost everyone had been paid earlier in the day. Every bachelor on the island, it seemed, and a good number of the married men, had come to spread the wealth around, bidding more than usual on the card games and buying extra rounds of drinks. All of the ladies of the evening eventually disappeared, either upstairs or out the front door, and Rachel's pockets were full of extra tip funds. It was a good night.

Time passed quickly, and she was constantly busy, either wiping down the bar and mopping up spills or filling drink orders for thirsty patrons who bellied up to the crowded bar. As she found time, she made rounds of the tables, taking more orders and gathering even more tips. At one point, she discretely counted her take, and was pleased. Fifteen dollars was nothing to sneeze at, and probably more than she would have made gambling, unless she counted cards.

Late in the evening, the first keg tapped out and she picked it up, hoisting it over her shoulder to take out back and exchange it for a full one. She stepped into the alleyway and looked up at the twinkling stars. She whistled as she set the keg down on the sandy ground, and fumbled with the latch on the storage shed, tugging at the rusty bent catch that always seemed to stick in the evening humidity. *Drat it.* She dug in with her heels and pushed with both palms against the unforgiving metal. Without warning, rough hands grabbed her and spun her around, pinning her against the shed door.

"What in blazes?" Three men held her, one at each arm and one at her legs, and as she started to try to kick, yet a fourth one moved in, helping to immobilize her completely. A large shadow stood over her, blotting out the friendly night sky, and before she had time to think or scream, a huge fist drove into her gut, forcing the air from her lungs. She made a sound, somewhere between a groan and a whimper, unable to double over as her body desperately wanted to do. The large man worked her over, punching her several times in quick succession, and she felt a rib crack. She had no voice, no air to make a sound. Her muscles strained against her captors, and one final blow connected with her face, snapping her head backward and slamming it against the shed, causing her to see stars of a different kind. She felt warm blood trickle from her nose, and coughed violently, feeling as if she were choking.

At last, after only a few minutes, which seemed like hours, her tormentor stepped back and a lantern shone harshly in her eyes, momentarily blinding her. She fought harder, groaning, and felt a firm hand cover her mouth and nose, increasing her pain and making it almost impossible to breathe. She felt weak as a kitten, but continued to struggle, finding her voice, which was muffled against a calloused palm that stank of stale tobacco.

The lantern moved away and Adam's face came into focus, his features garish in the flickering yellow light. He grinned evilly and dug into her pockets, removing her tip money and stashing it inside his vest. Her mind scrambled, trying to comprehend what was happening. She tried to remember the last time she'd seen him sitting across the room, how many minutes had passed, and mentally cursed herself for letting her guard down. Her rattled mind grasped for reason. She knew he wasn't the one who had hit her. He wasn't tall enough, although he was obviously behind the attack. He laughed low and then his face grew still, his eyes cold as ice. "Stay away from my wife."

Her eyes grew wide and sparked with rage, but her words were unintelligible. He moved closer, his whiskey-tainted breath warm in her face. "Don't bother arguing. A young man in there was kind enough to strike up a conversation with me. Oh, and don't be angry with him. He was quite innocent in all of this. He did, however, tell me about a most delightful clambake he attended last weekend. One thing led to another, and he described a woman you were seen with. Fit my Mattie to a T. Fortunately I always carry my beloved wife's photograph with me, and he confirmed that she was indeed the woman you were with. Seems my Mattie charmed everyone at your little soirée, Miss Travis. That will be the last time, I can assure you." He looked around, and found an empty ale bottle. "Now, if you'll excuse me, I have a train to catch."

The last thing she felt was a horrible crack against her skull, before the world turned black and her body went limp. Her captors released her and she dropped to the ground, face down in the sand. Adam knelt, feeling her throat for a pulse. "Perfect." He stood and pulled a wad of bills from a money clip, whipping out payment to each man present. "With any luck she won't wake up until we're all well out of here. I suggest you all go home now, and lay low for a few days. I'd be surprised if she presses charges. However, if she does, trust me, her kind could never win against me. Good evening, gentlemen." He tipped his hat and strode away into the shadows of the alley.

HER HEAD FELT like it was going to split open, and her body as if it had been run over by a supply wagon. The inside of her mouth tasted like cotton and blood. She tried to swallow but her throat muscles wouldn't quite work. She was too parched. Slowly, she opened one eye and immediately shut it, groaning in pain as light from the window stabbed her sensitive eyeball. "Wha—what happened?" She forced out the words, realizing she wasn't alone.

"Oh, sweet lord, thank goodness you're awake." Lillie's voice crooned in her ear, making her head throb all the more.

"Lil." Her lips curled into a half smile. "Would you please quit yelling in my ear?"

"Sugar, I'm not—oh, never mind." She softened her voice and scooted her chair closer to the bedside. "Can you drink some water for me, Rachel?"

The eye forced itself open again, and rolled toward her would-be tormentor. "Do you have a headache powder to go with that water? Maybe a whole box of headache powders?" The eye closed again. "Better yet, just cut the head off."

"Shhh." Lillie eased an arm under her shoulders and forced her to sit partway up. "Come on, Rachel. Sip some water and if that stays down I'll talk to the doctor about headache powders, I promise."

Rachel complied and opened both eyes, immediately regretting it as the room began to spin. "Can't."

"At least try." Lillie continued to support her. "Doctor Mills said you have to take it slow."

"Doctor?" The word finally registered. "Lil, I can't afford to pay a doctor, and I don't have anything I can trade."

"It's paid for," a very quiet voice answered from the corner.

Her brain spun, but not from the headache, as the welcome familiar voice washed over her. "Mattie?" Suddenly it all came rushing back with vivid clarity, and she sat bolt upright, ignoring the stars in her vision, the pain in her side, and the churning in her gut. "Mattie, you can't go home. Adam—he—*augh*!" A sharp pain lanced through her temple and she flopped back down on the bed, forcing down a wave of nausea.

"Don't you worry about me." Mattie got up and sat cautiously down on the edge of the bed, so as not to jostle her. She felt the mug of water pressed into her hand as Lillie mouthed the words "you try" to her. She nodded, the tiniest acknowledgement, and inched closer until she could look down at Rachel's face. "Here." She slipped a hand around the back of Rachel's neck. "Drink this now. It'll make you feel better."

Rachel felt the warm touch tickling her nape hairs, and allowed herself to be lifted up, just enough that the water wouldn't spill. She sipped, slowly at first, then took a few great gulps, her dry mouth and lips welcoming the cool refreshment. She stopped in mid-swallow and carefully pushed the mug away, reaching up to touch a pale bruise on Mattie's cheek. "I'll kill him."

"You'll do no such thing." Mattie's fingers curled around the ones caressing her face. "Don't think about it right now, please, Rachel? You should concentrate on getting better."

"Be-because of me." Steel eyes misted up, and her fingers moved further back, stroking silken red hair.

"Because of me." Mattie echoed her words, tracing a much darker bruise on Rachel's face, which banded her eye and blended from black to blue to purple as it covered most of her right cheek. "Because of me." A bare whisper, as she gave the slightest touch to a large lump at Rachel's right temple, along with a row of stitches at the edge of her hairline.

"I-I need to..." Rachel tried to sit up, only to find a gentle touch to her shoulder, holding her down.

"You don't need to go anywhere. You're safe in your own bed, and the doctor will be by later on today to re-wrap your ribs." She fluffed Rachel's bangs, riffling them through her fingers.

"Ribs?" So that's what was hurting so badly. "Broken. How many?"

"Just one." Mattie watched Rachel's face scrunch up in painful thought.

"Won't be able to work. They took my tip money, too." Thought turned to fear. "I probably have enough saved to get by a month."

"Sugar," Lillie chimed in, "don't you worry your pretty head about anything. You have a whole bunch of friends, and we will make sure you're taken care of. You're hurt pretty badly. You've got to rest."

"How bad?" The frown returned.

"Broken rib, big knot and gash on your head, and the doctor thinks you might have some bleeding inside. You came to for a bit earlier and coughed up some blood. And you have a fever, although he thinks you might have some illness that isn't related to the injuries." Mattie clasped her hand. "We thought your nose was broken, at first, but you managed to escape that."

"Hard to believe." Rachel gingerly touched the bridge of her nose, which was very sore. "Smacked me good there." She ran her tongue along her teeth. "No teeth missing." She smiled as proof. "What day is it?"

"It's Sunday morning," Mattie answered quietly. "You missed Saturday."

"How'd I get back in my room?" She closed her eyes and tried to remember, but her head hurt too much, and she whimpered as the pounding increased. "Hurts." She wrapped a hand around Mattie's leg, automatically reaching out for someone she had come to associate with comfort. "Might need to sleep again for a little while." She looked back up, one more time. "Stay?"

"Sleep now." Mattie patted the hand on her leg. "I'll be here when you wake up."

Satisfied with her answer, Rachel closed her eyes and settled back into the pillow, shifting until the pain was somewhat bearable.

Mattie watched, and listened, until shallow breathing became longer deep breaths, and felt her own body relax in response. She looked over at Lillie, who sat across the room, silently observing them. "You should get some dinner."

"Yes. I guess I should." She stood up, feeling the weariness in her body from too little sleep. "I don't believe I'm welcome downstairs, so I'll slip out the back door and go across to the hotel. You want me to bring you back a plate?"

"That would be nice." Mattie reached for her pocket book on the night table, only to have her hand stopped.

"I've got it." Lillie smiled.

"Thank you." Mattie smiled back, wishing the discomfort between them were gone. She had so many unanswered questions.

"I'll be back shortly." Lillie stepped out the door, closing it quietly behind her.

Mattie sighed heavily and looked around the sparse room. It had been a very long weekend, so far. Flashes of memory flitted through her mind and she closed her eyes against a vague unsettling terror.

Adam had come home, rousing her out of bed in the middle of the night and dragging her across the room, pinning her against the wall and shouting questions that her sleepy mind didn't fully grasp right away.

One solid slap to her face had quickly brought clarity.

He continued to scream at her about Rachel, wanting to know how they met, how much time they had spent together, and if "that unnatural woman" had touched her in any unseemly way. She didn't fully understand what he meant by that, or how he knew she had befriended Rachel. He wouldn't allow her to ask questions in return, and she finally convinced him Rachel was merely a client at the tailor shop who had invited her to a party as partial payment for a work order, and that she thought it would have been rude to decline the invitation.

"You weren't home to consult, so I had to decide on my own."

He bought the story, she hoped.

"Poor judgment on your part, Mattie, but it doesn't matter now." Finally, his lips curved into an evil smile. "She won't be bothering you anymore. I made sure of that."

"What did you do to her?" Mattie's eyes were fearful, as she tried to hide the shaking in her voice.

"Taught her a lesson she won't soon forget. If she wakes up and is able to remember it." He watched her like a cat taunting a mouse, daring her to show more than a measure of concern for a stranger.

"Where is she?" She managed to keep her words steady.

"Never you mind about that, Mattie." He picked up his carpetbag. "She's probably already back inside that whore house where she works. I'm taking the midnight train out to Houston, and I'll be back Monday night." He moved closer, until she could smell the whiskey and cigar smoke on his breath. "You're to stay in the house until I get back, except to go to the tailor's. Do you understand me?"

"Yes." Her face was impassive, her eyes cool golden hazel. "I understand perfectly."

"Good." He pecked her on the cheek—the one he hadn't hit. "I'm glad we have that matter cleared up."

She watched him leave, counting silently in her head, her heart racing, until she was certain he was well on his way to the train station. She had never run so fast in her life, hurtling down the road, seeking a ride, any ride, to the far end of the island where Rachel had said the saloon was. She finally got a ride in one of the new automobiles, thanking the driver absently when he dropped her off directly in front of the saloon.

She tore inside, gasping for breath. The place was mostly deserted at the late hour, with only a few stray workers remaining, mopping the floor and wiping down tables and the bar. A woman with blonde ringlets came down the stairs with an older gentleman, laughing giddily at something the man said. Their eyes met and the woman quickly dismissed her companion. Lillie approached her first, as if she knew her.

"Can I help you, ma'am?" A smile shone in her eyes that didn't meet her lips.

"I-I'm looking for my friend. Rachel." She looked around. "I need to find her."

"Haven't seen her in a while, Miss...?"

"Mattie." She saw the recognition on Lillie's face, but had no time to worry about why the blonde prostitute seemed to know who she was. "I fear she may be in some kind of trouble."

Lillie had seen it then, the rising welt on her cheek, with just the slightest shade of blue. Without a word she took Mattie's hand and dragged her across the saloon, where she gathered a handful of the workers who searched the saloon from top floor to bottom. It was Mattie who finally thought to step into the alleyway.

Her heart lurched at the dark figure curled into a ball against the back wall of the saloon. A trail of blood pooled from Rachel's head back across the alley to the storage shed, where a shattered bottle lay on the ground, more blood glistening off its surface in the moonlight. There was so much blood under Rachel's face. Kneeling next to her very still friend, she had at first thought Rachel was dead.

She had screamed, she thought, which brought the others running. Some of the men had gotten Rachel up into a cart, which Lillie herself drove back to the boarding house while Mattie sat in back, Rachel's head cradled in her lap.

Rachel's friend Billy had carried her up to her room, then gone running for the doctor, who came out in the wee hours of the morning to tend to her injuries. He had done all he could with Rachel being unconscious, and had left them until later on Saturday afternoon. He had been quite concerned as to how the blow to the head might affect her when she woke up.

"But you're going to be just fine," she whispered softly, brushing her thumb against the soft skin of Rachel's forearm resting against her thigh. "Because if you're not, I just might kill Adam myself."

She had missed work at the tailor shop. Had missed mass, and wasn't sure how she would cope with Adam when he returned. She had so many questions, but nothing mattered if Rachel didn't pull through. "And you will, you hear me?" She lifted a limp hand, kissing the knuckles. "I haven't learned to swim yet, Rachel Travis, and you promised you'd teach me, so you'd best get all better."

As if in answer, Rachel shifted, rolling toward her as her arm wrapped more solidly around Mattie's leg.

Chapter
Five

MATTIE SAT IN a chair next to the bed, pushing fried chicken and mashed potatoes around her plate. Lillie dozed quietly in a chair on the other side of the night table. The doctor had come by and given Rachel a headache powder, which had brought some relief to her throbbing head. She was sleeping soundly, with one hand resting lightly on Mattie's leg. Occasionally, her eyelids fluttered and she made little whimpering noises that reminded Mattie of a newborn puppy. It was cute enough to make her smile, despite the circumstances.

There was nothing to do but think. About her life. About Adam. About a friendship that admittedly had become the most important relationship in her life. Of course, Adam knew nothing of the depth of that friendship, and she was determined to guard it for all it was worth. Assuming he believed her story about Rachel being merely a client, she saw no reason why the friendship couldn't go on.

They would just have to be more careful about being seen together in public, that was all.

She studied Lillie, taking in tightly curled gold ringlets, the low-cut neckline of her blouse, her womanly curves, and the slight hint of rouge at her cheeks. No respectable woman wore rouge, at least not in the circle of women in which Mattie grew up.

Yet Lillie seemed genuinely concerned for Rachel's well-being, and had even broken down and cried after they first found her. It was obvious the two women were very good friends. Mattie puzzled over that, trying to figure out how a tomboy like Rachel had come to befriend a prostitute. She frowned, wondering just how well Lillie might know Adam. Shrugging slightly, she decided that perhaps Rachel and Lillie were drawn together by the simple fact that in some ways they were both outcasts. As for Adam, she wasn't entirely sure she wanted to know. There would be plenty of time to ask questions later, if she got brave enough.

She planned to have a talk with Rachel about working at the saloon, just as soon as she was up to it. She knew Adam well enough to know that if he'd been frequenting the establishment for this long, he wasn't going to stop, and she feared for Rachel's safety if she kept working there. She wondered just how much Rachel earned there, and thought about what jobs might be available as alternatives. She wasn't sure it was her place to question Rachel on her line of work, but the overwhelming sense of dread in her heart was winning out over manners that told her to mind her own business.

Her mind turned back to Adam's questions about Rachel. He'd kept calling her "unnatural," and repeatedly asked if Rachel had touched her inappropriately. She couldn't imagine what he meant by all of that. She thought about her times with Rachel, and laughed quietly to herself. "If anything, I seem to be the one always touching her," she whispered softly, and shook her head in wan amusement. Even now, she had one hand lying protectively over the one curled over her thigh, and realized she had been unconsciously stroking the back of it with her thumb.

Carefully, Mattie moved aside and stood up, intent on taking their eating utensils down the hall to wash them. As Rachel's hand lost contact with her, she frowned and grumbled quietly, her lips moving in incoherent displeasure.

Lillie woke up and cocked her head to one side, watching in fascination. "I do believe you've become her security blanket, sugar. Here." She stood, stretching her neck from side to side. "I'll go wash those out. You stay here. She seems to need you." She winked and disappeared out the door with the dishes.

"*Mmph,*" Rachel mumbled again and her eyes opened slowly in dazed confusion. "Time?"

"Almost sunset." Mattie dipped a rag in a basin of water and wiped Rachel's very warm forehead. "You still have a fever."

"I'm cold." The tiny hairs on her forearms prickled up as goose bumps raced across her skin. She felt Mattie tucking the blanket securely under her chin, and smiled at the gesture. She snuggled down into the mattress and cried out as pain shot across her torso from her broken rib.

"Shhh." Mattie smoothed her hair back. Heat radiated off Rachel's skin, and Mattie frowned in concern. "Open your eyes for me, as wide as you can."

Rachel complied, despite the discomfort of the sunlight streaming in from the setting sun. She watched mutely as Mattie leaned close, her hazel eyes quietly appraising something. "What's wrong?"

"You're eyes are dull." She sat down on the edge of the bed. "Dr. Mills thinks you have a touch of the fever and ague. I'm going to go downstairs and get you some warm ginger milk. He left some quinine too, so I need to get you a dose of that."

"Don't leave me." Rachel's hand came out from under the covers, shaking as she clutched feebly at her skirt.

"I'll only be a minute, I promise." Impulsively, Mattie bent over and kissed her forehead, then hurried out the door and down the stairs. True to her word, she reappeared a short time later, to find Lillie back in the room, sponging Rachel's face with the damp rag.

"I declare I don't know when I've seen someone have worse luck," she clucked over her friend. "How you managed to catch the chills and get the tarnation beaten out of you all in one day is beyond me."

"Maybe I made God very angry." Rachel smiled weakly, trying to suppress another chill. She failed and her entire body shook while her teeth chattered.

"Nonsense. God loves you, Rachel. Here." Mattie moved closer and Lillie automatically stepped aside. "I need you to drink up this milk. You'll like it." She smiled.

"I will, eh?" Her words sounded far off to her own ears, and she chalked it up to the fever. She took a tentative sip and smiled. "Ginger and honey." She smacked her lips. "More, please."

Mattie laughed softly and scooted closer, supporting her shoulders against her lap as Rachel finished the warm drink. "Feel better?" She set the cup aside.

"Some." Her nose scrunched up at a slightly bitter aftertaste. "You mixed the quinine in there, didn't you?"

Mattie smiled almost evilly. "Yes, I did. Was that so bad?"

"Not as bad as taking it straight up." Rachel shifted, arranging herself until even more of her body was in contact with Mattie's lap. "Need to sleep some more."

"Then let me..." Mattie eased out from under her.

"No." Rachel pouted, a full lower lip poking out pathetically. "Warm."

Mattie sighed. "Hold on." She raised a questioning eyebrow at Lillie, who shrugged back at her. With a heavier sigh, Mattie slipped off her shoes, then stood and removed her skirt and blouse, leaving her in her full slip and chemise. "What if I take a little nap with you? Will that help you get warm?"

Steel eyes peered up at her in mute gratitude, and Rachel nodded slightly. Her ears were starting to ring faintly, a side-effect of the quinine. She felt miserable, every muscle in her body crying out in pain, not only from the beating she had taken, but from clenching up from being cold. Mattie lifted the covers and slid in beside her, and Rachel immediately relaxed. She snuggled up until her head was resting on Mattie's shoulder. Within minutes she was asleep, her breathing slow and even.

"Guess I'm staying here tonight." Mattie stroked her head and settled in, feeling her own eyelids grow heavy. "If you want, I can take care of her tonight. I'll have to go to work tomorrow, at least for a while, and of course be home before Adam gets back from Houston. I have a feeling she's going to need you a lot in the coming days."

Lillie stood silent for a moment, observing Rachel's quietly peaceful face. "I suppose you'll only be able to come by during the noon hour this coming week?"

"I'm going to see how much time I can get away from the tailor shop." Mattie smiled as Rachel shifted, wrapping one arm across her waist. "I might be able to stay with her during the day this week, as long as I'm back at the shop before Adam picks me up."

Lillie's eyes met Mattie's, Adam's name hanging uncomfortably between them.

"My husband." Mattie grasped for words. "Do you know him?"

"Yes." Lillie's eyes darted away from her, dreading further questions.

Mattie merely nodded. She didn't need to ask. "Get some rest. I'll see you in the morning?"

"Good enough." Lillie gathered her pocketbook and managed a smile before she left the two women for some much-needed sleep.

MATTIE DRIFTED AWAKE, her senses gradually taking in her surroundings. She was very warm, and felt a solid weight draped across much of her upper body. Her nose twitched, breathing in a scent she had come to associate with Rachel. It was a pleasantly sunny smell, with a touch of ocean breeze, along with clean-smelling cake soap, much nicer than the harsh homemade lye soap many of the town's workers used. She opened her eyes and looked down, to see chestnut hair spread across her body, and Rachel's face, open and peaceful in sleep, resting against her upper stomach.

Dawn's light streamed through the curtains, pale pearl gray. It was Monday, and her heart felt heavy, wondering how she was going to manage her job, taking care of Rachel, and Adam's return from Houston. She reached up, feeling her face where he struck her. The bruise had faded some, but the internal pain remained.

He had gone too far this time, and she felt a slow simmer underneath the surface, overpowering her usually placid acceptance of his treatment of her. It was different this time. He had hurt someone else because of her, and the guilt of that weighed solidly on her small, if capable, shoulders. She loathed him. There was no more denying the obvious. She just wasn't sure what she could do about it.

A quiet tap at the door stirred her from dark internal musings, and she sat partway up. "Come in."

Lillie peered around the door before she entered the room, bearing a basket that released delicious aromas — biscuits, eggs, ham, and sweet hot tea. "How is she?" She set the basket down on the bedside table and removed her hat and gloves, hanging the hat on a peg by the door.

"Resting quietly." Mattie felt Rachel's forehead. "Still warm, but not as warm as she was last night. We probably need to get some more quinine and another headache powder into her when she wakes up."

"Hmm. Probably do." Lillie opened the checkered cloth covering the basket. "Thought you might want breakfast before you go to the tailor's."

"Thank you." Mattie gently rolled Rachel off her, allowing one long arm to maintain contact with her legs. She watched as the tanned face first frowned, then relaxed again, as Rachel resumed even heavy breathing. "That was very kind of you." Mattie accepted a plate of food.

"Pshaw. Tweren't nothing." Lillie sat down in a chair, drawing it up next to the table. "It's the least I could do, after..." She stopped, looking down and catching herself, about to make a confession she couldn't quite bring herself to speak aloud. "After you stayed here all night." She saw the knowledge of truth in Mattie's eyes. Mattie knew.

"Listen, Lillie." Mattie sipped her tea, reaching deep inside herself for wisdom. "My husband is not a nice man. He's a scoundrel, and I think we both know that. I don't understand why you do what you do, but I don't hold you responsible for Adam's behavior, at any rate."

"I've spent no time with him since finding out he was married to you." Lillie interrupted, picking at her food and avoiding eye contact. "I know that probably doesn't raise your esteem for me much higher, but for what it's worth, I only saw him on one occasion."

Mattie slowly digested that. Hearing it confirmed was shocking on certain levels, but knowing she wasn't sharing breakfast with one of Adam's regulars was reassuring on a completely different one. Finally, she looked up and waited until Lillie did the same. "How do you know so much about me?" She swallowed. "You knew who I was, didn't you — when I walked into the saloon Friday night?"

"Yes, in answer to your last question." Lillie's lips hinted at a bare smile. "As to the 'how,' you're just about all Rachel can talk about anymore." The smile widened at the surprise on Mattie's face. "I do believe you're one of the best friends she's ever had. Rachel, she has many acquaintances that think highly of her. The boys on the dock, the regulars at the saloon, although she doesn't see it that way. She feels like an outsider — a misfit. She doesn't let very many people get close enough to truly know her. You're one of the few."

"She's a very special person." Mattie stroked the sleeping head. "I do think I'd do just about anything for her. I have been very lonely, for most of my life. When I'm with her, I don't feel so alone anymore."

Lillie shook her head, almost imperceptibly. Mattie's face shone quietly as she spoke, and her eyes softened whenever she looked down at Rachel. It was so hard not to smack Mattie up beside the head. That she loved Rachel was painfully obvious. It was equally obvious she was completely unaware of that love.

"She is indeed a very special person." Lillie nibbled at a warm flaky biscuit. "I have a few women friends, most of them other ladies like myself. Rachel—she's about the only one outside that circle who has befriended me without judgment."

"You two do seem very close," Mattie agreed. "How did y'all meet?"

Lillie almost choked on biscuit crumbs, coughing violently before picking up her teacup and downing most of its contents in two gulps. Gradually, she regained her composure. "We met when Rachel started working at the saloon. You might want to ask her about that, when she's up for some questioning. I do remember the first time I saw her. She was so young, and I could tell she was terrified, walking into that saloon. She was the only woman in there besides me and my kind. Took a heap of guts, I'll tell you that much. But it's a good job. Probably pays her almost as much as she makes on a few days at the docks, leastwise on a full-house evening."

"I suppose it would be difficult to give up those kind of wages," Mattie commented dejectedly, seeing her plans to talk Rachel out of the job fly out the window. "I worry about her, now that Adam knows she and I know each other. He's relentless. He'll watch her like a hawk. I don't think I could stand it if he were to hurt her again. I do believe I might have to shoot him if he did."

This time Lillie spluttered her remaining tea back into the cup. "You truly mean that?"

"A part of me does, yes." Mattie reached across the night table for her pocketbook. "Adam has no idea I own this." She withdrew a twenty-two caliber nickel-plated revolver with a rosewood handle. "Nor that I know how to use it. It only weighs seven ounces. I purchased it about six months after we were married. Used to go out behind my father's barn and practice while Adam was at work. I can shoot a tin can off a fence post at twenty-five paces."

Two blonde eyebrows shot into Lillie's hairline. "I am starting to understand why Rachel is so taken with you. How does that old saying go—'wise as a serpent, gentle as a dove'? Does she know about the gun?"

"No." Mattie placed it back in her pocketbook. "It never came up. I understood, very early in my marriage, that I might someday need to defend myself." She shared a meaningful glance with Lillie. "I hope to never test that out, but if I have to, I could." Her sight turned inward, knowing the truth. "I seriously doubt Adam has shot a gun in his entire life. He doesn't hunt. He grew up in polite society, despite it being West Texas. About the only time gentlemen of his class used guns was if they pulled out dueling pistols. I haven't seen a duel since I was a very small girl." Her nose wrinkled. "I hope never to see one again. It is a rather unpleasant business."

Lillie was silent, absorbing a side of Mattie she suddenly realized no one had seen, not even Rachel. Slowly, she smiled, wondering how her friend would react if she knew about the gun. *Probably start worrying Mattie will shoot herself on accident,* she chuckled to herself. *Old mother hen.* "I can only imagine," she finally commented.

"Well." Mattie finished her breakfast and placed the plate on the table. "I should probably go wash up and get to the tailor's. I'll talk to Mr. Vaughan this morning and explain the situation. I'll be back at the noon hour to let you know what he says." She slipped out of the bed and Rachel whimpered in response.

"Rachel." She bent over the sleeping form. "I know you're hurting a lot right now. I have to go to work, but I'll be back in a few hours, I promise." She kissed her forehead and stood up, gathering up her pocketbook and a change of clothing she had gone home to collect on Saturday afternoon. "I'll see you at noon, Lillie. If y'all need me before then, go ahead and send someone over to get me."

"I will." Lillie smiled. "Have a good morning." She watched thoughtfully as Mattie stepped into the hallway and the door closed quietly behind her. She looked over at her sleeping friend. "I hope this works out for you, Rachel. Mattie is a keeper."

RACHEL STIRRED, TRYING to free her arms and legs from tangled covers. She was hot and sweating, which, she reflected in a fuzzy way, was a good thing, because it probably meant her fever had broken. "*Umph.*" She felt a gentle touch to her forehead, as a damp cloth dabbed at her warm skin, and she immediately relaxed and opened her eyes. "Mattie?"

"I'm here." Mattie reached down, helping turn back both blanket and sheet. "We need to get you changed into a dry nightshirt." She moved to the armoire and opened a drawer, removing a well-worn blue and white striped shirt. She heard a grumble of displeasure and turned to see Rachel watching her in consternation. "You don't like this one?"

"Too warm." Rachel cleared a very dry throat. "I'd prefer a clean undershirt and bloomers." She gave a nod of approval as Mattie put the longer shirt away and located the requested garments. She dropped her eyes as she felt slender yet strong arms raise her up and begin to remove her clothing.

"You don't need to be embarrassed." Mattie's expression gentled as questioning steel eyes slowly looked up at her. "Lillie and I gave you a sponge bath yesterday, although you probably don't remember it." The dark head shook affirmatively. "We thought you'd be more comfortable if you were clean."

"Th-thank you." She tried not to think about Lillie and Mattie seeing her nakedness at the same time, and decided she was glad she didn't remember it, although a part of her was curious as to what Mattie's reaction might have been. She grimaced as she turned too sharply and her broken rib made its presence known. She looked down at the sturdy muslin binding around her chest just below her breasts, the ends pinned neatly in place instead of tied in lumpy knots. As she felt the clean cotton slide down her torso and settle into place, she looked back up, her eyes thoughtful. "I can do the bloomers myself."

Mattie turned her back, giving her some privacy. She could picture what she wasn't seeing—a feminine yet strong body, with nice muscles covered by smooth creamy skin—pale womanly skin that had never known sunlight. Rachel was very beautiful. There was no denying that. She realized that usually when she saw Rachel she saw her strength, most of all. Without her trousers and men's shirts, she was every bit as much a woman as Mattie was, and Mattie found herself wishing she could sketch more of her. She could almost feel the charcoal in her fingers, the slightly rough paper under her hands as she traced out the planes and curves of Rachel's body.

"I'm going to be bruised for a while, I think." Rachel lifted up her undershirt just enough to reveal blue and purple mottled skin that stretched from the top of her bloomers waistband to the bottom of her bandages. She watched Mattie turn, and saw the guilty pain on her face. "This is not your fault, Mattie."

"He beat you up because of me." Mattie moved to the bedside and dropped to her knees until their faces were on a level. She lifted one of Rachel's hands and brushed her lips across her knuckles. She looked up and watched Rachel swallow, an unreadable expression in her eyes. "I don't even understand why he did it. He—he kept saying you were 'unnatural' and wanted to know if you had touched me in an unseemly manner. I don't understand what he meant." She searched Rachel's face for answers, but Rachel looked away, her eyes studying the bubbled wallpaper, its edges curling in places that were once glued flat.

"I don't expect you would understand." She released a long breath, her mind a jumble of medication and fear. If they were to be friends, Mattie needed to know exactly whom she was befriending. "How could you understand?" she whispered softly.

Impulsively, Rachel drew Mattie's head forward, kissing her just above her thick fringe of bangs. She drew back, her hand still cupping Mattie's cheek. "I feel weak as a newborn kitten, and my ears are ringing with the quinine." She paused, licking her lips nervously. "I promise you, when I am feeling more myself, I'll explain everything to you—what he meant." She closed her eyes and her head dropped again, but her thumb kept up a slow gentle stroking of Mattie's soft skin. "Then you can decide for yourself if you want to be around the likes of me."

Mattie reached out, her fingers lightly trailing through Rachel's hair, careful to avoid the stitches at her hairline. "I have already decided."

Slowly, the dark head lifted, revealing two large blue-gray eyes brimming with unshed tears. Without a word, Mattie crawled in bed, scooting behind Rachel and pulling the longer body against her, rocking her, as she made soft shushing noises. She felt warm wetness against the skin of her neck and simply held Rachel while she cried. "I can't think of anything that is worth more than your friendship, Rachel."

Long arms reached around, clutching more tightly around Mattie's gingham dress. Oblivious to the pull in her ribs and the pain in her battered body, she held on, releasing what seemed to be a lifetime of loneliness. It didn't matter if she ever had any more from Mattie than what she had at that moment. It was enough. More than enough.

She gradually allowed more sober thoughts, wondering if the friendship so freely offered her would stand against her coming confessions. It simply must, she reasoned, half-hoping, half-willing it to be so. It will. Carefully, she pushed up until they were sitting side by side. "Sorry." She swiped the back of her hand across her eyes. "Don't know what came over me. Must be the fever." She laughed feebly and felt a handkerchief pressed into her hand. She dabbed at her eyes and nose. "I must be a sight."

Mattie's eyes drifted affectionately over her. "That you are." She felt another kiss to her head. "Whatever you need to say to me, it can keep until you're ready." She felt a squeeze to her hand, as long fingers interlaced with her own.

They sat together in comfortable silence, each lost in her own thoughts. Mattie reluctantly sat up taller and withdrew a small silver pocket watch from her skirt pocket. "Unfortunately, I must get back to the tailor's. Adam should be getting off the train at five o'clock straight up, and sometimes he comes to pick me up before he goes home."

"Is it still Monday?" Rachel's mind spun with the effort of trying to piece together the periods of consciousness she could remember.

"Yes." Mattie gathered her pocketbook and gloves. "I've been here since the noon hour. Mr. Vaughan has agreed to let me go each day at the noon hour until you're back on your feet again. Lillie will be by to fetch you some supper each evening, and she will stay nights until noon each day." She held up a hand against the beginnings of protest. "Tell me you're able to get food, and bathe, and change clothing for yourself." She placed a fist on her hip and tapped her foot expectantly.

Rachel's mouth closed abruptly, her arguments quickly forgotten. "Thank you," she mumbled. "I—I'm not used to counting on other folks to take care of me." Another thought occurred to her, and her eyes grew wide with fear. "Do you trust Mr. Vaughan?"

"He has promised not to say anything to Adam about our

arrangement." Mattie's eyes twinkled. "I do believe he and Mrs. Vaughan have taken a liking to you."

"They are very kind people." The Vaughans had offered her several refills to a mug of sweetened tea until she was no longer thirsty from the dock work, and had shared a slice of freshly baked lemon cake with her for dessert. When she left to go back to the port, Mrs. Vaughan had packed her up two more slices of the cake, and had patted her on the arm as she left.

"Yes, they are." Mattie stood over her, and felt a tug at her skirt.

"You be careful." Blue eyes flashed in anger.

"I will, but I'd best be going if I'm to keep him from suspecting where I've been all afternoon." She squeezed the hand that clutched at her skirt and turned, pausing in the doorway. "Lillie should be here shortly."

Someone tapped lightly at the door. "Must be her now. Come on in," Rachel called out. Slowly the door opened, and Rachel blinked in surprise as a gray head appeared. "Betsy?" She looked down self-consciously, well aware of her bruises and stitches. "What brings you here?"

"Heard you were laid up." She held out a hand toward Mattie. "I'm Betsy MacKenzie."

"Mattie Crockett. Pleased to meet you." She politely shook hands. Like Rachel, she knew the bruises on her own face told their story, and she blushed in shame, wondering what this stranger had heard.

"Mattie." Betsy tried to place her, and finally smiled. "You work at the tailor's on Broadway?"

"Yes. In fact, I was just headed over there. We were waiting for another friend to drop by and sit with Rachel for a spell." She glanced at Rachel in question, wondering if it was okay to leave her alone with Betsy.

"Go on if you need to. I'll visit with Betsy for a while. I'll be fine until Lil gets here." Rachel felt awkward, and knew Betsy had guessed at who Mattie was.

"Very well, then." Mattie restrained herself, merely patting Rachel on the arm. "I'll see you at noon tomorrow." She turned toward Betsy. "Nice meeting you again."

"You, too." Betsy smiled warmly.

Rachel watched Mattie wave a gloved hand at her, then felt her heart grow heavy as she heard the door click shut. "That was her," she offered shyly.

"I gathered as much." Betsy sat down in the chair next to the bed. "I can't stay long. I need to get home and start supper, but I wanted to make sure you were taken care of. I was at the market earlier today, and heard some of the dockworkers' wives talking about a woman who was beaten up, and heard your name mentioned. I met Angel for dinner and told her, and she said we should check on you. I see you're in good hands," her voice gently teased.

"I am, but I appreciate the visit." Rachel scooted to the edge of the bed, patting her on the leg. "It means a lot to have you and Angel as my friends."

"Angel wants to know who did this to you. I think she's ready to send a posse after them." Betsy frowned. "What kind of man would do this, especially to a woman?"

"Mattie's husband," Rachel sighed. "And before you say anything, I'm not doing anything about it. No posses. You saw her face—he found out we'd spent some time together, and he took it out on both of us. I think he's figured out about me. Mattie still has no idea. But I've decided I need to talk to her. He's said too much and she's confused by what he meant. He told her I was 'unnatural'." The word was bitter on her tongue.

"My goodness." Betsy's eyes sparked in anger. "What a vile man she's married to. You be careful. I must say, I was cautiously hopeful for you when you first talked to us, but now, I do hope you win her away from him. He doesn't deserve her, and she certainly shouldn't be living with him."

"I only hope she'll still be my friend after we talk." Her heart sank, wondering what she was going to say.

"Oh, I think she will." Betsy smiled. "Her eyes light up when she looks at you."

"They do?" Blue eyes grew wide in surprise.

"Absolutely." Betsy leaned over and gave her a loose hug. "I need to go, but I'll try to check in on you from time to time, until you get back on your feet."

"Thank you." Rachel returned the hug. "Give my regards to Angel."

"I will." Betsy left quietly, and Rachel curled up on her uninjured side. She drew up Mattie's handkerchief that she'd kept balled up in her fist, inhaling the scent of her toilet water. She smiled and tucked it under her chin before she closed her eyes.

Lillie found her that way thirty minutes later, her chest rising and falling evenly in sleep, as a tiny smile twitched at her lips. She placed the basket of supper on the table and pulled up a chair, retrieving some stockings and darning needles from a bag. "Sweet dreams, Rachel."

IT WAS VERY late—well past dark. The tide had risen and the gentle sound of waves lapping against the shore lulled Mattie into a brief sense of peace. Adam had yet to arrive home. It wasn't entirely unusual for him to take a late train out of Houston on Monday, but given their parting, she was a bit surprised he hadn't come home earlier, if only to check up on her.

Her mind was a jumble of thoughts, and she wandered aimlessly about the small house, picking up items and studying them, thinking about everything that had happened in one short weekend. She thought about Lillie, and admitted to herself that despite who Lillie was, and even despite the fact that she apparently had been with Adam once, she grudgingly found herself liking the vivacious blonde. Lillie had a no-nonsense approach toward Rachel and life in general, and she had managed to make Mattie laugh a few times even in the middle of bleak circumstances.

Lillie seemed very dedicated to Rachel and yet... Mattie frowned and went out on the front porch, taking a seat on the top step. She gathered in her skirts and wrapped her arms around her legs, hugging herself against a slight chill in the air. It felt good after the unusually hot days they had been having. Looking out at the vastness of the Gulf of Mexico, she felt very small and very much alone. She loved the island most of the time, but on dark lonely nights, she sometimes felt a hundred miles from the mainland, and her family might as well have been on the moon.

Her thoughts turned back toward Lillie and Rachel. They had been friends for a long time, yet Lillie seemed to defer to Mattie when it came to caring for Rachel. She found that to be odd. Surely Lillie and Rachel were closer than she and Rachel. They had been friends longer, correct? Yet she recalled Rachel telling her that she had never had a friend like Mattie before. It made her feel warm all over, and drove back some of the chill.

She and Rachel were so different from one another. She suspected the more rowdy Lillie had much more in common with her friend than she did. A part of her wondered why Rachel and she had become friends in the first place, and what had possessed her to extend that first invitation to tea. Yet the friendship worked, and there was no one she had ever been more comfortable with than Rachel. They talked easily, and their silences were comfortable. She felt she could tell Rachel almost anything.

Adam hated Rachel, and for what reason she hadn't a clue, other than he seemed to think she was different and that he might hurt her. She snorted softly. Rachel would never hurt her. Yes, she was different, but Mattie found herself drawn to those differences. A vision of Rachel laughing, her hair whipping wildly back in the wind as she stood in the surf with her trouser legs rolled up, made Mattie smile. Rachel lived fully in he moment, and didn't seem to worry too much about the future, or dwell upon the past. Mattie wanted so much to be like her.

The future always seemed bleak. It stretched out before her — a life with Adam and all the uncertainty and pain that came with being married to him. She shivered, a bone-chilling sensation that came from within. There was nothing to look forward to with Adam, no matter how hard she tried to think of something. She couldn't make a move without his permission. She would always be alone with him because she had no intention of bearing his children. Her family was so far away that she wondered if she would ever see them again. She felt an overwhelming sense of despair and hugged her arms more tightly around herself.

She had no idea how much time passed, but finally a jaw-splitting yawn forced her to go inside and dress for bed. With a weary sigh she retrieved the pessary box and slipped into the water closet. She loved children. If she had married the right man...she shook her head sadly. There was no point in thinking about it. What was done was done. She could never subject a child to having Adam for a father. It would be sweet, to hold her own baby in her arms, to know that someone in the world loved her and needed her, but she realized those were very selfish reasons to have a child, given her circumstances.

She had almost fallen asleep when she heard Adam drive up, the buggy wheels crunching across the crushed-shell and sand driveway. She listened, her heart beating loudly in her ears, until she heard the heavy thump that signaled the barn door closing, then heard the almost undetectable sound of Adam's boots in the drive. His steps on the wooden porch made her jump, then the front door opened and she heard him drop his carpetbag in the entryway.

She shut her eyes tightly and rolled toward the wall as he came into the room and removed his clothing. He moved quietly around, opening a drawer and retrieving a nightshirt. A heavy weight settled on the mattress next to her, as he pulled back the covers and crawled up close. This was the animal that had had Rachel beaten nearly to death. She wanted to cringe and forced herself to remain still.

"Mattie?" He stroked her cheek and her heart clenched in fear. There would be no feigning sleep on this night.

"You're late," she mumbled, slowly rolling onto her back.

"My business in Houston went very well this weekend. I stayed later than I intended, but it was profitable." He kissed her on the cheek.

"That's good to hear." She forced herself to return his affections as his lips moved to cover her own. Inside, she wanted to gag.

"I'm sorry I've left you alone so much, Mattie." His body pressed against her and the heat made her feel sick to her stomach. "Unfortunately, I may be spending even more time in Houston in the next few months. The business is doing too well for me to not take advantage of a good opportunity."

She managed not to smile. The more he was gone, the more she could do whatever she wanted to do, including spending time with Rachel. "You should do what you think is best." She felt him tugging at the hem of her nightgown, and began shutting her mind off as best she could.

"I think we should start our family, Mattie." He rubbed her belly. "Although I would have thought you would be with child by now. Maybe I haven't given you enough attention. Maybe I should remedy that during the times I am home." He pulled her gown up and rolled on top of her, pushing her bloomers down. "A baby would keep you focused on more important things, I think. Keep you home and safe. Keep you away from bad influences."

There, in the dark, she finally allowed the tears to fall. Adam would not be able to see them. At least it would be over quickly. It always was. For the first time in her life, she briefly wondered why she didn't end her life sooner rather than later. She knew she would go to Hell if she committed suicide, but it couldn't possibly be worse than the hell she was already living in.

A MONTH PASSED. Rachel's wounds slowly healed, and she began to recover from the chills and fever. During the first few weeks of her illness and recovery, either Lillie or Mattie had been with her diligently, almost around the clock. She was certain she would have died if not for their care. It was the first time in her life that she could recall when she wasn't able to be self-sufficient. Betsy and Angel had also dropped in a few times, and Rachel found herself rich in the novelty of female friendship.

Toward the end of the month she was finally up and able to walk for a few miles. Her ribs still tugged at her when she moved, and her legs felt weak, as if all the muscles were loose and flat. The doctor had determined she had no serious internal injuries, and had declared her on the road to recovery a few days before. He had cautioned her against overexertion, and advised she take up the quinine again if the chills or fever returned. He also suggested she walk to build her strength back up.

The thought of hefting the heavy bales of cotton on the docks made her weary. Luckily she had been offered an extended position on David Gentry's fishing boat just as soon as she was able to work again. It was Sunday afternoon, and she intended to give the fishing a try the next morning. She might need help hauling in heavier catches, but she could easily tend the lines and the nets, baiting hooks and watching for any signs of activity.

This afternoon, she was walking out toward Mattie's house. She knew Adam was out of town, as Mattie had been by to visit her for a few hours the day before. Once her fever abated permanently, and she was able to bathe and dress herself, and make it downstairs for meals, Lillie and Mattie had looked in on her less frequently, although she saw one of them at least once every day, and often both paid her a visit.

If not for pain and illness, the month past would have been

downright enjoyable, she mused. She felt a transition in both her relationship with Lillie, and with Mattie. Her friendship with Lillie was strong as ever, but the physical aspect of that friendship had cooled considerably. Before, they had touched each other often when they were alone. Now the touches were limited to hugs of greeting, and the occasional kiss on the cheek. She found her desire for Lillie's physical affections to be almost nonexistent.

At the same time, Mattie was touching her more and more frequently — a pat on the leg, a playful hug, and rarely, a brief peck on the cheek or lips. And they had spent a lot of time sitting close together, going over reading lessons since there was little else she was able to do to pass the time. She was finding it more and more difficult to keep her hands off Mattie as well, often mussing her hair or curling up with her, ostensibly for comfort from her injuries and illness. In truth, it was a balm to her heart and soul, more than anything else.

They needed to talk. She had put it off as long as she could, and knew it wasn't fair to Mattie to prolong the inevitable. Her heart was heavy. The talk could very well be their last, and she already felt herself building inner defenses in the event of rejection. On the other hand, if Mattie heard her out, and still wanted her in her life — her stomach fluttered — a part of her wanted to let go of her restraint, and allow their friendship to lead wherever it might.

Lillie had readily confirmed what Rachel had not allowed herself to see. "That girl is in love with you, Rachel. Now what are you going to do about it?" Lillie's words echoed in her head with painfully solid loudness.

What, indeed, was she going to do?

There were no easy answers, and so she trudged forward, praying for the best while emotionally preparing herself for the worst. Mattie had become somewhat withdrawn in the past few weeks, and often when she first woke up, before Mattie was aware she was being watched, she caught her staring sadly out the window. However, she always seemed to perk up when Rachel talked to her, although she had yet to be forthcoming with whatever was troubling her. Rachel fervently hoped that whatever it was could be helped, and that she wasn't the source.

At last she reached Mattie's house and almost timidly knocked on the door. It opened in a few moments, and she accepted a long silent hug from her friend. "Hello, Mattie." Her eyes took in an ivory-colored ruffled blouse and navy blue skirt. "You look lovely."

"Thank you." Mattie smiled sadly up at her.

"Are you all right?" Rachel couldn't help but reach out, touching a pale cheek.

"Yes." She blinked, feeling the sting of tears trying to form. "It's nothing. Adam will be home tomorrow. I've grown used to him staying over an extra day these past few weeks, and having four nights a week to myself. You must think I'm horrible. He is my husband."

Rachel's thumb delicately traced her upper lip, silencing her. She realized there was no more hesitation on her part at such actions, and that Mattie seemed almost to expect it from her. "No." She placed a kiss on Mattie's forehead. "I wish there was something I could do to make you feel better."

"We could go for a walk on the beach." Mattie tugged at Rachel's shirt collar. "Assuming you are feeling like it after walking all the way here."

"I feel much better than I thought I would. Perhaps some more fresh air will make me feel even better." She held out her arm and felt Mattie's hand slip into the crook of her elbow. "I believe I promised you I would talk to you about some things, and maybe this afternoon would be a good time to do that." Her eyes searched Mattie's face, begging for understanding.

"And I believe I promised you that there is nothing you could tell me that would change the way I feel about our friendship." Mattie squeezed her arm as they stepped onto the porch and made their way down to the sand. She let go of Rachel long enough to raise her parasol, then took hold of her arm once more, surprised when she felt the taller woman leaning on her slightly, as if for support. "If you tucker out, we can always sit and rest a spell."

Rachel felt the fear welling up inside and quickly decided to ride it out, as the words slowly began to spill out. "A while back, I confessed to you that I had been in a physical relationship with someone, even though I've never married. I wasn't completely honest with you about that."

"Oh." Mattie's brows furrowed. "Have you been with more than one man?"

"No." Rachel nibbled her lower lip. "I let you believe something that I probably shouldn't have. I have been with no man."

"I don't understand." Mattie looked up at her, watching Rachel's throat muscles work as she swallowed and looked out to sea.

"I was with a woman." She felt Mattie almost stop, before resuming their pace.

"Now I truly don't understand." Mattie's brows furrowed in utter confusion. "That is impossible."

"No." Another swallow. "It is quite possible, I assure you."

"But women don't have..." Mattie felt herself blushing and couldn't finish her sentence.

"Not necessary." Rachel knew exactly where her friend's thoughts had wandered. "Mattie, you have said enough for me to understand that you don't enjoy being with Adam, in that way. Am I correct in assuming you have never found it pleasurable?"

"That would be true." The blush turned bright crimson and Mattie looked down, wishing she could crawl into one of the sand crab holes that peppered the beach.

Rachel saw the red head duck down, and her free hand involuntarily reached across, tilting Mattie's face up as she stopped and turned to face her. "You could never say anything that would repel me, Mattie. Please don't be ashamed, and I'll try to do the same. It is very important to me that we talk about this. It isn't fair to you for me to hide this part of myself from you."

"I-I'll try." Mattie tugged at her hand. "Shall we go sit on that log over there?"

"That is a good idea." She allowed herself to be led to the log, where she sat down in tired relief, drawing slightly apart from Mattie. Rachel looked down, studying her own hands before she tucked them between her knees. She continued to look down as she spoke. "There are ways that women can touch each other, things they can do together, that are every bit as pleasurable as what a man and a woman can do together. Men can do those same things to women, if they wish to bring them pleasure in a physical relationship."

"I can't fathom enjoying it with Adam." Mattie dug the toe of her shoe into the sand and set her parasol aside. "So what you're saying to me, I truly can't fathom. Nothing Adam has ever done to me has brought me pleasure. It-it is painful, more than anything else."

Rachel felt the anger rise. *Bastard.* She pushed the emotions deep down inside. It wasn't the time or place. "It shouldn't be, if he's doing it correctly."

"What is there to do?" Mattie felt the heat rising up her neck, and was certain her face quite matched her hair. She wanted to curl up into herself, and she hunched over, speaking slowly and softly. "He comes to me late at night, usually when he arrives home from Houston, and he's always been drinking. He kisses me a few times, then pushes my nightgown up and my bloomers down, and does his business. I can't see that there is anything that would make me enjoy that."

Rachel released an angry puff of air. "I'm sorry, Mattie. There are ways he could touch you that would make you more ready for him. Is that truly all he does?"

"Yes." She finally looked up. "I wouldn't want it to last any longer than it already does. I lie there and pray for him to hurry and finish as it is."

"Could you discuss it with him?" She already knew the answer, and at the same time, couldn't believe she was actually offering some advice in this area, if Mattie wanted it.

"No!" Mattie stood abruptly, and began pacing the sand in front of them, gesturing wildly with her arms as she spoke. "I can't talk to him about anything. I can't do anything without asking him first. He watches everything I do. I can't even discuss breakfast with him without the possibility of him hitting me if he isn't satisfied with what

I serve him. Do you honestly think I could ever — ever — talk to him about things a lady isn't supposed to mention?"

She dissolved into tears, and felt long arms close around her, a solid warm body rocking her gently as she was drawn back to the log. "I'm sorry." She sniffled and sat down. "You are supposed to be talking to me about you."

"No." Rachel stroked her hair and kissed the top of her head. "No. Your life is just as important. I'm so sorry he hurts you."

"I've grown used to it, for the most part." She sniffed again and accepted a handkerchief, which magically appeared from Rachel's pocket. "Thank you." She pulled her emotions in and leaned against Rachel's shoulder, more comfortable without eye contact, but with the warm connection she felt as Rachel's arm slid around her waist. "Please continue."

"When Adam called me 'unnatural,' he was guessing, correctly, that I am drawn to women in the way that most women are drawn to men. I have known this about myself for a very long time. It's why I had to leave home. My father caught me with another girl. We hadn't actually done anything but kiss, but if he had not caught us when he did, we would have. That was when he decided to either send me to a convent or have me married off. So you see, I had no other choice but to leave home. Either of his choices would have made me more unhappy than I can possibly imagine." *As unhappy as you are, I suspect, Mattie,* she added silently.

"So who...?" Mattie stopped. "I'm sorry. It is none of my business."

"Lillie." The silence that followed was so long and deafening, she assumed she had just driven the last nail in the coffin of their friendship. "I pay her, just like any other customer." Her cheeks burned in shame.

"Oh." The shock of it was almost like one of Adam's punches to her gut. "That makes sense, I suppose."

"She approached me first, a long time ago, after I moved here. I don't know exactly how she knew about me, but she is the only person I've ever been with, in that way. She's six or seven years older than me. Until you came along, she was the only true friend I felt I had." She felt Mattie move aside, just a little, although their legs were still touching. "I should have told you sooner. I am a coward."

"No. You're very brave for telling me now." She allowed the thoughts to swirl through her head. "She's been with Adam, you know."

"Yes. I know." Might as well jump the rest of the way in. "Only once, though, right before I met you, although it was a while longer before I learned he was your husband. He hit her. I punched him and broke his nose."

"So that's how that happened." Mattie finally chuckled, just a little. "No wonder he wouldn't talk about it. He was bested by a lady."

"I'm no lady." Rachel smiled and their eyes met for a brief moment. "But I did injure his pride, and he has been out to get me ever since."

"Pride." She shook her head. "He has a great deal of that."

"So do I." Rachel tucked her hands between her knees again. She thought about Mattie's sadness of late, and the things Mattie had just revealed to her. "Is that why you've been so sad lately, Mattie? Because of how Adam is with you?"

"Partly." It was Mattie's turn to study her hands, clasping them in her lap as she spoke hesitantly. "He...wants to start a family, so he wants...to be with me even more often than he used to. He wants me to have a baby, I think so that I will stay home and have something to keep me busy. I don't want that with him."

"There are ways..."

"I know." Mattie cut her off. "It's taken care of. I talked to a woman back in El Paso and she told me what to do to prevent it. Adam has no idea, of course. Once I figured out how things were going to go between Adam and me, I had to do something. I don't love him. He doesn't love me. I couldn't bring a child into our relationship. It's hard enough protecting myself from him. I won't give him the chance to treat a child the way he treats me. I know it's a sin."

"No." Rachel hugged her close to her side. "It's one of the most unselfish things I've ever heard. I'm so sorry, Mattie. Any child would be lucky to have you as its mother."

"Thank you." She patted Rachel's leg. "But Adam wouldn't be capable of loving a child. He's not capable of loving anyone, I don't think."

"You deserve to be loved, Mattie." Rachel's voice was profoundly sad, repeating a sentiment she had shared with her friend on more than one occasion.

"So do you." She squeezed Rachel's leg. "Do—do you love Lillie?" Mattie glanced up, studying Rachel's strong profile, watching the play of the sunshine that danced across her hair, creating rich auburn highlights.

"She has been my friend, lover, and older sister at turns. I am forever indebted to her, both for the things she has taught me, and for accepting me. But I am not, and never have been in love with her, if that is what you're asking." She couldn't look up, and felt the sweat beading on her forehead, dreading questions she didn't want to answer.

"But you are drawn to her, physically?" Mattie tilted her head in question, trying unsuccessfully to catch Rachel's eye.

"Yes." She still refused to look up.

"Have you been drawn to any other women on the island in that way?"

"Yes." A painful whisper that Mattie barely heard.

Mattie thought about the way Rachel treated her, with such kindness it came close to breaking her heart at times. It was a completely new concept to her. She had never heard of women being intimate with other women. Her head told her it must be a shameful taboo, or she would have heard of it before now. Yet her heart told her that if two women could bring comfort, perhaps even love, to one another, then how could that be wrong? She acknowledged silently that part of what Rachel offered her, part of what made her feel so good in Rachel's presence, was the physical closeness they shared.

Even now, she felt it herself, though she had not yet defined it, a warmth and a connection that she had only ever felt with Rachel. She had certainly never felt with Adam the things she felt when she was with Rachel. She was so confused. Part of her wanted to take off running down the beach, run until her legs gave out. But the part of her that was her heart moved closer, touching Rachel's face, then stroking her hair until pained steel eyes looked at her. "With me, do you?"

Rachel's hand covered her mouth. "Please don't ask me that."

Mattie gently pulled her hand away from her mouth, but held onto it tightly. "Very well. Let me ask you a different question. Do you think I could be drawn to women in that way?"

The chestnut head snapped back down, as Rachel looked steadily at the packed sand between her boots. "Only you know the answer to that question." Her throat hurt as she choked out the words, and her heart twisted in her chest. She was certain she would faint from the resulting rush of blood that pulsed to her head and made her limbs feel like liquid. Mattie's firm grasp on her hand was the only thing that kept her from jumping up from the log.

Gentle fingers probed Rachel's jaw, then trailed along her face. "I think you know the answer as well." Slowly, she scooted closer, and placed a kiss on Rachel's cheek. The brunette turned toward her, her eyes wide and uncertain. She looked as if she was about to bolt, and Mattie touched her on the leg with one hand, while the other cradled her face. "Don't be afraid, Rachel. I care about you every bit as much now as I did before we went walking down this beach."

"You—you do?" Some of the fear receded, replaced by a warm glow that turned her eyes a deeper shade of almost navy blue. "You aren't repulsed by me?"

"I could never be repulsed by you." She moved closer still, until they were nose to nose, and she could feel the air between them as they breathed. She tilted her head and their lips met. Rachel's hands came up, holding her face reverently.

Rachel's mind protested, only for a moment, before she gave in to what her body craved, deepening the kiss, guiding Mattie, begging her silently for more as she heard her slight murmurs of pleasure. It was more than she had ever hoped it would be. It was something she could easily give her heart up to—being in Mattie's arms, feeling her gentle hands against her face, and her warm lips pressing against her own. It was a place where her dreams could come true, if only Mattie shared those dreams.

She didn't intend for the kiss to go on for as long as it did, and when they finally broke apart, they were both breathing hard, their foreheads pressed together and their eyes closed. "I—sorry, I..."

"Shhh." Mattie pecked her lips again. "I surely wanted to do that, Rachel, more than I've ever wanted anything. No one has ever kissed me like that. It was wonderful."

Rachel looked down, more confused than she'd ever been in her life. What she wanted, she knew she couldn't have. She gathered her wits and looked back up. "I'm glad I didn't scare you away, Mattie."

"You didn't scare me away, but you have given me a great deal to think about." Mattie stood and pulled Rachel up with her. "I am married." Hazel eyes grew sad. "If ever I were to be sorry for anything, it's that I've had a taste of something I fear I can never fully have."

Rachel wanted to say so many things—that Mattie could leave Adam. That she would take her anywhere she wanted to go. But she knew it was much too soon to say such things, and too much had just happened to heap more confusion on her friend. "I will always be here for you, Mattie," was what she said instead. "I want to be your friend, in whatever way you need me to be."

"What—what if I need you to help me ponder my way through what all of this means?" Mattie's hand left her arm, and she wrapped it around Rachel's waist as they continued to walk.

Rachel's heart skipped a beat, then her own arm landed across Mattie's shoulders. "If that is what you need, I will help you in any way I can."

"I love you, Rachel."

She knew Mattie didn't mean it, not in the way she wanted her to. Yet once again, Mattie was offering her friendship, despite all they had discussed. It was a gift she could only accept with wide-eyed wonder. "I love you too, Mattie."

The rest of the evening was spent in reading lessons, and a leftover fried chicken supper, and one more walk on the beach, that somehow led to another heartfelt kiss, followed by a warm comforting hug that neither woman wanted to end.

THE SUN BROKE over the horizon, warm and bright, as Rachel's boots hit the docks with a purposeful rhythmic clunking noise. It felt good to be out and about, to feel the ocean breeze on her face and smell the clean salty air. Even the pesky seagulls were a welcome sight after her month of bed rest.

Her ribs were bound securely, and other than the occasional pull if she turned too quickly, she felt good. *Heck*, she admitted, *I feel fabulous.* She was wearing the shirt she wore the day before, and if she inhaled deeply enough, Mattie's scent greeted her nostrils, sending pleasant happy chills across her skin. Her lips almost tingled in memory of sweet kisses shared under the friendly sky.

It had been so long.

She reached Mr. Gentry's boat and carefully hoisted herself over the side, keeping her weight off the arm on the side where her rib was still mending. Just as her feet landed on the deck, Billy's tousled morning head appeared from down below, his arms wrapped around a bucket of bait. "Hello, Rachel." He set the bucket down and approached her, holding out a hand in greeting. "You're a sight for sore eyes."

"That goes double for you." She grasped his hand and shook it. "The old man asleep?"

"Passed out, as always." He stood back, his eyes taking in her lean frame. "You've lost some of your color. If I didn't know better, I'd think you were one of those lily-white society ladies."

"You!" She playfully punched him in the arm. "I haven't grown that pale in only a month. It would take more than one mean ugly bastard to keep me down. You should know that by now."

"True." Billy's eyes grew thoughtful. Rachel had seen her share of scrapping, he knew, but never had she taken a beating like the one dealt to her by Adam Crockett and his gang. "Say. When are you going to take that sorry scoundrel up with the Sheriff?"

"I'm not." Her voice was determined, her eyes gone cold and hard.

"You don't mean to tell me you're going to just let him get away with what he did to you?" Billy moved closer, shielding his eyes from the sun with his hand. "Rachel, for crying out loud, they almost killed you. Murder. It's a punishable offense, last time I checked."

"I won't do that to Mattie." Her chin jutted out defiantly. "She's been through enough because of him. I won't add to her misery."

"You can't stand by and do nothing." Billy's eyes flashed in anger. "What if he comes after you again?"

Rachel bent down and pulled up her trousers leg, revealing a large Bowie knife tucked into her boot. "Let 'im try." A dangerous little smile tugged at her lips, and she dropped the leg back in place, hiding the well-sharpened weapon.

"I know you're pretty accurate with that, and it does make me feel better, but I still don't understand. You've never backed down from a fight in all the time I've known you." He shook his head sadly. "All you have to do is file a report with the Sheriff, and let him go after the low-life snake."

"And then I'll have to testify before the county judge, and Mattie might have to testify as well." Rachel stood back up, wincing at the pain in her side. "And after that he'll go home and beat the daylights out of her. And as his wife, she'll have very little recourse. Think about it, Billy. Even I don't have a ghost of a chance against someone with Adam's influence. He's got all the money and power. I'm just another no-account dockworker, and a woman at that. It's not worth it. I wouldn't win anyway."

"But to not even try — if that's what you want, I'll abide by it, but I'm not making any promises about what I'll do if he crosses my path in a back alley. Hey!"

Without warning, Rachel grabbed fistfuls of his shirt, hauling him close.

"You'll do nothing, do you hear me?" She shook him surprisingly hard, given her injury. "Do you? I mean it."

"Yes. I hear you." He held up both hands in defense. "I give. Just let me go." She released him and he stepped back, tucking his shirttails back in and recovering his breath. "I don't understand at all."

"You go after Adam, he'll take it out on Mattie." Rachel's hands were still balled into angry fists. "I'm just glad he chose to take out most of his anger against me on me. Even so, he slapped her around some after he was done with me in that alley. So help me God, Billy, I'm going to do everything I can to make sure he has no reason to hurt her on my account."

"What does he have against you, anyway?" He took up the bucket of bait and Rachel followed along, as they pulled up fishing pole lines and baited sharp hooks before dropping them back into the water.

She remained silent for several minutes, thinking about how to respond. She dared not tell the whole truth. Much as she trusted him, the fewer people who knew about her feelings for Mattie, the better. Above all else, protecting Mattie was the most important thing. "He thinks I'm a bad influence on Mattie."

"Well." His eyes twinkled, knowing her penchant for drink, gambling, and cigars. "Are you?"

Her eyes closed for a moment, remembering shared kisses yet again. She opened her eyes and smiled mysteriously. "I prefer to think that I'm broadening her realm of experience. She's led a sheltered life, Billy. She's curious about some very basic things. We have fun together, and she could sure use some fun in her life."

"Sounds like you two have become very good friends." Billy remembered Adam's comments about Rachel, and couldn't help but wonder at the nature of that friendship. He clapped her on the shoulder. "Just be careful."

Their eyes locked in a moment of silent understanding.

"I have to be." She looked down, breaking their gaze. "Too much is at stake."

Billy finished baiting the last hook and they moved to unfurl large nets from the back of the boat. "Whatever happens, you have my full support."

She swallowed a painfully large lump in her throat. "Thank you, Billy. You're a true friend."

"Hey." He rooted around in his front shirt pocket, digging out two cigars. "I've missed going for a smoke with you." He handed one over to her, in an attempt to lighten the mood. With a flourish, he produced a match and lit first hers and then his own, sucking deeply at the tangy-sweet smoke.

Rachel smiled between clamped teeth, wiggling the cigar into a comfortable place as the smoke curled up and around her face like an old friend. "Got any whiskey to go with these?" She winked at him.

"I think I just might, my lady." He pulled a small flask from his back pocket, and they sat down for a morning of watching the lines and catching up on dockside gossip.

MATTIE ARRANGED THE china on the table one more time, folding her fine linen napkins and setting a pitcher of fresh lemonade on a lace doily. She moved to the stove and stirred a pot of simmering clam chowder, and cut thick chunks of hot steaming cornbread, and placed them in a basket, covering it with a red and blue-checkered cloth. A china butter dish held a slab of sweet cold butter she had purchased from the general store the day before. She owned a churn, but hadn't used it since moving to Galveston, finding store-boughten butter to be worth the extra cost compared to the time and muscle saved at the churn.

Satisfied the meal was ready, she went into the water closet and fluffed her bangs one more time, peering at her complexion with great scrutiny. Dark circles under her eyes bore testimony to the sleep she had lost during the week—a week spent in much contemplation. A little face powder helped mask the circles.

She had seen Rachel exactly once since their evening of kissing and hand-holding on the beach. The tall woman had shyly appeared in the tailor's shop at the noon hour on Friday and they had shared a quiet meal of sandwiches and awkward conversation in the back room. Mr. and Mrs. Vaughan, sensing they needed some privacy, had stepped out for dinner at the hotel. She didn't want things to be uncomfortable between them, and hoped their Sunday afternoon dinner would restore their friendship to a state of normalcy.

But nothing felt normal anymore. Her entire world had been turned on end, and she was forced to consider possibilities she never knew existed. Did she care for Rachel in a romantic way? She had nothing with which to compare her feelings. She certainly didn't love Adam, and couldn't remember ever having feelings for anyone as strongly as the ones she had for Rachel. *So why am I standing here primping in the mirror like a young girl waiting for her beau to arrive? And what if I do love her? What can I do about it, even if I do?*

A light rapping at the door tore her from her thoughts, and she pinched her cheeks for some color before hastily entering the parlor. She took a deep breath and opened the door to find Rachel standing there, head down, idly kicking at the doorframe, both hands behind her back. Slowly she looked up, her eyes full of hope as she brought a large bouquet of wildflowers around and held them out. "Thought you might like something pretty for your table."

Mattie took the flowers, inhaling their sweet fresh scent, and drew Rachel inside, leading her by the hand into the kitchen. Rachel sat down at the table, taking in the dainty china, a bone-colored pattern with a sprinkling of tiny yellow rosebuds and gold scrolling around the edges. She tried to remember if she had ever dined at such a fine table. Maybe once in the Tremont Hotel, a long time ago, when Mr. Gentry had treated her and Billy to a full-course supper after a particularly spectacular catch.

Mattie arranged the flowers in a vase and filled it with water, pumping the copper handle and watching as the water slowly reached the rim. She turned and paused in admiration. Rachel's hair was partly pulled back with the hair clasp Mattie had given her, while the rest of it hung loose, long chestnut waves spilling over her shoulders and framing her tanned face, which set off her blue-gray eyes. She wore a crisp blue and white striped shirt, with the folded corner of a white handkerchief peeking out from her front pocket. "I think I already have something pretty for my table." She smiled as Rachel visibly drank in the compliment, her cheeks blushing with a dusting of pink that reached from her nose all the way to her ears.

"Thank you," she mumbled, and looked down, smoothing her placemat in a nervous gesture. "Um, dinner smells delicious. She eyed the basket of cornbread and watched mutely as Mattie set the vase on the end of the table so as not to obscure their view of each other while they dined.

"I hope you like clam chowder." Mattie fiddled with the flowers and started to sit down, when strong fingers gently clasped her hand, a calloused thumb brushing across the back of it.

"I'd like anything you cook for me." Rachel lifted her hand and placed a quick kiss on her knuckles, then released it and allowed her to take her seat.

"Oh." Mattie frowned and stood up. "The chowder. I forgot to get the soup bowls out. I'll be right back." She disappeared into the parlor where her oak china cabinet sat against one wall, removing two bowls and returning.

Rachel stood at the stove. "Here." She held out a hand. "You did the cooking, let me serve it up. Go on." She shoed Mattie toward a chair. "I can at least manage to use a ladle without spilling anything, I think." She smiled charmingly as Mattie relented, handing her the bowls. She quickly dipped up two healthy portions of the thick milky-smooth broth and placed them on the table before taking her own seat.

Mattie poured two tall glasses of lemonade and they dug in, both women still struggling with their awkwardness. Finally, they eased their way into small talk, discussing the upcoming Independence Day celebration the island had planned, along with tidbits of information Mattie gained at the tailor's shop, and Rachel's adventures on the fishing boat during the week.

After Rachel refused a fourth helping of chowder, Mattie got up and fished some fresh-baked sugar cookies from a jar, arranging them on a platter and motioning to Rachel to join her in the sitting room. After retrieving two cups of sweet hot tea, she sat down on the sofa next to her friend, not touching, but with very little space between them. "Cookie?"

Rachel took the top one and bit into it, rolling her eyes and closing them in pleasure as the sweetness washed over her taste buds. "Delicious." She smiled encouragingly and took a sip of tea.

"Thank you." Mattie cleared her throat and looked down, clasping her hands in her lap. "I hate this," she mumbled.

"Hate what?" Rachel knew exactly what Mattie spoke of, but wanted to give her the choice to talk or not talk, whatever she was comfortable with.

"I feel so close to you, but I can't seem to speak my mind." Mattie stood and moved to the window, looking out at the sun-sparkling waves as they washed up onto the beach.

Rachel was on her feet in a second, moving in behind Mattie and hesitantly wrapping her arms around her waist. "I'm glad you still feel close to me, because I feel the same, Mattie. I was afraid maybe we shouldn't have kissed last weekend — if it's going to make us feel awkward..."

"No." Mattie leaned back into her, closing her eyes and allowing the closeness to fill her up and give her courage. "I just don't know what to do. I want something I don't think I'm supposed to have. Is it wrong, Rachel? I'm married to Adam. I wish I weren't, but I am. And even if I weren't, what kind of life could two women have together?"

Rachel's heart skipped a beat and her tongue felt like lead. That Mattie had thought hard enough to even consider the possibility of them, or any two women, sharing a life, was more than she had ever hoped for. It made her head spin so much that she felt slightly dizzy. She longed to talk with Mattie about Betsy and Angel, but didn't want to betray the older women's confidence.

The silence was overwhelming and Mattie felt the body behind her go still. "I'm sorry." She moved to pull away from her. "I must have offended you. I shouldn't have presumed that you would want–oh." Rachel's arms tightened around her, unwilling to let her go.

"Don't be sorry." Rachel kissed the top of her head and briefly nuzzled her soft hair, which was pinned up loosely on top of her head. "I'm just surprised is all.   I hadn't dared hope that you might consider..." She couldn't bring herself to say it, for fear she had misunderstood Mattie's meaning.

"I've thought of little else." Mattie turned in her arms, reaching up and playing with her collar.   The top button of her shirt was undone, and a small silver chain was visible. Curiously, Mattie pulled at it and drew it out, revealing a tiny silver cross, surrounded by an open silver heart. "How pretty." She continued to study the charm, surprised that Rachel would wear such a thing.

"It was my mother's. I took it when I left home. Haven't worn it in years, but I pulled it out this week and decided to start wearing it again. Figured I could use all the good luck and guardian angels I can get, considering everything that's happened in the past month." Her heart skipped a beat again as Mattie gently dropped the chain back inside her shirt, and she felt a soft kiss at the hollow of her throat, followed by gentle fingers that probed at the thin scar at her temple.

"I'm afraid guardian angels won't do you much good where Adam is concerned." She lowered her head again as she fiddled with the rest of the buttons that ran down the placket on Rachel's shirt. "They sure haven't been around when I've needed them, at any rate." Her voice dropped to a whisper. "I don't know what to do."

"What do you want to do?" Rachel tilted her chin up, holding back her desire to kiss tempting full lips.

"I want to go back to when I was fourteen and not marry him." Mattie looked back down, the lips in question beginning to tremble. "I want to meet you first. I want to not be so confused. I want to know the right thing to do."

Rachel pulled her close, until Mattie's head was resting solidly on her shoulder. She stroked the red hair and placed another kiss on Mattie's forehead. "I wish all those things, too." She hugged Mattie tighter as she felt her begin to shiver. "Leave him," she whispered into her ear.

"It's wrong." Mattie mumbled against a clean-smelling bit of cotton. Mixed in with the clean smell was the scent of bay rum and tobacco. She decided she liked it and buried her face more fully into Rachel's shoulder, feeling herself being rocked slowly back and forth, almost as if in a dance.

"You don't have to leave him for me." Rachel continued to soothe her. "Just get out." She rubbed her hands up and down Mattie's back in an effort to calm her fears. "How long is he going to go on, before one day he hits you too hard?" She felt her own legs tremble and backed toward the sofa, landing on a plump cushion with Mattie cradled in her arms, sitting on her lap. "I couldn't bear it if that were to happen."

"I can't just up and leave him." Mattie sighed and sat up enough to look at Rachel's face. "I'd have to get a divorce, and the church — I know adultery is reason enough, but he could deny it. Then I'd have to bring in Lillie. She's the only witness, and that would get her in trouble with the law. I don't think he will give me a divorce if I ask him for one. More likely he'd beat me senseless if I did."

"Over my dead body." Rachel's voice took on a fierce protective tone Mattie had never heard her use before.

"My knight in shining armor," Mattie mumbled softly.

"Just leave him," Rachel pleaded. "Forget the divorce. I know you want to do everything in the proper way, but he isn't playing nicely. Sometimes you have to break the rules. I don't want him to hurt you anymore."

"Even if I did leave him, where would I go?" She looked sadly into Rachel's eyes. "I couldn't stay here, and the only other place I know anyone is back home in El Paso."

"I-I would go with you, if you wanted me to. No matter where you want to go." Rachel broke their gaze, and gasped, as soft lips brushed against her own.

"That is a very noble offer." Another kiss. "But I don't think I'm brave enough to do that. I need some time to think about all of this. My mind is all aflutter and I haven't been able to concentrate. I had to re-sew the buttons on a shirt three times yesterday because I kept placing them wrong. I haven't slept more than an hour at a time since last weekend. I'm so very tired."

Rachel studied her eyes more closely, finally noticing the powder-covered circles, and Mattie's blood-shot orbs. She looked weary, and Rachel unconsciously placed a hand against her ribs. She had felt them often enough during their swimming lessons for her to know that they were more prominent than they should be. "You haven't been eating well either, have you?"

"No," Mattie answered in surprise. "Not until tonight. Somehow, when I'm with you, I feel calmer."

"You need to rest, take better care of yourself." Even as she spoke, she scooted to the end of the sofa and urged Mattie to stretch out, her head pillowed in Rachel's lap. "We don't have to swim or read today." She gently began removing Mattie's hairpins, then ran her fingers through the long tresses, watching gratefully as the hazel eyes blinked at the soothing sensation, fighting sleep. "Rest, Mattie. I'll sit here with you for a spell."

"I could-" She yawned before she could stop it. "-stand some sleep." She rolled slightly, curling one hand around Rachel's knee.

"So peaceful," she murmured, and drifted off into dreamless slumber.

Rachel soon joined her, her head drooped back against the sofa's high back as her hand stilled against Mattie's head.

Outside, the waves continued to roll ashore, maintaining their own quiet lullaby as the early evening tide rose.

Chapter
Six

RACHEL JUMPED, HER body twitching awake from vague unsettling dreams. Slowly, she raised her head from the sofa back and looked around, blinking at her surroundings. She shook her head to clear it and winced in pain as her stiff neck protested her actions. A solid weight on her leg, along with gentle warm breathing that tickled her skin through her trousers leg, quickly reminded her she was in Mattie's parlor.

She looked down and couldn't help but smile. Mattie had rolled toward her stomach, and her face looked very young and very much at peace. The tension in her features had dissipated as she slept, and she looked like an angel to Rachel. "My angel," she whispered softly, hoping that perhaps saying it aloud might make it so.

The room was decidedly darker than it had been when they sat down, and looking out the window, the long shadows of palm trees and the red-gold sunlight which gilded the rolling waves confirmed that west of the island, night was beginning to fall. Adam wasn't due back until Tuesday evening, and she relaxed. She had nowhere she needed to be until sunrise the next day.

Mattie murmured in her sleep and pursed her lips, making frightened whimpering noises. Rachel instinctively stroked her head and trailed her fingers along her face, smoothing a slight frown. Mattie smiled and settled down again, one hand reaching up and curving around Rachel's upper thigh, perilously close to places she truly didn't need the hand to be. She groaned quietly and carefully lifted it and moved it, allowing smaller fingers to curl around her hip, a much safer and less distracting spot.

Her own hand continued idle exploration, roaming down Mattie's arm and side until she reached her hip. She patted it lightly before splaying her fingers around a too-prominent hipbone. Mattie needed to put on some weight, she noted ruefully. Just as her hand settled into place, Mattie shifted in her sleep, rolling even more toward her, and suddenly her hand was no longer on Mattie's hip, but was planted firmly against her backside. A very nice, very shapely backside. "I do believe you're trying to torture me," she muttered, and allowed one gentle pat to the firm derriere before moving her hand up and lightly scratching Mattie's back.

This elicited an appreciative purr as Mattie curled in toward her, drawing her thighs up against Rachel's hip. Mattie tucked the hand that had been on Rachel's hip under her chin and sighed with contentment. Rachel decided she was the most adorable woman in the world, and leaned over, planting a loving kiss on her cheek, causing another sigh as Mattie slowly drifted into wakefulness.

Two hazel eyes fluttered open, so close they startled Rachel, who was just pulling away from the pale cheek. Without further thought Mattie reached up, threading her fingers through the hair at the base of Rachel's neck and drawing her back down, kissing her softly on the lips. It went on for a bit, until both women began to find breathing rather difficult.

Mattie sat up and stretched, and found herself pulled into Rachel's lap. Long fingers traced her brows, then her nose, then gently caressed her cheek before tilting her chin slightly to the side. Rachel's eyelids lowered halfway and she whispered one word. "Please."

Mattie smiled and closed the distance, feeling Rachel's other arm wrap around her, stroking her back as she deepened the kiss. Mattie gasped as a warm tongue probed between her lips. Rachel ever so gently coaxed her, not pushing her or showing any sign of aggression. It was new and different from anything she had ever felt before, and she decided she liked it, opening up and doing her best to mimic Rachel's actions. She heard a low moan of appreciation and felt herself being lowered down on the sofa with agonizing slowness, Rachel's long body stretched out next to her.

It was comfortable and warm, and relieved of her own body weight, she felt herself completely relax, all thought pushed aside, save for the new sensations coursing through her blood, causing her to crave more of the closeness they shared. She allowed herself to get lost in it, returning kiss for kiss and touch for touch, pulling Rachel closer and grasping at handfuls of her clothing, desperately wanting something, and not knowing what it was. Strong hands and soft lips gentled her and at the same time drove her to a level of passion she had only read about in books.

Rachel on the other hand, in a very small corner of her brain, wondered fuzzily if she was losing her mind. She was taking things much further than she had anticipated. This was a long way from standing together on the beach as they had the week before. Those kisses had been chaste nibbles compared to what they were sharing now, and a fire ignited in her belly as she heard more of the pleasure-filled murmurs coming from Mattie's throat.

She forced her hands to stay in a safe area, either running through Mattie's hair or stroking her face and arms. She smiled against Mattie's lips, realizing that Mattie had no such inclination, her smaller hands running freely up and down Rachel's back and occasionally clutching at her shoulders or sides, holding her in place as they continued their mutual exploration. She felt her shirt tugging loose from her trousers and groaned quietly, knowing Mattie had no intention of actually removing her clothing; it was simply inevitable given the pulling sensation she felt at her back as Mattie crushed the cotton material into her fists.

Reluctantly she moved away from Mattie's lips, kissing her along her jaw line and down to her ear, planting a kiss on soft sensitive skin and whispering in her ear. "Thank you." One more kiss. "No one ever kissed me like that."

Mattie shifted, cupping Rachel's face. "But, Lillie?"

The invocation of Lillie's name seemed all wrong, but Rachel pushed that aside and focused on the moment and a very important truth she needed to share. "No." She smiled and stole one more kiss from still-moist lips. "We never kissed. It's one of her rules."

"Why?" Mattie felt Rachel grasp her hand and draw it around, and a tickling sensation against her knuckles as Rachel's lips brushed across them.

"Kissing is too intimate." Steel eyes warmed to vibrant blue, gazed at her with a mixture of hope and fear. "It conveys something that would be an untruth between Lillie and me."

Red brows knitted in confusion. "I don't understand." She felt Rachel move, resting on her side, still hovering over Mattie's face. A warm smile graced Rachel's lips and she leaned in, sharing another lengthy kiss.

"I don't kiss Lillie because I don't love her." She ducked her head, thick chestnut waves hiding her face.

"And with me—do you...?" Mattie trailed off and reached up, pushing Rachel's hair behind her ear.

The dark head turned and Rachel nibbled the inside of Mattie's palm before holding it against her own face. "Yes." Their lips met again, a gentle exchange that ended in a long rocking hug as both women slowly sat up.

Mattie curled into Rachel's lap, one arm wrapped loosely around her waist, her other hand running up and down a muscular arm, which she occasionally squeezed, enjoying the steely sensation against her fingers. "I don't know what to do." She buried her face into Rachel's neck, nuzzling the soft skin. The scent of her bay rum cologne was heavier, mixed with another scent she couldn't identify, but liked very much. A strong hand rubbed her back in comforting circles.

"You don't have to do anything you don't want to do." Rachel kissed her head. "I enjoyed what we just did very much, but I'd never expect it of you. If you're not comfortable with it, just be my friend. That's more than I could ever have hoped for."

"But you love me?" Mattie kissed her throat and felt it shift as

Rachel swallowed.

"Yes." She released a long breath. "I do."

"I think I love you too." Mattie kissed the spot again. "The way you love me."

This time she held her breath for a moment, allowing the knowledge to settle in. "This is new for both of us. I have no expectations. Take all the time you need to figure out your feelings."

"I don't know if I can ever do the things with you that you do with Lillie." Mattie sat up taller, her head down, as she played with Rachel's shirt collar, pulling out the silver chain and studying it while she spoke. "Maybe someday." She shook her head sadly. "I have to sort it out, what's right and what's wrong. If I wasn't married..."

"Shhh." Rachel hugged her more tightly before releasing her again into their comfortable loose embrace. "This is enough, I promise you. If all you ever give me are your hugs, that's enough."

"You can get the rest from Lillie." For some reason that thought settled in her stomach, making it hurt, and she felt like crying.

"I don't think I can." She stroked Mattie's face and waited until hesitant hazel eyes looked up. "Not anymore. You have my heart, Mattie, whether I have yours or not doesn't matter. What I feel for you — I just can't go back to Lillie's bed is all. It wouldn't feel right. Though I don't want to give up her friendship. She's been too good to me."

"I would never ask that of you." Mattie ran light fingertips down her button placket. "I don't feel like I should expect the other." She blushed, her fingers continuing to wander.

"Even if you don't, I expect if of myself." She gasped slightly as Mattie's hand unconsciously slid over her breast. She was about to gently remove her friend's hand when she felt Mattie pause, her expression one of great curiosity.

"Are you cold?" A hard nipple pressed back against her palm, and she blushed more furiously, before moving her hand down to a safe place against Rachel's ribs.

"Not hardly." A light nervous chuckle escaped her lips. "You — how do I put this? It's a reaction to your touch."

Quizzical eyes looked at her in consternation and the hand came back up. She pressed her hand in slightly and cupped Rachel's breast through the starched cotton shirt, feeling the ribbed undershirt beneath and the still-hard nipple. She looked back up and watched Rachel's eyes slam shut. "Remember when I measured you for these shirts?" Her hand rested in place.

"Reaction to your touch," Rachel squeaked out, keeping her eyes closed for fear she might die of embarrassment.

"And here I thought you were cold that day." She laughed lightly. "I had no idea."

Blue-gray eyes opened in amazement. "You don't mean to tell me that Adam has never...?" The utter confusion in Mattie's eyes was all the answer she needed, and it took all her considerable self-control to keep from showing her exactly what she had been missing with her inept husband. Sensing it might frighten her, she took a deep breath and reached up, unbuttoning her own shirt, allowing the crisp material to slide off her shoulders, exposing her soft cotton undershirt. "It's all right." She grasped Mattie's hand and kissed it. "You can touch me if you want to."

"Adam has never what?" Mattie's hand came up, the firm soft curve of Rachel's breast filling her cupped palm again. It was an interesting sensation, the firmness and softness mixed with the hardness that pressed against the cotton barrier separating her skin from Rachel's. It didn't occur to her to remove that barrier, much to Rachel's mixed relief and frustration.

"I..." She swallowed hard, forcing herself to concentrate on the impromptu lesson. "I told you that there are ways that women can touch each other that can be very pleasurable."

"I remember." Mattie grew braver and lightly squeezed Rachel. She felt the sharp intake of breath and watched goose bumps dance across her friend's upper chest.

"The way you're touching me right now." Warm eyes opened and Rachel smiled softly, not wanting Mattie to be afraid or to stop. "That would be one of the ways."

"Oh." Mattie blushed furiously and started to remove her hand, then felt a large one cover it, holding her in place.

"Don't be ashamed." Rachel's lips brushed past her ear on their way to her lips. They kissed again, a deep longing exchange which left Rachel breathing heavily, her eyes tightly closed as she pressed her forehead against Mattie's, feeling her hand drive her to almost painful distraction as Mattie freely explored the novelty of Rachel's response to her touch.

Rachel held back, allowing Mattie to take her time, both hands coming up and gently circling her breasts, hazel eyes occasionally tilting upward to see Rachel's face. Much as she wanted to return the exchange, she knew Mattie was not ready for it. There would be plenty of time, a part of her reasoned. Something deep inside of her knew that someday they would share so much more than what they had on this evening.

Finally, when she could stand it no more, she grasped Mattie's hands, kissing each one almost reverently and holding onto them. "I'd best be going home." She saw the uncertainty in her eyes and smiled warmly. "Otherwise I'm afraid I'll be too tempted to scoop you up and take you to that nice comfy bed in there, and I think we'd both regret that tomorrow, don't you?"

"Probably." Mattie's own skin was flushed and she felt an exhilarating tingle all through her body. "I don't know much about all of this, Rachel." She blinked shyly and looked down. "But I suspect if it does ever feel right...for you to show me how two women can touch each other... Anyway, I'd most likely want it to be in your bed, and not that one."

"We have all the time in the world." Rachel hugged her tightly as she stood, Mattie's feet coming off the ground in the process. "We need to talk some more. I know you're feeling all befuddled about things. I don't want you to feel that way. But I meant it when I said I don't want him to hurt you anymore." She dragged the backs of her knuckles along Mattie's cheek. "Think about that, sweetheart. I'll help you in any way you need me to, if only you'll get yourself someplace that's safe. Promise me you'll give it some thought."

Mattie hugged her back as she was lowered back to the floor. "I promise." They kissed again in the doorway, and Mattie watched sadly as Rachel walked away. She turned at the edge of the dunes and waved, smiling brightly as Mattie waved enthusiastically back. She turned then, and made her way on down the beach, her skin bronzed by the setting sun and her hair framed in a flaming auburn halo. "I declare, Rachel Travis, you look just like an angel in the sunlight," she turned and closed the door on the sweet vision, unaware she was repeating Rachel's own sentiment.

A DARK HEAD popped out of the surf, sleek hair plastered back, the long ends fanning out in the water. Rachel bobbed up and down in place, treading water, trying to sort out a myriad of thoughts and sensations. She hadn't intended on the impromptu dip into the ocean, but for some reason, the cool water against her overheated skin seemed very appealing. She had her suit with her anyway, rolled up inside a towel, just in case she and Mattie had decided on swimming lessons.

What they had done instead...

She smiled. It had felt wonderful—sweet—and had left her longing for so much more. She played it over in her mind. True, Mattie had initiated their exchange, but she had encouraged the lengths to which they took it. A part of her wondered if it had been a huge mistake, if Mattie would be overwhelmed by it later. Another part of her wanted to take a quick hike back to Mattie's house, scoop her up, and take her to bed. She felt vaguely like a cat in heat, her skin longing to rub all up against Mattie's.

She ducked back under the water, holding her breath until she thought she might explode, before surfacing again. There. She shook the wet hair out of her eyes and nodded with satisfaction. The stinging salt up her nose, the slight chill to her skin, and the beginnings of a headache from holding her breath so long served their purpose, dampening her ardor to a more tolerable level.

It was full dusk and time to get out of the water. The tide was rising, but nothing unusual or dangerous. She swam toward shore and stood when the water was at hip level, walking with the pull of the water back to where she had left her clothing, stashed safely behind a thick pillar of someone's private boat dock. She looked around and stooped down behind it, slipping out of the wet bathing trunks and top, and drying off briskly before re-donning her clothing.

She paused as she was pulling her undershirt over her head and closed her eyes, remembering Mattie's hands on her, teasing her and making her ache inside. She opened her eyes again and swallowed, looking regretfully back out at the water. All her good intentions in cooling off were completely undone, and she was once again longing for things they did not finish. She thought, shamefully, that when she got home there were ways for her to take care of the problem, at least temporarily. Just one more thing Lillie had taught her. It wasn't something she did very often — a sin almost as mortal as her desire for women.

She finished dressing and decided to walk the rest of the way home along the beach, rather than through the streets of the town. It was a beautiful night, though slightly warm. The truly hot summer nights would be upon them any day, and she had learned to enjoy pleasant weather while it lasted.

She picked her way along the shoreline just in the edge of the water, so that it occasionally washed up and covered her feet and ankles. As she walked, she whistled a tune and then began singing it. It was supposed to be called "Katie," but she changed the name to "Mattie," smiling as she sang:

Ma-Ma-Ma-Mattie,
Beautiful Mattie,
You're the only gi-gi-gi-girl that I adore.
When the mo-moon shines,
Over the cow shed,
I'll be waiting at the ki-ki-ki-kitchen door.

"If I ever have a cow shed of my own," she mumbled. "Or a kitchen."

She allowed her mind to wander along those lines, picturing herself buying her own little plot of land and building a house. It would be a large sturdy house, one that would be big enough for her and whoever else she shared it with, and anyone else they knew who might need to take shelter. It would be on stilts to protect from floods, and the first floor level would have a balcony wrapping all the way around. Large picture windows would face out to sea, and the second floor bedrooms would each have balconies as well. At the peak of the roof she would build a watchtower, so she could climb up and look out to sea, and be able to see the sunset over the mainland on the other side of the island.

She tried to picture herself in another job, maybe at the bank, or perhaps owning some sort of shop. Maybe she would make something in demand, like buggies or harnesses. Maybe she would go to school to learn how to be a druggist or a doctor. She smiled to herself, dreaming of the possibilities, and what it would be like to have a job where everyone respected her.

She'd come home and maybe be greeted warmly. Maybe by Mattie. Maybe someday they would find a way to be together, and Mattie could do whatever she wanted to all day long, be it work at the tailors or do her artwork, or something completely different. Mattie deserved to be loved and cared for, and Rachel wished, more than anything, that she could be that caretaker.

A splashing sound in the water brought her out of her musings, and she strained her eyes, peering down the shoreline toward its source. She was coming up on the orphanage's property, and realized that some of the boys were out playing on the beach and swimming. Most likely they weren't supposed to be there, she chuckled quietly.

As she drew closer to the boys, she recognized two of them, Albert Campbell and Frank Madera. They were known to spend time down at the port during the summers when they weren't in school, begging for odd jobs—sweeping boat decks and scaling fish. She had spent several afternoons cleaning fish with them. They roamed the town freely in the summer; however, the sisters who ran the orphanage kept a pretty close eye on their charges at night. She suspected the young hooligans had slipped out a first floor window of their dormitory.

"Hello, boys," she called out, and laughed as a half dozen young gangly bodies froze in the shallows. "It's me, Rachel Travis."

Two bodies relaxed, as Albert and Frank trotted down the shore toward her, stopping a few times to re-roll trouser legs that were sliding down. "Hello, Miss Rachel, what are you doing out here?"

"I'm going for a walk in the moonlight." She ruffled Frank's unruly head of thick black hair. "I should ask you the same thing. Do the sisters know you're out this evening?"

Albert ducked his head, digging his big toe into the sand and tucking his hands behind his back, trying to appear innocent. Frank merely crossed his arms over his chest and smiled at her, his two front teeth obviously missing even in the low light. "We's big boys now. We know how to swim."

"Can you swim faster than a shark?" Rachel's eyes twinkled mischievously.

"Sh-shark?" Four other boys joined them, quickly moving out of the water, all of them looking down fearfully into the shallow waves as they retreated.

"Yep. Shark." She dropped her bundle of clothing in the sand and draped an arm across Albert's shoulders, then the other across Frank's, steering them back toward the narrow trail through the dunes, which led to the orphanage, the other boys following closely behind them. "I hear tales that big ol' sharks come out after dark, looking for something tasty to eat."

"Are little boys tasty?" A wide-eyed lad looked up at her, his freckles standing out against his pale skin.

"I wouldn't know," she smiled. "But I suspect sharks would find them to be a mighty fine meal on a warm summer evening."

"Miss Rachel." Albert looked up at her and took her hand, holding on tightly. "I think it might be time for us boys to go to bed now. I'm awfully tired."

"I think that's a splendid idea." Rachel squeezed back and stopped as they reached the bottom step of the orphanage's back porch. "You boys have pleasant dreams." She laughed internally, wondering how many of them would dream of sharks. She knew she shouldn't find it so funny, but couldn't help herself. Their young faces were too precious. Besides, she justified to herself, she'd probably saved a couple of them from drowning with her shark story.

"I heard you was laid up for a while, Miss Rachel." Frank took her other hand, and she knelt down at boy-level.

"I was hurt pretty bad, but I'm feeling much better." Before she knew it, he wrapped his arms around her neck and gave her a hug.

"I's glad you's better, Miss Rachel." He stepped back. "We was looking for you on the dock and heard somebody had beat you up."

"Somebody did." She frowned, wondering just how much of the story had made it around the town. "But it won't happen again."

"Miss Rachel," Albert slid in and also gave her a hug, "when I'm big enough, I'll beat up any mean old man who tries to hurt you."

She took a deep breath, unshed tears blurring her vision. She hastily swiped her hand across her eyes and stood up. "Thank you, Albert." She sniffled. "I think you'll grow up to be a fine gentleman someday."

The young boy beamed, too shy to say anything.

"What about me, Miss Rachel?" Frank looked up hopefully at her. Four other pairs of eyes were immediately behind him, all of them trained on her, waiting eagerly for an answer.

"Y'all just keep studying your lessons and do what the sisters tell you too, and I think all of you will grow up to be fine gentlemen." She ushered them up the steps. "Now go on, and get some sleep. Get yourselves into bed before you get in trouble."

She watched as all six boys clambered up the steps and traipsed across the porch, crawling through an open side window, just as she suspected. Not until they had all safely cleared the windowsill did she notice the lone figure rocking in a porch swing across the yard at the girl's dormitory. She cleared her throat. "Don't be too hard on them, Sister. It's such a lovely night and the moon is almost full. Probably too much temptation for little boys to stand, I'd imagine."

The nun merely nodded graciously at her, and she turned and made her way back down to the beach, retrieving her bundle at the trailhead.

MATTIE SAT UP in bed, her sketchpad braced on her legs. She had splurged on the container of pastels from the general store, and was busily filling in color on a seascape. It was a dusky scene, drawn from memory, of her walk on the beach with Rachel the weekend before. She used a peach color to work in the sunset reflecting on the water, smudging it with her pinky finger until it blended in with the gray-green color of the water. She added a touch of white for whitecaps and held the picture up at eye level.

She smiled and used a brown pastel to color the hair on one of the two small figures she had sketched in. The figures were of her and Rachel standing hand in hand on the beach, facing each other, about to kiss. They were too small for anyone to tell who they were. It was her own little secret.

Her mind was racing so fast from everything that had happened, it was all she could do to stay focused. The two days of work at the tailor shop since Sunday had been a blur she barely remembered, her mind very far away from the task of sewing. Sleep was out of the question. Sketching seemed like a good way to calm herself, but the subject matter only served to distract her more.

Kissing Rachel had been like stepping into a raging river. It washed over her and through her, and she had very nearly drowned in it. It had been heavenly. She couldn't begin to imagine what other things women could do together. The kissing alone had been beyond anything she had ever dreamed of.

She smiled, remembering how it felt to touch Rachel, and the interesting sounds she had made during their mutual exploration. A few times she thought Rachel was going to stop breathing. And at least once she was certain she heard a squeak. However it felt, Rachel had seemed to enjoy it immensely. Mattie wondered what that felt like, and if she dared ask Rachel to touch her in the same way.

Adam never would, and a part of her was repulsed by the thought of him touching her that way. She puzzled over that, trying to decide if it was because it was too late for him to become the husband she would want him to be, or if it was because in her heart, she had already given that part of herself to Rachel.

This confused her even more, as she pondered what, exactly, it might mean. She had given something to Rachel that should be reserved for her marriage to Adam. Then there was the whole question of what she and Rachel had not done. No matter how hard she tried, she couldn't imagine Rachel doing what Adam did to her, because she knew Rachel wasn't equipped for it, and because even if she were, she couldn't imagine enjoying it. Trying to guess at what Rachel referred to regarding women touching one another was making her crazy, a great mystery beyond her understanding.

Her head hurt thinking about all of it, and she wearily closed the sketchpad and put the cover back on the pastel tin. It was growing late and Adam was due home from the train depot. Her stomach churned, knowing he was still bent on her having a baby, and what he would surely want to do when he arrived.

She had decided to feign illness for the few days he would be home before going back to Houston. She knew she couldn't carry on such a ruse indefinitely, but it would buy her at least a week. She smiled sadly and removed a note she had tucked into her bodice. It was a simple note from Rachel, who had started practicing writing along with her reading. Mattie had found the note tucked into the top drawer of the sewing table at the shop. It was folded over twice and her name was printed in carefully blocked letters on the outermost fold. Inside were three words, "I MISS YOU." The note wasn't signed, but the faint scent of bay rum told her clearly whom it was from.

She kissed the note and got up from the bed, placing the note and her sketchpad in the bottom drawer of the armoire, hiding them under the extra set of bed linens. She kept all her drawings of Rachel there, along with her pessary box. It was a place Adam never ventured. Changing bed linens was a woman's work. Even if he did have reason to go there, she had placed one old tattered blanket over the hidden objects, with all the newer linens on top of it.

She ran her fingertips along the pastel drawing and covered the lot before closing the drawer. Rachel had been out at sea all day both days since they had seen each other last, and she longed to talk to her. The note was brave on Rachel's part, she knew, and she wanted to assure her that it was well received. "I love you, Rachel, leastwise I think that's what I'm feeling. I sure hope I can see you before Sunday."

With a heavy heart, she began dressing for bed, hoping to be asleep by the time Adam got home. After slipping into a ruffled white nightgown, she took a brush to her hair, working out the snarls before she braided it to keep it from getting tangled during the night. She splashed her face with water and used her toothbrush and powder.

Once she was ready for bed, she placed items on the nightstand to aid in her deception. Nervously, she arranged a cup of water, a box of headache powders, and a small basin of water with a rag. She dipped the rag into the water and wrung it out, draping it haphazardly on the rim of the basin as if it might have been feverishly placed there. She would tell him she had been running a fever and coughing.

Before climbing into bed, she left a single lamp on, on a far table across the room. She lay in bed for a long time, her hands folded across her stomach on top of the covers. The window was cracked open to let in the salty ocean breeze, just enough to keep the room from being stifling in the warm night air. It had been abnormally hot during the day and hadn't cooled down much after sundown; all the more reason she didn't want Adam anywhere near her. It was just too hot.

Her weary mind continued to race, thinking about Rachel and Adam, until finally she fell into an exhausted sleep. Sometime around midnight she felt the bed shake and she stirred, mumbling in agitation before opening her eyes a crack.

"Mattie?" Adam stood over her, holding up the headache powder box. "Are you ill?"

"Oh." She forced a cough and picked up the cup from the bed table, sipping from it delicately. "Just a little cough and fever."

Adam felt her forehead. "You are a little warm."

She was grateful he seemed to believe her. If she was warm, it was her own natural body heat, which was often slightly elevated when she slept. "It was worse earlier," she lied. "Just came on earlier today."

"Long as you don't get that chills and fever that's been going around." Adam turned the lamp off, and pulled his nightshirt on. "I hear it takes a good month to get over it." He crawled into bed beside her and settled on his back, his arms behind his head.

"Haven't had too many chills." Mattie noted with satisfaction that Adam was keeping his distance. "Mostly just this nagging dry cough." She coughed again, just for good measure.

"Mmph." He rolled on his side, facing away from her. "Good."

"Goodnight, Adam."

A deep rumbling snore was her answer.

She smiled into the darkness.

"HEY SUGAR, I haven't seen you around here in a coon's age." Lillie patted Rachel on the back as she slipped behind the bar to talk.

"Oh. Hello, Lil." She finished stacking some clean bar glasses on a rack to dry, and wiped her hands on a towel tucked into her waistband. "Been kinda busy, working on Mr. Gentry's boat and doing my reading lessons. I..." She paused and looked down at her boots, gathering her thoughts. "I worked out a deal with Mr. Bullock for my job here. If Adam Crockett shows up, I am to immediately pack it in and go home. He said it was the only way he'd let me keep working here, after what happened." Her voice was bitter.

"You mean to tell me he's going to continue to let that low-life good-for-nothing yellow-bellied skunk of an excuse for a man into this place?" Lillie's face colored in anger, as her voice rose.

"Shhh." Rachel covered her mouth with a cupped hand, hearing a squawk of outrage as Lillie continued to rant. "I need this job, and so

do you.   Am I right?"   She watched the blonde ringlets shake
affirmatively, and removed her hand. Looking around, she poured up
two glasses of rich amber ale and steered Lillie to a table in the corner.
It was early and only a few Friday afternoon regulars had wandered in
to shoot the breeze until the poker games started up.

"I wish to high heaven I didn't need this worthless place." Lillie's
lips puckered in a full pout and she huffed, placing her elbows on the
table and cradling her face in her hands. "I'm a good mind to up and
quit anyway. Go find myself something more respectable."

"Maybe you should." Rachel sipped at her mug with one hand,
tracing a circle in a water puddle on the table with the fingers of the
other.

"Ain't nothing pays women better than what I do, sugar, and you
know it." She sat back and took a long draw at her ale.

"I know." Rachel couldn't meet her eyes. "And I hate that. I'm
going to find something better, Lil. I swear I am. I'm reading pretty
good now. I might even go back to school and make something of
myself yet."

"You are something, in my eyes, and I know you are in Mattie's."
She saw the slight grin tug at her friend's lips. "How is Mattie? You
been spending time with her?"

"Yep." She felt a blush creeping up her neck and flooding her
cheeks, and sat back smugly in her chair, tilting it back on two legs
and crossing her arms, as she propped one booted foot against a table
leg, although her head remained bowed as she studied the bleached
bone buttons on her shirt cuff.

"Oh, do tell." Lillie scooted closer, dropping her voice.

"Not that kind of time, Lil, although I suspect someday we might
reach that point."   She finally looked up, fully meeting Lillie's
cornflower blue eyes.   "I—Lil, I can't spend time with you upstairs
anymore. Wouldn't be right. I'd feel like I was being unfaithful to
her."

"Is she still with her husband?" Lillie touched her leg, curling her
fingers around it.

"Yes," she spit out through gritted teeth. "And I can't allow myself
to think about that. Makes me crazy, thinking about him touching
her."

"Why don't you grab her up and run away from here? There's
plenty of places you could go. East to New York, or out West. I hear
there's all kinds of land to be had, even for women in some places."
She watched the smile disappear.

"If Mattie were to say the word, I would." She drained her mug
and sat forward again, gratefully accepting Lillie's unfinished drink.
"She's all confused. I swear, Lil, I know I was naïve when you met me,
but Mattie—she's married and knows less than I did about things.
She's just now figuring out how she feels about me."

"And how do you feel about her?" Lillie squeezed her leg, feeling the tension just under the surface.

"I think I'm in love with her." Rachel's eyes watered and she blinked hard. "Don't have nothin' to compare it to, but when I think about her, I feel all light, as if I'm walking two feet off the ground, and when she touches me, it sets my skin on fire. I-I'd do anything for her. And when I think about the possibility that she might choose Adam, it makes my chest feel so tight I can hardly breathe. I don't know what I'll do if he ever hurts her again."

"You'll keep your head about you if you know what's good for you." Lillie stood and drew Rachel up with her, pulling her into a hug. "I'm so sorry she doesn't see things for what they are. Do you want me to talk to her? We became friends while you were recovering. Leastwise I think we did."

"No." Rachel released her and looked around. Only a few curious pairs of eyes had turned their way, and quickly looked elsewhere as she met their gaze. " I don't want to push her until she's ready. I think — hope — she will leave him. Even if she doesn't leave him for me, I hate the way he hurts her. I feel so helpless. If I could get away with it, I think I'd kill him on sight."

"But you wouldn't get away with it. In the eyes of most of the folks in this town, he's better people than you. We know better, but they don't. They'd tie a rope around your pretty neck and that wouldn't do no good to nobody." Lillie kissed her on the cheek and led her back toward the bar, her hand crooked in Rachel's arm. "Mattie needs you alive and in one piece, sugar, so don't you go doing anything stupid, you hear me?"

"I do." She grabbed a rag and began swiping down the bar top. "I — well I'll be damned." A familiar red head appeared in the doorway, looking uncertainly around until hazel eyes lit up with recognition, and Mattie strode across the saloon toward her.

"Hello, Lillie, Rachel." Mattie nodded to each woman in turn. "Am I interrupting anything?"

"Absolutely not, sugar." Lillie hesitantly patted her on the arm, glad when Mattie didn't flinch away from her. "I was just headed upstairs to change, so I'll leave you two gals to talk."

"You don't have to..."

"No, no." Lillie waved a hand at her. "Talk. I have things I need to be doing." And she was gone up the stairs before they could say anything further.

"Hello." Mattie smiled shyly. "I got your note." She felt Rachel's eyes roam over her as she talked, and dropped her eyes uncertainly, yet another new sensation washing over her as she wondered if what Rachel saw was pleasing to her. "I miss you too." She felt a touch to her hand and looked back up.

"I'm glad you came in." Rachel trailed one fingertip along the top of her hand. "I take it Adam is..."

"Gone until Tuesday." Mattie felt a pleasant tingle that shot from her hand all the way to her stomach, making it dance with butterflies. "Could you maybe come over tomorrow instead of waiting until Sunday? I can take tomorrow off at the tailor's. I already asked and Mr. Vaughan said it would be fine."

"I'd love to." Rachel noted a profound sadness in her voice, and tilted her chin up to get a better look at her face. Mattie's smile didn't reach her eyes. "What's wrong?"

"I miss you something fierce is all." Mattie looked around, glad that no one seemed to be paying attention to them. It was a great risk, coming into a place where so many people knew Adam, but she'd gone by the boarding house only to find Rachel missing. Rachel's friend Billy had spotted her in the hallway and told her where she was.

"Don't worry. No one in here talks to Adam." Rachel guessed at her fear. "I'll be over whenever you want me there." She reached up, cupping a freckled cheek. "Spend all day with you, if you'd like."

"I'd like that very much." Mattie felt a tug to her hand and then she was being steered out the back door into the alleyway. Long arms wrapped around her, pulling her into a hug. It felt so good, and she snuggled in closer, inhaling a mix of cologne and clean salty sweat that she greedily craved. It drew her in, and she had no explanation for it. She only knew that lately Rachel's scent invaded her dreams. "Wish I didn't have to wait until tomorrow. I wish..."

Rachel ducked her head and kissed her, a soft bit of contact that left her head spinning. "Come to my room tonight." She brushed a lock of hair out of Mattie's eyes, which were round with fear. "Not for anything like that." She kissed her again. "I miss curling up with you as we did when I was ill. You — we could sleep together. Only sleep. I'll never push you, Mattie. You have my word on that."

"Sounds heavenly." Mattie hugged her tightly, feeling Rachel lift her and spin her around once before setting her back on the ground.

"I'll be going home early tonight, I'm thinking." Rachel winked at her before releasing her. "I'll get one of the boys to cover for me. It's my first night back since..." She trailed off, unwilling to bring up unpleasantness in light of the evening to come. "Anyway, they don't expect me to be fully back on my feet yet, I don't think."

"I'll go home and pack up a few things." Hazel eyes twinkled with genuine happiness. "I'll see you in a few hours, Rachel."

"I can't wait." Rachel waved at her, as Mattie turned at the end of the alley, blowing her a kiss before she rounded the corner out of sight.

Rachel sighed in giddy joy. It was going to be a long night at the bar.

SHE TIDIED UP the small room a dozen times, not that there was much to be tidied up in the first place. She'd turned the lamp off, and a single candle burned on the bedside table, mysterious shadows dancing on the walls as it flickered. After thirty minutes of nervous pacing, Rachel finally drew a chair up to the open window and leaned on the windowsill with her nose pressed against the mosquito netting. A slight breeze made the room temperature tolerable, lightly riffling the pages of an open reader on the table, the fresh salty scent filling the room and driving away the oppressive heat of the day.

If she craned her neck, she could see a scattering of stars across the sky. A full moon, while not visible, painted the buildings and alley below in pale soft light, making the ordinary scene appear magical, somehow. Or maybe it just felt magical because Mattie was surely on her way.

After a quick bath, she had stood in front of her small armoire, trying to decide what to wear. She finally chose a short-sleeved ribbed undershirt and a pair of tan summer trousers. Her feet were bare and she had left her suspenders hanging down around her hips. Her hair remained in the long braid she had worn to work that morning. She considered that for a moment, wondering whether to take it down or leave it braided, then mentally slapped herself.

"We are going to sleep," she muttered to herself, "so quit letting your mind wander places it has no business going."

An almost inaudible rapping at the door interrupted her musings, and she hesitated, taking a deep breath before she stepped across the room and opened it. "Hello, Mattie." She held out her hand, drawing her into the room and closing the door. "Here, let me take that." She grabbed hold of a small carpetbag and stowed it at the foot of the bed. She looked up and smiled. "You look lovely."

Mattie stood to the side, her hands clasped behind her back as she studiously watched Rachel. She wore a white frilly shirtwaist and a pale green gingham skirt with a flounce at the hem. Polished shoe tips peeked out from the bottom of a full ruffled petticoat, and her hair was swept up on top of her head. At Rachel's comment she blushed and looked down. "Why do I feel like a girl seeing her beau for the first time?" Her voice was somewhat uncertain, and before she had time to speak further, a gentle hand tilted her chin up.

"Hey." Long fingers stroked her cheek. "It's me. No need to be afraid." Cool skin quickly warmed at her touch, and Rachel felt a slight trembling cease as warm hazel eyes lost some of their fear. "I will never, ever hurt you, I promise."

"I know." Mattie smiled and clasped Rachel's hand, kissing her knuckles. Her smile grew wider as Rachel's brilliant one matched it. "Just that this is something different than anything I've ever done before."

"Why is it different?" Rachel moved to the chair at the widow and sat down, pulling Mattie onto her lap. She felt her warm slight weight settle against her, in contrast to the coolness of the wood floor against her bare feet. "You've been to my room before and we've slept together before. You've sat on my lap before." She gave a playful tickle to Mattie's ribs and bounced her up and down a few times.

"Stop that." Mattie giggled and batted her hand away. "But that was before..." She felt a long arm snug around her back, Rachel's other hand unconsciously squeezing her calf through her skirt. She smiled. "Before we ever did anything."

"And we don't have to do anything you don't want to do." Rachel kissed her on the cheek. "Are you uncomfortable sitting here?"

"N-no. That's just it. I'm never happier than when I'm with you, Rachel. Never more comfortable. I think I might want to do—I don't know... I can't, not what you and Lillie did, but I told you that. But maybe some of what we did last weekend—that would be nice." Her eyes dropped in embarrassment and she almost whispered, "I kind of liked it."

"So did I." Rachel kissed her cheek again. "There is no rush, here, sweetheart. I don't care if we sit and talk all night. I only want to be with you."

At that the dam burst, and Mattie sniffled quietly as the first tears trickled down her cheeks. "I'm sorry." She began to cry harder and felt Rachel wrap both arms around her, rocking her and making tiny shushing noises, along with a few kisses to her forehead. "I want to be with you, too. I wish—I want to leave him. I do. I just don't know how. I still need some time. I held him off this week from..." Their eyes met in understanding and she continued, "but I don't think I can keep it up until I figure out what to do. I don't want to be with him like that, but he's my husband. He will expect it."

"Shhh." Rachel touched her lips, silencing her. "I don't expect that. You owe me nothing, Mattie. Nothing at all. Don't go trying to do anything that would make him hurt you. I'd rather..." She couldn't believe she was saying it, but pressed on, "I'd rather you do what he expects, than have him harm you in any way." Her eyes flashed in anger and helpless frustration, and she felt a return kiss to her head.

"You deserve better than what I can give you." Mattie talked softly, her lips near Rachel's ear.

Mattie's breath on her skin sent a pleasant chill down her spine, and her bowed head slowly came up. "You listen to me. I have never been as happy as since I met you. Don't you go saying things like that. You're everything that is kind and gentle and loving to me. You're my best friend, Mattie. There's no one I care about more than you."

"That feeling is mutual." Mattie finally smiled and dabbed at her eyes with her cuff. She looked around and spied a bottle of wine on the bedside table, along with two glasses. "What's that?"

"French red wine Lillie gave me before I left tonight." Steel eyes twinkled in the low light. "Would you like some?"

"I've only had wine a few times." Her interest piqued and she stood, walking over and picking up the bottle, reading the label. "Imported from Paris, no less. I'd love some." She held out the bottle and smiled fetchingly.

Rachel stood up, and took it from her, popping the cork and pouring up two glasses with a flourish. "I usually drink ale, sometimes whiskey." She handed Mattie a glass. "Haven't had wine much, but I do like it."

Mattie held up her glass and swirled the rich dark liquid around, then sipped daintily at it, allowing the tart sweetness to wash over her tongue before she swallowed. "Mmm." She took another sip. "Dangerous."

"Dangerous?" Rachel drank down half a glass in one swallow, calming jittery nerves.

"It's strong. I can feel it burning as it goes down." A devilish grin played at her lips. "Too much of this might make me wanton."

"Would that be a bad thing?" Rachel teased her, making sure her smile told Mattie she wasn't serious.

"Maybe." Mattie moved to the window. "Maybe not." She looked outside at the moonlit night. "What a beautiful evening."

"That it is." Rachel finished her glass and poured another one, setting it down for later and moving in behind Mattie. She circled her waist with her arms, resting her chin on Mattie's head. "Wish I had a nice ocean view here."

"The stars are view enough. And the moonlight." Mattie swallowed and leaned back into the embrace. "What do you do here in the evenings after working all day?"

"Oh." Rachel swayed slowly from side to side. "Some nights I'm so tired, all I do is come home, eat supper, take a bath, and go to bed. Some nights I work on my reading or practice writing my letters. Some nights I play my harmonica. On nicer evenings I might go sit on the fire escape and smoke a cigar. I don't draw or knit or anything like that. If it's too hot, sometimes I go walk down to the beach to cool off. What do you do on the nights you're home alone?"

"Read." Mattie felt Rachel nuzzle the back of her neck, and a thrill ran through her. "Draw. I just started working with pastel colors, so I've been experimenting, learning how to use them."

"Bet you'll make some nice pictures with those." She nibbled to the side of Mattie's neck and kissed her below her ear, before resting her chin back on top of her head.

"Some of them are of you." The arms around her tightened and the nibbling started up again.

"Truly?" Forgetting all vows to be good, Rachel began removing the hairpins from Mattie's hair, the long wavy locks slowly spilling down her back and over her shoulders.

"Truly." Mattie tilted her head up and to the side, warm blue-gray eyes sparkling back at her in the candlelight. "I think about you often when we're apart."

"I think about you often too, Mattie." Nimble fingers lifted the long hair, allowing it to sift slowly back down. "You're very beautiful."

"So are you." Their lips met in a slow sensual dance, and Mattie managed to set her wine glass on the windowsill before turning in Rachel's arms, pulling her tightly against her. The kissing continued for several minutes until both women struggled for breath. Mattie stood on her toes, hugging Rachel as she kissed her way across Mattie's jaw line and down the side of her neck, before returning the hug for a long mindless bit of time.

"I'm not doing very good at controlling myself, I don't think." She chuckled lightly and felt Mattie squeeze her harder. "Sorry."

"Feels wonderful." Mattie grew brave and did some experimental nibbling of her own, small uncertain nips at the salty skin of Rachel's neck, which was very warm. Her hands found both arms, squeezing strong biceps, enjoying the sensation of the muscles flexing under her fingers. "Should—should we get dressed for bed?" She pulled back, watching Rachel's nostrils flare. "Do I smell bad?" She tilted her head in question.

A grin spread across Rachel's face and she buried her nose into Mattie's hair. "No." She moved lower, kissing the base of her throat. "I love your scent. You always smell very sweet." She felt the blush at her neck and was glad for the low light. "Do you want to get dressed for bed?"

"It must be close to midnight." Mattie smiled shyly. "Are you tired?"

"No." Rachel smiled back, trying to ignore the thumping of her own heart. "But maybe if we get ready for bed, I'll eventually get sleepy. Do you need some privacy? The water closet is..."

"I know where it is. I stayed here with you, remember?" She patted Rachel's belly through her trousers. "I'll just go splash my face and come back. I'd prefer to change in here. Don't want to walk down the hallway in my nightgown."

Rachel pursed her lips inward. "Do you mind if I sleep in this shirt and my bloomers?"

"No, silly." She ruffled the dark head. "It's what you slept in while you were ill. Besides, I've seen you in less."

This time she couldn't hide the blush, remembering that Lillie and Mattie had given her several sponge baths when she was too weak to take one in the tub. "I forgot. Hurry back." She watched Mattie duck out the door, and leaned back against it after she closed it. She swallowed a few times and rolled her eyes toward the ceiling. "I am not going to survive this night, I don't believe."

She removed her trousers and hung them up in the armoire, then turned back the covers and flopped back on the bed. She sat up and fluffed the pillows, then laid back down, her arms folded back and tucked under her head. A soft padding of footsteps told her Mattie was just outside the door, and she smiled as she stepped back into the room. "I'll just turn toward the wall while you change."

"Thank you." Mattie waited, then stood in the corner and quickly divested herself of shirtwaist, skirt, petticoats and stockings. She drew a lightweight cotton nightgown over her head and turned back around. "Ready."

Rachel slowly rolled back over, her eyes drinking in Mattie's figure, which was backlighted through the window. "You look like an angel." Her words reflected her thoughts from the week before, and she watched a smile tug at Mattie's lips. She held out a long arm, beckoning Mattie to join her.

Slowly, Mattie sat down on the edge of the bed and scooted back, resting half-sitting, half-lying against a plump pillow. She was warm, and felt slightly giddy from the wine. She could feel Rachel breathing next to her, and she slowly leaned down, tracing Rachel's face with her fingertips, watching her eyes flutter closed. She continued mapping her features and leaned closer, placing a quick tentative kiss on her lips.

Rachel's eyes opened and softened, and she reached up, pulling Mattie's face back down for another kiss, taking her time until she felt Mattie opening up to her, her body relaxing as she sank lower, draped partly on top of Rachel. Rachel's other hand came up, gently stroking Mattie's back a she deepened the kiss, her hand stopping at the small of Mattie's back, careful not to move any lower. She gasped slightly as she felt Mattie's hands begin to explore, one running leisurely around the curve of her hip and up her side, coming to rest just below her breast.

Mattie curled in closer still, and tentatively brought her hand up, re-familiarizing herself with the soft firmness, and hearing Rachel make quiet noises of pleasure in the back of her throat. "You like that?" She brushed her palm across a taut nipple, feeling it through the ribbed cotton.

"Y-yes," Rachel managed to sputter. "Very much." She reached up, covering Mattie's hand, encouraging her explorations.

"How does it feel?" Mattie's eyes studied her intently. "I've never..."

"Would you like to find out?" Rachel kissed her soundly. "I won't push for more. I promised you that." She kissed her again and felt Mattie nod affirmatively.

Slowly she sat up and leaned against the wall, pulling Mattie up so she was sitting across her lap. She reached across, touching her face and tracing her lips. "So very beautiful." She kissed her one more time and trailed one hand slowly up Mattie's stomach, feeling the surface flutter under her hand. Even more slowly, she trailed the hand higher, feeling the combination of brushed cotton and tickling lace against her palm, then gradually took Mattie's breast into her hand, cupping it as Mattie's breathing stopped.

She peered at Mattie's downcast eyes and kissed her cheek. "Are you all right?"

"I—feels nice," Mattie whispered, a myriad of new sensations assaulting her senses. Rachel's thumb brushed across her nipple and she cried out softly.

"Still all right?" The thumb stopped and Rachel ducked her head to make eye contact. Fiery hazel eyes met steel, and Rachel smiled. "Guess so." She leaned in, nibbling lightly at Mattie's neck, and began gently caressing her through her nightgown. "Breathe, sweetheart."

"Can't," Mattie gasped, then complied despite herself, her breathing erratic as she felt another new sensation settle into her stomach. At the same time Rachel gently rolled her over onto her back, hovering over her as she continued to tease her. Soft lips thoroughly explored her face and neck, while the sensations Rachel's hand was causing made her feel as if she were losing control. Rachel moved from one breast to the other, and Mattie cried out again. It was heavenly and she went with it, until Rachel finally slowed down and then stopped, withdrawing her hand and rolling onto her back, pulling Mattie on top of her and hugging her tightly.

"Was that too much?" She stroked Mattie's head and then her back, feeling her breathing begin to return to normal, although Mattie's heart was pounding so strongly she could feel it against her own chest.

"No." Mattie pushed up until she was hovering over Rachel. "Is that what two women can do together?" She smiled a crooked smile and felt Rachel take her hand and kiss it. It had felt good, but left her longing for more, although she couldn't figure out what she was craving.

"That was only part of what two women can do together." Amused eyes lit up as Rachel spoke. She saw the question in Mattie's eyes, and kissed her softly. "And I think we'd best stop now, or I'll be tempted to show you the rest."

"I'm not sure I can." Another kiss stopped her.

"I know." One more kiss. "That's why we need to stop." She pulled Mattie down, tucking her head against her shoulder.

"I like sleeping with you." Mattie traced idle patterns on Rachel's bare forearm with her fingertips.

Rachel laughed, a silent movement of her ribs that Mattie felt rather than heard. "I'm glad." She kissed Mattie's head one more time. "I like sleeping with you too. Goodnight, Mattie."

"Goodnight, Rachel." Despite the newness of it all, she was

suddenly exhausted, and quickly gave in to sleep, feeling safer than she ever had in her entire life.

Rachel held her, feeling her breathing even out, and the warmth of it against her chest. She looked up at the ceiling, absorbing the newness of holding Mattie while she slept. A fierce protectiveness surged through her, and she pulled the smaller woman closer against her. Much later, she doused the candle and joined her in peaceful slumber.

THE FIRST THING she was aware of was that she was very warm. The second was that she was pinned down and could barely move. Memory flooded her brain and she smiled, before opening her eyes to see Mattie's face inches away, her eyes closed in sleep. The very early morning sun robbed the room of all but the brightest of colors, painting Mattie's skin a very pale pink, her red hair shining like fire where the light touched it. Her head was still tucked against Rachel's shoulder, and her fist was curled under her chin. The bow of her lip pushed out in concentration, and her brows were furrowed slightly, as if she were dreaming of very serious things.

Rachel kissed the top of her head and lightly rubbed her back, and the frown disappeared, to be replaced by the faintest of smiles. Mattie stirred, her hand dropping down and settling in the indention of Rachel's waistline in an almost-possessive gesture. She sighed in contentment and snuggled up closer for more sleep. "That's it," she whispered quietly. "I want you to have nice dreams, Mattie."

She pondered that, wondering if the abuse Mattie suffered at Adam's hands ever invaded her dreams. Probably, she realized. It angered her, knowing there was nothing she could do until Mattie herself was ready to take action. It was something she innately understood, that only Mattie could take the first baby steps toward changing her own circumstances, just as Rachel had made the decision to leave home, taking her destiny into her own hands. *I wish for you courage, sweetheart.* She kissed Mattie's head again and peered toward the window, wondering what time it was. Her body told her it was barely dawn. Her nose told her that downstairs, breakfast was cooking, and her stomach growled in anticipation.

Despite her hunger, lethargy won out, and her eyes fluttered closed again. She didn't fall completely back asleep, her mind chasing idle daydreams instead, while she lay there, simply enjoying the closeness. It was one of very few sweet moments in her life, and she didn't want to waste any of it by sleeping. A part of her wished time could stand still and she could always be as happy as she was right then. She wished she could wake up with Mattie every morning, and that they would never have to worry about Adam again.

Her thoughts turned back to the woman in her arms, and she

wondered how something that felt so right could be so wrong. Who was it hurting if she and Mattie loved each other? She refused to count Adam in the equation. She didn't care if he and Mattie were married, at least not when it came to who might get hurt. He was more than an abusive monster, he was a fool. He had Mattie, legally. If he had spent his marriage being kind to her rather than cruel, Rachel was certain he would have Mattie in every sense of the word, and they wouldn't be lying in bed together at that moment.

Numbskull. She shook her head silently. *You have no idea how lucky you are. Or what you're missing.* She couldn't help but smirk, remembering their explorations from the night before. A part of her was meanly pleased that she had privy to something Adam had never bothered to take for himself. Another part of her, the bigger part, was very sad for Mattie, that she was forced to share her bed with someone who seemed so cold and uncaring. She shivered, wondering what it was like to be touched by someone like that, and hoping she never found out.

"Are you cold?" A soft voice and warm breath tickled her ear, as Mattie tightened her hold.

"N-no." She rubbed Mattie's back again. "Just thinking about something unpleasant."

"Mmm." Mattie kissed her on the cheek and began rubbing her belly through her undershirt. "No unpleasant thoughts should be allowed this early in the morning."

"True." Rachel looked down, tilting her head as Mattie's neck craned upward, and their lips met in sweet affirmation of what they had shared the night before. "Are you all right? After last night?"

"Yes." Mattie smiled and pecked her lips again. "Last night was very nice. I wish..." she looked down and continued to rub Rachel's belly, trying to articulate her thoughts. "I wish I were brave enough..."

"Shhh." Rachel silenced her, guiding her face back for a lengthier kiss. "Don't fret. Last night was more than I could have hoped for. I love being with you, feeling close to you. I was just thinking, before you woke up, that this morning was one of the happiest mornings of my life, just because I was with you, and for no other reason."

"Truly?" Mattie sat partway up, leaning on her forearm and peering down at steel blue eyes. "It's one of my happiest mornings, too." She nestled back down against Rachel's shoulder and felt both long arms close around her, pulling her close. "It's almost like sharing the same skin, isn't it?" She dared to look up again as she continued. "I notice things the past couple weeks I never noticed before."

"Such as?" Rachel's long fingers played with Mattie's hair, enjoying the silken texture and the weight of it as she lifted the mass of it, before letting it fall a few strands at a time.

"How soft your skin is." Mattie nuzzled the skin in question. "I love the way you smell." She blushed but forged ahead. "And when we're together as we were last night, a part of me feels like it's all mixed up inside of you." She sighed in frustration. "I know I'm not making a bit of sense."

"You are making perfect sense." Rachel rolled her over, hovering over her, tracing Mattie's face with her fingertips. "Because I notice all those things about you too, and I feel the same way, as if you're a part of me."

"Are we crazy?" Mattie's hand reached up, mimicking Rachel's actions, trailing over high cheekbones and full lips.

"We must be." Rachel dropped lower, nipping at Mattie's throat before moving higher, meeting her lips. "Must be," she repeated, kissing her deeply, restraining her hands from doing what they wanted to do. It was sweet torture, and she grudgingly broke away and sat up, pulling Mattie along with her, holding her in a rocking embrace. "I might best go down and get us some breakfast."

"Do you need me to get dressed and help you?" Mattie scooted to the edge of the bed, thinking to retrieve her skirt and shirtwaist.

A grin tugged at Rachel's lips. *On the contrary, I'd like for you to get undressed.* She kept that thought to herself, holding out a hand to stop Mattie from standing up. "No. I can manage it. You just sit here and I'll be back in a jiffy. Have you ever had breakfast in bed?"

"I don't think so. I—oomph." A pair of soft lips silenced her. She licked her lips thoughtfully as Rachel stood, donning her trousers and tugging her suspenders up over her undershirt.

"Allow me to pamper you, my lady." Rachel's voice took on a playful tone. "One breakfast fit for a queen, coming up." With a wink and a smile, she scampered out of the room, leaving Mattie laughing behind her.

"KEEP PUSHING, WE'RE almost there!" Rachel kicked backward, slicing through rolling waves as they swam deftly toward the sand bar set as Mattie's swimming goal. Lessons had progressed at a nice pace over the almost-three months, even with losing a month while Rachel recovered from the beating and the chills. She watched her friend make a credible effort, her arms drawing her forward, her face scrunched in concentration.

"I'm tired," Mattie spluttered. Her arms were beginning to ache and her nose and eyes burned from the salt water. Despite the coolness of the water, she was quite warm, the sun shining mercilessly down on her back and legs. She dared not stop. Several yards behind her she had discovered the water was too deep for her to touch bottom without becoming completely submerged. "You promise me we're close?"

"See those waves breaking and the white foam just ahead?" Rachel looked back over her shoulder. "That is where we need to go. I promise you can stand up when we get there."

Mattie blew out a frustrated breath, bubbling the water, and redoubled her effort, increasing her pace so quickly she almost collided with Rachel.

"Whoa, Nellie." Rachel held out her hands, gently guiding Mattie past her, keeping hold of the hem of her bathing suit top. "Slow down." She laughed. "You're about to swim over it. Stand up."

"Oh." Mattie cautiously let her feet drop and felt the shifting sandy bottom between her toes. "My stars." Her eyes grew wide. "What a queer sensation, to be standing so far from shore." She looked around in wonder, her chest heaving as she caught her breath. "Oh." A large wave knocked her off her feet and she felt a strong arm catch her around the waist, keeping her from going under. "Thank you."

Steel eyes twinkled. "You're most welcome." Rachel reeled her in closer, tilting her head and placing a few tentative pecks on first her cheek and then her mouth. "Mmm. You're all salty." She dove back in for more, oblivious to the breaking waves around them. She felt Mattie's arms circle her neck, and she lifted her up at the waist, as Mattie's legs came up, wrapping around Rachel's waist in a motion that seemed as natural as breathing. Her hands came to rest on Mattie's backside and she resisted the urge to squeeze her, concentrating instead on the intimacy, and how nice it felt.

"You did it!" Mattie yelled in triumph as she came up for air. "I can swim, Rachel!" She felt herself whirled around in a circle and laughed in dizzy happiness.

"On the contrary." Rachel hugged her tightly, speaking into her ear as Mattie's chin rested on her shoulder. "You did it. You swam all the way out here without any help."

"Couldn't have done it without you. Maybe I can go on a boat now and not be afraid." Mattie pulled back, making eye contact and enjoying her perch, her legs balanced on Rachel's hipbones.

"You've never been on a boat?" Rachel's voice was incredulous.

"There aren't many bodies of water in El Paso." She teased her friend, tugging at the wet braid running down her back. "No, I've never been on a boat."

"I could take you out on Mr. Gentry's boat, sometime." She thought ahead, and took a deep breath, plunging forward. "Maybe for the Independence Day celebration next week? I believe he's planning on going up to Waco for a spell, to visit family, so I don't think he would mind. He already told Billy and me to fish while he is gone, if we can't get other work at the port."

Mattie's smile disappeared, and her voice dropped to an almost inaudible level. She looked down, one finger tracing the neckline of Rachel's swimming top. "Adam will be in town for the celebration. It falls on Wednesday. He has already informed me I am to accompany him to the festivities, as he expects to see some clients out and about, and wants to make a favorable impression on them."

Rachel's soaring heart suddenly began to dive like the pelicans she had seen diving from cliffs, and she swallowed, maintaining a brave front. " When does he come home?"

"Tuesday, the day before the celebration. Three days from now." She looked up, her eyes shining as she managed not to cry. "I'm sorry." She looked down again. "I was looking forward very much to spending the day with you. I didn't realize until last week that the holiday is in the dead center of the week."

"Listen to me." Rachel cupped her cheek, her thumb brushing across chilled skin. "We wouldn't have been able to stroll freely around town anyway. You know that. This way, at least you'll get to see everything."

"I wanted to watch the fireworks with you." Mattie forced a trembling smile. "It — it sounds so romantic. I wanted to come down to the beach with you and see the show. Just us two." She remembered the party on the beach, and the couple they had seen kissing in the sand dunes in the dark under the stars. Her heart ached at something that seemed lost to her.

"You need to be safe." Rachel hugged her and shifted, until she was supporting Mattie and they began paddling back toward shore. "The town will be all spruced up, with red, white, and blue banners hanging from the buildings, and there will be barrels of lemonade and all kinds of food to be had. We could not have gone to that together, and you know it. With Adam in town, at least you will be able to go. It will be fun."

"It will not be fun." Mattie pulled away from her and swam the rest of the way to shore, her anger driving her with surprising speed. Rachel followed close behind, sensing that something was terribly wrong.

"Mattie." She watched Mattie reach the shallow area and stand, making determined strides back to the waiting blanket they had spread out before going into the water. Mattie reached down, retrieving a towel and wrapping up in it, before she sat down on the blanket, her ankles crossed and her knees up, her arms wrapped around her legs with her forehead pressed against one knee.

"Mattie." Rachel called to her again as she reached the blanket, plopping down next to her, but leaving a safe amount of space between them. "I'm sorry." She reached down, plucking a small conch shell from the sand and inspecting it closely, finding a tiny hermit crab inside, its spiky legs poking out from its safe haven. Impulsively she held the shell down in Mattie's line of sight, between her knees.

"*Yah!*" The red head shot up and Mattie jumped backward. She looked first at Rachel and then at the shell, and burst out in helpless laughter. "I'm sorry too." She scooted closer, until the sides of their legs were touching. "You did nothing wrong. I'm just so very disappointed about the holiday. I don't care if I get to see the festivities." Pained hazel eyes looked to the side, meeting steel. "All I care about is being with you."

"And I'll help you in any way you need me to." Rachel felt the familiar helpless frustration, twisting her stomach into knots and making her temples ache vaguely. "But if Adam is planning on you going to the celebration with him, I don't see a way around that, not without putting you in danger."

"And you as well." Mattie dug a toe into the sand, giving it a vicious kick and sending a spray of the fine pale brown grains across the blanket. "What all do they do at this party, again?"

"Well," Rachel casually draped an arm around her shoulders, pulling her closer, her own body relaxing as she felt Mattie's head drop down, tucked against her neck, "it's a large celebration along the Strand, with all the food and lemonade I mentioned. They'll have some boat races near shore — rowing and sailing contests and such. In the afternoon everyone will gather around and someone, most likely the Sheriff, will read the preamble to the constitution, and folks will probably sing a few songs. There will be other readings and music, and all kinds of fancy speeches. After the sun goes down, they'll shoot off some fireworks from the pier area. It's glorious, with the lights reflecting off the water."

"Sounds lovely." Mattie closed her eyes. "That's the part I wanted to share with you — the fireworks. I thought we might come down here and still be able to see them."

"Maybe not here." Rachel stroked her hair, enjoying the sleek damp locks against her fingertips. "But we could have found a private spot to watch from."

"I wish..." Mattie stopped herself. *And if wishes were horses I'd own a stable,* she ruefully realized. "Maybe by next year, Rachel. I want — if you can be patient with me, maybe I can..."

"Stop fretting." Rachel kissed her head. "If there's even a chance, I'll wait for you forever, Mattie, you hear me?"

"You'd do that for me?" Hope sparked anew as Mattie dared to open her eyes and peek upward.

"I'd do anything for you." The words were sure and solid, and Mattie believed without question. Suddenly the world spun and she was looking up at the blue sky. Just as quickly it was blocked out by Rachel's tanned face hovering over her. "Anything."

Mattie reached up and pulled Rachel down to her, kissing her soundly. She felt Rachel's body press against her, and decided she liked that, feeling the solid firmness of her in her arms, as time stood still. Her hands found Rachel's back, running up and down, then sliding underneath her swimming top. It was another new sensation, as her fingers explored the smooth warm skin of Rachel's back. She heard murmurs of pleasure and felt a familiar fire in her own gut, a longing she couldn't place. "I..." She blushed as Rachel pulled up for air. "I'm sorry. I shouldn't have—I don't know what came over me." She had never touched anyone's bare skin in such a manner, and felt her cheeks burning in shame.

"Don't be sorry." Nimble fingers found Mattie's face and traced its softness. "I'd never have found the courage to ask you to touch me like that. Probably would never have found the courage to touch you, either." Her own fingers ached for similar contact, and she soothed it with her continued exploration of Mattie's face. She frowned, reading confusion in Mattie's eyes. "Whatever you're puzzling over, you can ask me. I'll give you honest answers. I hope you know that by now."

"You and Lillie, you touch each other's bare skin?" Mattie shivered pleasantly, imagining how it might feel.

Rachel sighed, remembering Mattie's description of Adam's fumbling intimacies. She didn't need to ask. It was obvious this was yet a new facet of their physical relationship that Mattie knew nothing about. She decided to skip any delicate explanation. "Lillie and I, when we were together," she frowned for emphasis, "we got completely undressed." She watched Mattie's throat work in an audible gulp. "We got naked." She smiled as Mattie's pink cheeks darkened to red. "It was very nice, and it felt wonderful."

"You weren't embarrassed by it?" Mattie's own skin tingled, thinking about Rachel's soft brown skin, and the muscles she had seen when she and Lillie bathed her. She wondered what it would feel like, to have all that firm softness touching her.

"It's difficult to explain, but no." Rachel's fingers trailed lower until it came to rest on the pounding pulse at Mattie's throat. "We didn't take all our clothes off right away." She smiled. "At least not most of the time. We undressed each other slowly, while we spent some time touching. By the time we got naked, there was no embarrassment. Rather, we were aching to touch each other. Does that make sense?"

Aching? Mattie had felt that sensation all too frequently of late. "I think I understand." She slipped one hand beneath the top again, gliding up Rachel's back. "Seems like sometimes all I want lately is to kiss you, and touch you. It just never occurred to me, until today, about the bare skin part, that is."

Rachel groaned and slid her hand down, cupping Mattie's breast through her bathing suit. She would not return the bare-skinned touches without invitation. *Patience,* she reminded herself. *She asked for patience.* Then she was divested of thought, as she heard Mattie whimper, and felt a firm hand pulling her down, as they spent a leisurely time in more kissing. Ah, well. She tossed up a mental hand. There would be plenty of time to explore bare skin on some other day. For the time being, kissing on a secluded beach under the warm summer sun was akin to paradise, she was certain.

Chapter
Seven

INDEPENDENCE DAY DAWNED hot and muggy. Thin clouds brought no promise of refreshing rain, but rather served to increase the humidity and the discomfort of both man and beast. Horses and buggies, and the occasional team of oxen, were tied at every available hitching post along The Strand, as holiday revelers arrived to partake of the island's annual festivities. The horses clustered together in what little shade the buildings had to offer, their long tails switching at large blood-sucking flies. Dogs lay motionless under covered porches, and there was nary a cat to be seen.

Mattie looked around anxiously before lightly touching Adam's proffered hand and stepping down from their buggy. She tried not to shrug him off as he reached out with both hands, grabbing her around the waist to steady her as she landed solidly on the ground. It was not even noon, yet Adam had already put up the folding buggy top to protect them from the sun during the short ride into town.

"Well?" Adam held out a crooked arm and she reluctantly wrapped her hand around it. "What shall we do first?"

"Whatever you wish, darling." Mattie tried very hard to take the sarcastic edge off the endearment. "I suspect it will be much like celebrations back home."

"Perhaps." He began walking, guiding them through the already-sizeable throng that milled along the board sidewalks. "But back home we didn't have to deal with this blasted humidity." He mopped his brow with a handkerchief.

"True." Mattie clutched a delicate lacy fan in her free hand, but chose not to use it until she was desperate. It was only going to get warmer. Like every other woman of any status on the island, she had started the morning with a tepid bath, followed by a liberal sprinkling of sweet-smelling talcum powder. She felt vaguely like a dewy sugar cookie, the sweat and talcum sticking to her skin beneath her clothing, releasing a floral scent. Her hair was pinned up well off her neck and shoulders, in a tighter twist than she usually wore. She had chosen a pale lavender skirt with a matching shirtwaist, and had decided on only one petticoat in deference to the heat, despite what fashion dictated.

She put on a brave face and mustered up her sociable smile, nodding in greeting each time Adam stopped to introduce her to one of his associates. She found herself listening intently for clues as to what, exactly, her husband did for a living besides gamble. At various times, his associates mentioned shipments, trades, and payments, but what they were shipping and trading was never mentioned. She wondered if the other wives they met were as much in the dark as she was, or if she was the only one who wasn't privy to the means of her own livelihood.

Ever the gracious wife, she smiled sweetly, laughing in all the appropriate places, whether she was amused or not. Underneath the sham of her mirth was a profound melancholy. Once there had been nothing more in her life than housekeeping, sewing at the tailor's, reading, drawing, and attending to Adam's whims and desires. It had never been enough, and now she knew why.

She had ridden a bicycle, swum in the ocean, run on the beach, and knew now what it felt like to be alive. She had given and received touches and kisses from someone she knew cared for her deeply. Her mind wandered pleasantly over the weekend past, which had been spent reading, drawing, and swimming, as well as a whole lot of kissing. She hadn't been brave enough to explore any further than stroking the soft skin of Rachel's back, and was much too embarrassed to articulate her own desires.

She wanted Rachel to touch her in the same way, and to show her so much more than what they had done thus far. She had thought of little else, and how she might find the courage to ask for what she wanted. She chuckled ruefully to herself, realizing that she didn't know exactly what it was that she wanted. She wanted to be lost in Rachel—the feeling she got when Rachel took her into her arms and kissed her senseless—she wanted to feel that sensation tenfold.

A tug at her arm drew her out of her daydreams, to find Adam almost, but not quite, glaring at her. "Say farewell to our friends, Madeline." Adam gestured toward the couple they had been talking to, both of whom were looking at her in puzzlement.

"Oh." She blushed furiously. "I beg your pardon." She smiled in turn at each of them. "I thought I saw Mr. Vaughan from the tailor's shop across the way, and was distracted. It seems it was someone who only resembled him from the side. I do apologize." She didn't mention that he was her boss, assuming either they knew, or else that Adam probably didn't want them to know. Her employment was still a point of contention, and she sensed he felt her working to be a slight to his manhood. She suspected he allowed it only because he knew where she was when she worked, rather than leaving her to her own devices during the day.

"It's quite all right, Mrs. Crockett." The man—Mr. Wells, if she recalled—tipped his hat to her. "A good day to both of you. Perhaps we'll see y'all again down at the pier for the fireworks."

"That would be delightful." Mattie fully recovered, giving the couple a little wave as they departed.

"I'll not have you embarrassing me again." Adam squeezed her arm so tightly she had to clamp her jaw shut to keep from crying out. "Pay attention, Mattie, and get your head out of the clouds." He released his grip and she felt her skin tingle painfully as blood returned to the surface. She knew she would have a bruise around her forearm when she undressed that night.

"I'm sorry, Adam." She had sensed she was in trouble when he had addressed her by her more formal name. "I fear the heat may be causing me to feel addled. Could we find some lemonade and sit down for a spell in the shade?"

"We're already in the shade," he groused, but steered her toward a lemonade stand nonetheless. She stood politely to the side as he ordered two cool mugs, her eyes taking in the colorful red, white, and blue banners hanging from almost every window along the street. Several flags were flying, and somewhere out of sight she heard a fiddle playing patriotic tunes. Suddenly mixed in with the music, a familiar laugh rang out behind her. Turning ever so slightly, she spotted Rachel, Lillie, and Billy standing around a large wooden pickle barrel, all three of them munching on the salty sour treats, causing her mouth to water in sympathy. Rachel and Lillie were both laughing in between bites, as Billy told what was obviously a funny story, too far away for her to hear his words.

"Shall we go find a bench?" Adam turned and followed her gaze, his eyes darkening in anger. "I suppose there's no banning the riffraff from these affairs. Come along, Mattie. I'll not have that whore or her friends bothering you."

"Yes, darling." As he turned his attention toward some tables and chairs that had been set up in a vacant lot, her eyes lingered on her friends, her heart longing to be with them. At the very last minute Rachel looked up and their eyes locked. She ducked her head almost shyly, then looked back up and winked, flashing Mattie a brilliant smile. She bit her lip before returning the smile, then allowed herself to be led away. Adam had missed the entire exchange.

Rachel watched her walk away and looked down again, kicking savagely at the bottom of the pickle barrel. She felt a light touch to her shoulder and glanced behind her, to spy Angel's smiling face. The light touch became a shoulder clasp, as Rachel spun around to face her. "Howdy." She raised a brow in question.

"Howdy yourself. I need to speak to you about some business at the port." Angel drew her aside, away from the others, into the shade of the side of the mercantile building. "Don't you go feeling sorry for yourself." Kind but stern eyes admonished her.

"I-I guess I do, don't I?" She hunched over a little, jamming her hands in her pockets. "I feel so helpless."

"You're no such thing." Angel patted her on the arm. "She may be with him, but it's written all over her face. You have her heart. Now you need to figure out what to do about the rest."

"In the middle of this crowd, there's not much I can do but watch while he leads her about like some decorative ornament." She spit to the side in disgust.

"Now, now." Angel tisked at her. "You seem like an intelligent sort. I imagine if you put your mind to it, you'll figure a way to steal some time with her. Now." She glanced across the way where Betsy was sitting on the ice cream parlor porch. Betsy waved at them, and Rachel hesitantly waved back. "I believe I promised someone a dish of something sweet." She clasped Rachel's shoulder again. "Take the sweet parts where you can find them. That's my advice."

"Thank you. I think I needed to hear that." Rachel shook hands with her, then watched as Angel dodged her way through the crowd mingling in the street, and followed Betsy inside the sweet shop. She turned and spotted Mattie and Adam a few buildings down. "Hmm." She smiled and whistled a little tune, as she rejoined her companions. "Hey, Billy, I need to ask you a favor."

MORNING SLOWLY SEGUED to afternoon, the ever-present sun shining down relentlessly on the growing crowd of hot and sweaty townspeople. Many of the elderly had retreated indoors or down to the beach to escape the heat, while the more delicate women chose to settle in chairs and swings on the porches of businesses and houses. Most of the men had removed their jackets and rolled up shirtsleeves, while the women broke out parasols and wide-brimmed hats.

Mattie had retrieved her parasol from their buggy and was just about to suggest a detour to the shore when Billy approached them uncertainly. Mattie peered apprehensively at Adam until it became clear he didn't recognize him from his earlier association with Rachel. She smiled and waited, wondering what the attractive young man might be up to.

"Excuse me." Billy stopped a polite distance away and bowed slightly. "I'm sorry to interrupt you, sir," he smiled at Adam, "but I was hoping I might persuade your lovely wife to let me into the tailor's shop for a few minutes. I was in there yesterday afternoon and I believe I left my hat on the counter." He glanced up at the blazing sun. "As you can see, it would be a great help to me at the moment if I could retrieve it."

Mattie looked up at Adam hopefully before she spoke. "I believe he's correct, Adam. I was thinking of popping into the shop for a bit anyway, to touch up my hair. It feels like it might be coming loose, and in this heat, it would be unbearable hanging down on my neck."

"Very well," Adam answered slowly. "I see one of my colleagues across the way, and need to discuss a business matter with him." He gestured toward a man in a ten-gallon hat. "I'll be over there when you return." He released her arm. "Don't be too long."

"I wont." She had to fight the huge smile that was lurking just under the surface. She stopped and turned, walking back and whispering in Adam's ear. "I have the need for the outhouse, so I'll take care of that while I'm over there." She smiled as he nodded his agreement. She had just bought herself some time.

She barely spoke to Billy until they were around the corner and out of Adam's sight and earshot. "Thank you." She finally smiled fully, taking his hand and squeezing it quickly.

"You don't know what you're thanking me for, yet." He laughed at her obvious good spirits.

"I have a fairly good idea." She looked up at him, her eyes twinkling from beneath the brim of her yellow straw bonnet.

"You know, I do believe my hat may be in the hotel after all." He gestured toward the hotel across the street. "Just to be on the safe side, you'd best look inside the tailor's, though." They reached the shop and he left her to herself, as he dashed across the street to the hotel for a sarsaparilla.

Mattie looked around anxiously and shrugged, finding the tailor shop key in her pocketbook. She had barely slipped inside when a pair of warm hands grasped her shoulders from behind. Before she could stop it, a muffle little cry of joy escaped her lips, and she turned, burrowing into Rachel's embrace. Joy dissolved into tears, and she heard quiet shushing, and felt long fingers rubbing her back and arms, as Rachel rocked her in comfort. "S-sorry." Mattie sniffled. "Just missed you terribly these past couple of days. I didn't realize how much until now."

"Oh, Mattie." Rachel's voice caressed her name. "I've missed you, too." She tilted Mattie's chin up and kissed her soundly, holding on tightly as she drew out the exchange. "Whew." She finally pulled back. "I was already warm, but I do believe you've thrown another log on the fire." They kissed again and Rachel drew her into a soundless hug.

"Take me away from here, Rachel." Mattie nibbled at a patch of exposed collarbone, something she had not done in the past, but instinctively wanted to do. "Take me anywhere."

Rachel's heart skipped a beat as Mattie's lips delicately explored her skin. "That's why I had Billy get you in here." She licked her lips nervously. "I know we don't have much time before Adam comes hunting you down. When does he leave for Houston again?"

"Not until Saturday morning." Mattie looked down at her feet, studying her polished black shoe tips. "Dratted holiday forced him to rearrange his usual schedule."

"But he'll be gone by Saturday night, then?" Rachel moved to the chair at Mattie's sewing machine and sat down, pulling Mattie onto her lap.

"Yes." She trailed one finger up Rachel's shirt, reaching her neck and tracing her jaw line. She watched the steel blue eyes flutter closed for several minutes, while her fingertips danced along a high cheekbone, even daring to circle Rachel's full lips. She giggled as white teeth snapped at her finger and captured it.

Rachel raised one saucy eyebrow and released it, laughing back at her. "How would you like to spend Saturday evening on Mr. Gentry's boat? We'll only go out a little ways from shore and drop anchor, just relax and maybe I'll get some fishing in."

Mattie felt giddy. "It sounds lovely. Can we go out early enough that I can have some sunlight to sketch by for a few hours?"

"We can do whatever you want to." Rachel kissed her again. "I have a little surprise for you after the sun goes down, but we can make a day of it if you'd like — take a picnic basket and blanket out. Maybe even a bottle of wine. And pack up your swimsuit. We can swim off the back of the boat."

"I'd like that very much." Mattie hugged her fiercely. "I wish I didn't have to go back out there, but I'd best, or we might get caught in here."

Rachel grew quiet and looked down, finding Mattie's fingers and twining them with her own. She felt Mattie's lips brush across the top of her head, and buried her face into her shoulder, inhaling the smell of talcum and Mattie's own scent that set her senses spinning. She kissed the pale soft skin on Mattie's neck and ran one hand up her arm, intent on pulling her even closer. She gave her a little squeeze and pulled back when she heard a sharp intake of air. "What's wrong?"

"Nothing." Mattie rubbed her wrist.

"Sounded like I hurt you." She delicately touched Mattie's arm again. "Did I?"

Mattie sighed. "No. Just — my forearm hurts a little."

"Damn him!" Rachel carefully unbuttoned her sleeve and pushed it up, revealing a series of finger-sized red marks circling her arm, just above the wrist. "Did he twist it?"

"No." Mattie closed her eyes as Rachel gently probed her muscles. "I embarrassed him. He squeezed me a little hard is all."

"Hard enough to do this?" She gritted her teeth in anger. "I can't stand it, Mattie." She lifted the injured arm, kissing it all along its length before she carefully re-buttoned the cuff. "I hate that he puts his hands on you at all, I think you know that by now."

Mattie nodded slightly and re-twined their fingers. She didn't think of what she did with Adam and what she did with Rachel as the same thing. What she felt with each of them was so different. Rachel touched her to make her feel good—make her feel special—so she could see how the thought of Adam's callousness in his attentions would probably drive Rachel to distraction.

"But when he touches you to hurt you." She released a long frustrated breath. "I want to kill him." She buried her face into Mattie's neck again. "Never wanted to kill anyone before."

"I know." Mattie stroked her head and tugged gently at the long braid hanging down Rachel's back. "You can't. You simply mustn't."

"Would solve a whole lot of problems." Rachel's muffled voice hummed against her skin, tickling it.

"And would create a whole parcel of new ones, and you know it." Mattie kissed her head again. "I'm puzzling through all of this, Rachel, and when I figure it out, I need you to be here for me. Your neck is much too lovely to be hanging from the end of a rope. Please?"

Rachel hugged her fiercely. "Very well, if you insist." She felt gentle stroking against her back and sighed, then looked up hopefully. "You truly think my neck is lovely?" She batted her long dark lashes fetchingly, her earnest expression almost enough to make Mattie laugh.

"Yes." Mattie tilted her head and nibbled the neck in question. "I-I'd like to..." She trailed off, unable to express her feelings.

Rachel found her lips and captured them, gasping as Mattie's hand slipped up and circled her ribs, just below her breast. "Whatever you'd like, Mattie." She pressed her forehead against Mattie's, looking down, her stomach fluttering as Mattie's hand slid up a little higher. "I—you—can do whatever you like." She smiled. "But we'd best not do it here and now."

"I want..." Mattie couldn't look up, her cheeks flushing bright red. She felt Rachel's hand cup her face, forcing eye contact.

"Me, too." Rachel kissed her quickly. "More than you can possibly imagine. But right now I want you safe. So kiss me, and then let's go before he finds us here."

Mattie took her face in both hands and complied, a slow and promising contact that ended with both of them breathing hard, arms wrapped tightly around one another. "I'll see you Saturday, then?" Mattie sat up, straightening her shirtwaist. "Might be best if I come to the boarding house after Adam is gone."

Rachel stood, depositing Mattie on her feet. She took her hand and led her to the door, where she pressed her against it and kissed her soundly one more time, her body wanting to stay right where she was, feeling Mattie moving against her. She forced herself to stop, and patted Mattie's hip. "Go on and lock up. I'll stay inside a little while so as not to draw suspicion. I can slip out a side window after you make it around the corner."

"I can hardly bear to wait for Saturday." Mattie opened the door and stepped outside, looking around before she locked the door.

Across the street Billy and Lillie sat on a bench in front of the hotel, sipping sarsaparilla through two straws from a common glass. She waved, and Lillie waved back and smiled, while Billy tipped his hat, which had magically been found.

"I can't wait either, Mattie." Rachel watched through the shop window until she was out of sight. "Be careful." She swallowed, feeling her eyes sting. "I love you."

THE LATE AFTERNOON sun reached out across the sky in red and orange streaks of light, gilding the waves as they rolled ashore. A slight breeze picked up, bringing some relief after the scorching heat of midday. Most of the revelers had moved to the beach area near the pier, setting up blankets in preparation for the fireworks display which would start just after sunset. Families partook of picnic suppers, while some of the more resourceful vendors had moved barrels of lemonade, oranges, and pickles down to the pier, to take advantage of the last round of patrons for the day.

Rachel walked along the beach, her eyes absently taking in her surroundings while her sight turned inward. Billy walked next to her, keeping up a steady stream of conversation to which she managed to pay an adequate amount of attention. They were headed toward the docks to sit on Mr. Gentry's boat and share cigars and whiskey during the fireworks. Lillie had left them a while earlier to go to the saloon. Holiday evenings tended to be profitable, as some of the island's bachelors would end up there to delay going home alone after the long day of festivities.

"Can I ask you a question?" Billy stopped, turning toward her, his body blocking the sun from her face.

"You can." She studied his serious expression. "I may or may not answer."

"It's not that kind of question." He looked down and kicked a shell across the sand. "I think I know how you feel about Mattie." He looked up and held out a hand to forestall her cutting him off. "Hold on. I'm not finished. It must hurt to know she's with that horse's behind of a husband, when you'd rather she be with you."

"It does." Rachel's eyes snapped in angry memory of Mattie's bruises.

"What do you think about Lillie?" He watched her brows furrow at the sudden change of subject. "What I mean is, what if someone had feelings for her? With what she does at the saloon—how would someone deal with that?"

"I never had those kinds of feelings for Lillie." Rachel guessed at the reason behind the question, and its tie to his comments about her and Mattie. "Although there were times when I felt very protective of her. But if I had those kinds of feelings, I'd make sure I could be with her as often as possible. After all, the more I'd be with her, the less she'd be with others. As for what I think of her, she's a kind, decent person, Billy. She does what she does because it's the best money she can make. Anyone who has feelings for her, if they are going to pursue those feelings, they will have to forgive and forget her past. And not be judgmental."

"I see." He tucked his hands into his pockets. "Would you be all right if I take off for the saloon tonight?"

Rachel grinned knowingly at him. "I would be." She playfully punched him in the gut. "Um, Billy, have you ever been with Lillie?"

His blush was answer enough.

"She said something to me once." Rachel closed her eyes for a minute, remembering. "That the men she entertains, that it's always all about their pleasure, and not hers. I think she's looking for two things. Someone who can offer her a decent life, and someone who will make it about her. Do you understand?"

"I think so." The blush deepened. "I'd better get going. With Gentry gone, I've taken the rest of the week off, so I guess I won't see you again until the crab boil Saturday night."

"No. I won't be there." It was Rachel's turn to blush. "I have plans." She reached up and clasped his arm. "Thank you, for what you did this afternoon. It means a great deal."

"I'll always help you out if I can." He smiled and patted the hand at his arm. "Guess I'll see you Monday on the docks, then."

"Go on." Rachel gave him a little shove. "Get moving before she's otherwise engaged for the evening."

He grinned and took off at a trot toward the road. She watched him go, a part of her slightly envious that he would get to be with someone he cared about for the evening. She sighed and wandered on listlessly, still intent on watching fireworks from the boat. She passed a grouping of blankets that were occupied by nuns and children from the orphanage, and smiled as Frank and Albert ran up to her, stirring up the sand as they came to a halt and both boys hugged her around the legs. "Howdy, Miss Rachel. You going to come sit with us and watch the show?"

"Hello, y'all. Have you had fun today?" She eyed the nuns who were watching them with a small measure of disapproval.

"Oh, we did." Albert held up a small American flag. "We all gots these flags from one of the nice men on The Strand, and another nice lady, she boughts all of us lemonade and pickles."

"Come sit with us a spell, Miss Rachel." Frank looked up at her, his brown eyes beseeching her. "We done ate our supper, but Sister Mary, she says if we are real good we might get some ice cream when we gets back to the orphanage. Maybe you could come have ice cream with us."

Rachel looked down at her sweat-rumpled white shirt and her

dusty trousers. She could feel tendrils of hair sticking to her neck and knew her braid needed attention. She'd left her hat at home and her face felt tight with sunburn. The staunch nuns, their tall starched collars looking crisp even after a day in the sun, stood out in stark contrast to her own appearance. She knew she wasn't welcome there, and the nuns didn't appreciate her small amount of influence on the boys. "I appreciate the offer, boys, but I need to get going." She smiled sadly. "Maybe some other time."

"Awww." Frank's lower lip protruded in a pout. "We like you, Miss Rachel."

"Frank thinks you're pretty." Albert teased him.

"Do not!" He blurted back in embarrassment. "I mean, I..." He looked up at her, realizing what he had said. "You have nice eyes, Miss Rachel."

She blushed in spite of herself. "Thank you, Frank." She patted him on the shoulder. "Ladies always like nice compliments like that."

Frank beamed and stuck his tongue out at Albert.

"You'd better put that back in your mouth before one of the sisters takes your ice cream away." She chuckled as the pink tongue quickly disappeared. "Go on. And be good. You be nice to the sisters. They take good care of you, don't they?"

"Yes." Albert smiled at her adoringly. "They do. See you, Miss Rachel." He grabbed Frank's hand and they ran back across the sand to their group.

As she watched them go, the same sister who had been sitting on the porch the night the boys escaped looked at her and smiled. Rachel merely nodded her head in acknowledgement and continued on her way. Much later, she sat alone on the back of Mr. Gentry's boat, her feet dangling in the cool water. She nursed a half-full bottle of whiskey between puffs from a fat Cuban cigar that Billy had slipped to her earlier in the day.

As the first fireworks went off, she held up her bottle in a toast. "Here's to you, Mattie." She took a sip. "I hope you're enjoying the fireworks, wherever you are." She knew she was getting drunk, something she didn't do very often. She'd most likely sleep on the boat and wake up with a headache. *Well,* she mused fuzzily. *Maybe the headache will take my mind off the pain in my heart.*

Back on shore, Mattie jumped as a particularly loud explosion shook the ground, sending a flaming ball of light skyward, which burst into hundreds of bright sparkles. She felt Adam's arm around her, along with a rising lump in her throat. He'd talked more of wanting to start their family, and she knew there would be no holding him off for the nights remaining until he went back to Houston. She closed her eyes against the heavy ache in her chest, picturing a secluded summer beach, and a pair of warm steel blue eyes smiling down on her.

THE BOAT SAT a good way offshore near the end of the island, facing the beach area where the last crab boil had been held. If they looked very carefully through Mr. Gentry's magnifying scope, they could make out minute details of the post-holiday Saturday crab boil being set-up, and occasionally if the wind shifted just right, the smell of the cook fires wafted over the boat. Otherwise, to the naked eye the few people milling about on shore were no bigger than ants, with neither form nor detail.

It suited Rachel just fine, as she poised at the stern of the boat, flexing her leg and arm muscles and stretching out tall before she performed a high arcing dive into the water below. They had their privacy, but were still close enough to shore for the surprise that would come later. Mattie bobbed up and down in the water next to the boat, watching Rachel as she swam back to the little platform installed about a foot above water level at the back.

Rachel gave her a playful splash as she approached the platform. "Hey!" Mattie splashed back, watching in wicked delight as she spluttered the water out of her nose and mouth. She watched with a delight of a different kind, as long arms braced themselves, the muscles flexing nicely as Rachel hauled herself up onto the platform, turning and landing neatly on her behind.

She held out her arm invitingly. "Want a hand up?"

Mattie reached up and felt herself pulled partway out of the water, Rachel's hands grabbing her around the waist. An evil glint in the blue eyes told her of her mistake as Rachel laughed heartily and lifted her, tossing her back out into the water. "That'll teach you to splash me, you wench. Hey!"

Mattie surfaced right under her and before she could grab hold, felt a decided tug to both ankles, and she landed in the water herself. "Ha." Mattie laughed, backing out of reach and holding onto the platform. "Now, Rachel." Hazel eyes grew round as the evil grin reappeared, and Rachel snared her. "Remember. Oh." she felt a tickle at her ribs. "I just learned how to swim. You wouldn't want to drown me, would you? Ah—eeeee!" The tickle torture continued, gradually becoming more sensual strokes against her back and stomach. "Oh."

Full lips captured hers and she quite forgot the water, and the boat, and everything but the welcome warmth of Rachel's body in the water, pressing against her and lifting her until suddenly they were both stretched out on the wooden platform. "You wanna go back in the water, or stay right here with me?" Rachel smiled, her face mere inches above Mattie's. She watched Mattie's breathing catch as she caressed her face with the backs of her knuckles.

"Stay...here." Mattie got lost in a long sensual kiss, her body on fire yet again.

It was a beautiful day, with clear blue skies and hot temperatures, which made swimming in the cool salty water all the more enjoyable.

They had been teasing each other all afternoon, with gentle touches through their swimsuits, and occasional stroking of the bare skin of their backs, along with numerous kisses. In between, they had played with reckless abandon, swimming and fishing and laughing under the summer sun.

She had sketched several drawings of the boat, and of Rachel as she practiced her diving, enjoying the long clean lines of the lithe body as it arched and spun and leaped in mid-air. Now, as she felt Rachel's touches become more insistent, she longed not only to feel the broad muscular back, she wanted to see it as well. She remembered the day she had visited Rachel on the boat, and the way her muscles flexed in the sun while she worked hanging from the mast.

Suddenly, she had an idea, and wondered if she dared ask for what she wanted. She slowly broke away from the kiss, watching Rachel's chest rise and fall with uneven breaths. "Did you mean it, when you said we could do whatever I want?"

"Sure I did." Rachel's voice gentled, and she lifted Mattie's hand, kissing her palm on the inside. "What do you want, sweetheart?"

"I want to draw you from the back again." She watched twin brows furrow in question. "Up there on deck, with you climbed partway up the mast." One brow hiked up. "With your swimming top off." She giggled as both brows disappeared under Rachel's bangs.

"Whatever you wish." Rachel sat up and they both silently climbed the ladder. Mattie went up last, and she could swear Rachel's legs were shaking as she climbed ahead of her. Rachel padded over to the mast and looked over her shoulder, watching as Mattie took up her position on one of the benches bolted to the side of the boat, opening her sketchpad and resting it expectantly in her lap. When Mattie was settled, Rachel slowly drew her swimming top over her head and dropped it on the deck next to her. Keeping her back turned, she climbed up on the first set of rungs, her bare toes curling around them to hold on, as she reached up with her arms until she was supporting part of her weight with her upper body. "Like this?"

She was more beautiful than Mattie remembered, the afternoon sun burnishing the smooth skin to a golden color. Rivulets of water ran down her body and dripped on the deck below. Her biceps and corded forearms flexed, and the muscles all up and down Rachel's back stood out in the effort of holding on. Broad shoulders tapered to a trim waist, which flared back out slightly at the hips. Without the longer swimming top, the form-fitting bottoms revealed a nicely rounded behind, and Mattie realized that Rachel's buttocks and leg muscles were also flexed, her bare calves bulging below the hem of the swim suit bottoms. "Just like that."

Mattie licked her suddenly-dry lips and began to sketch, watching as Rachel's back muscles occasionally twitched, she assumed in the effort of holding herself up. She worked quickly, her fingers mapping out detail that was easier to capture, now that she had actually felt the subject she was working on. She finished the first sketch and stood, intent on moving to the side for a profile sketch, before she realized it would mean seeing Rachel's naked breasts. Not that she hadn't seen them when she was sick, but that was before...

"Are you too tired to stay up there for one more drawing?" Mattie moved in behind her, lightly touching her on the back, which caused an interesting reaction. Rachel was sweating, the light moisture beaded across her back, yet at Mattie's touch, goose bumps raced across her skin.

"I'm...good." Rachel's voice cracked and she gripped the mast rungs more solidly in her hands, hoping the sweat wouldn't cause her to slip.

"What if I draw you from the side this time?"

Rachel felt her nape hairs prickle pleasantly at the prospect, wondering where the game was leading.

"That would be fine." She closed her eyes as she felt Mattie move away from her, and kept them closed as she felt her nipples harden, knowing Mattie was watching her. She listened, hearing the scratch of Mattie's pencil against the rough paper. Overhead she heard a flock of seagulls fly by, their calls carrying on the wind well after they were past. The water slapped lightly against the sides of the slightly rocking boat, and a light breeze disturbed the ropes hanging from the masts. Underneath all of it Rachel's own blood pounded loudly in her ears.

"I'm all finished," she heard Mattie call out softly, and she opened her eyes, gathering her courage.

She stepped down to the deck and turned, exposing her front to Mattie, and heard her swallow audibly in reaction. "You want a front view?" Her voice was almost a whisper, and Mattie merely nodded, her hands shaking slightly as she sat back down and began to sketch the third drawing. Rachel quickly unbraided her hair, the damp locks spilling over her shoulders, then leaned back against the pole and rested her weight on one foot, drawing the other foot back and up against the pole, as she reached up and held onto the rungs just above her head, stretching her chest and torso out, making nice lines and curves to Mattie's visual delight.

It was hard to concentrate on the picture, and the infernal tremor in her fingers didn't help any. She looked up, sketching out Rachel's hair and face, the long lines of her arms, and the nice slope of her shoulders, then gradually began to shape the soft curves of her breasts, remembering the weight of them in her hands, and the ribbed cotton that had separated them from her skin. She thought to feign the need to touch in order to draw, but knew she simply wanted to touch Rachel, the drawing be damned.

She set the sketchpad aside and tucked the pencil against it so it wouldn't roll away, and stood, gliding as if in a dream toward Rachel, who didn't move as she approached. She drew close and realized Rachel's breathing was shallow, her nipples constantly hard since she had done the sketch from the side. *She's just as nervous as I am*, Mattie realized in wonder. "Can—can I...?"

She reached up, trailing her fingers along the soft curves, then grew bolder, cupping Rachel's breast and brushing her thumb over the nipple, watching more goose bumps dance across the tanned arms and the paler skin of her torso. Blue eyes slammed shut and Rachel made a noise deep in her throat, something between a squeak and a groan. It was an interesting sound, and Mattie moved to the other breast, hoping to hear it again. She wasn't disappointed. "Can't believe I've barely touched you, and you're all quivering."

"Oh, my darlin'." Rachel's arms dropped and she wrapped them around Mattie. "I beg to differ. You've been caressing me with your eyes ever since I took my top off. Before that even. Your eyes on me— it makes my skin burn."

"Burn?" Mattie's own knees were starting to grow weak, as Rachel hugged her tightly and found her lips, kissing her with a new and hungry fierceness that made her whole body want to feel those lips. "All I know is when I look at you, I ache all over."

"Shhh." Rachel moved away from her lips and kissed the top of her head. "Me, too."

"Is this what love feels like?" Mattie nuzzled the warm skin of Rachel's upper chest and burrowed further into the comforting hug. She wanted to stay there. She wanted more. She was dizzy with the deluge of emotions and sensations racing through her mind and body.

"I think so." Rachel pulled back, just enough to see her face. She watched as her own fingers reached out, and with a mind of their own, stroked Mattie's cheek, then drew her closer until their foreheads were touching. "I think so," she whispered, then tilted her head and brushed her lips against Mattie's again, this time with gentle promise and intent.

It was so soft, and she took her time, holding back the overwhelming desire to devour the warm mouth. She kissed Mattie, tentatively and slowly at first, then faster, with questioning nips, until Mattie opened up, and their souls merged in a kiss that left both of them breathless.

Rachel broke off, once again touching her forehead to Mattie's, while one hand wandered up the front of her swimming top, finding her breast with a soft sigh, mimicking the questing strokes that Mattie's own fingers had once again taken up against her skin. She closed her eyes and wondered if she could die from breathing too much. Then she quit breathing altogether as she felt Mattie take her hand and guide it under her swimming top.

She opened her eyes and slowly stroked Mattie's stomach,

gradually moving up until she reached her goal, feeling Mattie's breast in her hand, the taut nipple pressing against her palm in contrast to the firm softness, as she delicately played against Mattie's skin. She heard a small whimper and felt Mattie's ribs contract sharply. "Feel good?" She nibbled the sensitive skin of Mattie's neck, her voice burring into the younger woman's ear, as she stroked Mattie's sensitized skin, a slow motion from her stomach all the way back up to the perfectly-shaped breasts. "Is this what you wanted?"

"Y—yes." Mattie's own hands wandered freely, gliding up and down Rachel's back and down to her behind, then around and back up, pressing against her stomach as she sought contact. "P-partly." Rachel's touches moved from one breast to the other, and her free arm reached behind Mattie, pulling her close and pressing their bodies together.

Rachel felt her own ability to reason slipping away. It was the strongest sensation of her life, her need to touch and stroke driving her quickly to a place where there would be no turning back. Rachel groaned as Mattie's hands slipped upward, cupping her breasts again and making her entire body shake. "I..." her fingers moved higher, trailing along Mattie's jaw line. "I can't do this in half-measures, Mattie. We need to stop now, or..."

Two fingers pressed against her lips. "Or you can show me what two women can do together." Mattie's thumb traced a full lower lip, and she felt a tiny nip from Rachel's teeth. "I'm not afraid, Rachel. Show me," she whispered fiercely.

"Are you sure?" Rachel was close to not caring if Mattie was certain or not, and pulled away to regain her sanity, save her hands resting lightly on Mattie's hips. "What about Adam? I don't want to do anything you're going to regret tomorrow. Don't want you waking up and feeling like I led you to do something that goes against your morals."

"I—don't—care." She grasped Rachel's hand, and held it against her heart in a fist. "I don't love him. I never did. You know that. All I know is that when I'm with you, I am longing. Simply longing, and I don't even know what it is I want. It hurts, Rachel. It's the most lovely pain I've ever felt. When I look into your eyes, I feel more with a single glance than I've ever felt in the whole rest of my life. The only thing I'm afraid of is going through the rest of my life and never again feeling as much as I feel right now." She threaded her fingers through long chestnut locks and pulled Rachel's face within inches of her own. "With him I'm dead," she whispered. "With you I'm more alive than I ever dreamed possible."

Rachel's final defenses crumbled, and she pulled Mattie to her, kissing her fiercely, tasting and savoring the sweet mouth until she was certain both their lips were bruised. She moved away, kissing her way across Mattie's face, before ducking lower to sample her neck, greedily tasting the salty skin with light flicks of her tongue. Her fingers moved of their own accord, lifting the swimming top and drawing it over Mattie's head, tossing the top negligently to the side where it slid across the deck and stopped against the side of the boat. At last, Mattie stood before her, clad only in her split swimming skirt.

"You're beautiful." Rachel ran her flat palms up Mattie's stomach and cupped both breasts. "Beautiful." She wrapped her arms around the younger woman.

Mattie gasped as her breasts brushed against Rachel's stomach. Her entire being ached, and once again, she wasn't sure what could ever soothe it. Certainly nothing she and Adam had ever done had made her feel like she did at that moment. It was almost like a hunger, and she thought, fuzzily, as she felt Rachel reach around her, unbraiding her hair, that if she could somehow crawl inside Rachel's skin, that maybe then the ache would go away.

Her fingers unwittingly found the waistband of Rachel's swimming trunks, tugging anxiously at them as Rachel drew her close for another kiss. "You trying to take these off?" Rachel chuckled, a rich throaty sound that hummed against the skin of her neck.

"I don't know." Mattie felt Rachel's hands drop next to hers, and watched the long fingers quickly unbutton the bottoms, then reach to the sides, slipping them down until they dropped down Rachel's long legs. Rachel kicked them aside and her hands rested against her thighs as she looked at Mattie uncertainly.

She had seen Rachel unclothed before, but this was the first time Rachel was awake enough to watch her reaction, as she took in her naked body, her eyes roaming over tanned skin and firm muscles, then wandering over the curves of Rachel's breasts and hips. Normally steel blue eyes had taken on a much more vibrant hue, closer to navy blue, shining back at her with something she couldn't quite read. "You're beautiful, too," she commented shyly, her eyes drinking in soft-looking skin that begged to be touched, and inviting muscles that she wanted nothing more than to...

Rachel's fingers tangled in her hair and she crushed herself against the taller woman, drawing her face down for another kiss, which they became lost in. Her thoughts were at best sketchy, her mind racing along with her heartbeat, as she took in the sensations randomly. Rachel's lips, devouring her own, an insistently probing tongue parting her lips, then swirling with hers, causing her skin to tingle all over. She felt Rachel's hand against her lower back, gently stroking her bare skin. Then the hand slipped down and cupped her backside, squeezing it and pulling Mattie still closer. She realized a tickling sensation against her belly was Rachel's wiry patch of dark hair. Another squeeze of Rachel's hand brought them even closer, and she felt an odd wet sensation against her stomach as well.

Rachel slowly backed her toward the picnic blanket spread out on the deck, where they had shared their afternoon meal earlier in the day. She was vaguely glad they had already cleaned up the leftovers and packed everything away, leaving the blanket wide open for them, as she slowly lowered them down to the soft quilted material. Now that it was actually going to happen, or at least she hoped it was, she mentally banked the fire, allowing her mind and body to calm enough to have the discipline to take things slow and easy, and take the time with Mattie she deserved.

She knew it wasn't Mattie's first time, but it was the first time Mattie had been touched in love, of that much she was certain. She wanted it to be gentle and soft and wonderful, and wanted Mattie to feel safe and unashamed. Mattie lay stretched out on the quilt, her eyes at once trusting and shy. "You're blushing." Rachel lowered herself, stretching out on her side and tracing the dusting of pink along Mattie's cheeks. "Are you all right, so far?" She stroked the shiny red hair. "With what we're doing."

"Yes." Mattie's hands couldn't help but reach out, one coming to rest on a bare shoulder, while the other hesitantly brushed over an enticing breast, enjoying the view from the different angle, as Rachel hovered over her, her eyes shining warmly back at her.

Blue eyes fluttered closed for a moment, her entire body reacting to Mattie's touch. She realized, vaguely, that what was true for Mattie was true for her. The sensations were stronger than they'd ever been with Lil. With Lil, there was physical pleasure and friendly affection. With Mattie... She opened her eyes and found a pair of hazel eyes looking back at her, filled with wonder and something more. This was love. It made all the difference.

"I love you, Mattie." She dipped down, nibbling at the sensitive skin below a pink ear. "I want to show you just how much." She nibbled lower, across a collarbone and down. She paused and looked up at Mattie's face, then back down, and flicked her tongue over a brownish-pink nipple.

"Ahhh." Mattie's body arched up. "What are you doing?" It was heavenly and she wanted more.

Mischievous blue eyes peered back up. "Showing you what two women can do together." She flashed a fetching grin, then closed her lips around the nipple, sucking gently, while her other hand came up and traced the other neglected breast. Mattie's tiny whimpers of pleasure confirmed that what she was doing was more than acceptable, and she moved the hand from Mattie's breast, running it slowly down her flat stomach and across the top of her leg, before stroking up the inside of a surprisingly muscular thigh, at least what she could feel through Mattie's swimsuit-covered legs.

Rachel's mouth on her breast was quickly rendering Mattie incapable of intelligible thought. She thought she would die if she ever stopped. Nothing could feel as good as this, she was certain. A decided throbbing sensation settled between her legs, and she gasped with pleasure as she felt Rachel's fingers playing against her, the pulsing growing even stronger. Rachel shifted, and lightly straddled Mattie's left leg, keeping most of her weight off the younger woman.

Slowly, she slid one hand up Mattie's right leg, pushing the wide leg of the swimsuit up until her hand rested on Mattie's upper thigh, at the juncture of her hip. She stroked slowly and tenderly, moving inward, and felt Mattie's body grow tense. She stopped her hand and rose up on one elbow, seeing fear in the hazel eyes. "You want me to stop?"

"No." Mattie lowered her eyes. "Just—I'm afraid it might hurt is all."

Rachel forced down the surge of anger. It wasn't the time or place to invoke Adam's name. Instead she ducked her head, kissing Mattie until she felt her relax again. "I would never hurt you, Mattie." She tentatively stroked Mattie's upper leg again. "Never." Her fingers wandered lower, toward the soft skin of Mattie's inner thigh. "That doesn't hurt, does it?"

Mattie shook her head negatively, finding that quite the opposite was true. She didn't want the touches to ever stop, her body reacting strongly, wanting to feel Rachel touch her everywhere.

Rachel frowned, realizing she had one critical question to ask. "Has he hurt you recently, sweetheart?"

A tear squeezed out as Mattie closed her eyes and nodded affirmatively. Rachel quickly kissed the tear away, planting more kisses on Mattie's forehead. "I'll not touch you where he does. I promise you."

Mattie had already guessed at where Rachel's fingers might be headed and she opened her eyes wide in question. "But how can you...?"

"I don't need to." Rachel cupped her face reverently. "Do you trust me?"

"Yes." Mattie smiled, turning her head and kissing Rachel's hand.

"Good." Rachel's fingers played delicately against her skin. "Because I love you, Mattie, and I only want to touch you in ways that will make you feel good. Will you let me do that?"

"Yes," Mattie breathed against her skin, pulling her down for a long kiss, giving herself over to gentle hands and a warm heart, and relaxing into the knowing touches her body craved.

Occasionally, as Rachel moved, Mattie felt the odd wetness again, against her leg, on the bare skin just above her knee. She boldly reached down, touching Rachel's inner thigh, and felt more of the moisture there. She also felt Rachel stop completely for a long moment, a tiny gurgle erupting from the back of her throat as Mattie touched her. "You're all wet." Hazel eyes searched blue curiously.

"Yes." The word came out on a husky note. "Yes I am." Slowly,

Rachel shifted again and kissed her with great intensity, drawing it out, as she unbuttoned Mattie's split skirt, and slipped a hand inside. Her fingers trailed through soft curls and dipped between Mattie's legs, eliciting an almost silent whimper. "So are you." Rachel drew her fingers up and held them out for her inspection. "It's what happens when a woman feels desire." Her eyes were on fire and she tilted her head, a rakish smile gracing her lips. Her features softened as she traced Mattie's face. "And I've never desired anyone as much as I want you right now."

"Oh." Mattie blushed furiously.

"Sweetheart." Rachel cupped a bright red cheek. "There is nothing shameful about what you're feeling — what we're doing. I've only recently come to understand that. This is love, Mattie. God is love. God is perfect. This...is perfect."

"I never thought of it like that," Mattie's voice trembled.

"Can I take this off?" Rachel tugged at the waistband of the swimsuit.

"Yes." Mattie lifted her hips and felt the suddenly constrictive material slide away. A light breeze blew pleasantly across her bare body, right before Rachel lowered herself again, her skin gliding against Mattie's, causing her to cry out at the almost overwhelming sensation. She felt Rachel's lips at her breast, while her hand wandered up Mattie's oversensitized legs and slipped between them.

Rachel's skin continued to brush against her, at times feather-light and at others in a grinding motion, Mattie's body craving her lover's touch over every inch. She felt Rachel's lips against her ear, whispering quietly, while her fingers were drawing out strange new and powerful sensations. *And I thought it felt good when she touched my breasts.*

"Remember that ache?" Rachel nipped at her earlobe. "This is what your body wanted. Let me take you somewhere you've never been, Mattie." She kissed her soundly, then came up for air, studying Mattie's face as her fingers found their goal. She watched the hazel eyes grow wide, then slam shut at the pleasurable sensations.

"I think I shall die if you stop," Mattie gasped out, her eyes opening again partway.

Rachel chuckled. "Don't fight what you're feeling. Let your body do what it wants to do. I promise, it will be the greatest pleasure you've ever felt." Her own body reacted, hearing Mattie's breathing coming in short gasps, her hips moving against her in an age-old rhythm. Rachel lowered herself, partly covering Mattie's body, craving the feel of the younger woman's skin against her own. She found the ear once more, whispering comforting words, as Mattie cried out, finding sweet release at Rachel's gentle touch.

"Shhh." Rachel rolled to her back, pulling the smaller woman against her. "Shhh." She stroked Mattie's back in soothing circles. She felt Mattie's chest heaving and heard a tiny sniffle. "You're going to be fine."

"What...?" Mattie looked shyly up into her eyes, blinking away tears brought on by intense emotion. "What was that?"

"Did it feel good?" Rachel cupped her cheek, brushing away the tears with her thumb.

"Yes." Mattie turned her head and kissed the thumb.

"That was me loving you, Mattie." She felt the boat rocking them, and a lethargic peace creeping over her. As Mattie's cries had reached her ears, Rachel's own body had exploded in empathy, and she felt quite sated.

"I had no idea." Mattie rubbed Rachel's belly in idle circles, needing the continued skin on skin contact. "Never knew it could be like that."

"I want it to always be like that for you." Rachel kissed her head, and pulled the edge of the quilt over their sweat-dampened bodies, staving off a slight chill. She had no idea how long they'd been lying on the quilt, but somehow the sun had gone down without them noticing. A loud noise, like a cannon going off, made both of them jump, then hundreds of white lights streaked across the sky and sparkled as they fell to earth. "Oh." Rachel laughed quietly. "I forgot. Surprise."

It took a minute for it to register, then Mattie joined in her laughter. "More fireworks?"

"Yes." They watched another ball of light burst overhead. "One of the dockworkers helps run the Independence Day show each year, and he gets a crate of fireworks as part of the deal. He always brings them to the next crab boil and we get to have a second show."

"I thought watching fireworks with you would be romantic." Mattie snuggled up, resting her head against Rachel's shoulder. "I suspect it doesn't get any more romantic than this."

"I suspect you're right," Rachel agreed, wrapping her arms around her as they watched the remainder of the pyrotechnic display, after which they shared a bottle of wine, still cuddled up in the blanket together in a pleasant tangle of naked bodies. And much later, they explored one another some more, as they became acquainted in a new and wonderful way.

SUNDAY MORNING DAWNED in a pleasant haze of tangled limbs. "Don't go." Rachel pulled Mattie close, hugging her tightly and showering her face with kisses. "Just stay here with me."

"I have to." Mattie snuggled up, tucking the light blanket around both of us. "But not until later on today. Breakfast would be nice." She tweaked Rachel's nose. "Although that means one of us, namely you, would have to get dressed and go downstairs and get it for us."

"Oh, all right." Rachel mock sighed. "If I must." She kissed Mattie quickly, then rolled away, slipping out of bed and across the room to retrieve her clothing. "See, if you lived here with me, we could take turns fetching breakfast. Wouldn't have to sneak you in and out of here."

"If I lived here with you, I can assure you we would not survive the scandal." It was out before she thought about how it sounded, and she regretfully watched the smile disappear from Rachel's face. "I'm sorry." She stood and sidled up to her, hugging Rachel from behind. "We'll find a way. We will. I can't just up and move out on Adam. He'd come kill both of us. We need to talk about this, don't we?"

"Nothing to talk about." Rachel pouted. "You and I pack up our belongings and move away from here. End of story."

"It's not that simple," Mattie fretted. They'd left the boat around midnight and ended up back in Rachel's room, where they'd spent the remainder of the night in relative bliss, although they had lapsed into one argument about the future, which had quickly passed. She sorely hoped to get back to the bliss and leave the arguments for another day. "Thought you said you'd give me as much time as I need." She felt the tears coming and swiped her hand across her eyes in frustration. "This is all new to me. I need some time to let it simmer. I'm feeling a little overwhelmed."

"Are you sorry about what we've been doing?" From the tone of her voice, it was obvious Rachel's usual confidence was more than a little shaken.

"No." Mattie hugged her more tightly and felt Rachel turn so they were face to face. She burrowed into her, drawing in the familiar clean scent of bay rum. "I've never been happier, than when I'm with you. I never dreamed I could feel this good." She kissed the hollow of Rachel's throat, and felt long fingers combing through her hair.

"Good." Rachel nuzzled Mattie's hair. "Because I've been waiting my entire life to be as happy as I am with you. I just didn't know it."

"But it's difficult." Mattie drew her over to the bed where they both sat down, facing each other and crossing their legs. She reached out and took Rachel's hands in her own as she spoke. "If we are going to do anything at all, we need to plan very carefully. Where we would go. How we would get there. When we would leave. How we would live after we get wherever we go. What can we take with us of what we have now."

"I guess it is a bit more complicated than packing a carpetbag and leaving, isn't it?" Rachel sighed, the reality of their situation setting in.

"It is." Mattie chaffed the hands she held. "I'm not saying it can't be done. I still need time to think. I never even considered the possibility of spending my life with another woman until the last month or so." She watched Rachel lower her head, chestnut bangs hiding her downcast eyes. "Not that spending my life with you doesn't sound very appealing."

A timid smile appeared, and Rachel looked hesitantly up, her eyes full of hope. "Until a month or so ago, I figured I would be living alone for the rest of my life." She scooted closer, until their foreheads were almost touching. "I'm sorry I've acted impatiently toward you. I guess I know what I want, and I'm hoping you want the same thing."

"I think I do." Mattie bit her lower lip and continued to brush her thumbs back and forth over the top of Rachel's hands, admiring the combination of softness and strength. "But I don't think we can up and have that tomorrow. I'd like to spend some more weekends together." She blushed, a warm soft pink dusting of color that spread slowly across her cheeks. "Could I have some time to get used to this — to us — before we do anything further? We can keep talking about it, and start planning."

"I meant it when I said we can do whatever you want." Rachel leaned over and kissed her cheeks, first one and then the other. "I do want more time with you." Her eyes grew stormy — a vibrant gray with tiny blue flecks of color dancing on the surface. "I hate the thought of you being with him. After we...just makes my blood boil thinking about it."

"I can't refuse him completely." Mattie's voice edged on despair. "Not without incurring his wrath. Especially with him thinking we're going to start a family. I must at least pretend to go along with that notion. Otherwise my life would become a living hell, more than it already is."

"I know." Rachel was trembling inside. In a very short time she'd come to feel a new emotion — a proprietary protectiveness of Mattie that was much fiercer than anything she had felt with any of her friends or family, even Lillie. "I hate that he hurts you. Hate that he hits you, and the horrible things he says to you. I can't help feeling the way I do. You're warm and bright and beautiful. I can't believe I ever won your friendship, much less anything more. The thought that anyone would hurt you—"

"Shhh." Mattie gently covered her mouth with her hand, then pulled Rachel's head to her shoulder, holding her and rocking back and forth. "I do believe you're my savior, Rachel Travis. All my life, no one has ever come to my defense, even my mother and father. You're the only one who ever cared about how I feel or what I want. The only one."

"I love you," a soft, almost shy voice answered.

"I love you too," Mattie kissed her on the head, then shifted as Rachel looked up, capturing her first with her eyes and then with her lips.

"Mmm." Rachel deepened the kiss and slowly stretched out, bringing Mattie down with her and slipping a hand inside her nightgown, feeling warm skin and muscles that fluttered at her touch. Her own body trembled, as Mattie's hand stroked up her inner thigh, and she shifted, giving the inquisitive hand more room to explore. "I love the way you touch me," she breathed against Mattie's skin.

Mattie laughed softly, her touches becoming much more intense, as for a short while, breakfast, and the future, and everything else but each other, was forgotten.

THE MID-SUMMER DOLDRUMS set in, and business at the tailor shop tapered off. Mr. and Mrs. Vaughan assured Mattie there was no need to worry, that things would pick up later in August, a few weeks before school began for the fall term. For the time being, beginning the week after the Independence Day holiday, Mattie's hours were cut back to half days, leaving her free to go home at the noon hour.

Monday at precisely noon, she politely wished her employer a good afternoon, and made her way down Main Street to the general store. She absently checked off odds and ends on a shopping list, restocking her supply of sugar, flour, and a box of charcoals for her drawings. She smiled as she passed a shelf bearing toilette articles, including a bottle of fresh-smelling bay rum. She picked up the ceramic canister and uncapped it, inhaling deeply and closing her eyes. She could almost feel Rachel's arms around her, her soft skin brushing against her own, and Rachel's distinct scent enveloping her.

She knew very little of the world, having seen El Paso, Houston, and Galveston, and every train stop between the three towns. A part of her missed the stark dry deserts and hills surrounding El Paso, but another part of her had come to love the Gulf of Mexico and the pale brown sand beaches, the rustling sea grasses and the beautiful shells, along with the invigorating scent of the ocean water. Despite her miserable marriage, Galveston had become home, perhaps because of Rachel, and perhaps because it would always be the place where, for the very first time, she dared to hope she could live her life as she pleased, and not as others directed her to. She tried to imagine where, in all the world, she and Rachel might go where they could be together and out of Adam's grasp. She was certain they would have to go somewhere very far away, and that they would have to leave by darkness of night some weekend when Adam was in Houston.

Even then, she wondered if he would find her. He was relentless that way, when he felt something belonged to him, and she understood all too well that to Adam she was his property. His, to show off in public, and to be at his beck and call as he saw fit. Her leaving with Rachel, if he were to find out, would infuriate him. She feared that her and Rachel disappearing at the same time would rouse his suspicion, even though she was fairly certain he believed the only time she had ever spent with Rachel was at the clambake back in the spring, and as her tailor at the shop.

She placed the cork back in the bay rum canister and set it carefully on the shelf and moved quickly down the aisle to sign for her purchases. Leaving the store, she stepped out into the hot dusty road and briefly peered toward the port just out of sight behind the buildings of the downtown area. Rachel was out at sea fishing, so they could not eat dinner together, although she had left a short note for Mattie, tucked inside her sewing machine drawer, just like the first note. She pulled it from her skirt pocket and unfolded it, smiling. Rachel had simply drawn a heart and carefully printed Mattie's name in the middle, in even block letters. She kissed the note and slipped it back in her pocket, and began wandering toward the trolley, bound for home.

Home.

She shivered, despite the heat. It was a house, not a home. Home, she realized, should be a place filled with love. She knew she had some very nice things, and fine clothing, and never wanted for food, or shelter from the elements. Her lifestyle, on the surface, was much more elaborate than Rachel's, yet she'd never felt more at home than in Rachel's small room, amid its sparse furnishings, and the comfort she found in Rachel's arms was the first true comfort she'd ever had.

Impulsively, she decided to walk home, and raised her parasol against the white-hot sun. The sky was a thin blue color, devoid of clouds, and as she reached the beachfront road, the Gulf sparkled like emeralds. Heat shimmered off the broiling sand, which burned slightly, even through her sturdy shoes and well-knit stockings. She could feel the scant ocean breeze against the sweat on her neck and forehead, and she longed to be swimming in the cool water.

When she reached the house, she settled instead for a tepid bath and a liberal dusting of talcum powder. She donned her lightest housedress, a simple yellow gingham frock, which left her neck more exposed than the traditional Gibson girl shirtwaists she typically wore, with their proper high collars. The dress had sleeves that belled slightly at the wrists to allow more air to circulate, and she wore only one plain petticoat beneath it, choosing to leave her feet bare for the time being.

She picked up her sketchpad and flipped through its pages, which had become a chronicle of her time spent with Rachel. She smiled at the drawing from their very first meeting, chuckled at the one of the tall woman frolicking in the shallow waves, and felt her stomach flutter pleasantly inside at some of the more intimate portraits, the first one of Rachel sitting with her bare back turned toward her in her bedroom, and the series from their time together on the boat only two days before.

She couldn't believe it had only been two days. In that very short time, her view of what life could be had changed irrevocably, and her heart hurt at the thought of the sham that was her marriage. She knew she should probably go to confession for the things she had done, yet couldn't find it within herself to feel guilty about any of it. She loved Rachel and Rachel loved her. Rachel had said it herself, "God is love." If God was love and she loved Rachel, then surely there must be something divine in what they shared.

She wondered which laws were more honorable to God, the laws of man, or the love that now governed her own heart. More importantly, was there an honorable and legal way to end her marriage? She knew women had run away from marriages before without legally ending them. Did she truly have it in herself to run away, even if it meant there would always be a piece of paper out there legally tying her to Adam? Did the piece of paper matter? She had some difficult decisions to make, and her head was beginning to hurt thinking about it.

A solid knock at the front door surprised her so much that her heart skipped a beat. She set aside the sketchpad, and reached up to smooth her hair off her face as she made her way into the parlor and cautiously opened the door.

Three strange men stood on the porch, their eyes and faces very serious. They each had a pistol holstered at the hip, and she wished she'd had the forethought to get her own pistol before answering the door to strangers. "May I help you?" She heard the slight tremor in her own voice and cleared her throat nervously.

"Is Adam Crockett at home?" The tall man in the middle asked. He stood ramrod straight with his arms tucked behind his back. He wore a starched white shirt, a black string tie, plain black trousers, and black cowboy boots that were polished to a dull gleam.

"No." She eyed him curiously. "What do you want with him?"

"We're federal marshals, ma'am," he folded back his coat lapel to reveal a shiny silver badge. "We wanted to ask him a few questions. Would you be..." He fished a piece of paper out of his pocket and glanced at it. "Madeleine Crockett?"

"I am." She swallowed, willing down a wave of fear. "Would you like to come in?"

"No, Ma'am." The same man answered, and Mattie wondered if the others were incapable of speech. "When do you expect your husband back home?"

"I'm not sure." It was a small fib. She expected him home the next day. She just didn't know exactly what time the next day. "He's away on a business trip."

"Where did he go, Mrs. Crockett?" The same man persisted, relaxing his posture just a bit in an effort to appear friendlier.

"Oh," she answered blithely, "I'm not privy to his business affairs." She smiled her most charming smile. "I've not much interest in such matters."

The marshal smiled in kind, and retrieved a small scrap of paper and a stub of a pencil from his pocket. He scribbled out something and handed it to her. "Here's my room number at the Tremont Hotel. We'll be here another day, so if he comes home before tomorrow evening, would you ask him to come see me? Otherwise we should be back this way in two months, after we tend to some business in New Orleans."

"Yes, sir." She lay the scrap on a side table and looked back at him expectantly.

"Thank you, Mrs. Crockett." The man tipped his hat, and his silent companions did the same, before turning and stepping off the porch and walking back toward the road behind the house.

Mattie watched them until they were out of sight, then closed the door and leaned against it until her heart quit pounding. She picked up the piece of paper, studying it thoughtfully. "What has Adam gotten himself into?"

Chapter
Eight

A SOFT KNOCK at the door drew Rachel's nose out of her reader. She sighed and set the book aside, clipping the top of the page with one of Mattie's hairpins. She was making great progress; so much so that Mattie said they might want to start concentrating more on writing skills than reading. "Now who could that be at this hour?" she muttered, as she swung her long legs over the side of the bed and made her way to the door, opening it a crack and peering out. A huge smile involuntarily lit up her face. "Mattie?" She opened the door wide, drawing her inside. "What a surprise. Although it's a very nice one." She stopped, studying Mattie's drawn features. "What's wrong?"

Mattie handed her a large round paper bundle tied up with thick twine. "Partly, I wanted you to take these for safekeeping." She bit her lower lip and looked down at her feet. "They're all my drawings of you, and a few of the pastels I've worked on. I decided it might not be safe to keep them at my house anymore. There are too many of them at this point."

"Certainly." Rachel placed the bundle on the bed and took Mattie's hands. "I can do that, but you still haven't told me what's wrong."

"Some federal marshals came by the house this afternoon, looking for Adam." Mattie looked up, the fear evident in her eyes. "They wouldn't say exactly what they wanted, only that they wanted to talk to him and would be back around in two months. They were on their way to New Orleans. I'm afraid, Rachel. I lied and told them I don't know where Adam is. What if he's in some serious trouble? What if it involves me somehow? Do you think I should tell him they came by? He'll be home sometime tomorrow."

"First of all, you've done nothing wrong. If Adam is in trouble, it's something of his own doing that shouldn't involve you, I wouldn't think." Rachel guided her over to the bed and sat down, pulling Mattie down next to her. "As for telling him, you have to decide what's best for you. If they do take two months to come back around, maybe you won't even be with him by then." She looked earnestly at Mattie, every fiber of her body urging her to consider taking off with her before two months were up.

"Maybe." Mattie offered her a trembling half-smile. "But if something happens and they come back sooner than they said they would, Adam would probably kill me if he knew I knew they were looking for him and didn't tell him. Rachel," she drew in a deep breath, releasing it slowly, "the last time he got into trouble, he packed me up and moved me here. He didn't even tell me why we were moving. Just came home one day and started packing up our belongings and told me we were leaving."

"What if he does that again?" Rachel shifted, facing her and taking her hands again. "What if he wants to pick up and move in the middle of the night? What if he takes you away?"

"I've thought about that already." Mattie scooted closer, and reached out with one hand, touching Rachel's face, idly rearranging some errant locks of hair around her eyes. "If I do tell him, I'll do it while he's driving me to the tailor's, on a day when he's leaving for Houston. I can pull it off innocently enough, pretend it slipped my mind that they came by, or act like I didn't realize it was important. He seems to get less angry when I feign ignorance, for some reason. That way he'll have a few days to brood over it before he does anything, and it would give me a few days to make some arrangements if I need to."

"And what if he does decide to run?" Rachel grasped her hand and held it against her own cheek. "How will you keep him from making you go with him?"

"I-I have a gun." Mattie watched Rachel's jaw drop. "I know. Not what you would expect of me. It's just a small revolver, but I do know how to use it, very well, actually. I have it with me nearly all the time, in my pocket book. Adam doesn't know about it. If he tries to make me go away with him, I'll threaten him—do whatever I have to do, to get away from him."

"You can't kill him." Rachel placed her hands on Mattie's shoulders, squeezing them to emphasize her point. "You're his wife. There is no defense for shooting your husband because he wanted to move away. They'd hang you."

"I wouldn't kill him. Just threaten him, as I said. I think I can use the gun effectively enough to make him believe I mean business. I could probably shoot his hat right off his head without disturbing a hair on it." She smiled at Rachel's wide-eyed reaction. "Hopefully it won't come to that. But if I do have to run from him, I'll most likely come running to you. I don't know where else I'd go, unless I ran home to El Paso, and he'd probably just come after me if I were to do that."

"You run to me anytime you feel the need to." Rachel pulled her into a hug, rocking her back and forth. "I wish you'd run to me and just stay here, but you already know that." She kissed Mattie's head and continued to hold her. "I wish you could stay here tonight."

"So do I," Mattie murmured against a patch of warm soft skin. She felt her worries receding, replaced by comforting warmth, and Rachel's slightly sweaty, slightly spicy scent. She was wearing a white ribbed sleeveless undershirt and lightweight tan trousers. Mattie wrapped one arm firmly around Rachel's body, while one hand ran lightly up and down the curve of a solid upper arm. Solid. That was a good word for Rachel in general. She was dependable and she always seemed to keep her wits about her, logically thinking through each situation as she faced it. "I'd best get back home sometime tonight, though. Adam occasionally takes the morning train home."

"But you can stay here for a little while, can't you?" Rachel ducked her head, lightly kissing Mattie's lips. "I missed you today, something fierce. Billy kept teasing me. I couldn't concentrate on fishing to save my life. He was almost as bad. Seems he spent a good part of his weekend with Lil."

"Truly?" Mattie closed her eyes as Rachel's lips moved lower, nibbling the sensitive skin just below her ear. "They're both nice people. They deserve to be happy. Oh."

"Oh?" Rachel chuckled, her voice burring against Mattie's shoulder, taking advantage of the lower neckline of her dress. "Was that a good 'oh' or a bad one?"

"A good one," Mattie's own hands began to wander, tugging at Rachel's undershirt until it was free of her waistband. "We shouldn't..."

"I know." Rachel found her lips again for a long moment. "I need to let you go home in a little while. I can hardly help it. Feels so good when you're in my arms."

"I like being in your arms." Mattie felt herself being lowered down onto the soft mattress. "But maybe we'd best keep our clothing on, just to be on the safe side. I'd hate to get carried away and fall asleep afterward."

"All our clothing?" Rachel's undershirt was halfway up her torso, and she smiled as Mattie blushed and hastily pulled it back down.

"I'm sorry." She buried her face into Rachel's shoulder.

"Don't ever be sorry about this, Mattie." Rachel kissed her, getting lost in the sensation of Mattie's body moving against her own. After a long while, she reluctantly came up for air, feeling Mattie's head settle against her upper chest as she wrapped one arm around Rachel's stomach. She frowned, realizing she'd allowed herself to get distracted from helping Mattie with a very real problem. "Do you have any idea what kind of business Adam engages in when he goes to Houston, besides gambling?"

"I used to think he was in banking." Mattie rubbed random circles against Rachel's stomach with the flat of her hand. "It's what he did in El Paso, at his father's bank. But those papers I found in his desk—he had to leave because of some sort of problem there. I think he may have taken some money from his father or from the bank itself."

"But you don't think that anymore?" Rachel stroked Mattie's hair, enjoying the silky sensation against her fingertips.

"No." Mattie rolled over, resting her chin on Rachel's collarbone. "I sometimes think all he does is gamble, that perhaps our living is made off his winnings. But during the Independence Day celebration, I heard snippets of conversation between him and some of his business associates. They are in some sort of trade, I think, although I have no idea what sort of goods they might be trading. Cotton, maybe, since we have the mill here."

"Maybe," Rachel agreed with her, her voice thoughtful. "I only deal on the end where we ship the cotton out, so I have no idea who works on the other end of that. The business owners don't generally come down to the docks. They leave the physical aspect of loading the boats to the port bosses. I could nose around, ask some questions."

"That would be wonderful, if you could manage it without getting in trouble." Mattie's fingertips brushed lightly back and forth over Rachel's upper chest, causing tiny pleasant internal shivers in Rachel's gut.

"That's nice," Rachel commented with a smile.

Mattie smiled back and peppered her skin with a series of kisses, before resuming her tracing, her chin back against her collarbone. "If I knew what Adam does for a living, it might help me decide what to do about those marshals. But I can't wait very long before I tell him."

"I'll ask around tomorrow, see what I can find out." Rachel grasped Mattie's waist, drawing her up and forward, and engaging her in another lengthy kiss. She broke off and studied hazel eyes at close range, observing the warm affection and deep passion there, and suddenly realized she was the object of all that. "I love you, Mattie."

"Love you too," Mattie answered shyly. "Never thought I'd get the chance to love someone, not after..." She stopped, unable to speak his name. "Anyway, I kept wanting to pinch myself today. Couldn't believe my good fortune. No matter what happens, I know what it is to love someone, and to be loved in return." Her voice wavered and she swallowed.

"And no matter what happens, I'm never going to stop loving you." Rachel hugged her tightly. "You can depend on that. It's not something I'll take away. I'm not like him." She averted her gaze, feeling her chin tilted back toward Mattie.

"Not even close." Mattie held her gaze, watching until Rachel's eyes shone with unshed tears. "Not even close." She kissed her intently. "I'd best be going."

"I'm going to walk you home." Rachel sat up, bringing Mattie up with her. "Don't want you out alone in the dark trying to hitch a ride. "Better yet, I'll take you on my bicycle. How'd you like that?"

"That would be fun." Mattie smiled. "We haven't ridden it in a while."

"Very well then." Rachel quickly tugged on her boots and a shirt, buttoning it up and tucking it into her trousers. "My lady, your two-wheeled carriage awaits you." She motioned Mattie out of the room with a flourish, and soon they were riding down the road, laughing merrily as a blanket of stars twinkled overhead.

AS THEY PULLED up to the house, Mattie's thoughts grew somber, and she shivered unconsciously. Rachel slowed the bicycle, and stepped down, straddling it to balance it until Mattie could slide down to the ground. She watched as Mattie crossed her arms over her chest, facing out toward the Gulf, as a light breeze blew back the loose tendrils of hair around her face. Silvery moonlight shone down, illuminating her pale freckled skin and burnishing her hair with copper highlights. She was breathtaking.

"Mattie?" Rachel propped the bicycle against the porch and stepped closer, moving in behind her and reaching out hesitantly, touching Mattie's shoulders. She felt the smaller body melt back against her, and she wrapped her arms around Mattie, resting her chin on her head. "What's wrong?"

"I used to like it when I was home alone without him," Mattie mused quietly. "Now when I'm alone it only makes me wish I was with you." She looked up and over her shoulder, and smiled. "I was just wishing you could stay with me tonight. We could get up early, give you plenty of time to leave before he comes home, even if he were to take the early train home."

A dozen emotions tore at Rachel's heart, and a part of her was sorely tempted. Pride and common sense won out, however. It would feel wrong and she knew it would probably hurt things more than it would help between them. "I won't sleep in his house." It was the one place she had to draw the line when it came to Mattie. "Not in the bed you share with him." Her chest felt tight and her throat constricted. "I can't," she whispered. "I'm sorry. I love you, but I can't."

"I know." Mattie wrapped her arms around Rachel's, hugging them to her tightly against her stomach. It occurred to her that she had never desired to be that physically close to anyone before. Now her body craved Rachel's touch, and the closeness they shared, not just on a physical level, but on an emotional one as well. "I don't suppose the sofa..." A faint negative nod of Rachel's head was her answer. "I didn't think so. But you could stay with me for a little while, couldn't you?"

"As if I could leave you." Rachel smiled, and kissed her on the cheek. "Maybe we could go for a walk on the beach."

"Maybe we could take a blanket down to the dock and sit together for a spell." Mattie turned in her arms and batted her eyelashes fetchingly. The dark head nodded in agreement, and soon they were walking hand in hand toward the dock Rachel had been sitting on the morning they met.

Rachel took the blanket and fluffed it out, spreading it over the weathered boards, and took Mattie's hand, tugging her down on the blanket with her. They removed their shoes and dangled their feet in the refreshing water, feeling the waves lap at their legs as they held each other close, wordlessly watching the moonlight shimmering on the surface of the Gulf further out.

They became acutely aware of each other's breathing, and Rachel turned her head, nuzzling Mattie's hair, then moved lower, brushing her face against Mattie's neck before planting butterfly kisses on the tempting soft skin. Rachel knew she was lost, that there would be no going back from what they had started. In a few short days they had bonded well beyond anything that could be described as merely friendship. She would love Mattie forever. Mattie owned her, heart, body, and soul.

"What are we going to do?" Mattie stroked Rachel's stomach, as much for her own comfort as Rachel's. She felt tense muscles relax under her touch, and she gently pecked Rachel on the shoulder, inhaling her cottony-clean scent in the process.

"I'll do whatever you want to." Rachel blew out a frustrated breath. "I'd leave with you tonight if you wanted that. I'm waiting for you to decide."

"I know, and it isn't fair to you, to keep you in suspense like that." Mattie took Rachel's hand, twining their fingers.

Rachel reached up, tracing full lips with her thumb, then moved to stroke a downy soft cheek. "I'll wait for you forever, as long as you give me hope. There is still hope, isn't there?" She looked away, at the sprinkling of stars overhead, her throat moving in an audible swallow. She was suddenly unsure of herself, afraid that the dream had come true much too easily. She could hear her own breathing in her ears, waiting for an answer she almost dreaded.

Mattie shifted, sliding up, planting soft kisses at Rachel's jaw line. "There's always hope." She cupped Rachel's face, turning it back toward her. "Don't ever give up on me, Rachel. Please?" Her eyes brimmed with unshed tears and she blinked, sending a scattering of them down her face and onto Rachel's shirt. She ducked her head, feeling Rachel's fingers brushing them off her face.

"Don't cry." She realized that if she was feeling unsure of herself, Mattie must surely feel as if she were drowning. *I taught her how to swim in the ocean,* she mused. *It must be up to me to teach her how to swim these waters as well.* "No matter how frightened you are, sweetheart, no matter how uncertain you are, no matter what you decide you have to do, I'll always be here for you. You can count on me, Mattie. I promise you that. You've got some decisions to make. I'll admit I wish things were settled between us, but something is holding you back. I suspect it's your fear of Adam, am I correct?"

"Yes." Mattie bit her lower lip, her eyes hesitant as they met Rachel's. "Mostly. I'm afraid he'll find us, no matter where we go — afraid he'll kill you if he ever finds out about us. I could never forgive myself if anything bad happened to you."

"First of all, I can take care of myself." Rachel combed her fingers through Mattie's hair. "He caught me off guard once, but it won't happen again. I'm much more aware of my surroundings at all times. If we go away together, I'll find us somewhere so far from him, he'll give up before he finds us. We can go to Mexico, or Canada, or Europe, if we have to."

"That's where the 'mostly' part comes in." Mattie closed her eyes and dropped her head, afraid of the repercussions of her thoughts. "It frightens me to think of moving so far away. A part of me wants so very much to share my life with you. Another part of me is terrified. I suppose it doesn't make much sense. It's not as if I have many friends here. My family isn't here. I feel as if..." She struggled for words, her heart warring with itself. "As if moving so far away, I might get swallowed up, that I'll never see home again, or my sister. I want to be with you. I do. But it isn't fair to you for me to do anything until I'm absolutely certain it's a decision I can live with. Once we leave here, I have a feeling there will be no coming back. I know you're willing to give up everything for me. No one has ever sacrificed anything for me. Being cared for so deeply, it feels wonderful and frightening all at the same time. And it makes me feel selfish that I'm not as certain about all this as you are."

"Don't feel that way." Rachel drew her head down and kissed it. "I meant it. I don't want you to do anything you're unsure of. If the day comes when you can't be with me, like this..." she gestured at their closeness, and smiled half-heartedly, "I don't ever want to lose your friendship. It would hurt, for a while, I think, because I love you deeply. I'll not lie to you. I want to build a life with you, and I don't much care where we do that, as long as we can be safe and happy together. I very much enjoyed the things we did this past weekend." She smiled warmly then, allowing her eyes to speak for her. "But I do fear it will make me crazy if we don't move one way or the other, eventually, either toward sharing our life under the same roof, or back to our friendship without the physical intimacy we've shared."

"Why?" Mattie's eyes flashed, almost in anger, and she consciously softened her voice. "Isn't that what you've had with Lillie for many years? Why can't you be happy with that with me? At least for a little while?"

"I might could, for a very short while. But it isn't the same. Lil and I — we shared friendship, and affection. I've never been in love with Lil. I recently walked away from that part of my life, rather easily, I might add. I'll always care for Lil, and be her friend, but it's caused very little emotional consequence to either of us to give up the physical aspect of our friendship." She sat partway up, resting her weight on one forearm, while holding on to Mattie with the other. "Is that what you want? Something that means so little to me that I could walk away from it just like that?"

"N-no." Mattie flopped down on her back, covering her face with one arm.

"Good." Rachel hovered over her, softly stroking her hair in comfort. "Because I don't think I can walk away from this. I need you in my life, one way or the other, but I don't think I could settle for anything in the middle. I hope that makes sense."

"It does." Mattie moved her arm up, peeking timidly at the beloved face over her. She saw so much in Rachel's eyes—love, fear, pain, patience. She couldn't remember invoking that much in anyone before, and it warmed her all over. "I do love you, Rachel. That much I'm sure of."

"I waited so long to hear you say that to me." Rachel smiled, willing away her own fear for the time being. "And it give me hope." She bent down, tenderly brushing her lips against Mattie's. "I'd best go home. I have a feeling it's near midnight, and I need to be at the docks tomorrow at dawn. I'll be unloading some boats tomorrow— couple of freighters coming in from New York with goods for some of the stores. I should be able to ask around about who the cotton traders are during the noon hour. There are several folks I trust enough to ask without them prying into why I want the information."

"Oh." Mattie sat up. "I'd almost forgotten all about that. You took my mind right off it." She smiled and ran her hand up and down Rachel's arm. "I'll not tell Adam about the marshals' visit until I hear from you. If he's dealing in something truly bad, I'll have to decide what to do about that. Turn him in, tell him they're looking for him, or run like the dickens."

"I'd settle for turning him in and running like the dickens," Rachel replied, her face somber with worry.

Mattie looked deeply into Rachel's eyes, seeing her frustration and fear, and she moved closer, kissing a tanned cheek. She felt two arms close around her, and melted into the embrace, laying her head against Rachel's chest and inhaling deeply, imprinting her warm exotic scent in her mind. "You have a natural perfume." She nuzzled salty skin. "Draws me in like a bee to honey."

"It's not perfume." Rachel wrapped her arms more tightly around her. "It's the scent a woman gives off when she's aroused. You have your own special scent, too."

Two shocked eyes peered up at her before Mattie buried her face into Rachel's shoulder in embarrassment. "I do?"

"Yes, and it makes me crazy, in a good way." Rachel pecked her on the forehead, unwilling to break away from the warmth that enveloped both of them. "Can't seem to tear myself away from you," she mumbled.

"Some day, you won't have to leave me," Mattie vowed, looking up and pulling Rachel down for one last promising kiss.

"And I hope that day isn't too far in the future." Rachel took her hand and led her back to the house. The moon was high in the sky and much smaller than it had been earlier. They paused in front of the house and hugged each other as if for dear life, finally breaking apart. "I love you, Mattie. Hold on to that."

Mattie merely nodded and watched as she mounted her bicycle and pedaled up to the road and around a dune into the night. She sighed heavily and entered the house. It was indeed almost midnight, but she drew herself a bath and spent another hour soaking in the tepid water, rinsing off the sand and salt from the dock, and contemplating her options.

THE ROOM SEEMED empty, and much too quiet, as Rachel entered it and switched on the bedside lamp. She very much understood how Mattie felt when she went home to her empty house. When she left Fort Worth, she had relished being alone. It was a novelty after spending her childhood in the company of all her siblings. Now, she longed to have Mattie in her arms.

She was giddy from their time on the dock, and knew sleep would be long in coming to her. After a quick trip down the hall to the water closet, where she washed her face and brushed her teeth, she returned to the room and stripped down to her bloomers and undershirt. She carefully hung up her trousers and smiled as she caught a whiff of Mattie's toilet water on her shirt. She held it up to her face and inhaled, closing her eyes in pleasant memory before she reluctantly placed the shirt on its hanger. She closed the armoire door and turned, spying the wrapped up bundle on the bed, the crisp paper catching the lamp light.

She had seen some of Mattie's drawings of her, but apparently not all of them, judging from the thickness of the bundle. Curious, she sat down and untied the thick twine that bound the papers, and carefully unrolled the drawings to avoid smudging or wrinkling them. The first few she had seen—a drawing from their first meeting, the one of her bared back from earlier on, and some from one of their picnics on the beach. There were many more she hadn't seen. Ones Mattie had obviously drawn from memory when Rachel wasn't around to pose.

She smiled at a few, in which Mattie had drawn herself into the scene. In most of the drawings of them together, they were either holding hands or else Rachel had her arm around Mattie's waist. All of them were beach scenes, with the ocean crashing in the background, or the sand dunes rising behind them.

Rachel's heart skipped a beat when she came to the drawings from their time on the boat. She had seen the longing in Mattie's eyes. What she wasn't prepared for was how well Mattie had captured the fire burning in her own eyes. Had she truly been looking upon Mattie with such open desire? She had certainly felt it. And how often had she looked at Mattie like that prior to their time together on the boat? She appeared almost as a starved thing, her eyes at once desirous and begging. Mattie had managed to capture that. It was a wonder Mattie hadn't melted into a puddle under such an intense gaze.

She moved her attention from her face to the rest of her body, studying it with a critical eye. Mattie's drawing was flattering, and she found herself wondering if she truly looked like that. She moved in front of the mirror and slowly removed her undershirt, raising her arms so that they were extended as they were in one of the drawings. *Yep,* she mused silently. *Same muscles.*

It was indeed the same body, but Mattie had captured her through the eyes of a lover, she realized. In the photo her breasts were high and proud, her nipples tight and puckered, and she felt herself blushing as she studied all the tiny details — the shadowing under her breasts, the indention of her waistline, the curve of her hips in the form-fitting swimming trunks, and the long muscular lines of her lower legs. Mattie had even somehow sketched in the fine sheen of sweat on her chest and face.

"You're a talented little vixen, Madeleine Crockett." She chuckled. "And I love you."

Slowly, she rolled the drawings back up and tied them securely. Looking around the room, she pursed her lips, pondering where best to store them, settling on a lower drawer of her armoire, one that contained only a few odd personal possessions. She tucked them away and closed the drawer, then stood up and moved to the middle of the room. She still felt warm, and removed her bloomers before crawling into bed and pulling up clean fresh sheets that she had just changed that morning. The cool cotton felt delicious against her bare skin, and she fell into contented sleep.

MORNING BROUGHT CLOUDY skies and thick humidity, which settled over the town with an uncomfortable heaviness. Rachel awoke in a mass of sweaty tangled sheets, a testament to the outside weather conditions. She slowly rolled toward the window and opened one eye. Not even a hint of a breeze stirred the perfectly still curtains, and she could see the almost mist-like quality of the air. She sighed. The docks were going to be unbearably hot.

She slipped out of bed and blotted her body with a towel,

removing the coating of sweat. A morning bath would have felt good, but was almost pointless given how little time the fresh feeling would last. She had bathed right after work the day before, and planned to do the same again on this day. Choosing her lightest pair of work trousers and a white shirt, she quickly dressed and braided her hair, then chose a straw cowboy hat that was loosely woven to allow air to circulate around her head. If there were any air blowing, she acknowledged ruefully.

She rode her bicycle to the docks, enjoying what little breeze her brisk pace allowed. As she parked the bicycle, she looked up to see Billy also riding up on his bicycle. "Good morning," she smiled. "Murderous day ahead."

"So true." Billy parked next to her and they headed toward their assigned boat together. "Wish we were going out to sea instead of unloading cargo today."

"Maybe we can get in the water during dinner." Rachel swung her dinner pail as she walked. "At least wade in and get our feet cooled off."

"That will feel mighty fine." Billy swiped the back of his hand across an already sweaty brow.

"Here." Rachel retrieved two broad green magnolia leaves from her dinner pail, treasured pilfered from a tree in the churchyard on her way to the docks. She handed over one and removed her own hat at the same time.

"Thank you." Billy also removed his hat, and they simultaneously pressed the cool leaves against their foreheads, replacing their hats to hold them in place. "Got more in there?" He eyed her pail hopefully.

"A few, yes." She chuckled. "Might be a four-leaf day before all is said and done."

"At least." They reached a large unfamiliar freighter, and stood quietly to the side, waiting for instructions from the ship's captain, who was nowhere to be seen.

They both sat down on the dock next to the ship, their feet dangling over the side, not quite reaching the water's surface. "Billy." Rachel decided to begin her questioning with the person she trusted most on the docks. "Do you have any idea what Adam Crockett does for a living?"

"I've heard a few things, yes." His eyes shifted, studying her profile curiously. "Why?"

"I promised Mattie I'd try to find out. She thinks he's in some kind of trade or shipping, but can't figure out what his product is." She felt Billy shift, and heard the long release of an almost silent breath, followed by a faint clucking of his tongue against his teeth. "So. You going to tell me what you know?"

"I'm not supposed to know anything." Billy looked down, plucking at the crease in his trousers leg. "But I've got good ears, you know?"

Rachel bit her tongue, willing him to get to the point.

"I don't know. The less you know about him, the less Mattie knows, the safer it might be for you. He's a no-good skunk, if what I've heard is true."

Rachel touched his arm, her eyes pleading as he looked over at her. "Please?"

"I hear his cargo comes in from Cuba." He pushed the brim of his hat up, dabbing away fresh sweat with a handkerchief, and re-adjusting the magnolia leaf. He felt a prickling sensation over his skin, more sweat, a product of nervousness more than the pressing humidity.

"What? Nothing is supposed to come out of Cuba except through the U.S. government." Rachel's patience wore thin. "What is it? Sugar cane? Coffee? Tobacco? Tropical fruits? What is it?" She saw the hesitation in his eyes. "None of those things are so scandalous that you can't share with me. What? Is he in the diamond trade? I hear tell there might be some diamonds to be had in the jungles down there."

"It's not just his cargo, although he may be dealing in a little of all of that." He eased into the conversation, feeling his way carefully. "It's what you said—he ships through Cuba and they supposedly go up to Houston and sell their goods on the black market. They avoid port charges, taxes, and cargo inspections. Heard bits and pieces of conversations in the saloon here and there." He hesitated. "There's more."

"Tell me!" Rachel resisted the urge to simply wrap her hands around his neck and shake him senseless. "The law is looking for him. Mattie's terrified. She doesn't know what to do."

"Oh." Billy gazed off toward the horizon. "The law." He squinted, looking up and over the boat to the rose-tinted clouds. "Doesn't surprise me. Who's after him?"

"Federal marshals, from what Mattie said." She remembered the fear in her friend's—*no, lover's*—eyes, she mentally corrected herself. That's what they were now, weren't they? "She hasn't told him they came calling, and hasn't decided if she will or not. What is he into?"

"It's what he sends back to Cuba." He turned, looking her squarely in the eye. "Weapons."

Her eyes widened. "We're on shaky ground with them at best. You mean to tell me he's arming their rebel military?"

"Shhh!" Billy clamped a hand over her mouth. "Not so loud. Don't know who all around here might be in on it with him."

Her brow furrowed in anger and her muffled curses came out as hot breath against his palm until he finally dropped his hand. "Why in tarnation have you kept this from me?" she bellowed in outrage.

"For your own gosh-danged good, for one," he snapped back at her. "And because I didn't hear enough to know if all of what I've heard is true or not. I can't validate any of it, because I've heard none of it from Adam himself. Just heard talk from some of the men I've seen him talking to from time to time."

"All right." Her voice was low and even. "You're going to tell me what all you've heard, and help me figure out how we can find out if it's true or not. Please. If this is true, Mattie needs to know."

"If she turns him in, she needs to get away from here." Billy propped one foot up on the edge of the dock, wrapping his arms around his leg and resting his chin on his knee, turning his face toward her. "These are nasty people, Rachel. They'd kill anyone who betrays them."

"You think I don't know that?" Her ire rose all over again and she forced herself to remain calm. "Tell me what you know."

"I don't know much else, other than what I've told you." He sat back up, leaning back on his hands.

"She needs to turn him in." Rachel spoke more to herself than to Billy. "I can help her with the getting out of town part."

"You two planning on taking off?" His face registered complete surprise. "I mean, I knew you were sweet on her and all, but I had no idea..."

"We've talked about it, yes. But she can't make up her mind." She looked up at the sky, her voice almost a whisper. "Maybe this will help her make her decision. Can you put out some feelers? Help me find out if he really is dealing in illegal arms?"

"I'll see what I can do," he reluctantly agreed. "But it's a dangerous business. I don't much relish the thought of disappearing from my bed some fine night. I'll have to be very careful who I talk to and what I ask."

"Oh." Rachel wrapped sympathetic fingers around his forearm. "I don't want you to do anything to get yourself hurt. Didn't mean that. Just—do what you can as long as you can stay safe in the process."

"I'm no coward." His jaw jutted out defiantly.

"Didn't mean that, and you know it." She soothed his ruffled ego. "Just don't want to see anyone I care about hurt."

"Give me a week or so, then, will you?" He slowly stood, spotting what appeared to be a ship's captain walking toward them. Other dock workers were arriving, and their conversation could no longer be carried on in safety.

"Of course." Rachel also stood, and they lined up with the other workers, listening as the captain greeted them and began giving instruction on handling of his cargo.

MATTIE SWIPED HER hand across a damp brow, and pushed back her wilted bangs. She could feel her shirtwaist sticking to her back between her shoulder blades, and her stocking-clad legs and feet were absolutely miserable. She thought about Rachel and the cool waters of the Gulf, and fervently wished they were both playing together in the ocean.

Instead, she was cooped up inside the tailor's shop, buried under a mound of heavy black material, making a dress, a rush order for a woman who was attending the funeral of her great-grandfather. The tailor had asked her to work the full day in order to complete the job in a timely fashion. That was fine with Mattie, not only because she would earn more for the full day, but also because it would keep her away from home longer, in the event Adam arrived on the late morning or early afternoon train.

She knew neither the deceased nor the person for whom she was sewing, but felt sorry for the loss, and sorry for all the people who would have to attend a funeral mass and a graveside service, dressed in black in the July heat. She had started on the skirt of the dress that morning, while Mrs. Vaughan worked across the room on the bodice. They hoped to finish the entire outfit by noon the following day. The funeral was to take place two days afterward.

It was close to closing time, and she worked quickly to hand-sew the hem on the very full skirt. It was a double-layered skirt, a thick black cotton underskirt covered by a sheer black overskirt. Not the wisest of choices for summer, in Mattie's opinion, but it was what the customer wanted. She couldn't imagine wearing the dress, along with the customary two petticoats that would be required.

Her own corset boning was digging into her sides, adding to her discomfort, and she longed to go home and discard some of her underclothing. Another cool bath sounded divine as well.

She smiled as she worked, thinking about Rachel. Their time on the boat had been sweet. Rachel was an amazingly gentle lover, and her wide-eyed honesty and vulnerability when they were together worked magic to keep Mattie relaxed and comfortable in Rachel's arms.

Mattie had forced most guilty thoughts aside, justifying her relationship with Rachel to herself with the knowledge that Adam was doing the same thing, although she suspected he did not love the women with whom he committed adultery. Adam loved no one, not even her.

She wanted to leave. She had never wanted to marry Adam in the first place, and that, perhaps, was the one thing she was sorry for. That she had not had the courage, at the age of fourteen, to speak up for herself and save herself a lot of misery, and perhaps give Adam the chance to marry someone who did want to be with him. Although she thought she would probably pity anyone who married Adam.

She wondered, secretly, if she had been older, if she had known more of the world, or of love, if that would have made a difference in the way Adam treated her. When she learned he spent time with prostitutes, she had wondered if part of the reason for that was her own naivety, if she simply was too young and too unresponsive to him to satisfy him.

She had known nothing of the physical aspect of marriage when she and Adam exchanged their vows. It was, after all, the man's responsibility, wasn't it, to teach his bride the ways of love? Adam had only taught her the way of pain and humiliation.

After being with Rachel, she understood, more than ever, that Adam either hadn't tried very hard with her, or else he had been just as ignorant in those matters as she was. With Rachel, she had no choice but to respond. She smiled again, shaking her head as she worked. The way Rachel touched her when they were together, the kind and gentle words she spoke, her kisses, it made her blood race just thinking about it.

It was like a dream. She could never have imagined what it was like to be loved the way Rachel loved her. Rachel had never pushed, never forced, never asked anything of Mattie or done anything with Mattie that she wasn't willing to do.

She couldn't help but love Rachel, and she halfway wondered if she even had a choice. There was no logical reason in the world they had become friends, much less lovers. It had happened slowly, settling over Mattie like a warm familiar old blanket on a cold evening. There was no one moment when she knew she loved Rachel. She quietly thanked God each night for bringing Rachel into her life, and prayed just as fervently that she would know the right thing to do.

Mr. Vaughan slid his chair back, the scraping noise against the wooden floor bringing her out of her thoughts. She looked out the window, surprised at the long shadows that indicated it was later than she expected. A glance at the clock on the wall revealed it was six o'clock, and past time to go home. "I think we should close up for the evening, ladies." He folded up a pair of trousers he had been working on, setting them aside for the morning. "It's been a long day."

They quickly put away the rest of their work and walked out into the street. It was busy with the usual early evening bustle of people going home from work, or shopping. Mattie said a hasty farewell to the Vaughans and looked around for Adam's buggy. It was nowhere to be seen, and she assumed he was coming home on the late train.

Despite the heat, she decided to walk home. If Adam were home, it would keep her away that much longer. If not, it would make for a shorter evening alone. She adjusted her hat against the long low rays of the sun, and trudged down Broadway toward the beachfront road. Everything seemed to be paler in the hot summer air, and other than a few odd seagulls flying overhead, no wild creatures were out and about.

After a long hot walk, she finally reached her front porch. A few windows were open, though she had left them closed, signaling her that Adam was, indeed, home. She sighed and opened the door, peering around the room hesitantly as she entered the parlor. She remembered the visit from the federal marshals and renewed her vow to say nothing until Rachel reported back to her of her findings on the docks.

She frowned in puzzlement. The sitting room was empty, although Adam's ten-gallon summer straw cowboy hat was hanging on the rack in the parlor, and his small leather satchel sat beside the door. "Adam?" she called out softly, hoping maybe he had gone out again, although he rarely left the house without his hat. The house remained quiet, and she moved into the bedroom to remove her own hat, along with her sticky petticoat.

She stopped, studying the bed. The top quilt was turned back, and the sheets were rumpled. A half-full glass of lemonade sat on the nightstand, the sliced lemons still floating at the surface, and a book was resting open, pages down, on one of the pillows. Adam sometimes took a book to bed to read, and she wondered if he had arrived home early and taken a nap. If he were home, he was either in the kitchen or in the barn, but the house seemed awfully quiet. Maybe he had taken the horses out for some exercise.

She shrugged and sat down on the edge of the bed as she slipped her shoes off, sighing in utter relief as she rolled down her stockings and removed them, wiggling her bare toes, which reveled in being released from their hateful hot prison. She changed out of her work dress into a more comfortable pale blue housedress, glad to be rid of her petticoat. Even her bloomers and corset seemed too much, but it was much better without the dreadful petticoat and high neckline of the work dress.

Her heart sank as she realized that, one way or the other, Adam was home, and she reluctantly stooped down and opened the bottom drawer of the armoire, digging beneath the folded blankets there for her pessary box. She frowned and felt her way deeper, still not locating it. With slowly rising panic, she removed each layer of clean bedding until she reached the bottom of the drawer—empty, save a couple of Rachel's tiny folded-up notes, which were tucked into cracks.

"Is this what you're searching for?" a low, even voice asked.

Her heart lurched into her throat and her skin felt prickly all over, the adrenalin rushing through her system at rapid speed. She hastily dropped the bedding back into the drawer and stood up, turning to face him. "Adam." Her eyes went from the box in his hand to the hard lines of rage that etched his face. She was certain he intended to kill her, and cursed inwardly, realizing her pocketbook—and her pistol—were in the parlor.

"Yes, I'm Adam. Your husband." He moved closer, the box still clutched in his fist. "Where shall we begin, Madeleine? I was very disappointed to find this. I'm wondering how long you would have continued to deceive me, had I not spilled lemonade on our bed and gone searching for dry sheets."

"I-I can explain." She knew there was no good explanation, and inched backward until she was pressed against the wall next to the water closet door, trapped, with no where else to go. He was between her and the door, and the open window was on the other side of the armoire. She could see the sheer curtains fluttering out away from the sea breeze that blew in through the mosquito netting.

"It's a mortal sin, Madeleine, to prevent the natural God-given birth of children. And you lied to me, another mortal sin. Shall I also remind you of the admonishment that you are to obey your husband? You know I want children. And here, all this time, that's what I thought you wanted, too." He stalked toward her, his eyes a brooding storm, his neck veins standing out against angry red skin.

"I-I love children."

"Shut up!" He backhanded her so quickly she had no time to duck. Her face turned with the force of the blow, slamming into the wall. She felt the blood begin to trickle from her nose, and her cheek throbbed. She whimpered quietly and shrunk further away until she was in the corner.

"Only harlots have physical relations with no intention of bearing children." He held the box in her face. "This tells me I married a harlot." He shook it at her, then grasped her face with his other hand, forcing her chin around until she was looking at him again.

Her eyes were wide with fear, and the color drained from her face. He grabbed at her hair, yanking it until the bun came lose from the pins. "Adam, please," she whispered, her voice trembling and her knees shaking so badly she feared they would give way. He was pulling so hard, she was afraid he would pull her hair out by the roots.

"I said, shut up!" He slapped her again and she slid halfway down the wall, covering her face with one arm, holding the other out in defense. He backhanded her one more time for good measure, then flung the pessary box to the floor, sending it clattering across the hard wood until it hit the far wall. He watched it land, then grabbed her outstretched arm and wrenched it until she shrieked in pain. "Is that what you are, Madeleine, a filthy harlot? Maybe I should make a profit off you, loan you out for a fee, since you have no desire to bear my children."

"N-no... Pl—please." He pulled her up, grabbing her collar, and with one strong jerk, ripped the front of her dress open. "Please." She wrapped her arms around herself and felt his fist connect with her upper stomach, forcing the breath from her lungs, as his blows continued to rain down upon her. She doubled over in pain and he grabbed her, pushing her onto the bed where he held her down with his knees against her stomach and his boots digging into her legs.

She cried silently, the tears streaming down her face. Out of breath, her lips moved in pleas that were too soft for him to hear. She watched as he dropped his suspenders and unfastened his trousers, then closed her eyes, bracing herself for the pain that was to come. She felt the blood continue to flow across her upper lip and down her cheek, mixing with the hot tears that fell with them. Her stomach churned and she forced down a wave of nausea, as his foul whiskey-tainted breath brushed across her face.

"You will bear my child, Madeleine." He pulled her bloomers down and tossed them to the floor. "And you will obey me, no matter what it takes." He squeezed her wrists tightly, his blunt nails digging into her skin. "Do you understand me?"

"Y-yes." She briefly opened her eyes, her words coming through clenched teeth.

"You may be a filthy whore, but you are still my wife, and you will start acting as such." He pulled her tattered dress aside, observing her trembling body. It was one of the few times he had ever actually looked upon her nakedness. He slowly unlaced her corset and also pushed it apart. "Are you afraid of me, Madeleine?"

She was shaking too hard to answer, and merely nodded her head affirmatively.

"Good." He pulled his trousers down. "You should be."

THE DAY PASSED much too slowly, the oppressive heat making each minute seem like an hour. At last, the freighter was unloaded, and the dock boss indicated they could all go home. Rachel flexed her hands, wincing at barked knuckles on almost every finger. She had no idea what all was in the heavy crates they had unloaded. All she knew was that the wood wasn't sanded properly, and she had the splinters to show for it. She couldn't wait for a long soak in the tub, and a fresh change of clothing.

She'd spent the afternoon mulling over her new knowledge of Adam, and worrying about Mattie. If Adam was involved in illegal arms trading, she hoped Mattie would find the fortitude to turn him in. Rachel knew she could never bring herself to turn him in without Mattie's blessing. He deserved punishment for a lot of things, but trading with the enemy took him to new depths of lowness in Rachel's book, if that were possible.

"Are you going to the saloon tonight?" Billy sidled up to her, nudging her slightly with one elbow. "Haven't seen you there in a while."

"No. Best if I not run into Adam or any of his posse." Rachel used the thin end of her pocketknife to pry some of the larger splinters from her palms as she talked. "Ouch!" She dropped the knife as she tugged at a particularly deep one, drawing blood. She shook her hand before bringing it to her lips. "Guess I should wait on those 'til I can get my hands under lamp light and see them better."

"Those look bad. Why didn't you wear your gloves?" He tugged at the heavy leather mitts hanging from her waistband, then bent down and retrieved the wayward knife, handing it back to her. "Are you sure you can take care of them by yourself? Tough to work alone when it comes to hands."

"Thank you. I'll be fine." She folded it and placed it back in her pocket. "And I tried to wear my gloves, but they're worn through at the palms. And they got so sweaty inside, my hands kept slipping around and I was afraid I'd lose my grip. Leather's stretched out 'til they're too big for me. I'm getting some new ones with Friday's wages."

"Good thing that fishing boat needs us for a few days. You won't need the heavy gloves for that. Although the owner wants to leave too gosh-darned early for my tastes." He shoved his hands in his pockets.

"True." Rachel began walking toward their bicycles. "But it makes sense. If he wants to catch marlin, he needs to go out further and deeper. An hour before dawn can't be too bad, can it? Two whole days of smoking and fishing? At least he doesn't want to do a live-aboard."

"Too right. I always feel like I have to keep an eye on any other crew at night. Don't sleep too well unless I know everyone." They reached their bicycles and began the short ride to the boarding house. "Will I see you at supper?"

"Um. No." Rachel veered off toward the tailor's shop. "I have an errand to run first, then I'm taking a bath. Too hot to eat a cooked meal. I have some apples and soda crackers in my room. I'll be fast asleep in two hours. See you on the docks early tomorrow."

"Well." He watched her ride away, guessing at where she was headed. "See you then."

Rachel reached the tailor's shop, which was already closed for the evening. The sun was almost set, and she tugged a slip of paper and a stub of pencil from her pocket, scratching out a short note to Mattie. She unconsciously stuck the tip of her tongue between her lips to one side, concentrating on spelling the words correctly:

> *Deerest Mattie,*
> *I will not sea you at noon for 2 days. I will be fishing. We will go early and come home late. I learned some thing today. Do not talk about what we talked about. Wait for me to talk to you furst.*
> *I love you and miss you.*
> *R*

She went around back and looked for neighbors, then raised a

window, crawling inside and quickly slipping the note into the top
drawer of Mattie's sewing machine table. She pinned it to her
pincushion, just to make sure she would see it. A deep breath brought
her the lingering smell of Mattie's toilet water, and she smiled at a
subtler note she recognized as Mattie's own unique scent.

Slipping back out the window, she finished the short ride home
and quickly retrieved a clean change of clothing before making her
way down the hallway to the tub, which was blessedly unoccupied.
She filled it full and dropped down blissfully into the tepid water,
immediately feeling better just knowing the day's sweat and dust was
washing away. She had just closed her eyes and collapsed further
under the water when she heard a brief rap at the door.

"G'away. Just got in here," she called out, just loud enough for
whoever was on the other side to hear.

"Rachel, sugar, it's me, Lillie." Rachel's eyes flew open. "Can I
come in, please?"

"Lil?" Rachel looked down at her nakedness, uncharacteristically
shy for Lillie to see her that way. She warred internally with herself,
then shrugged. "Nothing she ain't seen before," she muttered quietly.
"Sure. Come on in."

The door opened and a blonde head popped around. Lillie smiled
and moved in, sitting down on a chair and closing the door. "I was
supposed to meet Billy here. He was going to take me to a nice supper
at the hotel across the street, but it's early yet. He told me about your
hands, sugar. Said you might could use some help."

"Dang it." Rachel groused. "I told him I'd be fine." She looked
up, chagrined at Lillie's patient expression.

"Let me see." Lillie held out her hand expectantly, smiling as
Rachel grudgingly offered up one of her own. "Oooh." She tisked
softly. "Here." She pushed the lamp on the table beside the tub closer,
and removed a needle from her cuff. "Let me take care of these for
you, and no complaints, missy. You should know better than to let
your gloves get in such bad shape that you can't use them."

"I know." Rachel's jaw clenched tightly as she felt Lillie removing
the angrier splinters first. "I've been kind of busy."

"So I hear." Lillie smiled slyly at her. "Billy doesn't miss much,
and he says you and Mattie must be spending an awful lot of time
together. Said he saw you piling up a large breakfast plate a few
mornings ago. Too large to be a meal for one. Said you took it back
upstairs."

"Maybe I was just extra hungry and wanted to eat in private?"
Rachel blushed from the tip of her toes to her hairline. "Thought we
were more careful than that." The blush turned to anger at herself.
"Can't risk Adam hearing about it."

"Shhh. Don't you worry. Billy and I won't say a thing to anyone
and I doubt anyone else noticed." She removed the last splinter and

turned Rachel's hand over, clucking in dismay at the damaged knuckles. "You need to take better care of yourself, sugar." She kissed a knuckle without thinking, then released Rachel's hand. "Wash 'em up good. Now. Let me see your other hand."

Rachel groaned and complied, closing her eyes as Lillie took care of the rest of her splinters. A thought occurred to her and she peered up, grinning evilly. "And just where were you when Billy told you about my large breakfast?" The grin grew broader as Lillie looked up, a blush dusting her own skin.

"In his room." She smiled coyly. "He frightens me sometimes, Rachel."

Rachel sat up in angry alarm. "What did he do? I told him to..."

"Oh. No, no, no." Lillie was warmed all over at Rachel's ire on her behalf. "He frightens me because he's the most kind and gentle man I've ever met. He doesn't care about who I am, although I swear he's doing his darnedest to keep me too busy to spend time with anyone else. He must be spending every last dime he makes on me."

"Is that important to you?" Rachel frowned in concern. "Money?"

"I used to think so, yes." Lillie finished up with the needle and carefully set it aside, dropping Rachel's hand back into the water. "Now I'm starting to understand that a kind heart may be worth more than a wealthy one."

"And?" Rachel nodded approvingly at her answer.

"And I think, someday, if things go as nicely as they have been, I might be Mrs. William Blaylock." She ducked her head in embarrassment, blonde ringlets hiding her face. "If he'll have me, that is."

"You're in love so soon?" Rachel teased gently.

"Doesn't take very long." Lillie looked back up and smiled, her face shining. "You should know."

"Guess I should," she answered quietly. "I'd best get out of this water before I turn into a prune, Lil. And you should probably get to your supper. Thanks for helping me out."

"Don't you ever be afraid to ask for my help." Lillie patted her on the shoulder. "No matter what, I'll always be your friend."

"Likewise." Rachel stood and wrapped herself in a towel. "Go on. I'll be fine now, thanks to you."

"You have yourself some sweet dreams, sugar." Lillie kissed her on the cheek and slipped out of the room.

"Oh, I think I will." Rachel smiled to herself, a pair of passionate hazel eyes flashing through her mind.

MATTIE HAD NO idea what time it was. All she knew was that it was cold and incredibly dark. It was amazing how cold she could feel in the middle of July. She hurt all over from the beating she had taken, and from Adam's attentions to her afterward. He had been rough with her, and told her she had it coming to her, that she deserved it for behaving like a whore. Despite the countless times he had pushed, slapped, and punched her since their wedding day, he had never been rough with her before when it came to lovemaking. Inept, yes, she now realized, but rough, no.

He was asleep. Her back was turned to him but she could hear his heavy even snores and she could smell him. He stirred and she felt him move closer, his back pressed against hers, although he continued to snore. His skin brushed against her, and it made her sick to her stomach, but she pushed down the waves of nausea, scooting away as much as she dared until they were no longer touching. She had hated his touch before, but now she couldn't bear it.

Everything had changed.

She felt dirty and she couldn't wait until Adam was gone and she could take a bath in private. Maybe if she scrubbed hard enough, she could scrub him away. She thought about Rachel and her chest felt so tight she had to bite her lower lip to keep from sobbing out loud. Suddenly her rebellious stomach won out, and she barely made it to the water closet, her abused abdominal muscles screaming in pain as dry heaves wracked her body. Adam had punched her hard, and her head pounded even as her stomach churned.

Finally the sickness passed, and she stood weakly, grasping the sink pedestal for support, her legs shaking like a newborn colt. There was no light in the water closet, and she was glad of it. She had little desire to see the bruises she could already feel on her face. She fumbled for the water spigot and rinsed her mouth out, cautiously sipping just a palmful of the cool, soothing liquid. She waited a moment, and when the water stayed down, she tip-toed back into the bedroom.

Adam had slept through the entire incident, and she released a tiny breath, deciding she had no desire to continue sharing the bed with him. She donned a soft worn old nightgown, grabbed a patchwork quilt from a rack in the corner, and made her way to the sofa in the parlor, where she curled up into a tight ball, lying on her side and hugging her knees up to her chest. She tugged the quilt up and caught a whiff of a hauntingly familiar scent.

It was the quilt they had taken down to the dock, and Rachel's bay rum lingered there, permeating her senses with memories too sweet to allow. She could still feel his hands on her and taste his breath against her lips. Those were her memories now. This time the sob welled up, choking out as her eyes stung and the tears came unbidden, streaming down her face. She dared not cry out loud, so she bit her lip, and rocked back and forth, holding the blanket tightly to herself as she cried in silence.

For the first time in a very long time, she felt sorry for herself.

She cried for her stolen childhood, and for a mother who valued appearances over her own children. For a sister that was all but lost to her, and a father who saw her unhappiness but did nothing. She cried for the freedom she had never known, and for a life she had never truly lived. For a husband who knew her not at all and loved her even less.

She closed her eyes and almost laughed at the absurdity of it all. Now on top of everything else, her eyes would be puffy when she got up in the morning. One eye, she was fairly certain, was already starting to swell from one of Adam's blows to her face. She had some of the fancy make-up some women were starting to wear. She used just a touch of it every now and then, and suspected a heavier coating of the facial powder might help mute the appearance of some of the bruises.

Far off, she thought she heard the church clock chime two o'clock. She had a few more hours until dawn, and despite the fury of thought and emotion racing through her brain, her tired body won out, and she fell into fitful sleep, grasping the edge of the sofa lest she roll off it, even as she dreamed vague dreams full of dark frightening images.

The images turned to nightmares, as she relived the night Adam's men had beaten up Rachel. The memories twisted in her dreams, and she watched Rachel die in her arms. Just as she started to scream in her dream, she awoke in a heavy sweat, gasping for air. Had she screamed aloud? She cocked her head to one side, listening carefully, relieved when Adam's faint snores reached her ears. She shook her head to clear the images, and got up, padding quietly into the kitchen to get a drink of water.

Rachel was alive. Now she just had to make sure she stayed that way.

Chapter
Nine

THE FISHING BOAT pulled into port late on the second day, and the weary crew de-boarded, all of them taking a share of fresh fish as part of their wages. While on the way back to the island, they had cleaned most of a considerable catch of marlin, sailfish, tuna, and even a few sharks. The captain thanked them as they passed him on the gangplank, and he promised their monetary reward would be forthcoming on Friday.

Rachel and Billy approached their bicycles in silence, sore arm muscles protesting as they lifted the vehicles and mounted them, placing their fish packets in the cargo baskets. When Rachel arrived back at her room, she made quick use of the tub in the water closet, and sank into bed less than thirty minutes later. She flexed her legs and arms, then relaxed, feeling the day's aches and pains slowly fade away, overcome by the need for sleep. It felt good to be clean, and even better to be off her feet and out of the hot sun and salty air. She was certain her skin was several shades darker than it had been two days before. The open sea and the burning sun were a relentless torture on the human body.

A rooster crowing in the alley woke her, and she slowly sat up, rubbing both eyes in confusion. The sun was indeed rising, although it seemed as if she had just gone to sleep. She groaned as she swung her legs over the edge of the bed, her muscles still stiff. She slowly pulled on her work trousers and shirt, and splashed her face in the washbowl before plodding downstairs, her body slowly coming fully awake.

After a quick breakfast, she was out the door and on her bike, headed for an open field down the road, where she was certain she had spotted some nice pink buttercups and yellow daisies growing beside the road. She smiled as she saw the bright flowers blowing in the gentle morning breeze, and jumped off the bike, grasping the flowers at the base of their stems, and picking them, filling her bicycle basket full. She could already picture the smile on Mattie's face as she handed them to her, and her own face broke into an involuntary grin.

It was still early, and she decided to ride by the tailor's shop and see if Mattie might have gone in early herself. As she approached the shop, she could see that the windows were open, indicating that at least someone was already there.   She parked her bicycle and hesitantly stepped into the shop, blinking as her eyes adjusted to the lower light. "Hello, Mr. Vaughan." She stepped forward, and nodded her head in greeting, as the tailor turned from his sewing machine and stood up.

"Miss Travis." He wiped his hands on his apron. "What brings you here this morning so early?"

Rachel frowned. She had become a fixture in the shop, her visits to Mattie as regular as clockwork, schedules permitting. "I don't suppose Mattie is here yet?" She looked around hopefully, as if she expected her friend to appear from the back room. Instead, Mrs. Vaughan popped out from behind the curtain, her face lined in worry.

"You don't know, then?" She looked first at Rachel and then at her husband. "Tell her, Matthew. I think she needs to know."

"Know what?" Rachel's smile disappeared, and she felt a vague sense of uneasiness settle over her.

"Mrs. Crockett isn't working for us anymore."   Mr. Vaughan moved to a side table and poured up a cup of tea, and handed it to Rachel. "Strangest thing happened two mornings ago.   Her husband showed up here first thing and told us she wouldn't be coming in anymore."

"I think something queer is going on," Mrs. Vaughan cut him off. "Mattie has always been so dependable. We were busy with a rush order for some funeral clothing the day before she quit, and Matthew and I had to work until almost midnight to finish up Mattie's part of the work. It's not like her to shirk her responsibilities."

"Eliza." Mr. Vaughan's voice took on a warning tone.

"Don't you 'Eliza' me!" She snapped at him. "That man is up to no good. I've seen the bruises these past months. I have eyes, don't I?"

" 'Tis none of your business."

"That girl needs a friend, Matthew, and Miss Travis here appears to be one of the few she has." She turned to Rachel, whose boneless fingers quickly set her teacup down lest she drop it.

"You haven't seen her since Monday afternoon?" Her voice shook with fear.

Mrs. Vaughan's eyes rolled upward in thought, then looked directly back at her. "That would be correct."

"Have you seen Mr. Crockett since Tuesday morning?" She was already headed for the door as she spoke.

"No." Mr. Vaughan joined in. "I believe he was headed up to Houston when he came by."

"I've got to go." Rachel opened the door and was gone, the hats on the hat rack fluttering behind her as she closed the door.

She didn't know how she got there so quickly. The town flew by her in a blur and she was on the beach road in no time, the air blowing her long braid back and making tears stream from her eyes, she was riding so fast. The soreness in her legs was forgotten as they pumped double time, carrying her to Mattie's house with no thought save one — she had to see her. What if Adam had indeed packed up and taken her away while Rachel was gone? Maybe the federal marshals had come back. Maybe... She gritted her teeth and pedaled even faster, refusing to think the worst.

At last she approached Mattie's house and forced herself to slow down before she jumped off the bike and propped it under a palm tree a good distance behind the barn. Cautiously, she crept to the barn and slipped around front, spotting no movement through the windows at the back of the house. The barn door was cracked open and she pushed it just wide enough to wriggle inside. A quick glance around revealed the horses and light buggy missing, with only the larger wagon left, parked off to one side.

She swallowed hard and gazed back toward the house, as she left the barn and walked warily across the open space between, feeling as exposed and naked as the day she was born. She would have been easy pickings for anyone with a gun, and her ears perked up, listening especially for the crank of a shotgun or the click of a pistol.

She rounded the corner of the house and eyed the porch briefly, a sheen of nervous sweat breaking out across her brow. Her boots sounded much too heavy as she climbed the steps and crossed to the landing. She drew a shaking breath and knocked, softly at first, then waited. She heard nothing and reached up with a trembling fist, knocking louder. She was well aware of the Bowie knife tucked into her boot, as she mentally prepared herself to reach down and grab it, if need be.

A rustling noise on the other side of the door almost made her leap off the porch, but a soft, familiar voice caught her ear, and she moved closer, waiting for the door to open. It remained closed.

"Rachel?" Mattie called out from behind a curtain at the open window beside the door.

"Mattie?" She moved to the window, anxious to see her face. "What's going on? I went by the tailor's shop and they said..."

"You need to go." The front door cracked open just a finger's width.

There was a note of utter defeat in her voice, and Rachel's heart turned over in her chest. "Not until you let me come in." She stepped forward, pressing against the door. A surprisingly strong grip held her at bay, and she eased off, and backed up. "Mattie, it's me, Rachel." She gentled her tone. "You're scaring me something awful here. Please. Let me come in."

"I can't." Her voice became desperate. "Just go away, Rachel. It isn't safe for you here anymore."

"No." Rachel stubbornly crossed her arms over her chest. She was certain Mattie was watching her from behind the door.

"He'll kill you if he finds you here." Her voice quivered and Rachel thought she heard a sniffle. "He's having me watched. Someone could come by at any time. You have to go. Please."

"Is that what you want?" Rachel moved closer, until she was a step away from the door.

"Y-yes." Nonetheless, the door opened just a bit wider, and Rachel saw the hem of a pale green skirt peek out.

"You don't sound too certain of that." She watched the door open wider still, until she could just make out Mattie's bowed head. "You look me in the eye and you tell me you want me to leave, and I will."

She waited and watched, as a pair of slumped shoulders heaved in a silent sigh, and Mattie stood up taller, still facing down and toward the inside of the room. "I can't."

"So you want me to come in?" Her voice grew hopeful and it was all she could do to stand still.

"You can't." Mattie began to cry, her head still bowed. "You need to go."

"I love you." Rachel took the last step, reaching out, only to have her hand slapped away.

"Go." Mattie brought one clenched fist up to her own turned face, and an audible sob escaped her lips. "I love you too much to put you in such danger."

"Don't you worry about me." Rachel reached out again, and this time her hand made it to Mattie's shoulder. She felt a shudder and quickly withdrew it. "Mattie, look at me."

"I can't." She wrapped her arms around herself and rocked back and forth, looking down at her feet. "You can't look at me," she whispered. She cried harder as she felt gentle fingers probing her chin, and slowly, her face was tilted up until she looked into a pair of steel blue eyes filled at first with sorrow, and then with rage.

"I'll kill him." Rachel spat out. Her eyes flicked over Mattie's face, taking in bruises at both eyes and cheeks, and a painfully swollen upper lip. A close appraisal noted what looked like healing fingernail-shaped puncture wounds at Mattie's wrists, and what appeared to be the bulk of a bandage wrapped around her right forearm beneath her sleeve.

"No. You. Will. Not." Mattie's eyes snapped. "You're all I'm hanging onto right now, Rachel. You do something to get yourself hanged, and I'll walk out into that water out there and drown myself. I swear I will."

"Please, Mattie." Rachel stepped closer, cupping Mattie's face against her palm. "Let me in before whoever is watching you comes by."

Mattie looked down and with a trembling sigh, opened the door and stepped back, making room for her to step inside. As soon as the door was closed she cried out, and fell into Rachel's arms, sobbing, her body shaking as three days of horror began to wash away. She felt hesitant arms close loosely around her, and realized Rachel was afraid she might hurt her if she held on tightly. "Just be careful of my ribs," she whispered, and felt Rachel pull her closer.

She buried her face into Rachel's chest, inhaling her bay rum and crying harder as she finally allowed herself to feel a small measure of comfort. "I want to die," she choked out.

"You hang on for me." Rachel cradled Mattie against her, hesitantly stroking her head with one hand, and simply allowed her to cry for a long while, until tears turned to hiccups. "Shhh." She looked down at an ashen face.

"Rachel, I think I'm going to..."

"Hold on." Rachel somehow scooped her up, rushing through the bedroom and depositing her in the water closet just in the nick of time. She held Mattie's forehead as heaves wracked her body, but nothing came up. "You haven't been eating."

Mattie shook her head negatively, feeling the edges of a damp towel as Rachel dabbed at her lips, then sponged her forehead. "Haven't been hungry," she replied weakly, as Rachel guided her toward the bed. "No." Her eyes grew wide in panic. "Not there. The sofa."

"Bastard." Rachel could only guess at what she had suffered, but shoved down her anger as best she could, forcing herself to focus on taking care of Mattie. "What did he do to you?" Her fingers ran lightly over the bruises. "What happened?"

Rachel sat down on the sofa, sitting back and pulling Mattie carefully down with her.

"He found my pessary box." She settled against the familiar warmth, trying to believe that Rachel was there, holding her. "You can see the rest." Her eyes darted up, then quickly looked downward in embarrassment. "I-I thought he was going to kill me that first night." She closed her eyes, feeling the shivers come again. "I've wished he had a dozen times since."

Rachel's jaw twitched with the effort of containing her fury. "When does he come home again?"

"Tomorrow night, far as I know." Mattie unconsciously clung tighter, and felt Rachel pull her closer.

"I should go get Dr. Mills." Rachel carefully prodded Mattie's bandaged arm, unbuttoning her cuff and pushing the sleeve up. "This might be broken, for all we know."

"No." Mattie's voice grew panicked. "No doctor. Adam said no one is to come into the house and I'm not to leave it while he's gone. I've seen some of his men ride by. They don't come inside, but still, I can't risk it."

"If you're certain." Rachel unwound the bandage, wincing at the mottled skin and swollen wrist beneath it. "I know you've been through a horrible time. Can you let me check out your injuries? We need to know how badly you're hurt."

Hazel eyes looked up at her, the shame evident in their sad depths. She slowly nodded her agreement.

Rachel's voice grew gentle and she stroked Mattie's head as she spoke. "My brave sweetheart." She kissed her head. "Let's go get you a nightgown to change into, before we start. After we finish, you need to eat something and get some rest, and then we have a lot to talk about before tomorrow."

Mattie nibbled her lower lip and nodded again. Rachel rose up and felt a strong grip at her arm. She turned, doing her best not to break down and cry herself, as Mattie's eyes watered up again and she pleaded, "Don't leave me."

"Never." She carefully helped Mattie up, guiding her toward the armoire in the bedroom.

RACHEL SAT ON the sofa, Mattie's head in her lap. She idly stroked the long red waves, which Mattie had allowed her to wash and comb out. During a tearful examination, they had determined that for the most part, Mattie was only bruised up pretty good. Her wrist appeared to be badly sprained, but nothing was broken, not even her nose, although it was extremely tender. Mattie had talked very little, sharing few details of her time with Adam, although it did come out that he had left for Houston Wednesday morning, and not Tuesday morning as Mr. and Mrs. Vaughan had thought.

Mattie was sleeping, after consuming a bowl of clam chowder and several soda crackers. It wasn't much food, but it was a start. Rachel could easily see her ribs during the examination, and could feel them, even through the light nightgown she was wearing. Her eyes were bruised, hiding any dark circles, but her features were drawn and haggard, sure signs she hadn't been sleeping well. She confessed to Rachel that every night, after Adam fell asleep, she had moved to the sofa, unable to sleep in the same bed with him, but even being in the same house while he was there robbed her of any true rest.

Rachel briefly thought of the Port. She'd not sent word and fervently hoped she would be forgiven for not showing up. It was the first time she had ever just not gone to work without sending word or having prior permission. She was not slated for any particular assignment that day, but there was always something available for her to do. She was a model dockhand compared to many, and tried to console herself on that point.

She was partially reclining, keeping in a position so she could easily duck down should the men who were keeping an eye on Mattie come up to the door. She was glad her bicycle wasn't in sight. They had drawn the curtains, but at least once Rachel had heard a buggy pull up in the driveway, and heard low male voices muttering for a few minutes before they pulled away.

Now Rachel's mind was turning, working on a plan. They had discussed the possibility that Adam was involved in smuggling, and that surely the federal marshals would be interested in that news. Meanwhile, she had to figure out what to do to get Mattie out of the house and safely out of Adam's reach.

She looked down, her face scrunched up in thought. In sleep, some of Mattie's worry lines had smoothed out, and Rachel could feel her relaxed under the arm that was draped carefully over Mattie's waist. Mattie's hand was wrapped firmly against Rachel's thigh, her body curled up against her hip. Every now and then she stirred and mumbled in her sleep, but a few shushes and more strokes to her head magically calmed her.

Gradually, thought turned to weariness, and Rachel's eyelids drooped, then closed, and her head lolled back against a sofa cushion.

She awoke an hour later and slowly raised her head, turning a stiff neck from side to side. She felt the change in Mattie's breathing and looked down, studying her face and closed eyes. "You awake?" She whispered softly.

"Oh." Mattie's eyes fluttered open. "Yes. I was just resting a spell. Didn't want to wake you up."

"You can wake me up any time you need to." Rachel shifted, and Mattie slowly turned until she was stretched out on her back, her head still in her lap. Hazel eyes peered up thoughtfully, then looked down, as Mattie's cheeks turned red.

Rachel cupped her face. "What's wrong?"

"All my fault." Mattie blinked, one tear escaping. "It's a sin, Rachel, I knew that."

"What's a sin?" Confused blue eyes peered down, willing Mattie to look back up at her.

"The pessaries." Mattie unconsciously grasped Rachel's hand, twining their fingers. She could smell the comforting scent of bay rum and a slightly musky scent that was simply Rachel's own skin, all mixed with the clean cottony smell of her fresh work trousers. Strong thigh muscles cradled her head, and with her cheek against Rachel's stomach, she could feel the slight sensation of her breathing. She burrowed further into her comfortable nest. She had been half-afraid she might reject Rachel's touch, but found instead she craved her comfort.

"It is not a sin to prevent bringing children into a miserable existence." Rachel tilted her chin up, studying Mattie's troubled eyes.

"But the church..."

Rachel covered her lips with two fingers. "Do you think what you and I have shared is also a sin?"

Mattie closed her eyes for a long moment, so long that Rachel feared the worst, her heart creeping slowly into her throat as the silence went on. Finally, two vibrant hazel eyes opened, conveying love that needed no words. "No. But the pessaries—I don't know. I should have at least been more careful with them. Now I've ruined everything. We can't run away now. I've lost my freedom. I can't live here, but I can't leave." Mattie sat up, slipping into Rachel's lap. Two sturdy arms wrapped loosely around her and she rested her head on Rachel's shoulder, playing with the buttons on her white shirt as she spoke. "Those marshals, they might not be back for weeks. I can't survive here that long. I'll die. What Adam wants..." Her cheeks flushed again and she looked down. "He's relentless. His touch makes my skin crawl and his kisses sicken me. When he..." She curled up into herself almost as if he were in the room with them and coming toward her. "I want to die. I can't bear it. I simply can't. Not for several weeks."

"I'm so sorry." Rachel hugged her as closely as she dared, mindful of the many sore spots on the thin body she held.

"Damn you." Mattie beat her fist lightly against Rachel's chest and Rachel jumped in surprise, more at Mattie's swearing than at her actions. She looked down to see a tear-streaked face, but there was a sad smile on Mattie's lips. "Now I know what love is." She looked up, tracing Rachel's face with gentle fingertips. "Before, I was prepared to live out my life with a man I didn't love and who didn't love me. I didn't know anything better. You came along and showed me everything I had only dreamed of. I don't know whether to kiss you or kick you."

"I'd prefer the kiss." Rachel managed to smile, wiping away a few of Mattie's tears. "But your lips might not be up for it right now."

"Damn them, too." Mattie pulled her head down, threading her fingers through chestnut waves, and lightly kissed Rachel's mouth. It was sweet and chaste, and about all her painful lips could take, but she lingered there, allowing a slight pressure before she pulled away.

Rachel's fingers lightly traced the bruises on Mattie's face, her thumb leaving the barest of touches against the injured lips. Her eyes were full of sorrow, and she felt her chin quivering. She shook her head in anger at her own weakness, and drew in a deep breath, feeling the emotions settle. "I'm so sorry this happened to you."

"What are we going to do?" Mattie lay her head back down on Rachel's shoulder. The comforting embrace, and the steady sound of the waves rolling ashore outside combined to lull her into a much-needed lassitude, tense muscles slowly relaxing after almost three days of constantly frazzled nerves. She burrowed her face into Rachel's neck and felt a kiss at the top of her head.

"I've been thinking on that, and something you said gave me an idea. Give him what he wants."

"Give—? But...have you gone loco?" Mattie's eyes flew open and she sat up, her hands grasping Rachel's shoulders as she glared at her. "If I have his child, I will be tied to him forever. I'll never get away from him."

"That's not what I meant. Make him think you're carrying his child. Make him think he's already accomplished that. Then tell him the doctor said further relations before you give birth would be bad for the baby."

"What if he checks with the doctor?" Mattie fretted. "And what do I do several months from now when my stomach is still obviously flat?"

"Shhh." Rachel kissed her head again. "We'll be long gone by then. We just need to buy some time until those marshals return. And no man I've ever known has willingly gone alone to a doctor to discuss his wife's delicate condition."

"Well." Mattie pursed her lips inward, her brows deeply furrowed. "It might work. I'll have to pretend to make a visit to the doctor. As for the other, he'll probably go to the saloon to satisfy his needs, which is fine with me. Not like he wasn't doing that anyway. But I don't know if..."

"If what?" Rachel watched Mattie's eyes tear up again.

"If I can bear to be with him in this house for very long, even if he doesn't touch me in that way. He flies into a rage over nothing. Or anything. He might not be able to restrain himself, even if he does think I'm carrying his child. Or he might just make sure to hit places besides my stomach. I don't know how many times I've had to wrap up this wrist."

Rachel's guts clenched and she felt her blood boiling, just under the surface. "Maybe they'll find him in a back alley with his throat slit."

"No." Mattie stroked her face, trying to calm her. "I'll manage to survive. We're too close to having what we want. I won't have you risk it."

"And what am I supposed to do?" She carefully lifted Mattie, shifting her until she was sitting on the sofa. Then she stood, pacing back and forth in front of the fireplace, gesturing with her hands as she talked. "Am I supposed to just go to the docks every day, knowing I might not be able to see you for weeks? Wondering how you're doing? Wondering if he's hitting you, or worse? You not able to get word to me? Me wondering if he doesn't get wind of the marshals and up and take you away? No!" She turned, stamping a booted foot in frustration, her fists clenched at her sides. "I won't have that. I can't."

As her boot hit the floor, Mattie cowered back against the sofa, her eyes wide with fear. Rachel's heart twisted and she lowered her head and relaxed her hands. "I'm sorry." She carefully stepped forward and dropped to one knee in front of Mattie. "I'd never hurt you. You know that, don't you?"

"I know." Mattie's voice shook nervously as she tried to smile. "I'm sorry, too. It's a reaction. I can't help it sometimes."

"I'm so very sorry." Rachel scooted forward, dropping her forehead against Mattie's lap and lightly hugging her legs. "Here you've been through a horrible thing, and I go and make it worse for you."

"It's horrible for you, too." Mattie combed her fingers through Rachel's hair. "You're perfectly right. It wouldn't be fair to you to not know what's happening here, and I'd be terrified if I thought I couldn't communicate with you. Let's think on this a bit more. Between the two of us, surely we can come up with a plan that will work."

"Forgive me?" Penitent blue eyes slowly looked up, and Rachel lifted Mattie's uninjured hand, kissing her knuckles a few times before holding the hand against her cheek. She felt Mattie's fingers, lightly stroking her face.

"Of course I forgive you." Mattie patted the space next to her and a tentative smile graced Rachel's face as she took the spot, and felt Mattie climb back into her lap. "You're my whole life, Rachel. Don't you know that by now?"

"I..." Rachel stopped. It was as close to a declaration of commitment as Mattie had ever given her, and she dared not spoil it with silly ill-chosen words. She hugged Mattie closer and buried her face in the clean-smelling hair. She rocked back and forth silently, careful not to jar her in the process. "I'll love you forever." The words finally came, muffled as she spoke against Mattie's head. She brushed her lips across Mattie's forehead before resuming her rocking.

She felt Rachel shaking, and realized she was crying. "We are a couple of weeping fools today, aren't we?" She pulled away and carefully wiped Rachel's face with her nightgown sleeve.

"That we are. I'm a fool for you, at any rate." She pressed her forehead against Mattie's. "We've got until tomorrow morning to come up with a plan that will work. What say we go try to eat a little bit more, take another nap, and discuss it some more over a late supper?"

"Truly? But you said last time you were here that you can't sleep in this house."

"Forget that." Rachel dredged up a smile. "I'll manage fine even if I have to sleep on the floor while you sleep here on the sofa. I'll sneak out a little before dawn and head for the Port."

Mattie eyed the plush cushions, measuring the space in her head. "I think we can both fit here. We might have to spoon, but I think we can."

"Might work at that. See." Rachel smiled fully. "We're coming up with good plans already."

PALE DAWN LIGHT filtered through a crack in the curtains, gently dappling Rachel's face in soft rose and golden hues. She blinked grumpily at the offending window, then closed her eyes and snuggled closer to the warm body she was curled against. It was past time for her to leave, but she had heard Adam's goons drive up only an hour before, when it was still dark out.

She'd slept lightly during the afternoon nap, and then through the night, timing their visits, and discovered that since the morning before, they'd been coming by every four hours, on the hour, for a total of six visits a day.

Duty got the best of her, and she sighed, stretching just a little bit. She was pressed against the back of the sofa, holding Mattie in the curve of her body and legs, surrounding her like a protective cocoon. Her heart was heavy as she studied the still very visible bruises on Mattie's face, and the paleness of the skin that was uninjured. As she silently watched Mattie sleeping, she felt the smaller woman's muscles begin to take on tension, and watched her eyelashes tremble and flutter open, as Mattie yawned and then swallowed, her body slowly coming to life.

"Morning." Mattie yawned bigger and turned, stretching out her legs. Rachel didn't miss the slight wince as she rolled over on her back.

"Your stomach and ribs still hurting?" She gently rubbed Mattie's belly through her light cotton nightgown.

"Some, yes." Mattie reached over, pulling Rachel's arm across her hips, nestling closer to the strong body, her mind spinning at everything that had happened of late, both good and bad. "I'm sore all over. He—he kept on coming after me. He forced me. I feel so ashamed—dirty. I can't seem to forget it. I'm sorry, Rachel. I don't know if I'll ever feel like..."

Rachel understood what her lover could not bring herself to say, and leaned up on one forearm, gently cupping Mattie's face with her other hand, closing her eyes as she struggled for just the right words. "You listen to me. You did nothing wrong, and have nothing to be ashamed of." Rachel opened her eyes and brushed her knuckles against Mattie's face, trying to ignore her anger at Adam's abuse. "I'll never ask you to do anything that makes you uncomfortable. That hasn't changed. I love you. We have all the time in the world, Mattie. And if we play our cards right, we're about to buy ourselves a whole lot more of it. We just need to make it through this next difficult bit, and then maybe we can have ourselves some peace for a while."

"Peace." Mattie tasted the word as it rolled off her tongue. Her eyes tilted up, sparkling in the early morning light that burnished her skin and created copper highlights in her hair. "The only peace I've ever known"—she caressed Rachel's face running her hand down across her shoulder and pulling her more tightly against her"—is in your arms."

"Careful." Rachel let the words wash over her, drinking them in and banishing any lingering fear that what they shared might suddenly vanish. "Don't want to hurt you."

"That would be impossible." Mattie trailed her other hand up a bare arm, tickling across the neckline of a ribbed cotton undershirt, then up and through thick morning-mussed hair. "You could never hurt me."

"I'll do my best not to, for as long as you'll have me around." Rachel kissed her lover's head and shifted, trying to allow for as much comfort as Mattie could have, given her injuries. They held onto each other for as long as they dared, until the sun was fully up. Rachel watched the soft shadows in Mattie's face slowly wash away, replaced with bright daylight. A few of her bruises were starting to fade, and some of the sparkle was returning to her eyes. "I need to go."

"Are you certain you can get another day off at the Port?" Mattie frowned in worry, her good hand plucking at soft, worn cotton.

"Yes." Rachel captured the hand, holding it against her heart. "Billy will cover for me, work a double shift if he has to. Especially given the circumstances."

"Can you get everything done in one day?" Mattie slowly sat up, feeling Rachel move with her, and smiling as she was pulled into a comforting side hug.

"I will get everything done today, and I'll get it done before the evening train comes in." Rachel projected as much confidence into her voice as she could. Truth be told, she had a lot on her plate, but she had no choice. Adam would be home by sundown, and they had to have their plan in motion by the time he arrived. So she smiled, and watched a hesitant mirror of that smile reflected back at her. "Don't you worry. You just be ready."

"What if..." Mattie looked down, her chin quivering.

"No 'what ifs'." Rachel tilted her face up. "You be strong for me, Mattie. You're the bravest person I've ever known, you hear me?"

"Yes." Mattie hugged her close. "I'll be waiting."

"I hate leaving you here." Rachel found herself unwilling to get up, despite the ticking clock.

"I'll be fine." Mattie stood, pulling at her hand.

"I left you alone for three days, and you were not fine." Rachel's face grew red in anger. "I should've checked in on you sooner. Maybe I could've..."

"No 'maybes,' either." Mattie cut her off. "This was not your fault. There is nothing you could have done to change anything."

"I could've taken you away before now." Rachel dug into the sofa with her free hand, her knuckles turning white.

"Against my will?" Mattie softened her voice to remove any sting to her words. "You're not the kind of person to do that, and even if you were, I wouldn't have stood for it. Until yesterday, I wasn't ready and you know it. You've given me more than I could ever hope or ask for. Don't you forget that and don't you go blaming yourself."

"Can't help it." Rachel slowly looked up, meeting hazel eyes that gently chastised her and loved her completely, all at the same time. "I've felt so helpless for so long when it comes to you."

"Well, you can stop feeling that way right now." Mattie leaned in, kissing her quickly. "Come on. The sooner you get going, the sooner I'll know what I need to do."

Rachel reluctantly stood, taking Mattie's hand and leading her to the door. She pulled her into a long hug, holding on and rocking back and forth for a timeless moment. "I'd best be going." She pecked the top of Mattie's head. "I love you. Be brave."

"I love you, too." Mattie peeked out the curtains. "All clear."

Rachel nodded and opened the door, looking around cautiously before dashing around the house and back toward the road and the tree where she'd left her bicycle.

Mattie watched her from a side window for as long as she could, then stood on the back porch and watched until the bicycle disappeared over a rise and behind a sand dune. With a resolute turn, she went back inside and firmly closed the door. For a little while, she simply meandered around, studying all the items that made up their house, occasionally picking up various knick-knacks, trailing her fingers over her shell collection, remembering the special times with Rachel on the beach. Her house. It was no longer a home. She knew that. Finally, she went into the bedroom and pulled a paisley carpetbag from under the bed, and set about the task of packing it.

MATTIE PACED NERVOUSLY back and forth in the parlor, waiting for Adam's arrival. Her bag rested on the floor beside the door, and she already had on her bonnet and travel clothes. She removed a small note from her skirt pocket and read it quickly before carefully folding it back up and tucking it away again. She had it memorized, having read it at least a dozen times since Rachel had delivered it. It was a list of instructions in an unfamiliar hand, and she hadn't even thought to ask who had written it, but she assumed it was probably Billy's penmanship, he being one of the few people they trusted.

Another crisply official-looking letter was folded up on top of the clothing in her carpetbag, in the event she needed it. She had no idea who Rachel had talked to, but somehow she had procured a piece of paper attesting to Mattie being pregnant, complete with Dr. Mills' signature on it. There had been little time for her and Rachel to discuss it, and it had been a surprise, sparing Mattie from having to go through the motions of pretending she'd been to the doctor with no proof. She trusted Rachel that someone at the doctor's office was looking out for her in the event Adam decided to see if it was authentic.

Now, if she could only pull off the acting job she was about to attempt.

Buggy wheels crunched across the shell drive, and she heard one of the horses snort. She parted the curtains at the back window and watched Adam jump down from the buggy and lead the horses into the barn. Her hand shook as she dropped the curtain and moved back into the parlor. She sat down on the sofa, then stood again, deciding standing gave her a bit more presence than sitting. After what seemed an hour, she heard Adam's boot steps on the porch, and watched the doorknob turn.

He removed his hat and hung it on a peg, then looked up and saw her standing there. "Hello, Mattie." He turned toward the bedroom and spotted the carpetbag, almost tripping over it. He spun back around, his face clouded in anger. "What is the meaning of this?" He gestured toward the bag and stepped closer, his jaw muscles twitching as he spoke.

"I'm going home." Mattie's head felt light and she swallowed, and took a deep breath to calm herself.

"The only place you might be going is the insane asylum, because it is obvious you've lost what little mind you had." He moved closer, his hand already drawn back to strike her.

Mattie's eyes never left him as she reached into her skirt pocket, her fingers resting on the handle of her hidden revolver. "Don't you hit me!" She moved backward. "I'm with child, and I'm going home to see my mother."

It took a second for her words to register, and for the first time in a very long time, she actually saw Adam smile, albeit a cautious smile. "You — you're carrying my child?"

"Yes." She was surprised at just how easy the lie was. She had lied to him before, but this was probably the biggest one she'd ever told. "You've gotten your wish already."

"You're certain?" He dropped his hand and stood in place, a profoundly surprised expression on his face.

"Yes. According to Dr. Mills, I am." She didn't move to get the letter, hoping it wouldn't be necessary. "And I want to go home and see my mother. There's a train leaving in an hour that goes through Houston and connects with another to Austin, then another to El Paso. Please, Adam. I'm afraid. I've not been around many babies and don't know much about caring for them. I want to talk to my mother about the baby while I'm still able to travel. In a few more months I might not be able to."

"I don't like the idea of you going all that way alone." He hesitated, though, his face still incredulous at her news.

"I won't be alone. One of the sisters from the church is traveling out there for some missionary work. She'll be with me the entire trip." Mattie could feel the sweat trickle down her back, between her shoulder blades, and hoped it wouldn't break out on her forehead or upper lip.

"Well." He eyed the bag, then looked back up at her. "I suppose there couldn't be anything safer than traveling with a nun. How long do you intend to stay out there?"

"I was hoping maybe five or six weeks, long enough to travel, get rested up, and maybe give mother and me time to sew some clothing for the baby, and order some nursery furniture." She smiled. "I thought a cradle might fit nicely under the front bedroom window. Please, Adam. Every woman wants her mother around when she's expecting. Mine lives so far away. This way she can help me make plans, then when it's time for the baby to be born, she can probably travel out here to be with me for a while."

"Five or six weeks, eh?" He tugged at his beard. "I suppose if you were in El Paso, I wouldn't have to worry about you being alone here while I travel." Secretly, the idea was growing on him for a very different reason. With Mattie safely in El Paso, he wouldn't have to continue to pay his men to keep an eye on her.

Mattie held her breath and waited, and prayed she wouldn't have to use the gun to press her point. She ran her thumb over the smooth wooden handle. She had taken a few practice shots out back earlier that afternoon, then loaded it again. She was fully prepared to throw a conniption fit and pull the gun on him, if necessary—pretend to be a crazed pregnant woman hell-bent on going home to see her mother.

Without further discussion, he suddenly bent over and hefted the bag up. "Come on. I'll drive you to the station. Wouldn't want you to miss that train."

"I can go?" Mattie felt almost faint. "Oh, Adam." She forced a gleeful smile, and threw herself at him, hugging him in feigned gratitude, silently wincing at the pain in her ribs. "Thank you. Mother and I are going to sew up the finest set of baby clothing in Galveston. Just you wait and see."

"I've met your mother," Adam mumbled. "I have no doubt of that." He shrugged off the unusual display and ushered her out the door and to the barn, where he re-hitched up the team and helped her into the buggy, dropping the bag behind the seat. In no time at all they were headed across the island to the train station.

On the other side of the house, away from the barn, Rachel drew a hand across a sweaty forehead, and tucked her Bowie knife back into her boot. She'd carefully listened to the entire exchange from below a side window, hidden behind a scrubby shrub that grew there. She'd done some practice tosses of her own that afternoon, and discovered she could still hit the knot in a tree trunk dead center from thirty paces.

"Billy," she muttered under her breath. "You'd better damned well be at that train station."

ADAM SPOKE VERY little during the buggy ride, but kept looking over at her with the most pleased expression she could recall. He appeared to be in mute happy shock. It almost made her feel guilty over her ruse. Almost, until she remembered the layer of face powder she'd applied earlier, and the deep-set bonnet she wore, all in an effort to mask the bruises on her face.

When they arrived at the train station, Adam himself purchased her ticket to El Paso, and jotted down her stops and train changes for her. She looked around surreptitiously and spotted Billy sitting on a far bench at the end of the platform, hidden behind a newspaper. He didn't dare look up at her, but she recognized him all the same. She knew he was there to make sure she got safely on the train without Adam, and made a mental note to bake him a huge batch of cookies just as soon as she had the chance.

Right before time for the train to pull away from the station, a nun appeared on the platform and introduced herself to Adam as Sister Francis. Mattie had met her once before. She had a stern face, but Mattie detected the slightest twinkle in her eyes, and knew that Sister Francis knew, and would never tell.

They engaged in safe small talk for a few minutes, then the train whistle blew, and they heard the final boarding call. Mattie stood on the bottom step and endured a quick peck on the lips from Adam. "You take care of my wife," he spoke to Sister Francis. "She's carrying my first child. First of a half dozen, I hope."

Mattie shuddered internally at the prospect, but Sister Francis merely nodded. "Congratulations, Mr. Crockett. I promise Mattie couldn't be in better hands."

"Send me a telegraph when you arrive in El Paso, Mattie, you hear me?" Adam handed her the carpetbag. "I don't want to be worrying about you any."

"I will." She blew him a kiss. "I'll miss you, and I'll be home before you know it with a whole heap of baby clothing." She forced a final false smile, then turned and ducked inside, taking a seat next to Sister Francis.

The whistle blew long and loud, and the engine shook with a great puff of smoke, then the wheels screeched as they pulled the heavy train forward, at first slowly, then faster until they were going at the incredible speed of twenty-five miles an hour, at least from what Mattie had read. She looked out the window until Adam was a tiny spot on the deserted platform, then continued to look out for a while, watching as they began to make their way over the bay to the mainland by way of the railroad bridge.

"Good-bye, Adam," she mouthed silently. She wondered if she would ever see him again. She hoped not.

"How does it feel?" Sister Francis patted her on the leg and she jumped at the touch.

"Oh. Sorry." Mattie turned to face her and folded her hands in her lap. "How does what feel? I don't understand."

"To know he's hit you for the last time?" She whispered, and clasped Mattie's hands and squeezed them.

Mattie looked up this time, meeting her dark brown eyes and finding nothing but compassion. She knew Rachel would have been forced to tell the sister of her dire situation, in order to get her to go along with their plan. "I-I don't know just yet. I suspect it hasn't sunk in." Her eyes widened. "I'm free, aren't I?"

"Almost." Sister Francis withdrew her hand and they fell into silence as the train passed over the two-mile bridge. Just on the other side was a small station where the train stopped to unload a few supplies and pick up additional passengers.

Mattie looked hesitantly at Sister Francis, then bent down and tugged her carpetbag from under the seat beneath her. "Thank you." She resisted the urge to kiss her cheek, uncertain if that were appropriate behavior with a nun. "You'll be all right for a few weeks until it's safe to be seen in town?"

"I hardly ever leave the orphanage. I'll be fine staying out of sight for a while." She patted Mattie on the leg. "You go now, while they're busy unloading those supplies. If they ask where you are, I'll tell them you went back to the sleeper car to rest. We're to switch trains in Houston, not far from here, but I'll not be re-boarding. I'll stay overnight at a convent in Houston, then one of the sisters there will help me get back to Galveston tomorrow, after dark."

"Thank you." Mattie gave into her urge, and swiftly kissed Sister Francis' cheek. She quickly made her way down the aisle and into the next train car, then out a back door. She peered around the car and as soon as no one was looking, ran to the back of the station house, and spotted a small wagon parked next to a water pump. "Bless you, Rachel," she spoke quietly to her absent lover.

She cautiously approached the buggy and the lone driver, who looked up as she approached, remaining silent until she was beside the tall front wheel. "Hello, Mattie. I don't believe we've seen each other since Rachel was sick with the fever. I'm Evangeline Sanders, but you may call me Angel. Everyone does who knows me. I apologize my Betsy couldn't come with me. She's back at the house preparing our guest room."

"It's fine." Mattie tossed her bag in the back of the wagon. "I'm ever so grateful to the two of you for taking me in. We promise it will only be for a few months, at the most."

"You listen to me, child." Angel offered her a hand up. "When your Rachel came to me and told me yall's story, I wanted to go whip that rat bastard myself, but she convinced me I could help in a much more constructive way. She's a brave one, she is. Told me only two others on the island know anything about what all is going on between you two. I also know she finally told you that Betsy and I are just like the two of you."

Mattie grew pale, and looked down at her lap, as the buggy pulled away from the station. "Is it worth it?" She peered up into a leathery face, lined with age. Most of the older folk in Galveston had deeply-etched skin, a result of living life on the sun-baked island. "Your life, I mean. Has hiding your life from everyone been worth it?"

"Do you love her?" Angel clicked to the horses.

"More than anything." Mattie finally smiled. "I'd do anything for her, I think."

"There is your answer. And from everything she's done today, it's obvious she would go to the end of the earth for you." Angel pushed her own straw bonnet back and ran her fingers through sweaty bangs before resettling it. "Betsy and I will share our whole story with you. We'll have plenty of time for that, I reckon."

"I'd love to hear it." Mattie frowned, as they approached the bridge. "How are you going to get me through town without anyone seeing me?"

Angel grinned and looked behind them. "In another minute here, you're going to get in the back of the wagon and hide under those horse blankets there, behind those sacks of grain."

"Oh." Mattie relaxed, enjoying the rays of the setting sun as they washed across her face. "I can do that." She smiled and closed her eyes, smelling the ocean nearby, and feeling the soft breeze brush over her skin, lifting her bangs and fluttering the ribbons on her hat. *I'm free.* She shivered with happiness.

THE SCRATCHY WOOL made her neck and face itch, and it was hot under the rust-colored blankets. She inhaled the scent of salty sea air combined with the chemical smell of dye, and reflected that at least they were clean. She could feel every jolt and jar as the wagon rolled over the railroad bridge and back onto the island, and she shifted, rolling to her side on the blanket beneath her.

It was dark and she was beginning to feel slightly claustrophobic. She dared not talk to Angel for fear someone would hear her. With her shoulders pressed against the front of the wagon beneath the seat, she could hear Angel whistling an unrecognizable tune, the clear clean notes drifting over the slight creak of the wheels as they turned. Every now and then one of the horses snorted, and she could sometimes hear their hooves crunching on the shell and sand roads. Occasionally she heard another wagon pass, and once an automobile tooled past, its engine sputtering loudly in her ears.

She felt numb. So much had happened since the prior evening, she hadn't had time to process it all. She needed to talk to Rachel, to make sure the rest of their plan had fallen into place. She was worried as to who all knew of her situation, and whether or not they could be trusted to keep her confidence. Billy and Lillie, she was certain of, and Angel and Betsy she knew would never betray them.

She smiled.

Just like us.

Who knew?

Calling upon them had been a stroke of genius on Rachel's part. Somehow she had just known that the two older women would be willing to help them. It was fortuitous they had a house large enough to accommodate her, and an extra guest room, and she had every intention of helping them out in kind, hoping they would allow her to do most of the housework while she stayed with them.

She was going to have to stay indoors until the marshals returned to deal with Adam. They couldn't risk her so much as standing in an open window for fear someone who knew him would see her. They had already determined she would always keep a carpetbag packed with the bare essentials in case they were forced to run at a moment's notice, and they would keep a wad of cash stowed in the bag, enough to purchase two train tickets and meals and hotel lodging for a few days, if necessary.

Exactly where they would run, beyond Houston, had not been decided, and they both hoped the marshals would lock Adam up and they could stay on the island. They'd talked until the wee hours of the morning and both expressed how much they loved Galveston, the friends they had made there, and the sand and the sea. Living so near the ocean made them both feel wondrously alive, especially when the waves pounded against the shore, rushing up and around their feet in frantic foaming swirls. Yet that same sea could bring incredible peace, the calm waters lapping into small coves and reflecting the slanted rays of sunrise, with the gulls dipping into the water for food, and the playful porpoises that sometimes chattered near the fishing boats.

The wagon rolled to a stop, drawing her out of her musings. She knew to remain still and quiet until Angel gave a clear sign. She could feel her breath against her own face as it pooled between her skin and the blanket. It was almost unbearably hot, and she felt sweaty everywhere. A bath would be heavenly, and she concentrated on that, closing her eyes and imagining tepid water and her lilac soap.

Suddenly, the blanket was drawn back and a face she would have known anywhere, even in the darkness, appeared over her, less than a foot away. She smiled in relief as the fresh air washed over her, and strong arms helped her up. "Rachel?"

"Shhh." Rachel swung her up and over the side of the wagon.

"Let's get you inside. Then we'll talk."

They rushed up what she assumed were the back steps of the house, entering a large airy kitchen that was filled with the scent of bread baking, and a fragrant seafood stew simmering on the stove. Dried herbs hung in bunches over a large deep sink, and several lamps cast a cheerful glow across hardwood floors and an inviting table, covered with a pretty pale blue table cloth, and set with four settings of fine bone china. Betsy turned from the stove and wiped her hands on a yellow-checkered apron. "Welcome, both of you." She gestured toward a staircase just outside the kitchen doorway. "Why don't you go freshen up? Supper will be ready in about thirty minutes or so."

"Thank you." Mattie's voice was soft and shy, her brain still trying to take in her new circumstances. She felt Rachel's arm wrap around her waist, as the taller woman expressed her own gratitude, before whisking Mattie up the stairs and down a short hallway, toward yet another small staircase which spiraled up into a large open third-floor room. She looked around, turning slowly, and ended up in Rachel's arms, peering up uncertainly into steel blue eyes that sparkled warmly back at her.

"Welcome home, Mattie." Rachel tilted her head and brushed her lips across her forehead.

"I—you—together?" She spied an open armoire door, and what she recognized as Rachel's clothing hanging inside.

"I moved." Rachel smiled and drew her over to a low sofa that was tucked into a round alcove, surrounded by windows, which were all covered by curtains. Rachel switched off the lamp on the table, leaving the room in temporary twilight, before she pulled the curtains back, revealing the final rays of sunset and the first scattering of twinkling stars overhead. "It's safe to have 'em open at night, as long as we don't have a light on inside here."

"You moved?" Mattie was still taking in the room, and beginning to recognize Rachel's scant possessions, mixed in with the rest of what she assumed were guest room furnishings provided by Angel and Betsy.

"That's my one big surprise in all of this." Rachel snuggled closer, draping an arm across Mattie's shoulders and pulling her close, turning and leaning back so they could look outside while they talked. "I'm paid up on rent through Saturday, so I gave notice for beginning of next week. Angel and Betsy agreed. They said I should save my wages for a while toward a house for just us two. For all outward appearances, it simply looks as if I left the boarding house to rent a room here. No one will be any wiser to us."

"I can't imagine it." Mattie closed her eyes, feeling a hesitant peace begin to settle over her, surrounded in the comfort of Rachel's arms.

"Imagine it." Rachel stroked her head, ruffling her bangs. "We can be together now, sweetheart."

"I feel like I've gone to sleep and am having the nicest dream." Her lids opened halfway and she spied a plump bed against the far wall under another window, the pillows propped invitingly at the head, and a pretty eyelet spread turned halfway down to reveal clean cotton sheets. "I get to share that with you?" She blushed and looked up, watching Rachel's eyes as they tracked across the room to the bed. "I mean, I..."

"Shhh. We have time, remember?" She spoke quietly and stroked Mattie's head in comfort. "I'll hold you as close as you need me to. I want to make your nightmares go away, Mattie."

"I think you already have." She snuggled close, closing her eyes as Rachel's arms circled her.

A rap at the door caused them both to pull apart self-consciously, their eyes wide. "Come in," Rachel called out, as she reached up, smoothing Mattie's slightly mussed hair.

Betsy appeared in the doorway with a tray in her hands. "I know you've both had a very long day. You must be plumb tuckered out." She smiled and Mattie immediately felt at ease. Betsy's face was tanned and deeply lined, just like Angel's, and her hair was mostly gray, with a few light brown streaks running through it. She was petite, quite a few inches shorter than Mattie, and her build was delicate in contrast to Angel's taller robust frame. "I though you might like to take your supper up here in private. I know you must have a great deal to discuss between you."

"I hate to be rude." Mattie hesitated.

"Pshaw." Betsy waved her off. "There will be many evenings for the four of us to dine together. Take your time, little one. You've been through many trials. It's time to give yourself some breathing room." She set the tray down on a small round table across from the sofa, lifting a cloth from a pretty pink-flowered saucer. "I made you a batch of sugar cookies, and I believe I dipped up enough chowder for both of you." She stood. "Bath is downstairs on the second floor, at the end of the hall, and I left two towels folded up in there for you. Please ask if you need anything. Our home is your home for as long as you need."

"Thank you." They spoke in unison, both women overwhelmed at the kindness of relative strangers.

"Our pleasure." Betsy smiled one more time and slipped out of the room, closing the door softly behind her.

"Mmm." Rachel stood and crept over to the tray, lifting the lid on the stew pot and sniffing appreciatively at its contents. "Smells wonderful. You want me to pour you up a cup?" She turned, only to see Mattie rocking back and forth, her arms wrapped around her knees and tears streaming down her face. "Mattie?" Her voice rose in alarm and she practically leaped back to the sofa, landing on her knees in front of her lover.

She took surprisingly chilled hands into her own and chafed them, guessing at Mattie's tears. "You're safe. No matter what, he's never going to hurt you again. I'll make certain of it."

"I-I can't believe it," she choked out, her chest so heavy she could barely draw breath. "Just like that," she whispered, her tears turning to hiccups before fresh ones appeared. "I'm afraid I'll wake up tomorrow and be back there, and him..."

Rachel moved up to the sofa, hugging her close and rocking her with one arm, smoothing her hair back with the other hand. "The only place you're going to wake up tomorrow morning is in my arms." She felt Mattie tremble against her, as more sobs welled up and she burrowed into Rachel's neck. "Shhh." Rachel continued to hold her. "Everything is going to be fine now. We're going to be just fine."

MATTIE WOKE UP, her heart racing from the edges of a rapidly fading nightmare. She couldn't remember what she had been dreaming, only that she had felt like she couldn't breathe. Her nightgown was damp with sweat and the light covers over her felt stifling. She could feel Rachel curled up behind her, her belly to Mattie's back, one long arm draped loosely over Mattie's hip.

She smiled and carefully rolled away from her, catching her arm and gently placing her pillow under it. Rachel frowned and mumbled in her sleep, then pulled the pillow close and settled down again. Mattie swung her legs over the edge of the bed, then stood and turned, simply watching Rachel for a long moment. She was beautiful, her strong features bathed in pale moonlight that filtered through the still-open window, and her chestnut hair spilled across the sheet, shining as it caught the odd moonbeam.

She softly blew a kiss in Rachel's direction, then turned and crept to the window, curling up on the sofa, her chin resting against her fist as she propped her elbow on the windowsill. The house was in an old neighborhood, just a little southeast of the business district. It was several blocks from the beach, on a slight rise, and although it was far away, if she cocked her head and concentrated, she could barely hear the hiss and roar as the waves broke into rushing foam against the sand.

They'd talked until midnight. Rachel had mailed a letter to Mattie's sister for her. She had asked Carrie to send a telegraph message to Adam as soon as she got the letter, pretending the message was from her. Then Carrie was to burn the letter, and was to be careful to watch the mail each day for any letters from Adam, and intercept them before their mother did, then forward them back to Angel and Betsy in a new envelope so they would look like letters for the two older women, rather than for Mattie.

She'd come partially clean to Carrie in the letter, telling her of

Adam's abuse, at least in terms of him hitting and punching her. She mentioned nothing of Rachel, and only described Angel and Betsy as two "widows" who had offered her shelter for a while until she decided what to do next. She'd begged Carrie to keep her confidence, and was certain her sister would honor her wishes. They'd shared too much growing up, and both knew their mother far too well. Carrie had mentioned in her last letter that she was thinking of leaving home someday before their parents married her off, and Mattie half-expected Carrie to show up on her doorstep in the next year or so.

Mattie focused for a moment on the simple knowledge that she had done it. She had broken free of Adam's grasp and was never going back to him ever again. It was mind-numbing. She had to force herself to focus on the conversation, until Rachel had finally figured out where her mind was, and had suggested they go to sleep and resume their discussion the next evening.

It had been so sweet. Rachel had combed out Mattie's hair for her and braided it, and brought her a glass of water for the night table, and made sure she had a comfortable pillow. Then she'd held her, stroking her head and softly singing to her—silly little lullabies Mattie hadn't heard since she was a child. It was Rachel whose voice had gradually tapered off first, into heavy even breathing that slowly lulled Mattie to sleep as well. It had been a rare moment of peace, and Mattie had fought to stay awake, lying there in Rachel's arms, wanting to savor it for as long as possible, not quite able to believe that it wasn't going to be snatched away from her.

A giddy shiver worked its way from her head down to her toes and she wiggled in pure happiness, drawing her legs up under her and resting both elbows on the windowsill. She knew there would probably be more nightmares, but for that one moment, she allowed herself to taste the truth of her own freedom. For a long while she sat there, watching the moon shadows on the ground below, and the odd cloud patterns as they blew slowly across the starry sky, as she listened to the sea further away.

Finally she got up and made her way back to the bedside, taking a healthy drink of water before she climbed back into bed. Rachel immediately snuggled up to her, drawing her close and kissing her head. "Do you feel all right, sweetheart? Your injuries still hurting you and keeping you awake?"

"I've never felt finer in my life," Mattie whispered, her breath mingling with Rachel's. "And sometimes, life is too wonderful to waste it sleeping." She kissed Rachel tentatively, feeling the sleepy body next to her gradually take on muscle tone and a wiry springy sort of movement, as Rachel woke up, not fully, but enough to have the presence of mind to reach out, reverently cradling Mattie's healing face.

A dark eyebrow quirked in question, as Rachel studied her eyes, her own brow creased with worry. "I wish I could make it so he never laid a hand on you." Her face scrunched up in anguish, and she swallowed hard, stroking Mattie's hair away from her eyes, her fingers lightly trailing along fading bruises.

Slowly, her expression softened, and she smiled sadly at Mattie, before planting a quick soft kiss on her lips. "It's a miracle, having you here with me." She closed her eyes as Mattie moved closer, nuzzling Rachel's chest and gently pushing her onto her back. Mattie curled up next to her and laid her head down, hearing Rachel's strong heartbeat and the quiet movement of her breathing.

"I kept praying for God to send me an angel to watch over me — keep me safe — take me away from ..." Mattie trailed off and kissed the warm skin next to her lips, feeling Rachel shiver. "I'd almost given up. Guess I was wrong."

"Wrong?" Rachel hugged her, tucking Mattie's head under her chin.

"Just when I thought I couldn't go on, along came the angel I'd been praying for all that time." She felt Rachel's hand, rubbing her back in comfort, and she sighed contentedly. "I got more than I ever hoped for when God decided to answer."

Rachel felt a lump in her throat, preventing speech. She blinked hard and drew in a long trembling breath, feeling Mattie settle against her, her eyelashes blinking against Rachel's skin as she fought sleep. Finally, she found her voice, a hoarse rasping sound. "I'm no angel." She stroked Mattie's head, tugging gently at the thick braid that ran down her back. "But I pledge to love you with all that I am, for as long as you'll allow me."

"Then you'll be loving me forever." Mattie scooted up, finding Rachel's lips again.

"Forever." Rachel breathed against Mattie's lips as they drew apart. "I think I like the sound of that."

"Together." Mattie closed her eyes and sank back down against Rachel, every fiber of her body relaxing for the first time she could remember. "Forever."

They lay together in silence, save the breeze, which ruffled the curtains and stirred across clean sheets. No more words were needed, as they drifted off into peaceful sleep.

Chapter
Ten

RACHEL AWOKE AND opened her eyes, her heart skipping a beat before she remembered where she was. She smiled at the warm weight next to her, and the soft breathing that tickled her chest. Mattie had one arm wrapped possessively around her, her hand splayed across Rachel's hip. It was sweet torture and she sighed blissfully, inhaling Mattie's scent and soaking in her closeness.

Her eyes and her body told her it was near dawn, as the palest light drifted into the room, casting deep shadows in the corners and overhead rafters. The ceiling sloped upward from the wall at an angle, giving the room an interesting shape. The room smelled vaguely of the ocean breeze and old warm wood, and the space had a cozy homey feel. She spied several crates tucked into the nooks and crannies above them, and wondered what it must be like to have a lifetime of things stored away in a house you owned and shared with someone you loved.

She hoped to have a personal answer to that question someday.

Now that they were together, her mind drifted logically to what they would do next, at least once the problem of Adam was resolved. They couldn't get married, not in the conventional sense, and she found herself wondering what she could do to make her intentions clear to Mattie. Her heart was in this for life. Most men gave their fiancés a ring when they proposed to them, and she wondered if Mattie would want one, and how they would go about explaining it to people, especially if Adam were in prison.

It might be easier if they ran away and started over somewhere. They could just say Mattie was a widow and the ring was from her marriage. Then again, if Adam went to prison and they stayed in Galveston, maybe she could get Mattie a new ring to replace the one Adam had given her. She frowned, realizing she didn't like the idea of Mattie wearing his ring, and she found her hand wandering down beneath the covers to capture the hand against her hip, drawing it up and studying it curiously.

Her brows hiked up as a quirky grin involuntarily graced her lips.

The ring was gone.

Mattie stirred at the contact and made a few little mewling noises

before she yawned, her hazel eyes blinking open. "Good morning."
She looked first at Rachel's face and then at their hands, which were
linked in mid-air between her face and Rachel's neck. "Something
wrong?"

"Where's your wedding ring?" Rachel twined their fingers and
rested their hands against her chest.

"I took it off last night when I washed my face, and tied it up in a
hanky and tucked it in a pocket in my carpetbag." She looked down as
a tremor ran through her body. "I figured I have to stay indoors away
from other people, so it won't matter if I don't have it on. I..." She
paused, drawing a breath into a suddenly-tight chest. "I couldn't bear
to wear it any more. It doesn't mean what it's supposed to mean."

She looked back up, catching Rachel in an unguarded moment,
her steel blue eyes regarding Mattie's hand thoughtfully. Finally,
Rachel took Mattie's hand and brushed her lips across her ring finger.
"Well then," Rachel swallowed hard, and Mattie could feel her
heartbeat pick up at a rapid pace, "maybe sometime we need to get
you a new one." Her lashes lowered. "That is, if you wanted one." She
looked back up, her eyes filled with earnest hope.

Mattie knew Rachel's heart hung by a thread. It was hers. She
could leave it hanging to fall, or she could pluck it to keep and
treasure like the gift it was.

She pulled at their clasped hands and held them tightly to her
own chest. With her other hand, she reached out, cupping Rachel's
face, her thumb gently caressing a downy cheek, then tracing full lips.
"I can't think of anything I could want more." She felt those lips curve
up into a smile, felt Rachel's heartbeat slow, and watched relief flood
her lovely features. She knew her own smile matched Rachel's, and
that they were speaking of something much greater than a ring.

Rachel pulled Mattie's head down, kissing it, then moved to
pepper her face with more tiny kisses, before finding her lips. It was
sweet, and she took her time, tasting Mattie as they moved together.
She felt Mattie's hands at her back, warm and firm, and she nuzzled
thick red waves. "I'll love you forever, Mattie."

Mattie smiled, the slightest hint of sadness reflected in her eyes.
"Can you make him go away, just a little bit?" She trailed her
fingertips along Rachel's lower back, coaxing her closer and conveying
her intentions. "I'll let you know if I need to stop."

"Are you certain?" Rachel noted Mattie's shy nod of confirmation,
and felt her hold tighten against Rachel's back, as one hand slid
around and lightly rubbed Rachel's belly. She kissed Mattie soundly
and pulled back, studying her concerned eyes. "You just make sure
and do that, you hear?"

Mattie smiled and nodded again, feeling nimble fingers work to
untie the laces of her nightgown, then felt a warm hand brush against
her skin, dancing across her chest and over the curve of her breasts.

Full lips kissed along her jaw line and up to her ear, and whispered comforting words as Rachel brushed against her, and her lips moved lower, nibbling at her skin and banishing all thought of the three days prior.

She found Mattie's breast, brushing her thumb across it, then following with her lips, her own body reacting to the little noises of pleasure so close in her ear. Her hand wandered down Mattie's waist, around her hip, and behind her knee, pulling her leg up and closer around Rachel. Her own breathing was quite uneven, and she had to keep reminding herself to take it slow, that this was about Mattie, and making her feel safe and loved.

Rachel shifted, her hand teasing up Mattie's inner thigh. "If I—I want so much—may I ...?" She felt Mattie's hand on top of hers, guiding her, and she smiled before kissing her again. The smile turned to concern as she pulled back from the kiss, her fingers gently stroking soft skin at the apex of Mattie's hip as she spoke. "I know he hurt you." She gazed intently into Mattie's eyes, her own desire rising at the honest open passion she saw there, Mattie's hazel orbs warmed almost to gold in the early morning light.

"I know you'll be careful with me." Mattie felt the strong clenching in her belly, every fiber of her body wanting Rachel's touch. "Touch me," she whispered, as she guided Rachel the rest of the way and stayed with her, her hand resting softly on Rachel's forearm. She thought fuzzily that it was an interesting combination of sensations, feeling Rachel's forearm muscles contracting and relaxing, and at the same time feeling the thrills and heat as Rachel very gently took her passion to a higher level.

And then all thought vanished and she simply felt Rachel, her touch and the love that flowed from it, and the shudders that rolled through her over and over again, pounding through her body like the waves against the shore. She heard a cry and realized it was her own voice, and she held on, her fingers in a vise around Rachel's wrist, her body pressed tightly into Rachel's. Gradually she became aware of quiet soothing whispers in her ear and Rachel's hand, now stroking her hair as she was rocked in a safe embrace.

Safe.

She mulled that over and vaguely wondered if it were strange that her first thought after making love was to think of how safe she felt

"Are you all right?" Rachel's voice rasped almost inside her ear, rumbling across her skin and making her shiver pleasantly all over again.

"If I were anymore 'all right' I'd be floating, I think. Thank you. You made me forget." Mattie smiled and ran her hand lightly up and down Rachel's side and over the curve of her hip. She could feel the coiled tension in her muscles, just under the skin. She placed her palm against Rachel's stomach and felt it ripple at her touch. "I do believe, though, that you could be more 'all right' than you are presently, Miz Travis." She trailed her hand slowly up, cupping Rachel's breast and hearing her breath catch.

"I..." Rachel's words were cut off as Mattie claimed her in a heartfelt kiss, and her touches moved down, tickling her navel before moving lower. She rolled slowly to her back, feeling Mattie settle partly next to her, partly on top of her, and her hands found Mattie's waist, hitching her up and settling her into a more comfortable position.

Their eyes met and locked, sharing their emotions as Mattie touched her, tentatively at first, then with increasing confidence, remembering things they had shared, things she had stored away, and what it felt like to see Rachel in the throes of passion — what it felt like to be the one to give that pleasure to her. It was empowering, and humbling, knowing she held another person's heart and soul. "I'll be careful with you too, Rachel."

She felt the first tremors as Rachel responded to her, and she dipped her head, kissing her soundly, as the sun rose on a very different day than the one before.

AFTER A QUICK wash-up in the water closet, both women made their way down to the kitchen, where wonderfully tantalizing scents wafted up the stairs, causing both their stomachs to growl in appreciation. "Good morning," Betsy called out pleasantly, as she heard their footsteps creak on the last few steps down. "I've cooked up a batch of griddle cakes and a mess of bacon, so I hope you're both hungry." She turned and gestured toward the table, which was already set with four place settings of the same pattern as the dishes they had eaten from the night before. "Have a seat, Angel will be in from the stable in short order."

"Oh." Rachel strode toward the back door. "I'll go see if I can help her out."

"Naw." Betsy stopped her with a hand on Rachel's arm. "We've only the two horses. No cows or chickens or such. We get our milk and eggs from one of our neighbors a few doors down. We trade. I make their baked goods, bread and such. Works out for all of us. He's a widower with two children, who has little time to cook, and we don't have the time nor energy to care for much livestock anymore."

"Well, I should help out somehow." Rachel almost pouted, feeling badly that they'd stolen their time together earlier, and missed early morning chores. She smiled, a tiny smile. Truly, she didn't feel all that badly. It had been a much-needed reconnection of hearts and souls that had seen far too much pain in the past week.

Betsy eyed her with a mischievous grin. "Oh, I'll be more than willing to take you up on that offer when I need the garden weeded.

My back can't take the bending and stooping like it used to, and poor Angel's usually plumb tuckered out after her day at the mill."

"I can help with that," Mattie offered, without thinking.

"No." Rachel and Betsy answered in unison, and Rachel sat down next to her at the table, taking her hand and stroking the back of it with her thumb. "Remember, we can't risk you stepping outside at all, not even one step on the back porch. If anyone sees you, it could spoil all our plans."

"I forgot." Mattie looked down at her lap, fiddling with a pretty linen napkin, folding it over in half. She knew she had to stay indoors, and the thought of seeing neither sun nor surf for a month was almost more than she could bear. She dredged up her best smile and looked back up. "To be with you is worth any sacrifice." She smiled, watching its mirror on Rachel's face.

"Well, aren't you two a couple of love birds?" Betsy chuckled and turned back to the stove, flipping over golden-brown griddlecakes that bubbled up around the edges, popping and releasing a wonderfully nutty-sweet scent.

Mattie blushed and looked back down, and felt a gentle touch to her hair as Rachel pushed it back from her face. She hadn't taken the time to braid it or put it up yet, and it hung in thick red waves down her back and over her shoulders, her heavy fringe of bangs hiding the scattering of freckles across her forehead. She wore a pale lavender shirtwaist and matching skirt, and as her blush began to fade, the lavender color complimented her milky pale skin perfectly.

"Don't be ashamed, child." Betsy brought a rasher of bacon to the table and set it down next to a cold pitcher of milk, sweat running down the thick crockery and dampening the napkin it sat on. "In our home, behind our doors, you don't have to hide your feelings for one another. It was the first rule Angel and I made when we bought this place. Out there when we're about town, we may be the widows Sanders and McKenzie, but behind our doors, we are like any other married couple, and we don't need a piece of paper to tell us how much we care for one another."

"It's so different from how I was raised," Mattie commented softly, auburn lashes blinking shyly over her hazel eyes. "Before I met Rachel, I'd never heard of two women being together."

"Imagine our confusion when Angel and I first discovered our feelings for one another." Betsy stacked the griddle cakes on a platter and covered them with a napkin to keep them warm, then joined the younger women at the table. She brought a pot of tea and poured up three cups, pushing the sugar bowl toward her guests. "Thirty-five years ago in Atlanta, where we come from, there was absolutely no one like us that we knew of. We had no one to talk to at all." She smiled and turned as Angel opened the back door and stepped inside, wiping the soles of her shoes on a thick rug before she sat down next to Betsy, kissing her on the cheek as she did so.

"Good morning." She nodded at Rachel and Mattie. "Did y'all sleep well up there? It has been a very long time since we've had any guests stay up there. Most times we just put people up in the guest room on the second floor."

"I thought y'all might enjoy having the entire third floor loft to call your own," Betsy chimed in, "it offers more privacy than our other guest room."

"Thank you," Mattie and Rachel answered at the same time, then turned and laughed at each other.

"We slept very well, thank you," Rachel continued. "We are both more grateful than we can say for y'all taking us in, especially on such short notice."

"You listen to me." Angel's features darkened. "When I heard what that bastard had done," she looked at Mattie, her eyes spotting the fading bruises around her eyes, "we had to do something."

"If we hadn't taken y'all in, my Angel was about to go after him with a pitchfork." Betsy patted her enraged lover on the arm.

"I've got a Bowie knife with his name on it." Rachel's own anger flared all over again, and she felt a tempering squeeze to her leg under the table.

"So, y'all are from Atlanta?" Mattie changed the subject.

"Originally, yes," Betsy answered, and Mattie could detect the remains of her softer Southern drawl, now tempered by a Texas twang. "I was eighteen and engaged to be married to my beau, as soon as he came home from the War of Northern Aggression. He was a private in the Confederate army. Angel, she was already a war widow at the tender age of twenty-two. We both volunteered as best we could in the ladies' social circle. I darned a good number of stockings for the soldiers, and Angel helped doctors treat any injured that came home."

"So you met during the war?" Rachel's grandfathers had both fought and survived to tell tales at family gatherings. "Those were some hard times, especially in Atlanta, from what I hear. Were y'all living there when the Yankees burned it down?"

"The burning of Atlanta was the single greatest miracle of our lives." The twinkle returned to Angel's eyes as she forgot her rage at Adam. "As far as our families know, Betsy and I died during that siege."

Mattie's mouth flew open in shock. "I don't understand." Rachel took her hand and squeezed it, then dished up griddle cakes to all four women as they listened to Angel and Betsy's story.

"We met about a year before Atlanta fell," Angel continued. "I already knew I had an attraction to women in general. My marriage was what I was supposed to do, in those times. When I got word my husband had been killed at Gettysburg, a part of me was sad, of course, but a part of me was relieved. I'd done my duty by society, and didn't ever have to remarry if I didn't want to. I could play the grieving widow for the rest of my life if I so chose."

"She never counted on meeting me." Betsy smiled charmingly. "And I most certainly never figured to fall for a woman." She reached up and patted Angel's arm again, keeping her hand there as she spoke. "It took us a while to figure out why we wanted to spend so much time together, and why we almost always seemed to snuggle up like two peas in a pod whenever we had some private time to talk."

"I finally got up the courage to talk to Betsy about my feelings." Angel blushed, something Mattie found endearing in the older woman. "I had to kiss her." The blush deepened. "I was simply going to die if I didn't, and I figured I'd best make sure it would be well-received first, so I gathered up my wits and told her I was in love with her."

Betsy laughed softly. "Once she said it, all my feelings suddenly made sense. For the first time, I understood why I looked forward to receiving little letters from her much more than I did mail from the front lines of the war. If I received a letter from her and my beau on the same day, I always read Angel's first." She gazed at Angel with warm affection as she talked. "I kissed her first."

"And I fainted." Angel laughed aloud. "Good thing we were in a hay-filled barn at the time. I woke up to her pressing a cold rag to my forehead. After that, we spent as much time together as we could, and began to talk about running away together."

"When the Yankees invaded and the town began to burn, Angel showed up on my doorstep." Her eyes took on a faraway look. "She took my hand and said 'now is the time'. I knew what she meant, and it took me all of ten minutes to pack a carpetbag. We snuck down an alley and disappeared in the chaos. We camped out in the countryside for a few nights and finally managed to hop a boat that took us around Florida and along the Gulf coastline. Spent a few months in N'Orleans and then came to Texas when we heard of jobs for women in the mill here."

"We never went back." Angel's expression was an odd mixture of joy and wistfulness. "Never looked back. No one from back then knows we're still alive today, far as I know. I managed to get a hold of the Atlanta newspaper right before we boarded that boat, and read our names among the civilian casualties."

"Ever since then, we've been the widows Sanders and McKenzie," Betsy finished the story. "Most folks from around here don't know much about our past, other than thinking we're a couple of war widows, which is halfway true, since Angel is."

Rachel and Mattie exchanged solemn glances. Rachel had already severed ties with everyone in her family except her brother, and she knew Mattie was prepared to do the same if she had to. Rachel swallowed and looked across the table at their hosts. "Do you have any regrets?"

"No."   Both women answered without hesitation, and Angel continued, "You ladies are about to embark on the adventure of your young lives. If you love each other as much as you appear to, you'll find that no sacrifice is too great to be together. You may have to lie and deceive folks in public, and that's a sad fact of our existence. But few married couples share the kind of love we share, and I'll wager few have had to work as hard or give up as much to be together as we have. It makes the love all the sweeter."

"And I've never doubted her love for me," Betsy added. "No one would go through what we have to be together, unless they truly loved one another."

Mattie peered thoughtfully at Rachel, just as the taller woman looked over at her with a new wonder and respect in her eyes. She smiled gently and saw Mattie's eyes warm as they fell on her face. They understood all too well, what Betsy spoke of.

Angel cleared her throat, breaking their gaze. "How about I give you a ride to the docks this morning? They're close to the mill."

"I'd appreciate that." Rachel hastily finished up her breakfast and stood. "I'll put my bicycle in the back of your wagon, in case we need to come back ho — back here at different times."

Betsy smiled at Rachel's stumble of words. "You can call it 'home' for as long as you stay here."

"Thank you." She turned, and took Mattie's hands. "You don't need me to take another day off?"

"No." She squeezed Rachel's hands in reassurance. "You've already missed two days on account of me. I'll be fine here. I'm sure Betsy has some more stories to tell, and I can help her clean up from breakfast and prepare a nice supper for y'all tonight."

"You two go on." Betsy shooed at Rachel and Angel, blushing as Angel snagged her in a bear hug. "Oomph." She let out a breath as the much taller woman released her. "I've got some fresh vegetables Mattie and I can chop up, and make a nice pot of stew for tonight. We'll manage to stay busy, so don't you worry. The day will fly by and you'll be back here before you know it."

"I look forward to it." Rachel ducked her head and pecked Mattie on the cheek. "I love you," she whispered ever so quietly into a pink-tinged ear. She winked and turned, following Angel out the back door.

Two thoughtful pairs of eyes followed them from the window, until the wagon pulled out of sight. Betsy turned and regarded Mattie. "How about we clean up these dishes, and then I've got some mending to do. I'll brew another pot of tea and tell you more about Atlanta and the war."

"I'd like that very much." Mattie smiled shyly, and moved to the sink, retrieving an extra apron and tying it around her waist.

AT THE NOON hour, Rachel hastily ate the dinner of ham sandwiches and pickles Betsy had packed for her, enjoying the hearty meal as opposed to the crackers and salt pork she was used to. After carefully picking off every crumb, she hopped on her bicycle. If Mattie couldn't go outdoors, she'd just have to bring some of the outdoors inside. She rode down to the beach and collected a dozen different shells to replace the ones Mattie had left behind when she'd left Adam. She gazed out to sea, slowly soaking in the knowledge that they were finally, magically together. It brought tears to her eyes and she blinked, scattering them across her cheeks before she could catch them with her shirt cuff. In all her life she'd never imagined she could be as in love as she was with Mattie. It was a miracle worthy of a few small sacrifices.

Feeling better about the situation, she made her way back to the docks just as the noon hour was over. She washed her face in a bucket of tepid water and moved to another one, drawing up a full dipper and gulping it down. Riding her bicycle in the noonday heat took its toll, and she could feel her undershirt sticking to her body. She looked around and decided no one was going to care if she shed her long-sleeved shirt.

She tied it around her waist and pulled a broad cool green leaf from her almost empty dinner pail, sticking it under the brim of her hat. Her hair was in a long braid, and she was wearing her lightest pair of work trousers. It was the best she could do to stay cool under the circumstances. Rivulets of sweat ran down her neck, dampening her undershirt, and trickling down her shoulders and over her biceps, making her skin feel sticky at the crook of her elbow.

She trod down the dock to a fishing boat she and Billy were repairing. The owner had gotten into shallow water and run aground, ripping a large hole in the hull. He had gotten lucky. The rudder remained intact and the hole consisted of missing boards, which were torn cleanly off. Some such accidents would have resulted in loss of the craft, but this one could be fixed.

The sound of sawing reached her ears, and she turned into the slip area where four sawhorses were set up. They had carefully measured out the lumber that morning, and now they were cutting it. It would be a two-day job. They would most likely get the fresh-cut boards nailed in place by day's end, and the next day would be spent painting the entire boat with a fresh coat of pale gray paint.

"Howdy." Billy looked up briefly, careful not to cut himself with his saw.

"Howdy yourself." Rachel took up another saw and joined him on the next set of sawhorses, retrieving a clean yellow board, the thick east Texas pine smelling sickly sweet in the sweltering air.

"Where'd you go?" Billy pushed his hat back, mopping his brow with a large red handkerchief.

"Went to collect some shells for Mattie." She blushed a little and smiled as she looked down. "I feel bad for her. She's going to get restless cooped up inside that house all the time. It's a nice house, and Betsy and Angel have been extremely kind to us, but I imagine Mattie may get a tad lonely, not being able to see anyone other than the three of us for the next several weeks."

"Maybe I can get Lil to pay her a visit a few times a week." His voice was hesitant. Billy had been with Lillie long enough that she had told him of her past both with Rachel and with Adam. It had taken some getting used to, and it wasn't something he liked to think about, but it was there, and he knew it was something Mattie was also aware of.

"I think she'd appreciate that," Rachel answered. "Truly."

"Good." He pursed his lips inward, making a decision. "I'm thinking of asking Lillie to marry me."

It was Rachel's turn to stop sawing. She looked up, studying the bowed head. "You going to stay here?"

"Tough to say." Billy finished one board and took up another one, resting the smooth, clean wood across the sawhorses and finding the penciled mark where he needed to cut it. "We've not talked about it very much, but it is a fact a lot of folks know who Lillie is. Or was," he corrected himself.

Lillie had given up her regular profession and was merely tending bar, taking on the shifts Rachel had once worked. Billy was helping supplement her income, and she had moved into the boarding house since she no longer worked for the room she had at the saloon. Mr. Bullock hadn't been happy to lose her as one of his "girls," but when she explained that he would either have to let her tend bar, or else she would leave, he reluctantly agreed. She was pretty, and having her behind the bar was better than nothing.

"Folks have damned long memories sometimes," Rachel agreed with him. "Might be tough for them to accept her as just another one of the married ladies on the island. That is a fact. Bunch of nosey old biddies with nothing better to do than gossip and make life miserable for anyone who doesn't fit in."

"That's what we've talked about." Billy continued to cut the board as he talked, keeping his eyes on his work, watching the sharp saw teeth grind into the hard wood. "She gets called names sometimes when she goes to the store, and some shops still won't let her in. Makes me want to go wale on a few people, but honestly, that would only make things worse. Might be best for us if we move away after we marry. If she'll have me," he added hopefully.

"I think she will." Rachel smiled warmly. "Listen. I was thinking of buying Mattie a ring myself. If you do decide to ask her, maybe we could go looking together. I don't have the first idea of what to buy, plus it will look strange for me to buy one. Maybe I can pick one out and you can get it for me. I'm saving up for one, starting this week."

"Um." Billy paused and looked up at her. "You do know you can't marry her, don't you?" He regretted the question as soon as it left his lips.

Pained steel eyes rolled toward him before Rachel straightened up, her chin jutting out just a little bit. "Of course I know that," she snapped. "We both know that. Know we're going to have to play-act in front of everyone for the rest of our lives. Act like we're just a couple of pitiful spinsters that no one would have." She finished cutting her board, giving the end a savage shove to free it from the part she needed to keep for repairing the boat.

Billy nibbled his lip and carefully withdrew a cigar from his shirt pocket, along with the whiskey flask from his boot. Without a word he walked around to Rachel, pausing and leaning back to sit against the sawhorse. She ignored him, retrieving another board and placing it across the horses, almost smacking him with it in the process. He sighed and held out the cigar, watching her lips twitch with the effort of trying to remain angry.

Long fingers slowly reached out and accepted the offering. She placed it between her lips and leaned over, allowing Billy to light it for her. It was a gesture on both their parts, a reminder that despite their relationship, he had just offended a lady, however unconventional a lady she might be. She raised her eyebrows and blew the first puff of smoke directly over his shoulder, her eyes softening in the process. The ruse was over, as he next held out the flask and she took a long soothing swig of the amber whiskey, enjoying the burn as it slid down her throat and hit her belly with a warm jolt.

"I'm sorry," Billy said quietly. "I don't know what I was thinking."

"I'm sorry I snapped at you," Rachel replied. "I...one of my greatest fears or regrets...oh, I'm not speaking very clearly." She stopped, working the cigar over to the corner of her mouth so she could talk and smoke at the same time. "Mattie deserves the best. Especially after what she's been through. I sometimes can't believe she wants to be with me when she could easily have some nice handsome man to take care of her. Her life would be so much simpler."

"But she loves you." Billy took a sip of whiskey and re-capped the flask, dropping it back into his boot. He reluctantly moved back to his work and took up his saw. "The way she looks at you. Whew." He shook his head and smiled. "Most men should be so lucky. That girl is smitten with you, Rachel. She looks at you like you've done gone and hung the moon for her."

"I'd give her anything." Rachel tried to shove down her bad mood. "The one thing I can't give her is my name. Or a baby, for that matter. What if she regrets that someday?"

"There are plenty of children who need a good home." Billy

looked over at her, gauging her reaction. "It wouldn't be so terribly strange for a spinster woman to take in an orphan or two."

"Hmmm." She peered at him thoughtfully. "That's a possibility, but right now we have bigger fish to fry. Gotta be careful not to cross Adam's path until those marshals return."

"Just be careful." Billy continued to frown. "I couldn't abide seeing you or Mattie get hurt."

"You know we have an alternate plan, if we need it." Rachel thought of the two carpetbags that would always stay packed sitting under the bed on the third floor, just in case. "If we need to, we are prepared to leave with a moment's notice."

"I know. Selfishly, I'd like you to be here long enough to witness my marriage to Lillie." Billy grinned at her, a slight blush coloring his tanned face.

"I wouldn't dream of missing it." Rachel flashed him a genuine smile. "And neither would Mattie."

They passed the afternoon in light-hearted banter, as the summer sun beat down on the docks of Galveston.

THE LONG, HOT day finally came to an end, and Rachel took off on her bicycle, winding through town and back into the older neighborhood streets, lined with stately Victorian homes, each yard etched with a white picket or wrought iron fence. After a short ride, she reached Betsy and Angel's house, pulling up around back and propping her bicycle against a post in the shelter of the covered back porch.

She carefully took up the shells, removing her hat and carrying them inside it, and wiped her feet on a braided-rag rug, before she opened the back door. The scent of spicy pepper and meaty white fish greeted her nose, along with fresh-brewed sweet tea. Her mouth watered in appreciation and she looked around, spotting Mattie's lithe form against the far counter, where she was removing fresh-baked oatmeal cookies from a pan. "Howdy." She sidled up to Mattie, holding her hat in front of her for inspection.

"Oh!" Mattie turned, wiping her hands on her apron. Her eyes sparkled in surprise as she took in the delicate pale shells, her fingers trailing lightly over them, lifting each one in turn and studying them. "How pretty." She looked up, just as Rachel reached out, wiping a smudge of flower from her freckled cheek. "Thank you."

"Pretty shells for a pretty lady." Rachel looked around. "Where are Betsy and Angel?" She leaned in, stealing a sweet kiss, lingering against Mattie's lips for a bit.

"Mmm." Hazel eyes fluttered open. "Angel took a loaf of bread down the street to the family they mentioned this morning, and Betsy is upstairs putting away some laundry. Supper will be ready in about half an hour."

"Good. Gives me time to clean up." She looked down at her sweaty sand-dusted clothing just as Mattie moved in for a warm hug. "I don't smell very good right now."

"I beg to differ." Mattie buried her nose into Rachel's shirt, inhaling the musky wind-blown, sun-kissed scent she had come to love. "Oh." She looked up in admonishment. "You smell like the ocean." She inhaled again, greedily absorbing the salty freshness that clung to Rachel's exposed skin.

It brought on an unexpected reaction, as Mattie found her body craving the closeness, and her cheeks turned pink at her own thoughts. It was a longing she was still getting used to, the desire to touch and be touched. "I missed you today." She nuzzled Rachel's chest, planting a quick kiss on the tanned skin there. "Let me go draw you a bath."

"You don't have to do that." Rachel gestured around the room. "Here you've been working hard all day, cooking up such a delicious-smelling meal for us. I can draw my own bath."

"I'd like to do that for you. Please?" Mattie straightened her collar, then adjusted the suspenders at her shoulders. "You can go up to the third floor and get a fresh change of clothes, and I'll have the tub filled by the time you get back down there. I'll wash your hair for you." She smiled charmingly.

"How can I refuse an offer such as that?" Rachel tilted her head, finding Mattie's lips again, then took her by the hand and led her upstairs.

A while later, she lay back in the tub, her eyes closed, as Mattie's fingers ran through her chestnut locks. Mattie hummed happily, and reached down absently with one hand to stroke Rachel's face for a moment, before she resumed the task of working out the wind-blown snarls in Rachel's freshly washed hair. Rachel relaxed into the touch and reflected that she was a most fortunate woman.

ONE EVENING, THREE weeks after they had moved in with Angel and Betsy, Rachel came home bearing a package, a mischievous gleam in her eye. She smiled at the two older women, both of whom were sitting on the back porch in the shade, sipping at tall glasses of cold sweet tea. "She upstairs?"

"She is, poor thing," Betsy shifted in the porch swing, facing Rachel as she stepped up onto the porch. "I think she's miserable in this heat. I finally convinced her there's no sense in wearing petticoats, stockings, shoes, and that godforsaken corset inside the house in the summer, but it's still real warm in there, especially in the heat of the day. She's been taking a cool bath every afternoon, and even taken to napping afterward. She's pale as a ghost, what with getting no sun or fresh air."

"You're looking a might tan, though," Angel joined in. "And, my lord, but if you don't start eating better, I do believe you're going to waste away."

"I do eat, just with this blasted heat, I sweat it off faster than I can put it on." Rachel smiled, patting her pocket. "Harvest was good this year, though, and I'll take the extra wages and overtime at the Port. Plenty of time to put back on weight this winter."

"Well, your Mattie is making up for it." Betsy laughed lightly. "She's so tiny, I don't know where she puts it, but she does have a healthy appetite."

"Glad to hear it. She ate like a little bird when she was living with him." Rachel shifted her package from one arm to the other.

"What do you have there?" Angel eyed the bulky paper-wrapped parcel.

"A little surprise for Mattie." She flashed a brilliant smile. "Don't suppose we could borrow the wagon and the horses for a while tonight, after it's full dark?"

"Ah-ha." Angel stood. "I'll go you one better. I'll go hitch the team up while you go show your lady her surprise."

"Thank you." Rachel patted her on the shoulder as she opened the back door. "I figure the risk is worth getting her outside for a while. I appreciate it. I promise to take good care of the horses."

"I've no doubt of that. Now scoot. She's been mooning about up there for over an hour. I think she's waiting for you."

Rachel ducked inside the house and crept quietly up the stairs. She stopped in the doorway to the loft to observe her lover for a moment. Mattie was curled up on the sofa next to the window, her chin propped on her arm. The window was open to let in the air, but the curtains were drawn against the remaining rays of sunset. As she watched, Mattie sighed heavily and sniffled, and reached up, swiping at her eyes.

Rachel's heart turned over in sympathy, and she stepped back, knowing Mattie wouldn't want to be caught sulking. She exaggerated her steps and entered the room. "Hello, pretty lady. How are you feeling?" Mattie had looked tired for a few days, and had been a little cranky, something Rachel chalked up to the never-ending heat as much as her forced confinement to the house.

"Sticky and hot. I'm sorry to complain, it's just that I can't ever seem to cool off, no matter what I do." Mattie stood to greet her, her eyes immediately lighting up as she spotted the package. "What's that?" Rachel's eager smile was catching, and her own lips turned up into a grin, playfully snatching at the brown paper and twine.

"A surprise." Rachel held it out of reach, doing a little dance before she relented and held it out. "Here. Open it up."

Mattie took it and sat down on the bed, untying the twine and opening up the paper to reveal — "Men's trousers?" She held up a small pair of canvas work trousers, and a long-sleeved white shirt, along with a pair of stockings, a pair of boots, and a wide-brimmed cowboy hat. Before she could catch herself, her face fell. "Um?" She looked up, not sure what to say.

"Go on, try them on." Rachel grinned, her eyes sparkling in the lamplight.

"Why?" Mattie was at a loss, but she stood and slowly began to unbutton her shirtwaist. She smiled as Rachel moved in to help her, playfully stealing a kiss in the process.

"You'll see." She helped Mattie undress, and showed her how to tuck in the shirt just so, and how to fasten the suspenders that were rolled up in the fold of the trousers. She'd forgotten an undershirt, and dug through her own clothing, finding one that was a little snug for her, but, while a little big for Mattie, would do. Once Mattie was dressed, Rachel picked up her box of hairpins from the dressing table, tucking Mattie's long braid up into a tight coil on top of her head and pinning it in place. She topped her head off with the cowboy hat and smiled.

"I look like a young boy." Mattie studied the loose-fitting clothing with a critical eye. None of her womanly curves were in evidence, and the only signs she was female were her slender neck, her delicate facial bone structure, and her smooth, milky skin. She watched as Rachel stepped in behind her, pulling up her shirt collar until it hid most of her neck.

"Precisely." Rachel gave her suspenders a tug. "It's almost full dark out, new moon tonight, but if we're going to go riding down to the beach, we'd best have you disguised, don't you think?"

Her words sank in, and Mattie spun around, wrapping her arms around Rachel's neck. "The beach? Truly?" She squealed with delight, as Rachel picked her up and twirled around in a circle, making her dizzy.

"Truly." Rachel smiled and held up a key. "I've got a small men's bathing suit out in the wagon, and this is the key to the Pagoda Bath House. We are going to walk on the beach, play in the water, and shower the salt and sand off afterward. You ready to go?"

"I've been ready for days!" Mattie kissed her on the cheek and gazed at herself in the mirror again. "You're sure it's safe?"

"It's a tad bit risky, I reckon, but I talked it over with Angel, and she thinks it should be safe enough. If we run into anyone, talk in a deep voice if you have to talk at all. You're Betsy's nephew visiting from up in Dallas. It's late enough we shouldn't see anyone out, but it's good to have a story, just in case."

"Yes, ma'am." Mattie gave the deeper voice a try and burst into helpless giggles. "What's my name?"

"Hmmm." Rachel tapped her chin. "How about Matthew? It's

close enough to your real name."

"Matthew it is, then." She took Rachel's hand, then dropped it. "Guess you wouldn't be holding Matthew's hand, would you?"

Rachel's eyes roamed appreciatively over Mattie. "My dear, there are many things I shouldn't do with Matthew, but will most likely try anyway before the night is over."

Mattie blushed, a dark pink dusting of her cheeks, and shyly tucked her hand in Rachel's. She allowed herself to be led down the stairs and through the kitchen, where Betsy draped a hastily prepared picnic basket over Rachel's free arm. "You two love birds go on now, and have a good time, spooning out on the beach."

Angel saw them to the door. She stood on the porch and studied the dark sky, as they made their way across the back yard to the barn. "Go on around the house. The team is hitched up and ready to go."

"Thank you." Rachel turned and waved at her. "I appreciate it."

"Me, too." Mattie blew her a kiss, and followed Rachel around the corner toward a much-needed outing.

THE BREEZE ON her face was heavenly, as the horses pranced along the beach road toward the bathhouse. They passed only a few other buggies, and two or three individuals on foot, but otherwise were alone on the long stretch of road. The tall coarse marsh grass rustled against the buggy spokes, and the mixed sand and shell road crunched in pleasant familiarity under the wide wood wheels. Mattie kept one hand tucked into Rachel's crooked elbow, while she held the hat on her head with the other.

Rachel road along in companionable silence, basking in the glow that practically emanated from Mattie's face as she drank in the fresh air and the warm summer night. Finally, they reached the bathhouse, which was deserted at the late hour. Rachel hopped down and ran around, grasping Mattie around the waist and swinging her down to the ground. As her feet hit the ground, a wave of dizziness made her lose her balance, and Mattie grabbed Rachel's shoulders, barely keeping from falling down.

"Whoa!" She took several deep breaths, clearing her spinning head.

"Sorry." Rachel saw the blood leave her face, even in the darkness. "Did I swing you down too quickly?"

"No." Mattie laughed, her voice shaky. "Guess I'm just not used to being outdoors. Too much fresh air all at once." She smiled and took Rachel's hand. "Come with me. I want to walk on the beach for as long as we can, and get my feet wet."

"Your wish is my command." Rachel led the horses over to a hitching post and tied them securely, leaving them both with feedbags to keep them occupied. She took Mattie's hand again, and they swung their joined arms as they walked through the loose sand on the upper beach, then reached the packed wet sand near the shoreline. They removed their boots, leaving them tucked behind a large piece of driftwood, and rolled up their trouser legs.

With a giant smile on her face, Mattie walked out until the rolling surf licked at her toes, then covered her legs to just above her ankles. It felt deliciously cool and refreshing, and she laughed in giddy happiness. Rachel chuckled along with her. "Darlin', it's a good thing we're alone on this here beach, because that laugh would never pass for a man."

"Oh." Mattie's smile disappeared. Much as she was enjoying herself, she knew they were taking a pretty big risk. "I'll try to be more quiet."

Rachel felt the change of mood, and silently kicked herself. *Just what she needs, for you to put a damper on the best time she's probably had in weeks.* "No." She sidled up to Mattie, then slipped in behind her, wrapping her arms around her and pulling her close until her back was pressed against Rachel's front. "Laugh all you want to. There's no one around to hear except me, and it's like music to my ears." She ducked her head, nibbling at Mattie's neck. "Does my heart good. I want to hear you laughing and see your beautiful smile for the rest of our lives." A few more nibbles. "I love you."

"I love you too." Mattie snuggled up against her and looked up at the sky. There was no moon, only an inky blanket covered in thousands of white twinkling lights. It was one of the most beautiful sights her starving eyes had seen, and they suddenly stung with unexpected tears. She blinked, closing them, and felt Rachel continue to kiss her neck, then her collarbone, then finally felt her nuzzle her hair as she removed the hat. "Feels so nice, being here with you."

"Likewise." Rachel slowed down, resting her chin on Mattie's head and releasing a sigh of contentment.

"Look." Mattie pointed up. "That one looks kind of red."

"Which one?" Rachel peered upward, trying to follow her gaze. She felt Mattie take one of her hands and lift it, as their joined hands pointed toward a large star.

"There." Mattie directed both their pointed fingers. "Near the center of the sky. See?"

"Oh. Yes I do." Half her attention was on the slightly pink-tinted star, the other half on the overwhelming headiness of Mattie's scent and her breathing. She could feel it, almost as if it were inside her instead of next to her. It was intoxicating, and she drew in great lungfuls, imprinting Mattie on her heart all over again. It went beyond the physical, a desire to merge with Mattie, and to pull her inside, with a fierce wave of protectiveness overriding all of it. She knew, in that moment, she would do anything for Mattie—jump in front of a trolley car, dive into a raging river, or climb any mountain.

She had no idea where the emotions came from, and shook her head, trying to re-gain her equilibrium.

"Are you feeling well?" Mattie turned in her arms, touching Rachel's forehead.

"Yes." Rachel removed Mattie's hand, kissing it in the process. Before she could think, Mattie moved in, gently tasting her lips, and she was lost all over again in a kiss that she felt from her lips all the way to her toes, with lots of nice tingling sensations in between. "I think I need to cool off a little." She pulled back, her body reeling from the contact. "Want to go for a swim?"

"That would be divine." Mattie cocked her head as Rachel began unbuttoning her shirt, sliding it down her tanned arms along with he suspenders, revealing her ribbed undershirt beneath it. "Oughtn't you to get our bathing suits from the buggy first?"

A playful smile tugged at Rachel's lips, as her thoughts turned to a vision of Mattie without her swimsuit. She shook it off and patted her lover on the arm. "Guess I should. I'll be back in a second." She retrieved the suits and made her way back toward Mattie, unbuttoning her trousers as she walked, and allowing them to drop to the sand, leaving her in her drawers, as she drew her undershirt over her head. "Care to join me?"

Mattie's mouth went dry at the sight of the strong body before her. "I might need some help with all this manly clothing." She smiled as Rachel quickly stepped up to the task, helping her out of the shirt and trousers, and picking up their discarded garments, folding them carefully and taking them up to stow them next to their boots. Mattie's body reacted so quickly it made her head spin all over again, as Rachel came walking back down to her, her lean leg and torso muscles shifting and sliding under her skin as she moved. It was a powerful body, one that felt more solid against her than anything else in Mattie's relatively short life ever had. In Rachel's arms, she could feel a hundred different emotions in the span of minutes — safety, love, and desire beyond anything she had ever imagined.

Rachel drew closer, not quite smiling, taking in the visible tiny shivers from her partner, as Mattie's eyes raked over her like hot shimmering coals. Her own body reacted to Mattie with a powerful surge of pure desire. Yes, a swim was definitely in order, because the sand and the salt water were certainly not the best places for what she was sure would happen if they didn't get in the cool water, and soon.

"We can't — not here." Mattie felt long arms wrap around her and gasped as their bodies made contact, warm skin against warm skin.

"I know." Rachel kissed her lightly, then released her and helped her into her bathing suit, then donned her own. She guided Mattie down to the water with a hand on the small of her back, her skin warm against her fingertips through the cottony bathing suit. As they reached the water, a large wave rolled ashore, crashing over them and breaking above their knees, almost making them lose their balance. They both laughed and held on to each other until it rolled back out, then they continued on until they were in waist-deep water.

"Best not go out much further. Too dark to see any sharks, but we're probably safe enough here." She smiled, watching Mattie's eyes dance as they looked up at her. The salt water worked its magic, cooling her skin and tempering her desire, taking it down to a more manageable level.

They held on to each other in timeless wonder, their bodies pressed tightly together as the water broke around them. It felt wonderful, reconnecting in a love of the purest kind, giving everything, and asking nothing in return. It was enough, sharing the closeness out there, under the laughing stars, in the ocean that had become home and mother to both of them.

They had no idea how long they stood there, the spell gradually breaking, as they pulled apart slightly. "How about that walk on the beach?" Rachel pushed a lock of hair out of Mattie's eyes, tucking it back with one of the hairpins that held the rest up on top of her head.

"I've been dreaming of walking on the beach with you." Mattie smiled, the corners of her eyes crinkling up.

Hand in hand, they walked almost a half-mile down, next to the edge of the water, before they turned back around toward the bathhouse. They talked very little, their hearts communicating well enough without words. When they reached the wagon again, they shared the contents of the picnic basket, sitting close together as they enjoyed the fresh air, and the night music of the breeze rustling the tall reeds in the dunes, and the water lapping against the shore. Mattie couldn't remember when she'd felt more peaceful.

"I can't thank you enough for bringing me out tonight." She finally broke the silence. "This night will go a long way in helping me endure the rest of this month."

"I'm sorry. I know it's been hard on you, and you've been so brave about it all." Rachel turned and helped her down from the wagon seat, leading them up for a much-needed shower. "I wish this month were over and we had things settled."

"They'll be settled soon enough." Mattie tried to sound chipper. "It hasn't been such a hardship. It's been freedom, in most ways." Her brows knit as she carefully chose her words. "If it means getting away from him, and getting to be with you, I'd stay indoors for the next twenty years. Truly I would."

"And I'd do the same for you if I had to." Rachel was relieved to hear the light-hearted tone in Mattie's voice. "But I'm very glad, darlin', that you won't have to put up with the current situation for twenty years. Seeing you out here tonight, you look much happier than you have in days. I don't think you were meant to sit inside knitting."

"True."   Mattie giggled.   "I'd much rather take my sketchpad
outside. Knitting makes my neck and shoulders hurt, if I do too much
of it."

They reached the bathhouse and picked up their clothing, then
went inside, using Rachel's contraband key.   She locked the door
behind them, then located some lanterns just outside the shower area,
so they could see to get cleaned up. She turned on a single spigot, as
the fresh filtered water came sprinkling out. It was cool, but not as
cold as the ocean water, and felt warm as it hit her skin. She beckoned
to Mattie, who joined her under the steady stream.

Ever so slowly, they undressed each other, kicking aside the
bathing suits as their bodies joined again.   Rachel touched her
forehead to Mattie's, looking down as she rubbed Mattie's belly. "So
good to see you eating right. I was worried you were going to waste
away."

"Couldn't help it." Mattie's stomach fluttered inside at Rachel's
touch. "He kept me all in knots. I sometimes couldn't keep my meals
down. Had to eat small portions to keep my stomach settled." The
flutter grew as Rachel's hand slid up to just below her breast, cupping
it lightly from underneath, as Rachel allowed its weight to settle in her
hand, noting a slight fullness that hadn't been there before.

"You're so very beautiful, my love." Their eyes met, almost shyly,
there, under the shower. Mattie reached up, stroking Rachel's face,
then drawing her in for a series of tentative kisses. They explored a
little further, before they reluctantly set about the task of actually
bathing. After playfully soaping each other up, they stood together,
allowing the clean stream of water to rinse them off.

Drying off led to another round of cuddling and kisses, ending
with both of them wrapped up in a towel together, as they stood just
inside the bathhouse door, out of sight of the road, but where they
could once again see the stars overhead. Rachel's nostrils flared, as
Mattie's distinct clean scent reached her nose, and the desire rose up
strongly all over again. She turned in the towel, pulling Mattie close
and kissing her almost senseless, stopping when they absolutely
needed to breathe. "I think I need to get you home, and soon." She
tilted Mattie's chin up, allowing her eyes to convey her intent.

Mattie swallowed. Rachel's eyes almost burned in their intensity.
"Is there a blanket in the back of the wagon?"

"Unfortunately, no." Rachel smiled at the implication. "But I'd
like to take my time with you, Mattie, in that nice soft bed in our loft,
don't you think?"

"I think that is a heavenly idea." She kissed Rachel on the nose.

They dressed quickly, then began the much-too-long drive back to
Betsy and Angel's house. When they arrived back, the only light on
was a single lamp in their loft window. They smiled at that, and at
each other, as they put the horses in the barn, then quietly made their

way up to their room.

As they fell into bed, the stars overhead continued to shine down on them through the open window, and off in the distance, the waves roared ashore.

THE DAYS ROLLED on, each one much the same as the one before. One afternoon, Rachel and Billy sat eating their dinner on the edge of the dock in the shade of a large boat. It was too hot to talk, and they were nearing the end of August, and the most unbearable days of summer. They'd brought their swimsuits in hopes of getting in the water to cool off after they ate.

As Rachel methodically worked her way through a second sandwich, her thoughts turned idly to home, and Mattie, and she wondered what she might be up to. She knew Betsy stuck to a schedule all week, doing laundry on Monday, baking on Tuesday, upstairs housecleaning on Wednesday, downstairs housecleaning on Thursday, and gardening on Friday. It was Friday, and since Mattie couldn't go outside, she figured she was probably napping, or drawing in her sketchpad. Her heart hurt for her lover, knowing it was miserable to be stuck inside.

Just as she was thinking of home, she felt a tap to her shoulder and turned to see Angel standing over her. She was breathing hard and her hair had come loose from the knot at the back of her head. "If you can, you need to get home right away." Angel bent over slightly to catch her breath. Her entire blouse was drenched with sweat, and her face was a ruddy red from working indoors in the stifling cotton mill.

"What's wrong?" Rachel jumped up, her dinner tumbling into the water, attracting a flock of eager seagulls, which began diving and swooping over the surface, snatching up the spoiled sandwich and cookies. She felt Billy at her back, his hand on her shoulder.

"I'm not sure." Angel stood upright, swiping her hand across her forehead. "Betsy sent one of the neighbor boys with a note that said to get you home if I could. That she'd called Dr. Mills for Mattie." She watched Rachel go pale, and paused, debating for a moment. She looked around to make sure no one else could hear her, and placed her hand on Rachel's other shoulder. "I suspect it's not life-threatening, or she would have said so. I've seen your Mattie swoon a time or two recently." She spoke very quietly. "She's not taking to the heat real well, and this summer has been a scorcher. I should've mentioned it to you, but I figured you knew."

"No." Rachel's voice grew cool. "She hasn't said anything to me about not feeling well." Her thoughts turned inward, remembering Mattie's dizzy spell when they went for their adventure on the beach. "Damn." She shook off her initial shock. "Billy, can you cover for me?"

"Sure." He frowned in concern. "Shall I send Lil by later on?"

"No. Let me find out what's wrong first. I've told her to take it easy in the heat of the day. Knowing Mattie, she's gone and overdone it." She forced a smile, trying to convince herself it was nothing serious. "I'd best get going." She ran up the dock to her bicycle, leaving Angel and Billy watching her.

The ride home was a blur, her legs peddling faster than they ever had, as she automatically wound through the streets toward the neighborhood where the large old house was. At last she drove the bicycle up the driveway and around the back of the house, dropping it on the lawn and taking the back steps up two at a time, tugging the door open. Dr. Mills sat in the parlor, chatting quietly with Betsy, whose lips were drawn into a thin, grim line. They both looked up as Rachel entered the kitchen, her boots sounding on the hard wood floor as she rushed into the parlor.

She spotted Dr. Mills and stopped in her tracks, re-grouping. She had no idea what he knew of their living situation. The letter she had procured from his office when they planned Mattie's escape from Adam had been the work of Billy's ability to charm Dr. Mills' young female assistant out of his official stationary, and Lillie's fine forgery skills with the doctor's signature. She was certain the assistant was to alert Billy if Adam ever came nosing around the doctor's office, but the doctor himself had been excluded from their plans.

"Hello, Miss Travis." Dr. Mills stood and shook her hand. "I'd heard you were boarding here these days. What brings you home in the middle of the day?"

Rachel just managed to keep her expression neutral, watching Betsy fret and mouth an 'I'm so sorry' behind the doctor's back. "I forgot my dinner pail." She looked around, as if she were searching for it. "Heard you talking and thought I'd stop in and say hello."

"Well, I was just leaving." He stooped down, retrieving his medical satchel.

It was all Rachel could do not to blurt out a half dozen questions. She remained silent, her eyes pleading with Betsy to say something, anything, to clue her in as to what was wrong, and what Dr. Mills already knew about their circumstances. She released a relieved breath as Betsy nodded her understanding and turned to the doctor. "Thank you so much for coming by, Dr. Mills. Mattie was just paying me a visit and fell ill suddenly. I was afraid to let her go home without you examining her first. Was afraid she'd collapse out on the road or fall off the trolley."

"Well, it's to be expected, given the circumstances." He smiled slightly. "Nothing she won't recover from, eventually."

Rachel's guts unclenched and she turned toward the stairs. "I believe I'll go up and change into a fresh shirt before I go back to the docks." She forced herself to keep her speech normal and steady.

Betsy's deep frown made her stomach twist back into a knot and she frowned back in question, getting the slightest shake of a finger in answer.

"Good-day to you, Miss Travis." Dr. Mills tipped his hat as Betsy escorted him to the front door.

"Good-day to you, too." Rachel took a few steps up until she was out of sight, and sat down on the stairs, waiting. It took all her willpower to not bolt up to see Mattie, but Betsy's wordless admonition had been clear. If Rachel had learned anything, she had learned not to ignore the warnings of a riled southern lady, and Betsy looked like she was close to exploding.

In a minute that seemed like an hour, Betsy returned and found her on the stairs. She sat down just below Rachel, patting her on the knee. "I need to talk to you before you go up there."

"Hurry, will you? I have to get to her. Is she hurt? What's wrong?" Rachel felt Betsy's hand clench around her leg, holding her down. She huffed in frustration, burying her face in her hands.

"Do you love her?" The question brought Rachel's head snapping up.

"Of course I love her. What kind of a question is that?" Her eyes flashed in indignant anger.

"A dead serious one, missy." Betsy's tone held her in place as effectively as her hand ever could. "Because you are going to need every ounce of that love when you get to the top of those stairs, and I swear by all I am, I will slap you into the next county if you turn out to be less than the woman I think you are."

"What?" Rachel felt like throwing up. "Is she disfigured or something? I love her for her. It doesn't matter to me..."

"No." Betsy released her grip. "Get on up there. She needs you. Don't you dare forget that."

"Of course not." Rachel leaped up, practically flying to the second floor and up the next set of stairs to the loft. "Mattie?"

She stepped carefully into the room, surprised when her eyes fell on an empty bed. She moved in further, to find Mattie sitting on the sofa, her legs curled up under her, looking out the window. The curtains were parted just enough for Mattie to see out, but no one could see in. Two things became readily apparent. Mattie was dressed in her traveling clothing, and her carpetbag was stuffed full, sitting at the foot of the bed. "You going somewhere?"

Mattie turned, her eyes swollen from crying.

Rachel rushed to her side. "Sweetheart, what's wrong?" She felt Mattie's forehead, which was clammy, despite the heat. "You should be lying down if you're sick."

"I've been throwing up my breakfast every morning," Mattie began.

"Well that would explain why you're eating like a horse but not gaining weight, at least not much." Rachel tried for levity, which failed miserably.

"I'm going back to Adam." Mattie shuddered, just saying his name. "I-I knew Betsy sent for you. I told her I could just come talk to you later."

"Whoa. Hold on." Rachel felt a wave of nausea, pushing it aside. Her ears rang as fear rose up. At the same time, her heart clenched up so tightly she thought she would keel over from the ache in her chest. *No.* "Can you start from the beginning, please? Why did Betsy call the doctor?"

"I fainted." Mattie lifted her bangs, revealing a bruise on her forehead. "Was out quite a while. When I came to, I told her about being sick almost every day. And I think I've fainted a couple of other times when I was alone up here."

"Why didn't you tell me?" Rachel took one of her hands, squeezing it lightly.

"Figured it was the heat." She looked down, feeling her eyes sting all over again. Her head ached from crying, and her nose was so stopped up she could barely breathe through it. "It's not the heat." She looked up. "Strange, how God manages to punish us for even the smallest of sins."

"What?" The change of direction made Rachel's head spin.

"Seems my lie to Adam wasn't a lie after all." She searched Rachel's face, hoping she wouldn't have to spell out the obvious. "I guess I wasn't meant to escape him."

The truth hit home, slamming Rachel in the gut like a sledgehammer. She gulped in air, trying to remain calm. "You're pregnant?"

"With his child." Mattie shook as fresh tears trickled down her cheeks. "I love you so much, Rachel. I wanted a life with you more than anything. I'm sorry."

"No." Rachel scooted closer. "Don't you be sorry, you didn't do anything wrong."

"I lied to him. Or I thought I was lying at the time." Mattie wailed. "And now I'm carrying his child in punishment."

"Not his child!" Rachel's voice rose in anger. She saw the fear in Mattie's eyes and tempered her voice. She reached out, stroking Mattie's blotched face. "Not his child," she whispered. "Do you still want a life with me?"

"With all my heart." Mattie broke into outright sobs, and felt Rachel pull her close, kissing her on the head. "All our plans are ruined. We almost got away with it, too."

"Hold on." Rachel stood, moving to the dressing table and opening a drawer to retrieve a small velvet-covered box. She quickly made her way back to Mattie, dropping to her knees in front of her. "Spend your life with me, Mattie." She held out the box, her hands visibly shaking.

Mattie sniffed and grasped it, brushing a fingertip over the navy blue material. "So soft." She cocked her head in question and opened it, revealing a gold ring with a large white pearl setting in the center, flanked on each side by two smaller triangular diamonds. "Oh." Her voice grew quiet. "It's beautiful." She looked up, her face a study in anguish. "I can't take it from you, though, not now."

"Do you want it?" Rachel persisted, taking Mattie's hand and curling it into a fist around the ring, her own hand encasing Mattie's.

"Yes." Mattie's voice quivered. "But..."

"My child." Rachel made the only decision her heart would allow her to. "I'll love it like my own, if you'll allow me to."

"But..." Two fingers pressed against Mattie's lips, silencing her.

"Maybe this is a blessing." Rachel swallowed. "What's the one thing I can't give you?"

"A baby," Mattie mumbled, as Rachel removed her fingers. "Can you love it if it looks like him?"

"How could I not love a child who is a part of you?" Rachel took her hand and kissed it.

Mattie watched as Rachel took the ring from her palm and slipped it on her left ring finger. It was a perfect fit. "I love it." Her eyes shone with renewed hope. "I love you."

"Then don't go back to him." Rachel moved back up to the sofa, pulling Mattie to her side. "Stay with me and be my family." She placed one hand on Mattie's belly. "Both of you."

"How did I become fortunate enough to find you?" Mattie turned in her arms, cupping Rachel's cheek and drawing her in for a kiss, which ended in a long silent hug. Somehow, in a sea of overwhelming fear, Rachel had thrown her a lifeline, pulling her ashore just in the nick of time.

"*Augh.*" Rachel jumped up. "What about Dr. Mills? What does he know?" She began pacing back and forth. "I need to go catch him and talk to him."

"No." Mattie stood, drawing her back to the sofa. "He doesn't know I've been gone, at least he didn't seem to. He truly thought I was just here for afternoon tea with Betsy. When he—he told me I was with child, I asked him not to tell Adam if he sees him. Told him I want to tell him myself, first. He agreed."

"That should buy us a little time." The color returned to Rachel's face. "Still, he'll probably eventually see Adam and congratulate him, don't you think?"

"Most likely, but Adam thinks Dr. Mills already knows. The only problem is if Dr. Mills mentions seeing me recently. Otherwise I'm hoping Adam will think it's just belated congratulations." She nibbled her lower lip. "Those marshals should be here any day now, shouldn't they?"

"Yes." Rachel closed her eyes, thinking and counting days in her head. "They should be here by the end of this week or next at the latest."

"So we wait for them?"

"As long as we can, but with everything that's happened, we need to be doubly prepared to leave at a moment's notice." She nodded toward the carpetbag. "Might as well leave that packed if you can."

"I'll double-check your bag, too." Mattie's face grew sober. "Make sure you have everything you might need."

"It's been ready ever since we moved in here." Rachel sat back on the sofa, smiling as Mattie curled up next to her, in the curve of her arm.

"I'm quite terrified," Mattie confessed, looking up at Rachel and tugging at her shirt collar. "A baby is something I never counted on."

"I'm certain I shall be terrified as well," Rachel smiled and kissed her cheek, "as soon as my mind comes back from wherever it disappeared to." She tightened her grip as her voice gentled. "I promise you, Mattie, whatever happens, wherever we end up, you and this baby have all my love, and all that I am, for as long as we live."

"And I pledge my life and my love to you." Mattie kissed her again and closed her eyes, resting her head on Rachel's chest, listening to her steady heartbeat. They might not ever be allowed to have a proper wedding, but there in that loft, in the most unexpected time, they had sealed their love with pledges as heartfelt as any marriage vows.

Chapter
Eleven

RACHEL HELD MATTIE close, watching as the sky out the widow gradually changed from gray to pink to the palest blue. She had taken to sleeping in the nude, in deference to the oppressive heat that seemed to have settled in to stay. She had tried to convince Mattie to do the same, but the younger woman was more comfortable wearing at least a light nightgown. Rachel smiled at that, a charming naiveté that made their intimate times all the more special, somehow, especially in those moments when Mattie allowed her desire to show in both her eyes and her response.

It was blazing hot already, even though it was still very early morning. It was September Seventh, and by Texas standards, summer was far from over. Nary a drop of rain had fallen in several days, sending islanders and vacationers alike flocking to the bathhouse and the beaches. The town burgeoned with visitors, many of whom had taken advantage of the Labor Day holiday to make a trip to the Gulf shores for blessed relief from the heat wave that gripped much of the country.

Rachel sighed, the slightest whisper of breath from her lips, and felt Mattie tighten her grasp around her waist. "Penny for your thoughts." Mattie patted her hip and snuggled closer.

"Oh, not worth a penny, I'd wager." Rachel smiled and kissed Mattie's forehead. "Just dreading working on the docks. I felt slightly nauseated by the end of the day yesterday. Been a long time since I worked hard enough for that."

"You be careful, please? Take a break and drink plenty of water. I hate that you're working so hard while I sit inside knitting booties." Mattie absently rubbed her own belly, her lips curving up as Rachel's hand closed over hers, guiding her. "Maybe you're having sympathy symptoms."

"Maybe." Rachel's hand moved upward, tracing a lazy circle around Mattie's breast. "I had a little talk with Lil. I feel so ignorant. I should have picked up on a few things."

"Such as?" Mattie's breath caught as Rachel brushed a thumb across her nipple. She squirmed, the sensation a combination of pleasure and pain. "Mmm. Careful, my love."

"Such as that." Rachel ducked her head and pushed the top of her gown aside, placing the barest of kisses on the other, neglected nipple. "They're very sensitive."

"My bosoms?" Mattie's brows furrowed as she looked down at Rachel's hand, which had dropped lower, softly lifting one breast.

"Uh-huh." She backed off, once again rubbing Mattie's belly. "And your nipples are darker, and your bosoms are fuller than before."

"So soon?" Mattie admitted she had noticed some changes, but had thought perhaps she was gaining weight due to eating more. With Adam out of sight, her constant nervous queasiness had all but vanished, except for what she now knew had been morning sickness.

"Yes. Things start happening pretty quick, according to Lil." Rachel rolled to her side so she could look at Mattie's face. "You missed your cycle too. You should have had at least one during the time we've been living here."

"Not necessarily." Mattie's own hands wandered, stroking Rachel's arm as she talked. "My cycles were never predictable. I think Adam scared them out of me. And the morning sickness. I used to lose my breakfast pretty often anyway, especially if he was in a truly foul mood."

Rachel's eyes darkened. She forced the ugly thoughts down. "He's never going to do that to you again, sweetheart. May God have mercy on his soul if he dares to try."

Mattie's words caught in her throat, and then she couldn't remember what she was going to say anyway, so she buried her face into Rachel's chest, feeling strong arms wrap around her and protective hands rub her back. She settled against Rachel with a soft grunt of happiness, allowing the touch to seep into even the remotest crevices of fear, banishing them from her presence.

Gradually, she felt one hand glide along her side, under her gown, and back to her stomach as Rachel laid one possessive palm against her, right below her navel. "Wonder when we'll feel it kick?" Her voice was muffled against Rachel's skin, but she was loath to move.

"Be a while, but I want to be there when it happens." Rachel pressed slightly against Mattie's soft skin. "Never thought I could have someone like you in my life, Mattie, much less a family to call my own. Don't know what I did to deserve all this, but I swear, no matter what happens in the rest of my life, nothing can compare to the miracle you have been."

"You loved me." Mattie answered simply. "All you did was show me what love is, Rachel. I would have died back there, and we both know it. This child..." She opened her eyes and looked down at Rachel's hand on her. "This child is fortunate beyond measure to have you. I still want to pinch myself sometimes. It all seems like a happy dream. Hey!"

"Heh." Rachel released the slight fold of skin she had pinched on

Mattie's backside, and resumed stroking her stomach. "See. No dream." She received a playful slap to her own behind, causing her to slide closer to Mattie. She gazed into shining hazel eyes at very close range, feeling such overwhelming love for both Mattie and their unborn child, that it brought tears to her eyes. "I love you so very much." She traced Mattie's face with her fingertips and threaded her fingers through her hair, urging her closer still for a long languid kiss. She pulled back and smiled, still stroking Mattie's hair. "How about I bring our breakfast up on a tray, and after we eat, I'll draw you a nice tepid bath so you can cool off a little?"

"I think I'll keep you forever, that's what I think." She wrapped her arms around Rachel's neck, kissing her soundly one more time, before the taller woman scooted out of bed and quickly dressed, blowing a kiss at Mattie before she disappeared down the stairs.

THE HEAT WAS almost unbearable as the sun beat down on the helpless laborers. Rachel had shed her long-sleeved shirt early in the day, working in her thinnest work trousers and ribbed sleeveless undershirt. Sweat ran down the cuts and curves of her shoulders and biceps, and her long braid was drenched, sticking to the back of her neck and upper shoulders. No amount of broad green leaves helped, and she knew she should take a breather.

But pride won out and she stuck to her task. The others were working diligently to load a huge cotton freighter. The heavy, bound bales were stacked all along the dock, their woody scent wafting through the shimmering air. *Well. It could be worse,* Rachel mused. *It could have been a cattle boat.* She envied the men around her, who were all stripped bare above the waist. She eyed her own torso and its telltale curves with regret, then smiled, realizing just how much at least one person in her life appreciated those curves.

No one looked at her the way Mattie did. Mattie took the time to express her love, with words, with touch, with shy gentle glances and blushes when she was caught looking. It had happened a few times before Rachel took the bull by the horns, and gave Mattie verbal permission to look all she wanted to. Mattie had been mortified until Rachel had sat down with her and told her all the nice things she appreciated about Mattie's appearance. The ducked head and furious blush she'd received in reward were endearing in the extreme. Then a very shy Mattie had — reluctantly, at first, then with growing confidence — shared several things she liked about Rachel's physical appearance.

It made her look in the mirror with new eyes as she gave a few extra strokes to her hair when she brushed it at night, made her feel her own arm muscles when they flexed, knowing how much Mattie enjoyed being held by them, and made her scowl speculatively at her own skin when naked, studying the odd contrast of milky white skin on her body with the dark brown skin of her arms and face. For some reason, Mattie liked that, puzzling as it was.

"You feel that?" Billy brought her out of her daydreams.

Her head snapped around, looking over a bale of cotton at his pale eyes. "Feel what?" She stood, and felt a ripple of slightly cool air blow over her skin. "Oh." She closed her eyes, drinking in the welcome sensation. Her eyes opened. "Blessed be."

"Indeed." Billy pushed back his hat, allowing the breeze to cool his damp slicked down hair. "What I'd give to be a young lad again, running bum-bare down the road in this wonderful air."

Rachel burst out laughing. "Maybe we can go down to the water during the noon hour. I didn't bring a bathing suit, but we can at least get our feet wet."

"Feet?" Billy turned in a circle as the breeze continued to blow. Relieved sighs could be heard all along the docks, as the workers paused for a moment to enjoy the refreshing wind. "I'll be diving in, clothes and all."

"In that case, so will I." Rachel set about her work with renewed vigor. Judging from the sun, the noon hour — and her dip in the ocean — was fast approaching. Sure enough, in no time at all, the long whistle blew, signaling dinnertime, and the groans of working men were replaced with low male voices in conversation and the tin sound of dinner pails being set on the wooden dock and opened. Just as quickly, the voices grew silent as the hungry men ate their meal.

Rachel and Billy practically ran up the dock and around toward the sand. They grabbed up their bicycles and took off at break-neck speed, pedaling across town toward one of the gulf-side beaches, the strong wind at their backs aiding their progress. The ride back was going to be more difficult against the wind, but Rachel didn't care. She was too busy taking in the pleasure of the wind blowing against her soaked shirt and her bare head. She'd placed her hat in her basket, allowing her hair to dry as they made their short journey.

With a whoop, Billy reached the sand first, leaping off his bicycle and dropping it, the back wheel still spinning as he ran for the water, slicing through the waves and then swimming out toward one of the sand bars with efficient strokes. Rachel was close behind him, her trousers only slightly slowing her progress. They reached the sandbar and stopped, standing in the middle of the water.

"Whoa." Rachel bobbed unsteadily, as water rose up to her armpits. "Deeper than it usually is." She looked up, noting a trace of feathery white clouds way out to sea. "Think it might rain?"

"Dunno." Billy leaned back, floating in the water, as he studied the mostly blue sky. "Odd." He squinted. "Clouds are downwind. Guess the rain has passed us by." He closed his eyes again, stretching out his arms and feeling the water rock him back and forth as the waves washed over and around them.

"Very odd." Rachel continued to stand, looking first at the clouds to the south and east, then back toward the north, where the wind seemed to be picking up speed. "Billy, shouldn't the water be shallower than normal, rather than deeper?"

"What?" Billy flipped his hand, splashing salt water at her, hitting her square in the chest. "Are you going to be assisting Mr. Cline, now?"

"Mr. Cline..." Her voice trailed off, as she considered the island's weatherman, the water, and the wind. "Billy, it isn't right. I'm going back up to the beach and walk down a ways. You want to join me?"

"Awww, Rachel." He reluctantly rose up, back on his feet, then followed the already-swimming Rachel as she pulled back toward shore. "Go and ruin a perfectly good swim," he muttered. Yet the gentleman in him would not allow her to go alone. He snorted. "Like she couldn't most likely protect me if needed."

"You say something?" Rachel squeezed the water out of her braid, then donned her long-sleeved shirt, leaving it unbuttoned so her undershirt could dry. She enjoyed the rare sensation of chill bumps, as the cooler air hit her wet skin and clothing.

"No. Nothing." He shoved his hands in his pockets, leaving his feet bare to enjoy the sand, as they walked silently near the shoreline. "Anything in particular you're looking for?" He glanced sideways at her.

Rachel's gaze was intent, scanning first the water and then the horizon where the ocean met the sky. Every now and then she looked back over her shoulder to the north. "It doesn't add up." She nibbled her lower lip.

"What doesn't add up?" Billy followed her gaze, which was back on the water.

"Strong wind from the north, yet the tide is higher than usual coming in from the south." She pointed toward the dunes ahead of them. "See those? They aren't usually that close to the water. And that log..." She swung her arm around, gesturing toward a large section of dead tree trunk that was below the dunes, the waves breaking around it as they rushed ashore. "That log—I've sat on it and eaten dinner many a time, and wasn't near the water."

"Maybe someone dragged it down closer?" Billy hazarded a guess, wishing he were back out at the sand bar.

"No. I don't believe so." Just then, a flock of seagulls flew past them, away from the beach and out of sight toward the mainland. *Hmmm.* Even as they walked, the waves seemed to be picking up, roaring ashore with unusual speed, and whitecapping out further away from shore. Yet the wind continued to blow steadily behind them, rippling across the water surface.

Something was very wrong.

"Billy, I'm going back early." She turned around, ducking her head against the increasing wind. "Think I'll go pay Mr. Cline a visit before I go back to the docks."

"Ah. So you are considering a change in profession?" He joked, trotting to keep up with his friend's determined strides.

"No," she almost snapped at him. Something didn't feel right. The odd weather was putting her on edge, and she forced herself to be civil. "I just figure Mr. Cline should come down here and see the tide for himself. He's always studying things like that, reporting them back to Washington. Maybe we're in for a big thunderstorm or something."

"Wouldn't that be a blessing," Billy mused. "We sure could use it."

Rachel sniffed the air. If she concentrated hard enough, she could almost smell the scent of rain on the wind. Her skin prickled at the thought. "I suppose," she finally answered, before picking up her bicycle and leaving him behind.

ISAAC CLINE HOVERED over the telegraph message, moving from the message to a map, plotting a path with a straight edge and pen. A quiet rap at the door startled him, and he brushed against a cup on the desk, spilling his tea on the telegraph paper. "Blast!" He stood, blotting at the paper with the hem of his shirt, which had been untucked since early morning. "Come in." He glanced at the door in annoyance, blowing on the message, hoping the ink wouldn't run. Then he sighed. He'd already received the information he needed. He dropped it on a pile of similar pieces of paper and turned, just as Rachel entered the small office.

"Hello, Mr. Cline." She looked around the chaotic office, peering first at the stacks of paper, then out the second-floor window of the Levy building. A few passers-by chatted on the street below, their conversation drifting up through the mosquito netting tacked over the window frame. "I'm sorry to bother you."

"Oh, no bother," he lied, shuffling around the desk and holding out his hand. "Miss..." He paused, trying to place her. "Travis?" He was surprised at the rather strong grip that met him, and his eyes roamed up her arm to take in powerful corded wrists, and wet clothing. "How can I help you?"

"What's all of this?" Rachel momentarily forgot her mission, dropping his hand and moving to the map on the wall next to the desk. Her eyes tracked precisely-drawn lines in blue, red, and black ink, each line connected by a pinpoint of ink, each pinpoint circled.

"Oh." He pushed a pair of wire spectacles back up his nose until they properly covered his eyes. "I'm plotting a storm out in the Gulf."

Her eyes followed the lines, blinking at the last set, which fanned out in three directions. She had little experience with maps, and she moved closer still, puzzling over words until she found some she recognized. "Galveston." Her finger followed from the island to the nearest line.

"Careful." His voice rose sharply. "I just drew that one. Don't smudge it."

"Sorry." She dropped her hand and turned intelligent eyes on him. "Is it a big storm?"

"I think so, yes." He wished the girl would leave him alone, but good manners precluded him sending her away. "Now." He looked pointedly at her. "What can I do for you?"

"The tide on the Gulf side of the island." Rachel gestured toward the open window and the sliver of ocean beyond. "It's behaving strangely."

"How so?" He looked out the window, suddenly interested in his impromptu visitor.

"It's higher than usual, even though the north wind is blowing against it." She turned back to the map. "Is that why?" She pointed to the odd web of colored lines.

"Perhaps." He picked up his stacks of paper, shuffling them and laying them back on the table. "Tropical cyclone, out in the Gulf."

Rachel's eyes widened. "Oughtn't you to warn folks?"

"Pshaw." He brushed her off. "If it stays its course, it will land well east of here. We've weathered many a storm here, young lady."

"I know." Rachel had been on the island long enough to know what a cyclone was. "But the tides — I've never seen anything like this. Gave me the willies." She crossed her arms, rubbing at goose bumps she could feel beneath her shirt. "Maybe you should at least raise the warning flag, give folks a chance to decide for themselves if they ought to board up their homes."

"The tides." He sat down on the windowsill, dust motes dancing around his face in the sunlight. "How much higher than usual?"

"Oh. Dunno. Three feet or so, best I can guess." She shrugged. "The air feels peculiar."

"Nonsense." He smiled. "The cyclone is a long way from here yet. You couldn't be feeling anything other than this refreshing wind." As he spoke, the breeze picked up, ruffling the curtains and blowing them across his face. He swiped them away and stood, stepping back to his desk. "If it will make you feel better, I'll take a walk in a bit and check out the tides myself. But I assure you, even in the worst of times, all we had to do was take shelter up near Broadway. It's a good eight feet above sea level. The tides have never risen high enough to flood Broadway. We'll be fine."

"If you say so." Rachel casually studied the top telegraph message in the pile on the desk, taking in words and phrases. Her scalp prickled again. She looked up. "This thing sank some ships?" Her voice was incredulous. "Not boats. Ships?" She pointed to the sentence. "Where is Cuba?"

Cline released a frustrated breath. "Over here." He approached the map, pointing to a small island way across the Gulf. He traced a line drawn through some tiny islands at the tip of—

"Florida," Rachel read aloud. "That's pretty far away." She studied tiny notes. "Went through there yesterday? And it's already over here?" She pointed to a spot much closer to Galveston. "That's awfully quick, isn't it?"

"That is a guess as to exactly where it is, based on reports from Washington, and yes, it is moving a bit rapidly." He shrugged. "But as I said, if it stays on course, we shall get some much-needed rain, and nothing more."

"Well. Guess I should get back to the docks." Somewhat reassured, she re-buttoned her now-dry shirt, shrugging to settle it over her shoulders. "Sorry for my appearance." She suddenly realized she must look like a sea monster. "I went swimming at the noon hour, and that's when I discovered the tides rising. Had to dry off." She ducked her head in apology. "I hope you do go check the water. Would make me feel a might better to have an expert take a look at it."

"Very well then." He smiled. "I shall. Good day, Miss Travis." He showed her to the door, watching as she took the wooden stairs down, then moved back inside and saw her take to the street on a bicycle. "What a most improper young lady." He shook his head. "Curmudgeons. This island attracts them in droves, I do believe."

Still. He checked the silent telegraph and sent out a message of receipt, then stood, donning his jacket and hat. Curmudgeon or not, he had no reason to believe Rachel would make up her tale about the tide. He might as well go see for himself, and put the matter to rest.

Later that evening, as Rachel pedaled home, she looked up as she passed the Levy Building. The flagpoles were empty, devoid of any storm warning banners.

THE FRIDAY NIGHT sky was almost clear, with a glowing moon that illuminated the ground below. The soothing breeze continued to blow, and Rachel and Mattie risked sitting on the swing in the corner of the back porch, hidden in shadows. It was unspeakably delicious to Mattie, to be out in the fresh air, in the moonlight, snuggled up against Rachel, who stroked her hair absently as they swung in silence.

It was beautiful. Rachel was beautiful, her brooding profile outlined against the navy blue sky beyond the porch. Even in the darkness, her brows were furrowed, and Mattie reached up, smoothing them automatically, watching a slight smile twitch at her lover's lips. "Are you certain we should be worried?" She looked around and up. "It's a lovely night. Loveliest one we've had in weeks. It feels delightful."

"I know." Rachel secured her hold around Mattie's waist, feeling her shift until her lips were within inches of Rachel's ear. She could feel Mattie's breath pleasantly tickling her skin, and she turned, unable to resist the urge to savor those lips and that breath for a long while.

It was divine, and Mattie whimpered, a happy little sound, and felt both arms close around her, holding her close. Rachel deepened the kiss, and Mattie melted into it, almost, but not quite, wishing they were upstairs in their nice comfortable bed. Still, she wasn't going to miss the rare chance to venture outdoors. Her body betrayed her, and she felt Rachel break away with a chuckle.

"Sorry, my love." Rachel pressed her forehead against Mattie's, feeling the smaller body heave in her arms. "I can't resist your charms."

"Nor I yours." Mattie stole another kiss. A thought occurred to her and she touched Rachel's cheek, tilting her face until she could see warm eyes shining back at her. "Those marshals should be here sometime soon, correct?"

"Yes. End of next week at latest." Rachel internally berated herself. She'd been so caught up worrying about the weather, she'd quite forgotten about the marshals.

"End of week!" Mattie sat upright. "Rachel, tomorrow is Saturday. That means..." She grabbed Rachel's shoulders, shaking her in pure happiness. "That means in a few days or so, I'll be free of Adam for good." She searched the steel blue eyes so close to her own. "Doesn't it?"

"Yes." Rachel lovingly brushed the hair from around Mattie's face. "One way or the other. We live here in peace, or we run. But we've been prepared for that for weeks, haven't we?"

"Yes." Mattie's thoughts turned to the two carpetbags under the bed upstairs. As time passed, those bags had been added to. In addition to a few changes of clothing, some money, and other necessary personal items, they now held a few books, and her beloved paintings and drawings were rolled up carefully inside her bag. Rachel hefted them every now and then, making sure she could still carry both of them at a run if she needed to. "Rachel, if we do decide to leave, will you please let me do my share?"

"I can carry both bags." Rachel stubbornly crossed her arms and looked directly ahead toward the garden and the barn beyond. The wind ruffled through the cucumber and tomato plants, dredging up the scent of sandy loam and a stronger hint of rain. She delicately sniffed the air and shivered, trying to ignore her roiling guts.

"And I can carry one." Mattie patted her leg, leaving her hand there and squeezing it slightly. "I've tested it. I can run up and down the stairs carrying mine with no problem."

Rachel's hand flew to her belly. "When did you do this?" She rubbed the soft cotton skirt. "You could hurt yourself. And the baby."

"Hush." Mattie brushed her hand across Rachel's mouth, feeling soft lips nibble at her passing fingers. "I only did it a few times, just to make sure." She cupped a tanned cheek. "Hopefully we'll sneak away quietly and slowly, if we have to. But if we do literally have to run, we'd both best be able to. You can't carry me and both carpetbags."

Rachel frowned, feeling Mattie's fingers stroke her face. She sighed heavily. "I know. I-I love you—"

"I know you do," Mattie interrupted.

"And I love this baby." She patted Mattie's stomach, feeling Mattie's hand close over her own. "It's my responsibility now. Both of you are." She bent down, kissing the spot just below Mattie's waistband. Fingers tangled in her hair, raking through it and on down her back, rubbing soft circles against her cotton undershirt.

"And you are mine." Mattie continued to rub her back as Rachel's cheek rested against her stomach.

"All yours," Rachel mumbled, her face slightly squished, her words muffled. "We have to take care of each other now, don't we?" She turned, stretching out on the swing on her back, her head pillowed in Mattie's lap. In answer, a possessive arm draped across her hips.

"Always." Mattie looked down at her, their eyes meeting in the soft muted moonlight. She held up her hand, allowing her ring to sparkle as she turned it up toward the sky.

Rachel grasped it and pulled it down, kissing her palm, then tucking it against her chest. She laughed as Mattie tickled her skin, then gasped as the hand moved lower, cupping her breast through her ribbed shirt. Mattie was pleased she'd managed the distraction, and glad to hear the laughter as it bubbled up at her teasing touch. She watched Rachel's eyes narrow as she tugged the soft brushed cotton from her waistband, slipping her hand beneath it to continue her quest. Rachel shivered, closing her eyes and giving in to sensations that rose up faster than she could have imagined. Her body was on fire, and she took deep uneven breaths, allowing her lover to slowly explore her skin, groaning as Mattie tugged at her suspenders, pulling them down and unbuttoning her trousers.

"Out here, on the porch?" Rachel grinned, her shaking voice giving away her desire. "Might not be the safest place, my love."

It was Mattie's turn to gasp as Rachel sprang up, turning the tables and pinning her against the high slatted back of the porch swing. She kissed her soundly, her own hands wandering in easy patterns over Mattie's body. "Inside," Rachel mumbled, pulling Mattie up with her. "Now."

"No." Mattie's hands stilled. "I can't."

"Um, but..." Rachel tilted her head in question. "I beg to differ. You certainly seem to me like you can." She smiled at the blush on her lover's face.

"I can." Mattie looked down. "That, I mean. I can't walk past Betsy and Angel in the parlor in there, and go up the stairs this early. Would be obvious."

"I think they have a pretty good idea of what we do up there from time to time." Rachel tilted her chin up, watching the blush deepen, even in the low light.

She looked back up, her eyes pleading. "I can't. Please? Let's sit for a minute and calm down."

"Or we could go in the barn." Rachel kissed her again for a bit, feeling Mattie drape bonelessly against her. "I just put clean straw down in there this evening. Got that one empty stall down on the end."

"The barn?" Mattie paused, looking up at the sky as she contemplated Rachel's suggestion. She felt the breeze lift her hair, cooling her and settling her racing heart just a bit. "So beautiful out here."

Long arms settled around her waist as they both studied the clear sky. "That it is." Rachel rested her chin on Mattie's head, her own body slowing to a low simmer.

"Can't hardly wait until I can go outside whenever I wish." Mattie smiled as Rachel nibbled at her ear.

"How 'bout we go on in the barn?" The low voice whispered. It rumbled in her ear, sending pleasant shivers up and down Mattie's spine. "We can open up that big window over that end stall. Watch the stars."

Mattie felt suddenly adventurous, and made up her mind. "You do have the best ideas." She took Rachel's hand, leading her toward their safe haven.

"Would I be correct in assuming there might be a nice soft blanket in here?" Rachel felt a gentle tug at her suspenders, and was dragged into the barn where she stood in the middle watching while Mattie opened a window wide, allowing moonlight to spill inside and over the fragrant piles of hay, providing both soft light and fresh air, which quickly drove away the heat of the day.

"Yes." Mattie pulled said blanket from a rail and fluffed it out, spreading it over a thick pile of hay in the corner stall. She crooked a finger and motioned for Rachel to come closer, smiling as the taller woman took her in her arms. She helped Rachel shrug out of her undershirt, enjoying the play of soft light against exposed skin. "This will be a new experience for me."

"Oh, I believe we've done this a time or two now, haven't we?" Rachel teased her, as she found the tiny pearl buttons at Mattie's back and unfastened them, slipping the gingham dress down until it pooled at Mattie's feet. "Do you have any idea how beautiful you are?" She began a thorough exploration of Mattie's neck and shoulders with her lips, groaning softly as Mattie's hands claimed her, finding sensitive places to stroke and touch. The groan became a quiet growl, as their bodies pressed together, the contact achingly pleasurable.

Mattie wasn't sure how they lost the rest of their clothing. All she knew was that one minute she was on her feet, and the next she was lying on the blanket with Rachel hovered over her, love shining from her steel blue eyes as she dipped down, tasting, teasing, and touching her, until all she knew was the pleasure and the passion between them. Rachel shifted, nibbling her way down Mattie's torso, stopping to trace her navel before moving lower. "Wh-what are you doing?" She felt tentative kisses at her inner thighs, a part of her thinking she shouldn't like that, and a part of her silently begging Rachel to never stop.

"You said this would be a new experience. Figured I'd show you something else two women can do together." Rachel turned and slid back up, kissing her deeply. Mattie could feel Rachel's heart pounding, and a slight tremor in the lean body. They had shared many things together. This, however, was one place Rachel had ached to take them, but had not yet dared. "I need to love you as fully as I possibly can. Trust me, Mattie. Please? I love you. I don't want you to be repulsed by the way I express that to you."

"I'm not repulsed." Mattie gently stroked Rachel's back. "I just never thought of...what you were doing. It's beyond anything I ever conceived of, is all." She smiled warmly, her body tingling in anticipation. "But it felt wonderful." She cupped Rachel's face and drew her down for another kiss, then whispered in her ear. "Show me more."

Rachel stretched out next to Mattie and curled back around, strong hands sliding down Mattie's torso to her legs. Her lips followed her hands, kissing her lover in a new and intimate way. Her senses were filled with Mattie, her warmth and her scent and her taste, and Mattie's gentle hands stroking her back. Rachel cried out softly, almost overwhelmed by the intensity of it all. "I love you, Mattie." She felt it, the moment when Mattie let go, her body relaxing and tensing against her as Rachel took her up to a new and higher place.

And then she was holding Mattie, rocking her as she shook against her, little kitten-like sounds escaping from her throat as Rachel brought her gently back down. Mattie trembled in her arms, and she felt Mattie's lips against her stomach, and then her chest, before they reached her mouth in a soul-searching kiss that took their breath away all over again. It was a long while before either woman could speak, but words were not needed. Gentle touches and soft nibbles spoke volumes, as they held each other there on the soft blanket in the springy fragrant hay.

Cloud-muted moonlight danced over the sheen of sweat-covered bodies, and a gentle breeze brought blessed coolness to overheated skin. "Are you all right?" Rachel finally spoke, feeling Mattie's body curled against her, and she pulled her even closer, pecking her lightly on the forehead.

"Mmm." Mattie nuzzled the hollow of her throat. "Very much so."

Rachel laughed lightly. "Glad to hear it." She released a long contented sigh and closed her eyes, pulling the edge of the blanket over them. "Let's just rest a spell before we go back inside the house, shall we?"

Mattie nodded vaguely in agreement, yawning and stretching lazily before she snuggled up in a warm embrace, her hair tickling Rachel's skin, as a calming lassitude crept over both women.

Far off to the south, lightning snaked across the sky as the water rose, and the clouds rolled ashore.

RACHEL STIRRED IN her sleep, swatting at annoying wetness that hit her face, pecking away at her skin and finally waking her. Her eyes eased open, then grew wide, as she tried to remember where she was. A soft blanket was beneath her, springy straw cradling her, and Mattie was curled against her, her naked skin delightful against Rachel's. Another pattering of water made her blink, and she realized rain was falling, hitting them through the open barn window next to them.

They'd fallen asleep, and she had no idea what time it was. She groaned, trying to get up without disturbing her sleeping lover. Carefully rolling from Mattie's grasp, she sat up on her haunches, raking her hands back through her hair and ordering her thoughts. She grinned. The barn had been a truly wonderful idea, and she realized that Mattie had been carefully controlling her reactions in the loft in the house. Probably afraid Betsy and Angel would hear them, she mused silently.

Not that Mattie was all that noisy. Rachel had no experience with such things, but Lillie had told several humorous stories of some of the men in town, who became rather vocal when at the height of passion. It wasn't like that between her and Mattie, but the little noises of pleasure Mattie made when Rachel touched her made her love Mattie all the more, and drove her own desire to new heights.

Just then, Mattie's face scrunched up, and a whimper of a different kind escaped her lips. The whimper became a low cry, and Rachel quickly moved closer, stroking her head to soothe her. Another nightmare. It couldn't be helped, not after everything Mattie had been through. It set Rachel's teeth on edge that Adam dared invade her lover's dreams. "He's disturbed her a damned sight enough," she whispered.

Mattie's eyes opened and she sat up, looking around wildly, then flying into Rachel's arms, burying her face into her neck. "It happened again. He was coming after me." She felt Rachel rocking her. "I hate that." Her heart slowly quit pounding, and she frowned again. "We fell asleep, didn't we?"

"Yes." Rachel kissed her head. "I need to get up and close the window there. It's raining." She reluctantly released Mattie and stood, stepping across the thick bed of hay. As she moved closer to the window, she realized a steady heavy rain was falling, the sky now completely covered in clouds, obscuring all light. It was pitch black, save the occasional lightning streak.

"We should get back inside the house." Mattie fretted, feeling around for her clothing, which had been tossed in a corner of the stall. "Guess Betsy and Angel will know what we've been up to after all."

"Guess they're probably asleep by now." Rachel studied the falling rain, watching lightning shatter the darkness. She counted the seconds, then heard the rumble of thunder that followed, off toward the north. *North?* She expected the tropical cyclone to be coming in from the south, then thought about the stiff north breeze. *Ah. Guess it brought us some rain after all.* She kept watching, and smiled as a warm body snuggled up behind her and Mattie's head ducked under her arm. She dropped her hand, scratching Mattie's back, and swore she could almost hear a purr of contentment.

"Is it bad out?" Mattie closed her eyes as the pleasant scratches traveled up to her neck and lingered a bit, then traveled back down her back.

"Falling mighty hard." Another flash of lightning crackled across the clouds, and the thunder boomed closer. "You sure you want to go inside, or would you rather bunk down here until morning?"

"Well." Mattie looked around at their comfortable nest, then back out at the menacing rain. "I suppose the damage is done. We'll hear about this at breakfast one way or the other, eh?"

"Most likely." Rachel kissed her cheek. "It's nice and dry in here. We'll be drenched out there, and have to dry off, and change, and get all woken up."

"That blanket is looking better and better by the minute." Mattie kicked at the corner of the soft, clean quilt.

"It sure did a few hours ago," Rachel teased. "Come on." She closed the shutters, blocking the rain. "Let's go back to sleep. We can run inside in the morning, and take our bath before we dry off. Not have to go through all of it twice."

"Very well." Mattie yawned, and sank back down on the blanket, reaching up and pulling a surprised Rachel after her. They wrestled for a moment, a happy struggle that caused Mattie to shriek with laughter as she was gently flipped onto her back, Rachel hovering over her on one arm, holding her wrists with the other. Her eyes were used to the darkness, and she could see the smile on Rachel's face, her steel eyes squinting, deciding what to do next. Mattie solved the problem by curling a leg up, using it to take out Rachel's braced arm with a firm shove of her foot.

"Oomph." Rachel landed on top of her, nose to nose with Mattie. She burst out laughing in surprise, grabbing Mattie and rolling her into a warm hug. They finally settled down on the blanket, Rachel on her back with Mattie once again curled against her side. "Can I tell you a secret?" Her lips brushed across Mattie's forehead.

"Anything." She lightly rubbed Rachel's bare belly with her fingertips. Something had changed between them yet again, and she realized all hint of formality was gone, replaced by a warm familiarity. There was no more embarrassment between them. Two months earlier, wrestling naked in a barn in the rain with anyone would have been unthinkable. Now, it had come easily, something she had fallen into without the slightest thought at all. "What's your secret?"

"In all my life, I never had as much fun as I've had with you." Rachel smiled as Mattie rose up on her forearm, looking down at her. Hazel eyes shone golden in the darkness, and Mattie's own warm smile bathed her in a loving comfort she craved beyond anything else.

Mattie stroked Rachel's face, tracing her eyebrows, then her nose, and then her lips. She memorized the moment, wishing for one brief second she could crawl right inside Rachel's heart, and feel what it must be like in there. She couldn't find words of response, and allowed her touch to speak for her. Slowly, she was pulled back down, Rachel's arms holding her close against her side. She kissed a bare shoulder, and fuzzily realized that she was already there, in a place no one had ever been before. It was the warmest safest place in the world.

The rhythm of the falling rain, and the warm embrace quickly lulled them back into contented sleep. Nearer the beach, a sleepless Isaac Cline stared out the window at the ankle-deep water rising in his back yard.

THE TRICKLING SOUND of water tickled Rachel's ears, and she wrinkled her nose in annoyance, burrowing down further into the blanket. She smiled, feeling Mattie's warmth pressed against her back. Her internal clock told her they really should get up, get dressed, and go back inside the house before Angel came out to feed the horses. She groaned and forced herself to sit up. While she enjoyed the occasional ribald joke with the older woman, she wasn't quite ready to be caught snuggled up with Mattie in nothing but their birthday suits, and Mattie, she was certain, would be mortified at the prospect.

"Mattie." She brushed long red tendrils from Mattie's face. "Time to get up."

"No-o-o-o." Mattie rolled over away from her, covering her head with one arm.

Rachel grinned. The cute round behind presented to her was

much too tempting, and she reached out, giving it a little pinch.

"Youch!" Mattie flew up in outrage. "That wasn't very nice." She turned, a charming full pout gracing her lips.

Rachel leaned in, kissing her, feeling Mattie's arms automatically respond, reaching out and pulling her close for a long minute.

"How about that?" Rachel pecked her on the forehead. "Was that nice enough?"

"Very nice." Mattie smacked her lips and stood up, stretching and stepping gingerly across the springy bed of hay to the window. She cautiously opened the shutter and peered out. "Um. Rachel?" She studied the steady heavy downpour. "There's water from here to the back porch."

"Huh?" Rachel joined her at the window, draping an arm across her shoulders. "Good heavens." What appeared to be a good half-foot of water was pooled across the ground as far as she could see. "Better check the barn door and see if it's getting in here." She grabbed up her clothing, tugging it on as she moved past the stalls and the two placid horses. As she pulled up her suspenders, she reached the barn door and lifted the bar, pushing it open just enough to poke her head outside. The roof overhang protected her from the elements, and she looked down.

The barn itself was raised up about a foot above ground, having been built up on a man-made bank of soil in deference to the low-lying island and the occasional seasonal floods. It was barely dawn, as far as she could tell—time was difficult to judge, due to the cloud-covered sky. Water lapped dangerously at the bottom of the sandy slope down from the doorframe, large raindrops peppering its surface and creating concentric circles all across the yard. Rachel scratched her head in consternation and looked over at the horses, which were munching contentedly from containers of oats, apparently unconcerned that in a few more hours it appeared they might be standing in water.

She looked back at the yard and the pathetically dripping garden, which would most likely be ruined if the heavy rain continued. The wind had picked up considerably and she mentally kicked herself for getting distracted and not noticing it earlier. Now it was clear to her sharp ears, whipping through the palm fronds overhead and blowing the sheets of rain at a decided angle. It whistled beneath the eaves overhead and stirred the tall grasses growing along the picket fence line. As she studied the water-logged expanse of yard, a familiar head peeked out the back door.

"Rachel?" Angel's voice carried over the wind. "What in tarnation are you doing out there, and how did I miss you going through the house?"

"Been out here all night!" She shouted back.

Angel stepped out on the back porch, hands on hips, her head tilted in question.

"Never came in from the porch last night." She shrugged and smiled sheepishly as Angel's face registered understanding, flashing her a devilish grin. "Go on back in. I'll take care of the horses while I'm out here." She shooed at the older woman until she disappeared into the house.

Behind her she heard the sound of frantic dressing, and knew she was in trouble. She turned to face a perturbed and embarrassed Mattie, who stormed toward her with intensive purpose, and grabbed great handfuls of the front of her shirt. "Did you have to let her know I was out here?" She frowned furiously, and Rachel had to fight a smirk. Mattie was adorable when she was angry.

"Sweetheart." Rachel closed her hands over Mattie's, gently removing her already wrinkled shirt from tightly clutched fingers. "I didn't actually say as much, but I have a feeling that was going to be obvious as soon as we step through the back door. You know if Angel's up, Betsy's already in the kitchen cooking breakfast. Short of scaling the side of the house and crawling through the third-floor window, I don't think there was going to be any hiding the fact we were out here together."

Mattie's features softened, though she still withheld a forgiving smile. A gentle hand cupped her face and Rachel stroked her cheek with her thumb. "We could've tried to convince them we came out here early this morning to spare Angel having to go out in the rain." She stubbornly held her ground.

"First of all," Rachel smiled, "they know me better than to believe I'd have let you come out here with me in this downpour. Second of all," she mussed Mattie's hair, "we both look like we've been rolling in the hay. Our clothes are completely wrinkled, and I have straw in places I'm pretty sure Mother Nature never intended. It's all in your beautiful hair as well." She plucked a long yellow strand and twirled it in Mattie's face as proof. "Gonna take a good combing to get it all out."

"Oh." Mattie relented, burying her face in Rachel's chest. "I have to go in there like this, don't I?"

"Yes." Rachel kissed the top of her head. "Unless you want to stay out here and swim in later. Which is what we'll be doing if this keeps up." She closed the barn door and quickly checked hay and oat levels in the stalls. Mattie busied herself combing down the two mares, and soon the animals were taken care of.

"Ready?" Rachel raised the door bar again. "I've never seen it like this." The water had risen what appeared to be another inch in the time it had taken them to care for the horses.

Mattie peered thoughtfully out the door at the dismal scene and audibly swallowed.

"Hey!" Without warning, Rachel swooped her up in her arms.

"Rachel!" She playfully pounded a sturdy shoulder. "Put me down. I'm going to get soaked anyway. No way around it."

"I can at least prevent you ruining your shoes in this mess, can't I?" A dark eyebrow edged up in question. "Hold on." She stepped outside and the rain slammed into them in thick sheets. "Whoa!" She kicked the barn door closed and ran for the back door, the cold, pelting drops dripping down her face and off her eyelashes, obscuring her vision.

They were greeted with two dry towels. Betsy clicked her tongue at them. "You young people today have absolutely no common sense. Go on." She shoved them both toward the staircase. "Angel's drawn you a hot bath. Get up there and get out of these wet clothes before you catch your death of cold. You should know better, both of you." She wrung her hands. "You've got to take care of that baby better than that. I'll have a hot breakfast ready by the time you're through. Land sakes."

Two guilty pairs of eyes glanced in Betsy's direction before both women trudged solemnly up the stairs. Angel ushered them into the water closet with a much friendlier conspiratorial grin. "Never mind her. She's cranky this morning. Rain's set her bones to aching something fierce. She's been jitterier than a long-tailed cat in a room full of rocking chairs. Says she's got a 'feeling' about the weather. I learned a long time ago there's no accounting for her strange notions. Best I can do is say 'yes, ma'am' and stay out of her way." She nudged Rachel in the ribs. "Lesson you might do well to learn early yourself."

"Hey!" Mattie's eyes shot sparks in Angel's direction. "I am standing right here."

Angel and Rachel bit their lips and covered their mouths to keep from laughing. "Here." Rachel nodded toward the water closet door, indicating Angel should leave. "Let me help you with all those buttons, sweetheart." She moved closer, helping her lover out of her clothing. The long skirt and full petticoat were so waterlogged they clung to Mattie's legs, making walking a difficult task.

Soon she was divested of the cold, soggy fabric, and felt a warm hand against her lower belly. "You feelin' all right this morning?"

Warm lips claimed hers, and she melted into a toe-curling kiss. "Mmm."

Rachel nuzzled her hair, making light circles against her stomach. "Thank you for last night, Mattie."

"I kind of enjoyed it myself." Mattie's cheeks colored. "Come on." She took both of Rachel's hands. "Help me into the tub?" Large capable hands steadied her as she stepped over the thick sides. Just as she hit the warm water, an even warmer body slipped in behind her, pulling her back into a comfortable nest of long arms and legs.

"I never dreamed bath time could be so much fun." Rachel picked up a soft sea sponge and a bar of fragrant store-boughten soap.

"Relax." She started at Mattie's neck, carefully scrubbing down and across her shoulders. "Wish I didn't have to go to work today."

"You can't be serious. It's Saturday." Mattie peered over her shoulder. "And it's raining cats and dogs out there. You can't be loading freighters in this weather, the cargo would be ruined."

"No." She lifted an elegant arm from the water and carefully squeezed soapy water across pale freckled skin. "But Billy and Mr. Gentry and I nearly always fish in the rain. Doozy of good weather for that. Fish'll be biting more than usual, and might be nearer the surface with the cooler temperature. Besides, Angel has to ride in to work at the mill, so I might as well ride along."

"What about the storm?" Mattie's forehead knitted in worry.

"It's just rainy wind right now. Mr. Cline said it was supposed to blow east of here. I figure it should've hit us by now if it was going to be real bad." She wiggled her feet in appreciation of the warm water, and the soft legs pressed against her own.

"You be careful out there." Mattie swiveled in the water and they switched positions, so she could return the favor, dragging the sponge across a well-muscled back. Impulsively, she leaned forward and peppered the smooth skin with kisses. "I want my Rachel back safe and sound with me tonight."

"And I'll most likely want to share another warm bath with you when I do get home." More kisses were her answer.

BY THE TIME they left for the warehouse and the docks, the water was starting to seep under the barn door. Angel fretted over that, and they took time out to move everything they possibly could into the loft. When they were done, only empty stalls filled with hay and two empty feed troughs remained on the ground level, along with the water troughs, which they left full. "Can't remember when the rain was this bad." She donned a long macintosh and stepped up into the buggy. "Thank you for driving."

"My pleasure." Rachel had insisted on taking the reins. Angel's sight wasn't what it had once been, and the strong winds were bothering her eyes. She hunkered down on the wagon seat and they both ducked their heads against the driving rain. "You still want to board 'em up in the public stables?"

"I think it might be best for a day or two. Ground is a little higher up there. Don't want 'em getting foot rot standing around in the water all night. I figure the barn will be flooded by afternoon at this rate." She turned, her concerned eyes meeting Rachel's. "Ain't never been this bad," she repeated herself. "Barn's never been flooded before. The bottom step up to the back door of the house only lacks an inch or two before it's covered. I told Betsy and Mattie to move upstairs if it gets too bad."

"I told them the same thing." They both grew sober. The long porch was a good three feet off the ground, and neither of them dared voice the unthinkable.

"Well, that should be good enough. In all the time I've lived there, though cyclones and all kinds of tarnation, the house has never flooded."

"Good enough," Rachel echoed her. They grew silent, lost in their own private, troubled thoughts.

ADAM CROCKETT LAY in his hotel room, listening to the monotonous sound of rain on the roof overhead and the annoying, whistling wind that had awakened him in the first place. He growled in frustration and stood, his long striped nightshirt falling down to his knees. Scratching his stomach, he shuffled over to the window and drew back the curtains. It was gray and dreary as far as he could see. The street below was obviously sodden, with large pools of standing water dotting the sandy shell surface.

A trolley car rattled past a block away, the damp wheels screeching as it neared its stop. He growled again and pulled off the nightshirt, as he moved to the washbasin and splashed his face. After quickly combing his hair and beard, he donned a lightweight black and gray pinstripe suit, and followed his nose down the stairs to the hotel dining room.

He had been trying to leave for Houston for two days. On Thursday, he'd been held up on business. The night before, he'd gotten caught up in a poker game and ended up taking an unknown whore to the hotel. He'd kicked her out shortly before midnight, despite her protests that it was raining too hard to be walking back to her shanty room a few blocks from the saloon. He'd dismissed her anyway, hoping to make the midnight train.

He'd missed it, and since the hotel room was paid up for the night and it was only a few blocks from the train station, he'd opted to go back to the hotel rather than all the way across the island, home, in the driving rainstorm.

Now he was glad, as breakfast was included with the room and smelled much better than his own meager attempts at fending for himself in Mattie's absence. He was growing irritated at her extended trip, and had sent off a letter a few weeks before, demanding she come home. Now he puzzled over that, as he sat down at a small corner table and accepted a hot cup of black coffee from a harried dining room server. He thanked her gruffly, then turned to the newspaper, but his mind kept drifting back to Mattie, wondering if she'd received the letter yet. "I'd best not have to go out to El Paso and fetch her home," he grumbled to the empty chair across from him.

He decided to give her one more week to answer or show up, or he would go out there. He had a contact across the border in Juarez he needed to meet with anyway, so a trip to El Paso was inevitable, eventually. Some of his Mexican sources closer to home were drying up. His island sources were still fairly strong, but he needed the new contact to keep his Mexican trade flourishing.

He drummed his fingers, waiting for his eggs and ham to arrive. The server delivered fresh hot biscuits and butter in a straw basket covered with a red and white checkered cloth. He drew out a biscuit, pulling it apart and slathering butter on the flaky, fragrant layers. With a contented bite, he mused on his good fortune. Even as he sat there, a freighter loaded with newly-made arms was coming in from South America, and would arrive due east of Houston, in a private well-hidden cove, sheltered by moss-covered low-hanging trees and protected by a native group of alligators.

His breakfast arrived, and he was just digging into a pile of fluffy scrambled eggs when Dr. Mills approached him, his face lined with worry. "Mr. Crockett?"

"Dr. Mills." Adam rose and shook the doctor's hand. "What brings you to the hotel on this cursed morning? Sit down." He gestured toward the table. "Have some breakfast."

"I wish I had time. Have you been here all night?" His pale eyes darted around the room.

"Yes. Why?" Adam's eyes narrowed, wondering if word was out regarding the whore he'd snuck into his room. "I got caught here when the rain set in," he lied.

"Beach is flooded out by your place. You'd best get home to your wife and get her to higher ground. She's in no condition to be dealing with a flood." He shuffled his black bag from one hand to the other. "I'm headed out that way myself, to see if anyone has been injured or needs help."

"My wife is safely in El Paso." Adam sat back down, taking a sip of coffee.

"That's good to hear." A server handed the doctor a cup of coffee, telling him it was compliments of the house. "Why, thank you." He sat down, adding cream and sugar to the rich dark brew. "She didn't mention a trip home when I saw her a few weeks ago. I'm surprised I haven't heard from her since she passed out at the widows Sanders and McKenzie's house. I assume she's feeling well?" He looked up, his brows raised in question.

Adam's face was frozen in an unreadable expression, and his fingers gripped the coffee cup so tightly that the handle cracked off before he released it. "When did you say you saw my wife?" His face was dark red, his voice a low controlled rumble.

"Why, a few weeks ago, I believe. I'd have to check her chart for the exact date. As I said, she was visiting and I was called out to see her after she fainted. I assumed she'd told you about..." He trailed off.

"Oh, my. You do know about the baby by now, surely?"

"Of course I know about the baby!" Adam roared. "She told me before she left for El Paso, in mid-July, some seven weeks ago."

"Seven weeks?" Dr. Mills frowned. "If I were a betting man, I'd lay odds I'd seen her only a few weeks ago. Are you certain she left that long ago?"

It was all Adam could do to remind himself the doctor had done no wrong. He restrained himself from flying across the table and choking him. "Exactly where, again, did you say you saw my Mattie?"

"Why, the widows Sanders and McKenzie's house." He gestured out in the general direction of the older neighborhood where their home was. "Nice place," he mused. "That young Rachel Travis has been boarding with them. Odd girl, but polite enough."

"What?" Adam rose up, knocking the table to one side, his breakfast and the doctor's coffee flying across the floor. Without another word, he stormed past the gawking patrons and out the front door of the hotel, oblivious to the driving rain, which quickly soaked him to the skin.

THE WIND INCREASED in velocity two-fold by the time Rachel reached the public stables. Her macintosh hood continually puffed full of air and blew back off her head, and her braided hair was drenched, along with her shirt collar, where the heavy rain had run down the back of her neck. She dropped Angel off in the shelter of the cotton mills and told her she would take care of boarding the horses. Luckily, she procured the last two available stalls and paid the stable boy on duty a little extra to assure the horses received proper care.

The buggy was left under a covered shelter as well, although the wind blew fiercely enough that the shelter was useless under the circumstances. She turned into the punishing deluge and began the tenuous walk to the docks. The wind swirled around her, pushing at her from all directions, and the rain was surprisingly cold, given the warm temperatures of the previous morning. Her dinner pail was tucked securely inside her coat, and she held it against her body as she trudged, head down, watching streams of water run past her feet from uphill behind her.

As she got closer to the docks, the water level increased until she was slogging through what amounted to an ankle-deep running stream. The water, like the wind, seemed to swirl around her, not coming from any one direction. She frowned and wondered if the winds were causing the strange flood patterns. She couldn't recall the last time that much rain had fallen on the island in such a short period of time, and it had been years since the port area was flooded.

Still, given the conditions a few blocks inland, she wasn't surprised to find the docks partially underwater when she arrived, the entire area a mass of chaotic activity as boat and freighter lines were let out to allow for the violent sea swells which rocked the vessels many feet up into the air before dropping them just as many feet back down. She groaned. There would be no fishing. The day was going to be spent in boat salvage. She recalled a similar day a few years before when a large tropical storm had destroyed several smaller boats that hadn't been properly maintained.

The water ran calf-deep along an area just above the docks that only the day before had been wide-open street. She fought the strong currents and wind tugging at her and found Billy at the end of the docks, helping their friend Mr. Gentry with his fishing boat. "Rachel!" His voice barely met her keen ears and she looked up to see him frantically waving at her. "We could use a hand here."

She nodded and made her way to the small fishing boat. Grabbing a thick rope, she swung up and over the railing, where she landed on a slick surface and almost lost her balance. "Whoa!" She held to the rope until her boots stopped skidding. "Gotta lose those." She eyed the ruined leather work boots, along with the basically useless macintosh. "And that."

In less than a minute she was down to bare feet, trousers, and her long-sleeved shirt. Her feet would hold to the slippery wood much more effectively than her boots would have, and the coat would only have restricted her movement. "Have you a plan here?" She sidled up to Billy, pulling on her leather work gloves to protect herself from rope burn.

"We're moving her around to the bay side of Pelican Island. The channel's too narrow to handle this rising water." He grabbed the railing as a strong swell lifted the bow, almost tossing him overboard. Rachel reached out and steadied him by grabbing a suspender and hauling him back from the edge of the railing.

"Thank you." He shook off a prickling sensation in his scalp. "Let's get moving."

"Gonna be tricky." Pelican Island was a small island directly northwest of Galveston. Together the two islands formed the ship channel that comprised the port area. Rachel began helping him let out line. She glanced along the dock, or more precisely, the water-covered area where the dock was, and realized most of the boat owners were preparing to do the same thing, the ones nearest the end pulling out in orderly fashion, one after the other, heading south out of the channel into Galveston Bay. The wind tossed the smaller craft mercilessly, and controlling sails was going to require some precise skills. She smiled. *Nothing like a challenge.*

They let out line as much as they dared, holding the boat to a controlled pitching motion. Finally, their turn arrived, and they cautiously pulled out, keeping the sails trimmed closely. Rachel manned the wheel, controlling the large rudder beneath the boat, while Billy and a partially sober Mr. Gentry hauled the sheets in and out, catering to the ever-changing wind velocity and direction. "Wind is behaving strangely," the older man commented, as he shuffled past her from one side of the boat to the other, tacking and jibbing as they neared the upper end of the island.

"Too true." Rachel could feel the swift current below them, her arms straining as she fought with Mother Nature to keep the boat on track. The wheel pulled against her, and more than once was almost wrenched from her grasp by sudden current changes, which were puzzling. Neither wind nor water were behaving in a predictable manner. As they exited the channel into the bay, and turned to go around the southern tip of Pelican Island, winds pummeled them from both directions and the truth hit home.

They were battling two converging storm fronts.

Other small craft up ahead of them were fighting the battling winds, and she could see some larger freighters rocking on the waves as if they were weightless. All the while, the rain and wind beat down on them, blinding sailors and sending some boats into helpless drifting circles as they fought to maintain control.

"This is gonna be no good!" She yelled over the squall, her voice carrying faintly toward Billy, who was busy with the mainsail. "Pull that one back in and we'll run solo off the jib!" She saw him nod and begin the difficult task of rolling in the heavy water-filled canvas. "Mr. Gentry!" She turned, facing fully into the southeast wind, rain hitting her face so hard it felt like tiny needles. "We need to get her to shelter pronto. Just anywhere we can tie her down."

As she spoke, a huge swell rocked under them, tilting the boat almost on its side. She grabbed the wheel with both hands, bracing her bare feet on the slick wooden deck, trying to stand upright and steer the teetering craft back in a forward direction.

"We've bigger problems than that, lass!" Mr. Gentry pointed over her shoulder and she looked back in horror, watching as a large freighter bore down on them.

"Billy!" She screamed as loud as she could. "Hold on! We're gonna be rammed!"

She couldn't decide whether to stay on deck or jump, but the freighter made the decision for her, picking up momentum and slamming into the small fishing boat with a sickening crunch of wood against iron. The impact sent her careening through the air, and she flew through space for a timeless moment before hitting the churning waves and going under.

Calm.

Her mind spoke as the frigid water sent a shockwave through her body. She tried not to tense up, trusting the air in her lungs to help her rise to the surface, although she had no idea which way was up or down. After what seemed an eternity, she felt the wind on her head and opened her eyes, drawing in a lungful of blessed salty, rain-filled air. She coughed, the saltwater she had swallowed burning her throat. Her eyes stung and it took a moment to gain her bearings.

She treaded water, fighting billowing waves that continued to obscure her view. At last a particularly large swell raised her up, and she saw the island, maybe fifty yards away.

Swim.

She began fighting the killer current, managing to lose the constricting shirt, leaving her in her trousers and undershirt. She was so cold her teeth chattered, but she pressed on, her mind focused only on the land ahead of her. Every few strokes she was forced to re-adjust her direction, the current threatening to draw her from the shelter of Pelican Island and out into the raging bay. She forced thoughts of Billy and Mr. Gentry from her mind. *Can't help them until I get to land,* she reasoned.

At last, exhausted, she crawled through the remaining shallows, practically kissing the packed sandy beach as she scrambled clear of the water. She lay on her back for a long moment, gulping in air and hearing her heartbeat race in her ears. The rain fell down on her but she barely felt it. "Almost didn't make it home for supper tonight, Mattie." Her thoughts went out to her lover and she smiled grimly. "Don't believe I'm ready to leave this life just yet. It just now got interesting."

Slowly, she sat up. The waves had carried her far north, and she couldn't see the fishing boat or the freighter that had done it in. She stood and walked at first, then ran down the beach as she spotted the freighter, run aground many yards away. She could make out its frantic crew, scrambling along the deck while others had already climbed overboard and were walking around the vessel trying to figure out what to do.

Her eyes tracked out to the bay and Pelican Island, and her stomach churned. There was no trace of the fishing boat anywhere, save a few pieces of floating wood she assumed were its remains. "Hey!" She reached the freighter. "Have any of you seen the old man and the younger one who were on that boat you ran over?"

"You were on there?" An incredulous sailor eyed her bedraggled appearance. "It's a miracle you survived."

"My friends. I have to find them," she persisted. "What in blazes happened? Can't your captain control his ship any better than that?" Her heartsick anger surfaced, and she resisted the urge to attack in blind fury.

"Cap'n was blown overboard. We couldna get to the wheel in time. Current blew us out of control. Sorry about yer boat. Maybe yer friends made it to land, eh?" His voice rose in wan hope.

"Maybe." She watched him wander away and realized he was in shock. "He's no help," she muttered. She shivered, feeling like a drowned rat, and she was nauseous, she suspected from ingesting seawater. She scanned the water slowly, watching other small boats fighting the gale-force winds, tossed about the waves like toys in a pond. At last her eyes fell on a wet dark-blond head as it rose out of the water from behind a large piece of driftwood. "Billy!"

She started running down the shoreline, oblivious to the sharp shells and rock crunching beneath her tough bare feet. "Billy!" She saw the wood begin to move with purpose as her friend kicked vigorously against the rough waters, propelled ashore by the sound of her voice.

She plunged into the bay, jumping waves to get to him, hauling him bodily out of the water across the last few feet. They collapsed on shore and Billy lay there speechless for a long while, as he recovered from a near-drowning. "I'm going to wale on the captain of that freighter in a minute here."

"Too late." Rachel reached over, smoothing plastered bangs out of his eyes. "Captain fell overboard out there. Most likely he's drowned."

"Oh." His face grew sober. "I'd have suffered the same fate, if not for that wood. I saw that freighter and dove overboard right before it hit. I think I passed out for a bit. Found myself hanging onto that board when I came too. Couldn't remember what happened at first."

Rachel gently probed at a knot on his forehead.

"You must have hit your head on something." She peered thoughtfully out at the growing storm. "Mr. Gentry?"

"No way he survived this one, Rachel." Billy's eyes grew sorrowful. "If it almost did me in, then...old man, half-full of whiskey as he was, I just don't think..."

"I know." Rachel's voice was quiet. "Damn." She slammed her fist into the sand. "We should have checked the weather with Mr. Cline before heading out of the channel."

"Don't go blaming yourself." He sat up more fully, rain water running down his face. "Who would've thought we had two storms?" He shook his head sadly. "Never happened before."

Rachel's thoughts focused inward. No one close to her had died since her mother, and she realized she'd cared about the old man in a gruff grandfatherly sort of way. She stood on shaky legs and after a moment Billy followed her, as they wandered a few hundred yards up and down the shore in either direction of the freighter. No sign of the boat or Mr. Gentry turned up.

The wind was growing stronger, and she was grateful for the excuse for the tears in her eyes. "Damned old man," she mumbled softly. "The one day you had to care what happens to that godforsaken boat of yours."

Her shoulders slumped in defeat, and Billy draped his arm across them. "Guess we might as well head back into town and send some help out here. Gonna be a lot of stranded boats before this day is over. We tried, Rachel." He ruffled her head. "Nothing more we can do here, not just the two of us."

Her heart hurt, and she looked up at the cloud-covered sky, studying the ominously darker edges of the ones to the east of the island. Thunder rolled overhead, and lightning snaked across the sky out over the bay. The weather matched her mood.

She nodded silently, tears streaming down her face along with the raindrops. Billy gave her a little squeeze and guided her away from the beach as they began the long walk home. Rachel felt as if she were in some bizarre nightmare. Her bare feet were killing her, she was freezing, and Mr. Gentry was most likely dead. That death weighed heavily on her shoulders. She played those few seconds out in her head over and over again, the moments from when she saw the freighter and when it knocked her overboard, trying to decide if she could have grabbed him, somehow saved him. "No," she mumbled, not realizing she'd spoken aloud. She shook her head sadly and felt Billy pull her closer.

"Rachel." His voice was very gentle. "Cut it out."

"Cut what out?" She looked up, realizing he was just as cold as she was, his lips faintly blue around the edges.

"Blaming yourself." He hugged her. "How can it be so chilly out in September?" He felt the goose bumps on Rachel's bare arms and rubbed the outer one vigorously as they walked. She stumbled and cried out angrily as she stubbed her toe on a rut under the water, and he grabbed her waist, steadying her. "Let's sit for a minute, shall we?" He looked around at the flooding neighborhood just south of the business district. "If we can find a place to sit."

Water was rising as they walked, creeping up almost to the calf-level depth they had experienced on the docks earlier in the day. They passed a church, the clock indicating it was around eleven o'clock. Rachel spotted a house with a high covered porch, and several children playing merrily in the yard, splashing through puddles and squealing in delight. "How about that porch over there? Bet they won't mind."

"Fine." He steered her toward the house and what appeared to be an inviting porch swing under cover. "Hello." He nodded toward the children, who ignored them, other than to wave before going back to their games. They sat wearily down in the swing, idly rocking and catching their breath.

"I can't wait to get a hot bath," Rachel moaned, examining her bruised and swollen feet. The skin was puckered and shriveled, making them even more vulnerable to injury, and she noted several cut and cracked places on the soles. "I'll be paying for this walk for a few weeks."

"Want my boots?" Billy held up his sodden foot covering.

Rachel eyed the boots, which appeared to be twice the size of her own feet. "That's very noble, Billy, but I suspect I'd just step right out of them and they'd wash away."

"I could carry you on my back," he half-joked, hoping she didn't accept the offer.

Rachel chuckled. "I'm smaller than you, but not that small. I weigh a darned lot more than I look like I do." She flexed her biceps, producing an impressively bulging muscle. "I'm pretty solid."

"That you are." He'd been around her enough to note her nicely-developed form, and had helped her on and off boat decks enough to have a general idea of her bulk.

An older woman, wrapped snuggly in a canvas macintosh, stepped out on the porch. "You poor things." She moved in front of them. "Come inside out of this wind and rain, and warm up. This flood is a blessing and curse, isn't it? I've got cookies and hot tea inside."

It was tempting. "Ma'am, we're soaking wet and filthy, but maybe if you could bring us the tea out here, we'd be mighty obliged to you." Rachel plucked at her clinging undershirt, and realized in its soaked state it was practically indecent. She crossed her arms over her chest and smiled in embarrassment.

"I'll do that." The woman stepped inside and reappeared momentarily with a tray, which she set on a table next to the swing. She pulled up a chair to join them, and handed Rachel an over-sized man's shirt. "Here. It's an old one you can keep. You look like you're cold."

Rachel blushed faintly under her tanned skin. "Thank you, ma'am." She donned the warm soft black and blue buffalo flannel and buttoned it up. "Been a long morning. Our boat was sunk out in the bay and we're walking home."

"Oh, my." The woman poured up two steaming mugs of sweet hot tea and handed them over to the grateful pair. "As I said, this rain is a blessing and a curse. We needed it badly, but my goodness, I've never seen rain water rise so quickly, and flood so badly. My children of course, are enjoying it." She smiled at the low din coming from the front lawn. "I wish my husband were home. He would give you a ride home. He works in the mills and left before sunrise this morning."

"We appreciate your hospitality, ma'am." Billy sipped his tea, in between bites of sweet crumbly oatmeal cookies, laden with cinnamon and brown sugar. "These cookies are mighty fine."

"Why, thank you." The woman preened a bit, smoothing back her windblown hair. "Just look at all that water," she fretted. "It's over the bottom step there. I don't think it's ever rained that hard here before. I surely do hope it doesn't flood the house. My James has a store of sandbags in the barn out back, but I can't lift them myself, and I've no idea how to place them to block the water."

Something had been niggling at the back of Rachel's mind, and she stared solemnly at the flooded yard, watching the rain and the brisk breeze ripple the surface, churning and swirling, drowning the grass beneath it. She peered down the street, squinting in each direction, seeing the same flooding as far as she could in both directions. It was troubling. With the water in the bay rising, and the tides in the Gulf already higher than usual, the rain certainly had nowhere to run off. The wind continued to blow, gusting so hard at times that it almost lifted the children off the ground as they ran splashing about.

She thought some more about the bay and the Gulf, and the torrential downpour that seemed like it had settled in. As she studied the water in the street, it seemed to be streaming from more than one direction. She frowned and suddenly stood up, setting her teacup down and stepping down to the bottom step, stooping down and cupping a handful of water.

"Rachel, what are you doing?" Billy watched in fascination, as his friend willingly left the covered porch.

Rachel ignored him and sniffed at the water. She carefully tasted it with just the tip of a pink tongue and wrinkled her nose, before moving out to the edge of the yard. She repeated her actions, cupping up some water, smelling it, and this time taking a healthier mouthful. She swirled it around with her eyes closed, then spat it out. "We need to get home, now." She turned, her face lined in worry.

"Why?" Billy stood, hands on hips, their hostess mimicking his pose.

"This isn't just rainwater." She held out her arms at her sides, looking around. "It's got salt water mixed in."

"So?" Billy scratched his head in confusion.

"So, what that means is, the rain isn't causing the flooding, Billy, the sea is rising from both sides. You've seen it yourself. We've got storms blowing at us from both directions." She kicked at the water. "This is the ocean closing in on us. Much more of this wind and rain, and it will cover this island completely. We've got to get to higher ground, just in case."

"My goodness." The woman wrung her hands in her apron. "What should I do?"

Rachel eyed the three-story house. "I'd start by moving my valuables up a floor, ma'am, but I think I'm going to go home, get my loved ones, and head for the mainland. Come on, Billy." She turned toward the small fenced edge of the yard. "We need to talk."

"Um." Billy bowed slightly to their hostess. "Thank you, ma'am. And good luck. You might ought to find your husband and fetch him home, I'm thinking."

"Maybe I shall." She watched in worry as her two guests abruptly departed.

Further away, across the island, Isaac Cline sent a frantic message to the weather bureau in Washington.

Chapter
Twelve

"I'M GOING TO go fetch Angel home." Betsy crossed her arms stubbornly over her chest, her parasol clutched tightly in one hand.

"It's not safe." Mattie tried to pull her back into the parlor and away from the front door. Outside, the wind whipped in a fury, battering the door and blowing so hard the tall thick palm trees in the front yard were bending over as if they were twigs.

"I know that hateful man who runs the cotton mills. He won't let them go. Well, I'm going to go get her, I don't care if I have to beat him over the head with my parasol." She tilted her chin up in defiance, daring Mattie to stop her. She seemed much taller than her scant five feet one inch of height, and Mattie backed off, her eyes beseeching her friend to reconsider going out in the storm.

"Please. This house is going to be flooded soon, but at least we've got two more stories to work with." Mattie gestured toward the back door, where water was starting to seep underneath, pooling near the icebox and soaking the rag rug. "Out there..." She cocked her head, listening to the wind as it whistled past the house and under the deep eaves, making her skin crawl with the eerie high-pitched sound. "You might not make it back before..."

"Listen, child." Betsy moved closer, cupping Mattie's cheek. "Tell me, if your Rachel weren't out on a boat where you can't get to her, what would you do?"

Mattie sighed, knowing the truth in her heart. "No storm in the world would keep me from trying to get her safely home." Mattie sat down on the sofa, her eyes watering and blurring her vision. "Truth be told, I think that's why I'm on edge. I've half-considered going to the docks myself. I want her home. And I feel helpless. What if..."

"Oh, Mattie." Betsy moved in next to her, patting her on the leg. "Nothing is going to keep that girl from coming home to you, even if she has to dive overboard and swim." She smiled sadly. "Angel— she's inside a large room with no windows. They might not even know how bad it is out. And she's just mule-stubborn enough to work until she finishes her quota of whatever they've given her to do today. She always did seem to think she was invincible."

"But what if something happens?" Mattie looked up, swiping the back of her hand across her eyes. "You've become such wonderful friends to us. I don't want to see y'all get hurt or anything."

Betsy closed her eyes. It was lunacy, and she knew it. In all her years on the island, the house had never flooded. Now water was almost three feet deep in the back yard. The barn was starting to lean, the last time she'd gone out on the back porch, and she was grateful they had no animals in there to worry about. The man down the street who traded milk and bread with them had already come by twice, warning them to move up to the second floor. They had hastily moved nearly all their valuables up to the third floor loft, leaving only the furniture to whatever lay ahead. She could only imagine how bad the flooding was nearer the beaches and the cotton mill.

"Hear me out, child. She's not come home, so I have to go to her." Betsy stroked Mattie's hair. "There are a lot of things worth living for, but very few worth dying for. I must go to her, because I'd rather die by her side, than live without her. I know that probably sounds foolish."

"No." Mattie felt the words to her very core. "No." Her voice softened. "I've known Rachel for eight months. I wouldn't trade those eight months with her for eight years without her. I understand." She stood, drawing Betsy up and into a hug. "I wish Rachel were here. We'd go fetch her for you."

Betsy snorted. "No you wouldn't, because I'd be damned if I'd stay here alone. I'd be going with you."

"Maybe I should go with you."

"No." Betsy squeezed her shoulder. "You have to be here when your Rachel comes home. You'd drive her insane with worry if you up and took off in this mess. Don't you fret over me. I'll be fine."

"You be careful." Mattie bit her lower lip in worry.

"I will be." Betsy paused and turned back, making her way to a small writing desk tucked into a corner. She opened up a drawer and withdrew a yellowed folded document. "This is the deed to this house. If anything should happen to me, to us — this place belongs to you and Rachel. We have no family, so I don't think you'd have to put up a fight as long as you have the deed. Take it up to the third floor where it's safe. If we don't come home..."

"Stop it." Mattie began to cry. "Don't talk like that."

"It's only a precaution." Betsy hugged her again, feeling her tremble as she sobbed even louder. "Silly of me to think of it. I shouldn't have upset you so. You've got that baby to think about."

"Rachel and I were discussing names, just the other night." Mattie smiled through her tears and sniffled. "If it's a girl, we're going to call her 'Rebecca Evangeline'."

"That's very kind of you two." Betsy smiled sadly. "I don't know that we deserve that."

"Yes. You do." Mattie drew in a deep calming breath. "You gave us shelter when we had no where else to turn. Took in relative strangers and showed us a great kindness."

"Ah, child." Betsy drew her cloak more closely around herself, preparing to go out in the growing cyclone. "And you gave hope for the future to two old ladies who had never known others like ourselves." She stood on tiptoes, giving Mattie a kiss on each cheek. "You've become like daughters to us. Family." She turned to the door. "Watch over our house until we return, you hear? And you make sure Rachel knows, every day, how much she's loved. She needs the reassurance. She's so like my Angel in that way—so brave on the outside, and so very vulnerable on the inside. They don't let many folks see that. Only us. It's why I have to go to her. I can't let her come home in this storm alone. Her eyesight..." She straightened up. "Well. I'd best get going before it gets any worse out there." She hugged Mattie one last time. "You take care of her. She'd be lost without you."

"Yes." Mattie felt the tears rising again, and she swallowed a lump in her throat. "I know." She resisted the urge to bolt out the door after Betsy. She closed the door behind her with a loud click of the latch, and peered out the window to watch her go, but the rain was so heavy, she could no longer see past the front porch. "Be safe," she whispered, then turned back to the kitchen and the large pot of hot tea that sat on the stove. She poured up a cup, her hand shaking as she lifted it and dropped in two sugar cubes.

She sat down in a large rocking chair, facing the back door, and watched in fascination as the water puddle grew, covering much of the kitchen floor. When it reached the edge of the parlor rug, she calmly got up and moved to the stairs, sitting halfway up. She'd been isolated from the world for so long, and now she felt completely alone. She shivered and sipped at the warm tea. She'd changed into the men's clothing she had worn for their beach outing. She wasn't sure why she felt the need to do that, only that she moved more freely in the trousers, and she felt comforted wearing Rachel's old soft undershirt beneath the long-sleeved blouse that was tucked into her waistband. If she concentrated, she could smell Rachel's bay rum on her clothing, and just a hint of the salty air. And she was definitely cooler in the trousers than she would have been in her skirt and petticoats.

"Rachel, where are you?" She dared not think about her lover out on a fishing boat in a cyclone. Surely they had come ashore by now, and Rachel was on her way home. Maybe she'd bring Angel and Betsy back with her. Maybe...her thoughts trailed off and she watched the floor below, as water now trickled slowly to the bottom of the stairs. It would be a while before it would cover the bottom step. It would have to fill the entire first floor, and she thought that might take a while. The house shook with a particularly strong gust of wind, and she thought she heard a tree fall in the yard outside, as a loud cracking sound drifted through the walls, followed by a tremendous splash.

It was near noon, the last time she'd checked the hallway clock. Her stomach rumbled and she chuckled at the absurdity of it all. "Life goes on," she mumbled, and patted her belly. "I must get you fed, little one, no matter what's happening outside." She removed her boots and stockings, rolling up her trouser legs before she traipsed back downstairs and waded through the kitchen to make herself a sandwich. She flipped the switch on a table lamp but nothing happened. Betsy and Angel had the entire house wired with the new-fangled electricity, but apparently it wasn't working. She could see well enough, and quickly made herself a roast beef sandwich, and poured a tall glass of cold milk.

She took her dinner back up to the second floor, and sat down on the top step of the first staircase, keeping an eye on the water while keeping her feet dry, as she began methodically devouring the sandwich. The wind and rain outside made such a racket that even thinking became difficult. She strained to distinguish the various sounds assaulting her ears — wind whistling around and under the porch roof, rain beating against the side of the house. That was an oddity. They usually didn't hear the rain at all unless they were on the third floor.

This storm was different, though. Very different. She shivered as she realized part of the noise was the sound of things being battered and broken outside. Many homes on the island had tile roofs, and she was certain she could hear some of them shattering as they were torn away and flung about by the furious wind.

She swallowed hard, as she realized that most likely, Rachel was exposed to all of it out there somewhere, and that if things were as bad as they were several blocks inland, how bad must it be nearer the water? "Please be on your way home, my love." She set the half-eaten sandwich aside and closed her eyes, leaning against the stairway wall and feeling the cool, somewhat damp wallpaper against the side of her face. Everything was damp and a little clammy to the touch.

Something crashed against the side of the house and she heard a window shatter somewhere behind her on the second floor. She jumped a little, her entire body coming off the step she sat on. Her heart thumped against her chest and she suddenly felt a little queasy. "No." She crossed her arms over her stomach and bent over, forcing her meal to stay down.

Gradually, the sensation passed, and she hesitantly stood and went in search of the broken glass. She found it — a large bay window overlooking the street in the second-floor guest bedroom. She only set one foot inside the room before she realized that going near the window would be foolhardy. Several loose shards clung perilously to the frame, while dozens of others were sprinkled across the now-drenched rug. As she watched, the wind whipped up and tore the curtains from the rod, sending them whirling about the room before they settled in a sodden heap on the floor. She simply closed the door against the wind, and stood out in the hallway, trying to determine what to do next.

It occurred to her that maybe she should move the food to higher ground, and she moved forward with heavy steps, stopping at the top of the stairs and steadying herself before she made her way to the first floor. It was completely covered in several inches of water, and she sloshed across the parlor to the kitchen, her feet still bare and her pants legs still rolled up. A picnic basket sat on the end of the counter, and she picked it up, shoving as much food as she could inside before making her way back upstairs, all the way to the third floor.

As she rounded the corner to go back downstairs and see about the food in the icebox, she nearly collided with a large figure, and screamed in reflex. As she realized who it was, she screamed again, in joy, and flung her arms around Rachel's neck, losing control as she sobbed against her. "Oh. I didn't hear you come in." She couldn't articulate much more, and Rachel held her for a moment, stroking her hair and making soft little comforting sounds near her ear.

"Hey. Don't worry." Rachel held her at arm's length. "I'm getting you all wet."

"Don't care." Mattie pulled her close again, drawing in her scent and the warmth that radiated back against her, even through her soaked clothing. "I was so frightened. I kept wishing you'd come home, and I just thought..."

"I'll always come find you Mattie, no matter where you are, or what may lie between us." She kissed her head and then her lips, briefly.

"It must have been horrible out there. It sounds so savage." She studied her lover with anxious eyes. "You look like you've been dragged behind a horse." She plucked at the soft flannel material covering Rachel's shoulders. "And where did you get this shirt? And where are your boots? Rachel." She tilted Rachel's face up with a gentle nudge of her hand. "Your feet are bleeding."

"Long story that I don't have time to tell right now." She urged Mattie up to their third-floor loft, and led her over to the bed, where they sat down. "We need to get off this island." Rachel took Mattie's hand, stroking it with her thumb as she spoke. "We're flooded from the bay to the Gulf. We are underwater. Just a bunch of buildings sticking up out of the sea. I saw a trolley car run off the track earlier. Most of the electricity is out. Billy has gone to find Lillie, and will try to meet us back here, but he told me to just go if it takes them more than a half-hour."

"Did you go past the mill on your way home?" Mattie suddenly remembered Betsy and Angel.

"No. I ended up far south of the business district. Out boat was taken out by a runaway freighter. I think..." She swallowed and looked down. "I think Mr. Gentry's dead. I fell overboard. Billy almost drowned."

"Oh, dear lord." Mattie covered her mouth with her hand, her eyes welling with fresh tears. "I'm so sorry about Mr. Gentry." She shook inside at the thought that Rachel had gone overboard in the storm. She reached up and ran a trembling hand through long dark hair. "What about you?" She touched an ugly bruise that peeked out from Rachel's shirt collar.

"I'm alive." Rachel brushed off the subject. "Where's Betsy?"

"That's why I asked about the mill. Betsy went to get Angel." A few tears spilled over, and she sniffled. "I tried to stop her, but she said she had to go to her. She talked to me about you, some. After that, I couldn't make her stay. I-I would've done the same thing." She grew quiet, unable to bring herself to share the entire conversation.

"Damn!" Rachel looked over at a small clock on the bedside table. "We have to go. Water's rising so fast." She reached across, touching Mattie's stomach. "I want us both to be around when this little one comes into this world, and I swear I am going to see to it that we all survive this thing."

"Is it as bad as it sounds out there?" Mattie covered Rachel's hand with her own.

"I think there are some more dead out in the water by now, yes." She pursed her lips inward. "Wind is blowing something fierce. I think I saw a man taken down by a piece of flying roof. Folks are walking toward the bridges in droves, carrying their things on their backs and heads. But the water..." She thought of the carpetbags under the bed. "We should take almost nothing with us."

"But..." Rachel brushed a finger across her lips.

"We need to be able to swim some, if we have to." She saw the fear in Mattie's eyes. "I can help you, sweetheart, if it comes to that, but we can't be loaded down with things."

"All that matters to me is that we both make it through this." Mattie leaned in and quickly kissed her. "What do we need to do?"

"We both need to put some boots and stockings on, and hightail it out of here while we can." She got up and moved to the armoire, withdrawing two pairs of clean dry stockings. "Wish these would repel water."

Mattie moved to her side. She still felt unsettled, and her head was spinning at everything that was happening. She touched Rachel's arm, seeking out tactile comfort. "I was so frightened today after Betsy left. I didn't know where you were and I wanted so badly to come find you. I need to tell you about my talk with Betsy, but we probably don't have time right now. Just know that you are the most important person in the world to me."

Rachel turned and wrapped her in a wordless embrace, rocking her gently back and forth and allowing the words to settle over her very tired body and frazzled nerves. "We've both had a very hard morning." She nuzzled Mattie's hair. "We still have a very long afternoon ahead of us." The wind whipped into a frenzy outside, rattling the roof, emphasizing her point. "When we get out there, we need to be covered so our skin isn't exposed to flying debris in the air. Need to tie our hats down and wear long sleeves and macintoshes. I'll have to wear Angel's old one. Mine was lost with Gentry's boat. And we need to stick close together. The wind is so strong, it almost took me off my feet a couple times, and the flood—in some places the currents are strong enough to wash you away, if you lose your footing. Don't let go of me, no matter what."

"Never." Mattie kissed her quickly, then set about the task of dressing to go out. "Next time I pray that I'll be able to go outside soon, I'm going to be a bit more specific about the circumstances." She smiled wryly and felt Rachel ruffle her head as she stepped past her and studied the clock.

"Billy should've been back by now." She squared her shoulders. "We—we have to go. No more time. If we don't hurry, the water might get too deep for us to get to the bridge. Of all the things," she spoke quietly, "to leave all our friends behind at a time like this."

Mattie shot her a look of quiet sympathy, and reached up, lightly scratching her neck. "Would you expect them to wait for you in a life and death situation?"

"Of course not," Rachel groused.

"Then I would hope they would forgive us for doing the same." She took Rachel's hand. "Come on. Let's get moving."

Rachel nodded in grim silence. Outside, the wind howled, as the sea continued to rise, slowly swallowing up the island. They quickly got into their coats and placed a few scant possessions in their pockets, mostly the cash they might need to sustain themselves once they reached the mainland. As they stepped outside into the raging fury, Rachel draped a protective arm around Mattie, pulling her close as they began the soggy trek toward the bay.

As they left, and turned down the sidewalk into the street, Adam stepped out from beside the house. He watched in disbelief and shouted in anger, but the wind carried his words in the wrong direction. He tried to run after them, taking high awkward steps through the rising water. As he reached the street, a roof tile tore free from the house next door, and with unerring accuracy, slammed into his side, knocking him to the ground with a great splash.

He lay there for a long time, coughing as water ran up his nose. He got up and sullenly trudged through knee-deep water after them, ducking his head into the driving wind and cold pelting rain. He knew what he'd seen, and somehow, some way, he intended to make Rachel pay for stealing his wife. It sickened him. He had heard tales of women doing disgusting things together, and seeing Mattie with Rachel only strengthened his resolve to kill the taller woman the first chance he got.

RACHEL HAD ONE goal—to get herself and Mattie across the bridge to the mainland and safety. The flooding made walking a slow, difficult task, but as they crossed Broadway the water level was lower. Nonetheless, Rachel noted the floods running through the street, the rivulets pooling and gathering, mingling with rivers flowing toward the street from both directions.   The tides have never risen high enough to flood Broadway. Isaac Cline's words echoed in her head and she shivered. She turned her attentions to Mattie, who was much too silent at her side. "You all right?"

Mattie nodded solemnly. She knew if she talked her teeth would chatter, giving away just how cold she was. She walked next to Rachel, one arm wrapped snugly around her waist, with Rachel supporting her in kind. It was agony, the cold, and the pull of the flood, and the constant roaring noise all around them. Her face stung from both rain and tiny bits of rubble that continually pelted her in the face. She pressed forward in silence. She had no other choice.

She felt dizzy, and she tried to place the source, other than her pregnancy. In their haste to be on their way, she realized she'd never finished her sandwich.   Now her stomach felt hollow, growling angrily at her from lack of food. She tried not to think about it, or about the unborn baby that was depending on her to provide it nourishment. It was surreal, walking through the raging water, the wind battering her from all sides, having to shout to hear each other talk.

She should be terrified, she acknowledged, but other than her physical discomfort, she felt a little numb, and under that, a layer of peace based in the calm assurance that Rachel would take care of her. All around her, people and animals were panicking, women weeping in fear, horses bolting, dumping their riders and taking off without them.   Men struggled along, carrying trunks and carpetbags, their harried wives and children trotting along behind.   Some of the younger children danced through the water with glee, oblivious to the coming storm.

She could feel it at her back, and if she glanced back toward the Gulf, she could see the rolling dark clouds, and the gray sheets of heavy rain pouring across the horizon for as far as she could see. Greater than the cold wet rain or the bothersome wind, or even her pain and hunger, was the solid warm presence at her side. Rachel had said little about her morning, but Mattie sensed she'd almost lost her. She swallowed hard, renewing her hold, slipping her thumb inside the waistband of Rachel's trousers and idly rubbing warm skin. She felt

Rachel's breath catch just a little, then even out as Rachel's own grip tightened around her.

"You certain you're all right?" Rachel's voice burred right in her ear, in an effort to be heard over the wind.

She nodded again, giving her lover a little squeeze of reassurance. She thought of Billy and Lillie, and Angel and Betsy, and even of the little house she and Adam had lived in on the beach. Judging from what she'd seen on the long walk to the bridge, she was sure the house was a loss, along with all the furniture and things she'd left behind there.

Good.

It was selfish, and absurd, to think of such a thing in their dire circumstances, but she couldn't help it. The less that remained to bind her to Adam, the better. A rueful smiled graced her lips as she thought again of the child she carried. *There is that,* she acknowledged. She shifted, turning more fully into Rachel's hold, and buried her face inside the edge of Rachel's macintosh, trusting her lover to guide both of them as they plodded forward. She felt Rachel's hand trail up her back and brush briefly across her head, before it settled once again at her hip.

"Almost there, sweetheart." Rachel's lips were at her ear again and she let it soothe her. She was weary to the bone, and the bridge was a long one. She could feel the crowd around them growing, as more and more people poured off the side streets, joining the desperate throng as it flowed toward the bay bridge and the promise of solid land. Somewhere behind her a baby cried fitfully, and next to them a horse whinnied and snorted, dancing sideways in the rising flood.

"I-I'm cold," Mattie finally spluttered out. She was soaked to the skin. They both were and there was nothing they could do about it.

"I know." Rachel hugged her tightly. "Hang on, Mattie, just a little ways further and one bridge, and we'll go find a warm dry place to ride this out."

It hurt to see Mattie so cold and exhausted. The life she carried was too precious to be in such peril. She should be at home in a warm bed with her feet propped up and a nice big plate of food at her side. She felt Mattie stiffen with every step, and felt the slight uptake of her ribs as she drew in each breath. Occasionally she felt a cold shiver work its way through Mattie's body, and the clutch of her hand at her side as she sought support in her struggle to simply walk.

The rain dripped down her back beneath her collar and pounded against her face, and the wind almost pushed them along at times. Overhead, the thunder rolled and lightning flashed across the dark, roiling sky. Flying debris constantly pelted them, and more than once she'd fended off larger bits—shingles and such—as they hurled perilously close to their heads.

And the water rose.

They neared the last few blocks before the bay, and the water was back up around their knees, making walking a chore. Mattie felt unknown objects brush against her legs under the water, and watched in numb shock as a small dog paddled past her, its eyes rolling in frantic fear as it searched for footing and found none. At the last minute, a man scooped it up and lifted it into the back of his wagon. "Glad I didn't have to watch that dog drown," Mattie smiled, and shouted near Rachel's ear.

Rachel looked down at her, surprised at just how much better Mattie's smile made her feel. She looked around before quickly ducking her head and giving Mattie a swift peck on the lips.

At that moment, Mattie felt someone grab at her, jerking her out of Rachel's embrace. A strong arm wrapped around her body and she felt cold steel at her throat. "You lying whore!" Whiskey-tainted breath drifted past her face. "I should beat the fear of God into you. You're going to burn in Hell, Madeline."

"Adam?" Mattie's knees almost gave out and she slumped back against him.

"Let her go." Rachel reached down and swiftly drew her Bowie knife from her boot. Mattie's face was pale as a ghost, her eyes wide with fear. She looked around and realized that no one was going to help them. As the frightened people passed, they gave them a wide berth. Everyone was too intent on their own survival to worry about what appeared to be a domestic dispute.

"Are you insane? What are you going to do, Adam, kill me?" Mattie resisted the urge to stomp down on his foot, realizing he might pull the wrong way and slit her throat. "Have you looked around? I think we both have bigger things to worry about right now, like surviving this storm. What are you planning to do, knock me over the head like a caveman and drag me across the bridge? That's what it'll take, because I'll not willingly go with you anywhere. How far do you think you could carry me in this mess?"

"You will come with me, and you'll be praying for mercy before this day is over." He eyed Rachel's knife warily, and glared at her in utter hatred. "You don't have it in you."

"You don't know that." Rachel stood firm, her fingers twitching against the knife hilt. She knew she could nail him easily, even with Mattie in his grasp, if not for the blasted wind.

"She's poisoned you, that disgusting harlot." He didn't move, turning his attention to Mattie, choosing to fight with words for a while instead. "Look at you in men's clothing, Madeleine. What's happened to you?"

"I learned that I don't have to stand for being hit." She blinked as the rain continued to sting her face. "And I finally learned what love is."

"Love? I could have both of you hung for your 'love'." He laughed mockingly. "You're coming with me, Madeleine. We're leaving here, and I'm going to be a proper father to our child, and you are going to be a proper lady, no matter what I have to do."

"Proper father?" She spat out. "You're not even a man."

"Why, I oughta..." His rage rose up, and he lost his concentration, loosening his grip at her throat.

Mattie felt the metal leave her skin and saw her opening, shoving at his arm and ducking under it, dropping as low as she could, his other hand still gripping her arm. She'd seen Rachel practice knife-tossing, and she closed her eyes in silent prayer. *Come on, my love.*

"*Augh!*" He shrieked in pain and dropped his knife as he looked down. Rachel's knife was driven all the way through his forearm, a wicked blade-tip protruding about two inches out on the other side. Blood spurted from his arm as he grasped the hilt, trying to pull it out. Mattie's eyes flew open. She saw two things—drops of blood hitting the water next to her, and his knife just below the surface. She grabbed it and swung around, stabbing him in the leg. "Oh, God! Dammit!" He stepped back, dropping the Bowie, and Mattie half-crawled, half-leaped forward, staggering into Rachel's arms.

"Gotta get my knife," Rachel hissed, releasing her and diving forward. Adam spotted it at the same time, and they both splashed around, wrestling for it. Rachel plowed into him, taking him out at his knees and landing on top of him. She got in two swift punches to his face, but he reached up, grabbing her by her braid and yanking her head so hard she saw stars.

She went with the motion and landed on her back in the water. Just as she got her bearings, he pounced on her legs, crawling up and slugging her hard in the stomach. She coughed violently and tried to scoot backward, out from under him. He crept up after her and she saw an opening, kneeing him solidly in the groin.

Adam groaned in agony and grabbed himself as he rolled off her. As he doubled over on his knees in the rising floodwater, he spotted the knife and grabbed it. "I'm going to kill you, you damned whore!" He turned and landed on her so quickly she had no time to react. Rachel looked up and saw him raise the knife, his eyes gleaming insanely. "Your kind don't deserve to live."

He had her pinned, his knees on her legs and one arm across her body. If she tried to fight him, all he had to do was stab her, and that would be the end of it. Her face hardened, and she said a quick silent little goodbye to Mattie. She kept her gaze fixed on him, refusing to die with her eyes closed. With one great breath, she yelled as loudly as she could, "Mattie, run!"

He raised his arm higher and she felt her gut clench, and almost threw up. Something exploded directly above her head, and blood flew over her chest in wet warmth. Adam screamed and dropped the knife, as he rolled off her and curled up in a ball in the water. She grabbed the knife and sat up, blinking into the rain and spotting Mattie a few feet away, her pistol still raised.

"Mattie?" Rachel stood on shaking legs and closed the distance, gently taking the gun from her grasp. "Didn't even know you brought this with you, but I'm sure glad you did." She tucked both knives into her boots, and pulled her close as Mattie buried her face into Rachel's chest, and great wracking sobs coursed through her body. "I got you." Rachel kissed her head, never taking her eyes off Adam. "You were supposed to run."

"The only place I'll ever run is into your arms," Mattie choked out.

A groaning noise caught their attention, and Mattie looked up as Adam slowly stood. His right arm and hand were both bleeding, as was his leg. His face contorted in pain, and he drew in several deep breaths. "You — you shot me." He stared at her incredulously.

"Didn't know I could do that, did you?" She shifted, standing a little taller, still sheltered inside Rachel's coat. "I always knew this day would come. First time you hit me, I went out and bought this." She took the pistol from Rachel and watched in satisfaction as he ducked. "Took me a long time, but I learned. All those whiskey bottles you left on the kitchen table in the evenings made damned fine targets."

"I am your husband and you are my wife, and you are carrying our child. Come with me," he pleaded. "We can leave here, start a new life."

"I've already started a new life." She glanced briefly up at Rachel. "I'm happy now, Adam. I've found the place I was meant to be, and it doesn't include you anymore."

"I love you." He edged just a little closer, careful to stay out of Rachel's reach.

"You love me?" She laughed bitterly. "You have a strange way of showing it. How many times have you twisted my arm? Slapped my face? Punched me in the stomach? Or the times you threw me across the room. There were the couple of times you knocked me out, back home. Do you remember that, Adam? How about the time you broke my ribs, or the time you cracked my back tooth?" Her anger grew and she felt the rage building up. "No more!" She roared, clenching a fistful of Rachel's shirt. "Don't you ever — ever — touch — me — again. Or I swear, I will kill you."

"But you're my wife!"

Rachel released Mattie and touched her on the arm "Stay put for a minute." She strode toward him, grasping his shirt collar and lifting him, as the water sloshed around their legs. She drew the Bowie knife, brandishing it in his face. "Not another word. You ever hurt her again, and I will see to it that you regret it." She flicked the blade dangerously close to his throat. "Mine!" she roared in his ear, causing his hair to stand on end. "Do I make myself clear?"

Cold steel eyes bore through him, the sparks almost visibly flashing from them. There was no doubt as to her meaning, and he nodded meekly. Her lips twitched in rage before she dropped him. He almost lost his footing as curious onlookers walked past them. Glaring at her one last time, he turned, facing the bridge area, feeling her eyes at his back.

The wind blew fiercely, and Mattie had heard only one word of their exchange, but it was the only one that mattered. She smiled as Rachel returned to her and held her closely against her side for the rest of the short walk, keeping an eye on the surly figure ahead of them. "Mine." She patted Rachel's hip, knowing Rachel heard her as the taller woman kissed the top of her head.

At last they reached the bay and stopped, staring at the churning water and the wreckage of boats bobbing in the whitecaps. More importantly, their eyes fixed on the arches of the bridge, and the waters below them.

"Rachel?" Mattie looked up uncertainly at her lover, then out at the bay. "Now what are we going to do?"

Rachel remained silent for a long moment. The bridge was covered by water. Its surface was still visible, but it was submerged. She heard the forlorn muttering of the people around them. "Dunno. Maybe the other bridge, or the railroad bridge."

"Don't bother," a man heard her and moved closer. "We've already been to both of 'em and they're covered, too."

"Well, then." Rachel forced down the rising panic in her gut. "We can't risk it. We can't see how deep it is out in the middle, but I'm pretty sure I see the water flowing freely out there. Tough to make it out from here, but I don't think it's safe."

"So we — we're going to die?" Mattie's throat tightened. "Is that what you're telling me?"

"No." Rachel hugged her. "We'll find another way."

"Fools." Adam practically spat at them. "There is no other way. Stay here if you want to, but I'm crossing this bridge and getting off this island. Mattie, come with me. You stay here with her, and you will die."

Mattie's eyes flicked sadly across his hopeful face. "No." She looked up at Rachel. "You do what you think you have to, and I'll do what I have to."

"But the baby." Adam dared move closer, well-aware of the powerful figure standing next to his wife. "What about our baby?"

"Our baby." Rachel enunciated the words carefully.

"Now, wait just a minute." Adam moved closer still, talking over the wind as his hands balled into fists. The rain dripped off the brim of his hat, obscuring his view.

"No." Mattie stepped between them. "It ends here, Adam. This is not your child and you are not my husband. Cross the bridge or go on your way, whatever you choose, but you're not a part of my life anymore."

"Out of my way!" He roared, shoving past her and barreling headlong toward Rachel. She merely met his head-butt, grasping his body and rolling with it, lifting him and dumping him on his back in the water.

With a yell of rage, he rose, coming at her again. She turned, cocking her fist back, and then swung forward, landing a solid uppercut to his jaw and sending him to his back again. She stood and watched as he got up yet again, rubbing his aching jaw as he circled her.

"Stand down, Adam." She took on a defensive stance, waiting for him to make a move. "I've got to get her and that baby to safety, and I'm not letting you or anyone else get in my way."

"My baby," he growled, and came blindly at her again, intent on using his body weight to knock her down. She suddenly shifted her stance, simply plowing into him and sending him to his back a third time, landing on top of him, holding his head down under the water for a brief second before she grabbed a handful of his shirt and hauled him back up. He spluttered and coughed, spitting out cold salt water.

Rachel dug her Bowie knife out again. "She may not have killed you back there, but I sure could." Rachel pressed the sharp side of the blade against his throat, her knees and one elbow holding him in place. "Fight me." Her eyes glinted wickedly, as the rain poured down her face. "I do so want you to fight me, and give me a reason to kill you right now, you sorry piece of pig dung. And that's an insult to pigs everywhere."

"Rachel." Mattie moved cautiously closer, but stayed well out of his reach. "Don't." She dropped down behind her lover, resting one hand on her back. "You can't kill him."

"But I so want to." Rachel's hand twitched and she felt a pressure, as Mattie squeezed her shoulder. "Fine. If you insist." She pulled the knife back, then suddenly and viciously elbowed him in the face. "My baby." She slugged him again with her free hand. "My wife!" Another blow and she let him fall back, as she rocked back on her heels and stood up.

He slowly stood, shaking his head to clear his ears of water — and perhaps a faint ringing sound from Rachel's blows. He looked first at Rachel, and then at Mattie, who instinctively moved next to Rachel and felt a protective arm drop around her shoulders. She stood up tall, seeing Rachel in her peripheral vision, her dark head held high and proud. "Goodbye, Adam." Mattie's words were soft but certain, and he growled one more time, then turned and headed toward the bridge.

Mattie clung to Rachel, feeling her ribs rise and fall with labored breathing. "Did he hurt you?"

"My stomach hurts from earlier, and my hand hurts from hitting him." She flexed her fingers and watched as Mattie took her hand and kissed the throbbing knuckles. "Other than that, I'm fine. He's in worse shape than I am. If he doesn't drown he just might bleed to death, though his injuries don't seem to be slowing him down much."

"Do you think he will be able to cross?" They both watched his progress as he made the first tentative step onto the bridge, the water washing over his legs at mid-calf. He clung to the railing on one side, taking one slow step at a time, careful to never completely let go of the railing.

"I suppose we'll know soon enough." Rachel blinked water out of her eyes. The wind battered tiny raindrops against her cool skin, and blew the tails of her mackintosh back. She snorted. The coat was useless, actually. A crowd was gathered at the bridge, and a few others bravely began to follow Adam on his trek across the bay. "If he does make it, we should try, too."

"Surely the floods won't rise high enough that we can't take shelter on the second floor of the house." Mattie looked worriedly up at her, watching Rachel's jaw work as she swallowed.

"It's a cyclone. We've got rain and wind to worry about. Powerful wind. Mr. Cline said Broadway has never flooded, but you saw it back there. This is the worst it's ever been. I-I believe our best chance of survival is going to be to get off the island."

"And if we can't?" She continued to watch Adam's painfully slow steps.

"Then we find another place to go. I think the house is sturdy enough—sturdy as most other homes here, at any rate. There's a few larger buildings downtown we might try to reach. I don't know. This flooding, the storm—they aren't predictable. They can leave little houses standing and destroy larger ones, with no apparent rhyme or reason." She pitched her voice high enough to carry over the wind, and realized the people around her were listening.

A glance around revealed terror, mostly. Women held onto babies and men shouldered bags and various other possessions. The children, who had been playing in the water earlier, now clung to their parents, their eyes solemn with fear. A few wagons were off to the side of the standing crowd, nervous horses snorting and sidestepping in the rising water. Down on the beach, huge waves slammed ashore, swirling and foaming as they spread out, mingling with the floodwaters that crept ever higher toward the center of the island. Whitecaps churned out in the bay, and a few small boats bobbed helplessly in the mayhem.

The handful of people on the bridge halted and appeared to be studying the path ahead with some trepidation. Only Adam plowed forward, the water well up to his waist. One by one, the others turned back, plucking their way toward their onlookers. "Damned fool," Rachel muttered, as Adam wobbled a bit, a large wave washing over him and covering him to shoulder level. He stopped for a long moment, then ducked his head and used the railing to pull himself forward. Finally, in a desperate move, he climbed onto the railing, and began inching slowly forward, using both his arms and his legs.

Suddenly, a large tidal surge swept across the bay, capsizing a boat out in the middle before washing over the bridge. Adam looked up and saw a wall of angry debris-filled seawater bearing down on him. There was no place to run and no time to escape, as it covered him in cold darkness, tearing him effortlessly from the bridge and washing him out into the bay.

"Damn!" Rachel saw it, and tore her mackintosh off, handing it to Mattie.

"What are you doing?" Mattie's eyes grew wide as Rachel next removed her long-sleeved shirt, leaving her in her trousers and undershirt.

"He's going to drown." Rachel gestured toward the dark head bobbing in the water, then looked around at the horrified crowd, which stood rooted in place. "No one else seems inclined to help him."

"No one else is foolish enough." Mattie grasped a suspender and tugged Rachel toward her. "Besides, I thought you wanted him dead."

"And I thought you wanted him to live!" Rachel snapped at her, her anger rising. She knew it was irrational. Mattie was a kind-hearted soul, but she felt it anyway, the boiling anger mixed with a jealousy she realized she'd harbored for a very long time. She watched as Mattie's hand moved up, cupping her face.

"Not at the risk of losing you." Mattie blinked, warm salty tears joining cold rainwater.

"And what if he dies?" Rachel looked down, crossing her arms over her chest. "Will you blame me for that later?" Hesitantly, steel eyes glanced upward, dark lashes blinking uncertainly over them. "More importantly, will you be able to forgive me for not trying to save him?"

Rachel might as well have slapped her. Mattie drew back a step. It wasn't the time or place to discuss the complicated emotions she knew lay beneath the argument. "Can you forgive yourself?" She stepped forward again, laying a hand against a cotton-clad stomach, feeling Rachel's heartbeat strong against her fingers.

"I can't let you down, Mattie." She pursed her lips inward. "And I've never killed anyone. I know I've expressed that particular desire in his regard, but truth is, I've never stood by and let someone die before my eyes, not if I could help them."

"No!" Mattie tugged at her hard, hooking her fingers inside her waistband. "Let me down?" She was furious and felt her blood rising, driving away all hint of the chill in the air. "What do you think will happen if you go out there, Rachel? Do you honestly think you won't drown, too? Look at it. We just watched a boat roll over and disappear. Are you stronger than that? Are you?" She pushed at her, shoving her backward a step.

Rachel's own eyes grew wide and she remained silent as the words rained down over her. She shook her head negatively in answer and looked down. "No," she finally whispered. "I just..."

"No!" Mattie yelled again. "I am with child, Rachel. If you go out there and don't make it, I am alone, do you hear me? I have no folks here. I don't know how to survive a storm like this—I've never seen anything like it. None of our friends are with us. And if I do survive, I don't want to raise this child alone. The most heroic thing you can do right now is live, for me and for this baby." She stopped, drawing a heavy breath, feeling her chest tight and her eyes stinging. "I need you." She moved closer. "I love you." Long arms wrapped around her, pulling her close.

"Shhh." It was the easiest choice in the world. "I'm not going after him." She kissed Mattie's head, oblivious to their curious neighbors, who were half torn between Adam's plight and the unusual exchange between the two women. "It was ignorant of me to consider it."

"It was very brave." Mattie sniffled and looked up at her. "I don't want him to die, because I can't wish that on anyone, no matter what they've done. But I won't lose you, even if it means leaving him to fend for himself. He made the choice to go out there. Sometimes we have to live with the choices we make." She cupped Rachel's face again. "And he might die for that choice, but I won't risk you. Letting you go out there—that is a choice I could not live with."

All the anger and the jealousy dissipated and Rachel closed her eyes, feeling the warmth of their joined bodies. "I choose you, Mattie."

They continued to stand there in the rain and wind, locked in the embrace, not caring if anyone saw or what they thought about it. Mattie turned and rested her cheek against Rachel's chest and they watched Adam's dark head as it bobbed out in the water. He made no sound that they could hear, and they were uncertain if he was dead or alive. Slowly, the waters carried him away from shore, tossing him back and forth until it finally closed over his head, and he disappeared from their sight.

"Do you think...?" Mattie stopped. "We need to find another place to go, don't we?"

"Yes." Rachel's eyes were still fastened on the spot where Adam had sunk. She nodded, her eyes taking on a faraway look as she made a decision. "Let's go home."

They turned their back on Adam's watery grave, and began wading back toward town.

SISTER FRANCIS PEERED out the window of the girl's dormitory. Heavy sheets of rain lashed the window, and she could see no further than a few feet past the porch, which was already underwater. Great creaking noises carried on the wicked howling wind, and she jumped as a large slate roof tile was hurled through the window, shattering the glass, which landed in shards at her feet. The rain poured in and she carefully stood back, stepping through the glass as she brushed off her habit. Her finger caught on a small sliver of glass and she looked down in odd fascination at the single drop of blood that appeared on her fingertip.

"Sister Francis?" Albert tugged at her skirt and she looked down. "You need to move back some more." He pointed at the rapidly growing puddle of water at her feet.

"Yes, Albert." She drew her finger to her mouth for a second, then turned to face a crowd of terrified children, and followed their gaze to another puddle of water, which trickled in under the door, pooling on the wooden floor, and soaking a large rug in the entry area. They were all in the girl's dormitory, even the boys, as the boys' dormitory was already flooded on the first floor. "Perhaps we should all move to the second floor. Come along." She managed a smile, and herded her charges up a narrow wooden staircase.

The noise of the storm was much louder up there, and it seemed as if God himself were reaching down with an angry fist, pounding at the dormitory, slowly scrubbing away at the building in a fury of rain, wind, and hail. The boards creaked as strong gusts battered the structure, and they could feel the entire building shake as a large wave rolled upward from the sea, breaking against the lower story. One of the younger girls began to cry, and several others quickly joined her. Water dripped steadily down in one corner of the room, from a leak where several tiles had been torn from the roof.

"Now, now." Sister Francis moved around among the children, urging them to sit down and huddle together for comfort as much as for warmth. Soon a few other nuns joined her from the first floor, and they led the children in singing hymns, and in reciting the rosary, and in petitions to the Blessed Virgin Mary to spare them. Small, brave voices piped up, pitched high to carry over the chaos outside, and Albert scooted closer to Frank and their friend William, taking their hands. The boys were too frightened for their usual show of bravery, and meekly clung to each other as they tried to concentrate on the songs.

Another tile flew through a window on the far side of the room, and all the children screamed. Sister Francis rose, picking up a blanket from one of the beds, and making her way to the window, intent on somehow covering it up. She paused in horror at the sight below. Despite the cold and the rain, she moved closer, peering out at a blackened sky, streaked through with lightning. Thunder rumbled over the angry Gulf, which was indistinguishable from the yard below. There was no more yard, nor any sign of the beach; only water as far as she could see, and a few lonely buildings peeking up above the roiling waves. She watched a small storage shed break apart, rended by the sea as if it were nothing more than a thin reed, the boards quickly spreading out in all directions as they were carried away.

"Sister Francis!" Frank's voice finally broke through to her. She was soaked to the skin, and water dripped down into her face. She wiped a hand across her eyes and took a deep breath, hoping to hide the hopeless fear that gripped her heart. "Children, let's all gather closely together, shall we, way over there." She pointed toward the corner furthest away from the outer walls.

The wide-eyed children obeyed without question, meekly scooting back until they were all piled into the corner. Most were openly crying, even the older boys, and the girls clung to one another, sobbing uncontrollably. Sister Francis left them briefly, returning minutes later with a large coil of clothesline.

"We're going to play a game." She unwound the rope, laying it out around them. "Each of you should take your turn, starting at the end, and see who can loop this rope around your waist, and tie the most secure knot."

"Why?" Albert piped up, his eyes on the rain pattering freely through the shattered window. One of the younger nuns quickly stood, taking the blanket Sister Francis had left behind. She raised the remains of the window frame, and managed to tuck the blanket in, partially blocking the growing storm.

"Because it will be fun." Sister Francis smiled at him, patting him on the head. "Come on, now." She moved to the far end of the group, helping a very young girl get the rope around her. The children began to chatter among themselves, some from increased fear, and some from the excitement of the new diversion.

"Frankie, Willie, come on." Albert moved to the opposite end of the group from the sisters. "Don't tie up too tight."

"Why?" Frank scooted up next to him, quickly followed by William.

"Yeah," William chimed in. "Sister Francis said to see who can tie the tightest knot."

"Just don't." Albert's sight turned inward. "It seems like it might be a bad thing to be tied to all of them, if we end up having to swim or something."

"You think?" Frank whispered, as Sister Francis drew ever closer to their end of the group.

"I'm not sure." Albert patted him on the leg. "It just don't feel right is all."

"I'm with you, Albert," Frank looked up as the boy next to him finished tying off, and handed him the next section of rope.

Despite their protests, Sister Francis tied them in tightly before she moved away from them and sat down next to the younger girls. The other nuns were tied in among the children, situated next to the very smallest ones, including a few who were barely old enough to walk. As they commenced with singing and prayers, three little boys stole furtive glances as they stealthily untied themselves, merely looping the rope around their waists.

IT WAS DUSK-LIKE, although sunset was several hours away. Mattie bleakly surveyed the turmoil overhead. There was no sign of the sun or even of the sky itself. Dark billowing clouds covered them, the rain growing colder and stronger with each step they took. She took one last glance upward, then hunkered back down in a protective fold of Rachel's coat.

Suddenly they were both lying face down in water that covered them. A loud crash splattered next to them, sending ripples of floodwater over their heads. Before she had time to think, Mattie felt herself hauled up as Rachel clung to her. "Sorry." She pushed plastered hair from Mattie's face. "Near miss." She indicated a palm tree, which lay next to them, ripped from the ground by its roots. "Had to shove you out of the way."

"Oh." Mattie felt shaky, and suddenly her stomach twisted inside. Her face felt hot, in odd contrast to the cold deluge of rain against her skin.

"Mattie!" Rachel patted her cheek gently. "You're kind of green. Or gray, maybe." She tilted her head in question.

"I don't feel well." Mattie swallowed as her stomach protested. She felt like vomiting, except... "I didn't finish my dinner." She felt a warm hand cover her belly. At some point she'd lost a few buttons, and Rachel's touch slid against her skin, taking advantage of the gap in the material.

"We need to get some food in you." Rachel's brow furrowed and she looked around. They were in a residential area, with no sign of a store in sight. "Can you stand?"

Mattie nodded as Rachel helped her up. She wanted to cry, and her insides were doing something akin to a hoedown. Her jaw clenched with another wave of nausea, and she swallowed several times. "Baby's angry with me." She stumbled, and sat down in the water again.

Rachel stooped down, helping her up again, this time supporting her with both arms. "I'll carry you if you need me to."

"No." Mattie shifted, taking advantage of the extra support. "Just having both your arms around me makes a big difference."

Rachel grinned, just for a moment. "I can think of much better places to have both my arms around you." She pulled Mattie close. "Let's get you home so we can feed you." She felt Mattie nod against her, and they continued on. Mattie shivered constantly, her teeth chattering at times, but Rachel made no comment. There was nothing that could be done. Their heavy wet clothing protected them from bits of flying debris, but otherwise they might as well have been naked. The cold rain was almost unbearable, and stung every inch of exposed skin it hit, and her eyes hurt from constantly squinting to see ahead of them.

The floodwaters were rising, and as they reached a lower area, rose above knee level, almost up to Mattie's hips. The slow pace against the strong current was exhausting, and Rachel felt Mattie's labored breathing as she tried to walk. After nearly an hour, she knew Mattie was crying, although the noise of the storm drowned out her sobs.

"Mattie." Rachel stopped, pulling her lover over to a house and up onto a high porch that was still above flood level. "Talk to me." She patted a cold cheek.

"I can't go on." Mattie's muffled voice sounded against Rachel's shirt. "I can't."

"You have to." Rachel's voice rose to near panic. "We're still too close to the bay. We have to get further inland, even if we don't make it home."

"Maybe — maybe the church." Mattie looked up hopefully. "It's halfway between here and home, isn't it? It's a nice big safe building, don't you think?"

"Maybe." Rachel nibbled her lower lip. "But we have to get to the church, and to do that, I need you to get up."

Two hazel eyes peered mournfully up at her, then Mattie drew in a long breath, releasing it as she slowly rose back up to her feet. "Al right." She wrapped one arm around Rachel's waist. "Let's get moving."

"That's my girl." Rachel kissed her on the head, and helped her down the steps and back into the free-flowing street. Others were out and about, moving in all directions, as people scrambled for any place that might provide shelter and safety. The wind picked up, and heavier debris began to pound at them. Rachel used one arm to continually bat at objects that flew toward them. She winced as a sliver of wood lashed against her forearm, leaving an angry gash that went clean through her clothing to her skin. Mattie had not noticed, so Rachel said nothing, feeling warm blood inside her sleeve.

At last they reached St. Mary's Cathedral. The water was running waist-deep in the streets, and a horse galloped past in panic, its rider long-gone. They heard a great ripping crunching sound, and a beam flew through the air, killing the horse instantly. It dropped into the water near them, and Mattie screamed, clutching at Rachel. They could no longer hear each other talk without shouting, and the wind blew so hard that each step was agony.

Rachel held on to her lover, and studied the cathedral, noting its obvious swaying. A good portion of the roof tiles were gone, and she could just make out the faces of frightened occupants who had taken shelter inside the large building. The bell in the tower overhead clanged constantly as the wind whipped around it, and she could hear the entire structure creaking, even above the roar of the storm.

"We need to move on," she shouted. "This is no good."

"Home?" Mattie yelled back at her.

"If you can make it that far." Rachel cradled her head, forcing eye contact. Two determined eyes met her. "It's closer to the center of the island, Mattie. I just have a feeling this isn't a good place."

"I trust you!" Mattie yelled, almost in her ear, then quickly pecked Rachel's cheek. "Take me home."

Rachel gathered her strength and led onward. She had been doing her best to practically carry Mattie, lifting her up as much as she could. As they passed the church, she noticed a small rowboat, tied to a tool shed behind the church. Without a word she turned away from the street area, fighting the current until they reached the boat. "I'm giving you a ride home." She scooped Mattie up, setting her carefully into the boat as Mattie squawked in outrage.

"You can't row against this current!" She lifted a long wooden oar that rested in the bottom of the boat.

"No, but I can pull it." She began untying the boat, affixing the thick rope around her own waist. She turned, facing Mattie. "Let me do this," she pleaded. "It will be easier than what we were doing before, believe me."

"If you're certain." Mattie's doubtful eyes appraised her.

"I am more than certain." She leaned in, stealing a quick kiss. Mattie's face was already losing the pinched, pained expression it had bore for the past two hours. "Rest, my love. Sleep, if you can."

Mattie snorted, an unexpected bubbling laughter. "I don't believe sleep will be possible until this storm blows over."

"All right, then. Home we go." Rachel stepped carefully back toward the more open street area. In some ways it was easier, as she had both arms free for balance. True, the current was strong, and she had to fight it to move forward, but she was moving faster than they had been before. Every fiber of her body told her they had to get home. She watched lightning streak across the sky, striking far enough away that she couldn't tell where, or what, it hit.

Back in the boat, Mattie settled against one of the benches, feeling safer sitting in the bottom of the small craft. She stretched out her legs, and sighed with relief. The rain still punished her face mercilessly, but being off her feet made a world of difference. She slowly felt a small measure of tension drain from her body, and her stomach settled down some, although she was a long way from being relaxed.

She watched Rachel moving ahead of her, her head bent against the wind, her long arms idly moving next to her sides, her fingertips grazing the floodwaters around them. Rachel had left her coat in the boat, and Mattie was using it as a cushion to sit on. She could clearly see Rachel's strong back muscles, shifting and moving against the white shirt plastered against her skin. Her braid was almost completely undone, and her long hair whipped back behind her. She looked like a wild thing, and Mattie found the sight to be irrationally appealing, there, in the middle of a storm that threatened to kill them both.

Her insides settled some more, and she looked down, resting a hand against her stomach. "She's going to take care of both of us." She found herself humming an old lullaby, and smiled for a moment, trying to imagine what it would be like when they were a family.

Halfway between the church and the house, she heard a series of sounds like gunshot, and jumped. Both women turned and watched as the bell tower of St. Mary's wobbled precariously in the wind. The iron bands that held the tower in place had snapped, and the structure threatened to give way at any minute. Suddenly, a smaller tower collapsed inward, smashing the roof of the church. The larger bell tower quickly followed, missing the church itself.

Mattie's eyes grew wide, remembering the people inside the church. She turned back around, sharing a grim look with Rachel, who shook her head sadly, then turned away, increasing her stride with a new motivation to get them home. They passed fewer and fewer people, as group by group, the islanders chose their places to wait out the storm. Most of them had been through their share of cyclones, but no one could remember anything like the one they were facing.

A few blocks from home, the wind picked up considerably, carrying a constant high-pitched shriek. As they rounded the corner on their own street, a large piece of slate tile came flying through the air, crashing against Rachel's back and sending her stumbling into the water. She lost her footing and felt the boat dragging her backward. In a blind panic, she reached around for the rope, trying to grab hold and pull herself back above the water.

Mattie watched and screamed as the dark head disappeared below the surface. They could no longer hear each other, even at a shout. She scrambled to the front of the boat, lying on her stomach so as not to fall overboard. Grasping the rope, she began desperately pulling at it, knowing that Rachel was hopefully still tied to the other end.

Bracing her feet against one of the bolted benches, she tugged with all her might. "Rachel!" she cried out, in spite of the wind, feeling the heaviness that pulled back against her, indicating Rachel was working just as hard as she was.

At last Rachel spluttered to the surface, her feet finding the ground again. She coughed violently, digging in with her heels so as not to lose her grip. "Dammit!" Her face contorted in anger. Mattie's pale face stared back at her and she softened her expression. "I'm fine." She coughed again and spit out some water. "Truly. I am." She moved to the side of the boat and felt her faced cupped between a pair of cold, but gentle hands.

"You could have drowned." Mattie stroked her cheek. "You scared the living daylights out of me."

"Sorry." She closed her eyes for a moment, drawing up reserves of strength. "Look." She gestured down the street. "If it wasn't raining, we could see the house."

"Can you make it?" Mattie's fingertips brushed across her face again.

"You bet I can." Rachel flashed her a smile and ducked her head into the wind once more. Three blocks away were warm blankets and dry clothing, and more importantly, food.

BETSY STOOD IN knee-deep water, watching as workers came out of the warehouses. She searched each face, blinking away the rain blowing in from the Gulf and pelting her face with icy-fine drops. She had long since discarded her useless parasol, and was drenched from head to foot. Her height wasn't helping any, as the throng of much taller people slogged past her, intent on getting to higher ground.

At last, a beloved lined face appeared in the warehouse doorway across from where she stood. "Angel!" She waved frantically, her voice lost on the wind. She began pushing her way through the crowd, practically launching herself into Angel's arms as she approached her. "I feared I would never find you."

"What are you doing here?" Angel squinted, trying to focus in the windy wet gloom.

"I came to lead you home." Betsy took her hand and began tugging her away from the buildings and back toward town. "Or at least that was my intention."

Angel stood her ground, unaccustomed to the rare public display of affection. "Why?" She grumbled. "I can get home on my own—been finding my way home for over thirty years now."

Betsy looked down, recognizing the chastisement for what it was, and allowing it to wash over her. She swallowed and looked back up. "Your eyesight." She reached up, her hand trembling as she pushed a lock of hair away from Angel's face. "I worry about you sometimes."

"I can see just fine," Angel groused.

"Is that why you allowed Rachel to drive the buggy this morning?" Betsy's gentle smile removed the sting from her words.

"Oh, well, so I might need to get some spectacles." She peered into the driving rain. "We need to get the horses and get home. I suspect I will have to drive, seeing as Rachel didn't see fit to come with you."

"Angel." Betsy took both hands in her own, chaffing them with her thumbs. "Rachel and Mattie are headed toward the bay bridge and the mainland by now. This storm — it's bad. I imagine the house is flooding. We can't get to the stables from here."

"What do you mean 'we can't get to the stables from here'?" She started in the direction of the stables, and felt a hard tug to her arm. "What?" she shouted over the howling wind.

"Please, just follow me?" Betsy's eyes pleaded. She had to stand on tiptoe, cupping her hand around Angel's ear and shouting her request as Angel stooped down to hear her.

Angel frowned and nodded, placing a hand at the small of Betsy's back even as Betsy urged her forward. They walked in mute silence, sloshing through the flood and dodging people and animals headed in all directions. The rain lashed at them from the back, quickly soaking Angel's macintosh and hat. Betsy led her up a few blocks and over, turning away from the direction of home, and toward more of the business district. At last they reached St. Peter's and Betsy pushed the heavy wooden door open, leading Angel inside and up the stairs to the balcony area.

A crowd had gathered in the cathedral, claiming pews and spots along the walls, hunkering down to wait out the storm. Babies fussed and the occasional dog whimpered, as mothers fretted over their children, and the men stood around in small pockets, talking and gravely listening to the din outside. Some water had seeped inside, but the building was solid enough that it was holding much of the floodwaters at bay.

Betsy drew Angel to a soft old blanket, which was folded over and tucked next to the back pew of the balcony, and covered a small area of the hard wood floor. The pews were all occupied, and the balcony walls were lined with even more people than the first floor.

"Would you tell me what in tarnation is going on here, so we can get home?" Angel crossed her arms and blew out a disgruntled breath of air, watching as Betsy removed her own coat and laid it across the back of the pew. "The water's only knee-deep out there, the horses can make it through this."

"The stables are underwater." Betsy pursed her lips inward, watching Angel frown. "I tried to go get the horses before I came over here. Ran into the stable hands. They had to let all the horses go, or else let them drown. They're gone. Rachel and Mattie are gone. I told Mattie they should go without us, if they were to have any chance of getting off the island. This spot..." she indicated the blanket and the corner. "I had to fight to claim it. It was the last place left on the second floor, and this kindly gentleman promised to hold it for me until we could get here. Thank you, sir."

An older man smiled. "You're more than welcome, ma'am." He had several children with him, and a younger woman who resembled him enough to be his daughter. She was hunched down behind the pew back in front of her, trying to discreetly nurse a baby.

Both Betsy and Angel turned, giving her a measure of privacy. "I want to go home." Angel looked around the tall room and up at the vaulted ceilings in confusion.

"We can't." Betsy made a move to unbutton her macintosh, and hesitated until she realized Angel was going to allow the assistance. With a gentle hand, she stroked a tanned cheek, just once. "We can't, because the flooding is such that we would have to walk for miles out of the way. The direct route is no longer passable. I asked." She worked first one button and then the next, watching Angel's face as she processed the information. Her lover shrugged out of the waterlogged canvas. "This storm, it's here, and we would not make it home in time."

"We've never had to run from a cyclone before." Angel looked around, trying to comprehend what she was hearing, refusing to believe her world had changed so much in a few short hours. "Is it truly that bad?"

"It is." Betsy reached up with both hands, straightening an errant shirt collar. "Most folks who could go have already headed toward the bridges. I think the entire island is flooded now."

"You should have gone with them." Angel felt Betsy's hands stop, going still for a long moment, as her head dropped down and she rocked slightly from one foot to the other. Finally, she looked back up, her fiery brown eyes sparkling with amber flecks. Slowly, they filled with tears and she blinked, once, drawing in a shaky breath as Angel caught the tears with her fingertips, then ran those fingers back through her damp hair. It mattered not who might be watching. Some things were too important to be left unsaid. "I'd have wanted you to be safe, rather than coming after me."

"I couldn't have." Betsy's lips trembled in a smile. "Because I made you a promise, a long time ago, in the woods outside Atlanta." She closed her eyes, remembering a quiet time of commitment, just the two of them, beneath a tall pine tree under a blanket of bright twinkling stars. Swallowing hard, she quoted a familiar verse from memory, "Whither thou goest, I will go, and where thou lodgest, I will lodge. Thy people shall be my people, and thy God my God. Where thou diest, will I die, and there will I be buried. The Lord do so to me, and more also, if aught but death part thee and me." She looked up, watching the tears pool in Angel's eyes, matching her own. "I don't break my promises."

Angel recognized the verse—from the Book of Ruth—and

remembered the first time she had heard her lover speak those words. She gasped, grasping the gravity of the situation. Without further thought, she pulled Betsy into a tight hug, kissing her on the cheek and nuzzling her hair. "My beautiful brave lady. How could I ever love you more?" She quickly brushed Betsy's lips with her own, not caring where they were. "My home has always been with you. Let's get some rest, and make the best of this, shall we?"

Betsy clung to her, absorbing the hug and the shared body heat. She felt herself lifted up slightly before Angel released her. "Good, because I am weary from walking here. I wasn't sure I would be able to walk all the way back home, even if we could."

The settled down on the blanket, and Angel rested with her back against the wall, holding Betsy close in an effort to help her fight off the chills from her wet skirt and shirtwaist. After a while a nun came along, passing out dry clothing and extra blankets, which had been taken from a dry goods store near the church. The women took turns holding up a blanket, using it as a makeshift changing screen.

"How does this look?" Betsy laughed, holding out her arms, which were encased in a man's shirt twice as big as her. Her hands were hidden, and the shirttail came down to her knees. Beneath the shirt she wore a plain skirt, which fit a bit better than the shirt, and she wiggled her toes in pleasure at the sensation of clean dry stockings.

"You're beautiful." Angel held out a hand. "Come here and let me comb out your hair and re-braid it." She sighed as the smaller woman did her bidding, landing lightly on the blanket next to her. They suffered a few curious glances from those around them, but most people were too busy tending to their own families. A hush had fallen over the room, as one by one, children and babies managed to drift off for afternoon naps, despite the roar of the storm which beat down on the building outside.

"It feels divine to be dry again." Betsy's scalp prickled pleasantly as Angel worked a wide-toothed comb through her hair.

"That it does." Angel tugged carefully at a snarl, and began separating the long strands of mostly gray hair into sections for braiding.

"I think I'll leave it down for a while," Betsy glanced shyly over her shoulder. She knew Angel loved it when she left her hair unbraided. "It needs to dry some more."

"Very well, then." Angel set the comb aside and settled back against the wall, half sitting and half reclining. Betsy scooted over, fitting herself under one arm and curling up with her head resting against a strong shoulder. Under her ear, she could hear Angel's heart, beating as strongly as it had the first time she'd ever heard it so close.

Angel idly stroked Betsy's head, feeling her breathing deepen and even out, and watched as her eyelids slowly drooped shut. Warm breaths brushed across the skin exposed above her top button, and Betsy's hand rested flat against her stomach. She lay her own hand over it and kissed the top of Betsy's head. "How did I ever manage to find you, Rebecca McKenzie, 'cause it's for darn sure I didn't do anything to deserve you."

Outside, the flood waters rose, and way out in the Gulf the waves began to gain speed, as the storm continued to batter the island. Inside, two women rested, taking shelter in a love that had weathered the greatest storm of all, life.

Chapter
Thirteen

IT SEEMED LIKE hours, but Rachel and Mattie finally reached the house. The water was up to Rachel's armpits, and threatened to take her off her feet and carry both of them away. She half-dragged and half-swam the boat around back of the house, and tied it off to a porch column. Making her way onto the water-covered porch, she tugged mightily at the back door, but it was held shut by a rushing current of water, which even Rachel's substantial muscle was useless against.

Mattie shivered, and tried not to pay attention to her stomach, which gnawed at her with hunger, and her head, which had started to spin with dizziness. She no longer even bothered to swipe the water away from her eyes, allowing the deluge to pour over her unhindered. It felt as if she would never be warm again. She realized some of the spots before her eyes were not raindrops, and swallowed as a wave of nausea rose up, bitter on the back of her tongue. "Rachel?" Her voice was weak and the howling wind carried it away, unheard.

Meanwhile, Rachel methodically tested the four windows off the back porch, all of which were kept locked against the vagrants that made their way to the island, riding the boxcars that arrived daily from the mainland. "Dammit all!" She yanked with all her strength, to no avail. The rain hindered her grip, and her fingers kept slipping. Finally, she sloshed back down the steps and swam over to the boat, intent on getting an oar to smash one of the windows. She clung to the side of the boat, well aware the water was rising. "Can you hand me that oar, sweetheart?"

Bloodshot hazel eyes blinked at her, as Mattie struggled to both concentrate and hear her. "Mattie?" She hoisted herself up as much as she could without tipping the boat over. "Mattie!" The combination of pale skin and blue lips did not bode well, and with no further thought, she tilted the boat, grabbing an oar and catching Mattie at the same time, as the smaller woman slid into her arms.

She dragged her passenger and the oar up the steps, getting Mattie situated on the seat of the porch swing, which hung only a few inches above water. "Stay there, please." She stroked a chilled cheek, then moved to the window furthest from the swing, hoisting the oar back and landing a hard blow to the middle of the window, shattering the glass and cracking the cross-pieces of the frame.

Working frantically, she cleared the window of stray shards and splinters, until there was only a large gaping hole. Just as she finished, the water rose perceptibly, and began flowing over the sill and into the house. "Mattie, let's get you inside."

Mattie nodded vacantly and gripped weakly at Rachel's waist, as she felt her lover guide her to the window, picking her up gently and lifting her up and inside the kitchen. Rachel quickly followed, picking Mattie up again and carrying her to the stairs. "Mattie, can you make it up there?" She sat down next to her lover, practically cradling her in her lap. "Come on, talk to me, will ya?"

"Baby needs some food," Mattie mumbled softly, patting her belly. Wide blue eyes signaled Rachel's worry, and Mattie managed a smile. "We're home, for better or for worse. Maybe there's something salvageable in the kitchen?"

"Oh. Right." Rachel practically leaped from the stairs to the rapidly filling room below. The first four steps were already covered, and she wasn't hopeful any food had been spared from the water that now covered the cupboard door halfway to the ceiling. The electricity was long gone too, meaning food in the icebox was most likely beginning to spoil. They'd watched the poles snap and fall all along the way, and had to dodge dangerous wires several times during the long journey home. Rumor on the streets was that they no longer had electricity or telegraph connections. With no bridges, the island was effectively cut off from the rest of the world.

She rummaged through the cupboard, which, to her puzzlement, was bare. "I know this was full this morning," she groused, too low for Mattie to hear. She frowned in confusion as she moved to the icebox, which was also empty. Her heart sank as the truth hit home. They were trapped inside a house with no food, and a cyclone bearing down from outside. They had no cows or chickens, and going outside again was out of the question. Wasn't it? Going back out was out of the question for Mattie. Rachel, on the other hand, was going to have to go out, or risk Mattie becoming terribly ill, or worse. She swallowed and made her way back to the stairs.

"Mattie." She gently cupped her lover's face. "Let's get you upstairs and then I'll get you some food."

Mattie nodded agreeably, understanding that Rachel's search had been fruitless. "Won't have you going out there again," she argued, even as Rachel practically carried her up to the second floor.

"And I won't have you and our baby survive this storm only to starve to death." Her tone was no-nonsense, daring Mattie to argue further. "I'll only go down a few houses and try to find something, I promise."

"Very well, but only for the baby." A stubborn lower lip poked out, and Mattie found a sudden surge of strength, as they rounded the banister and headed for the stairs up to their third-floor loft. She smiled wanly. "We're going to be a family real soon, Miz Travis." Despite her tiredness, and the cold, and the hunger, she could feel the warm affection radiating from her lover, and Rachel's beaming face easily reflected her feelings.

"I need to get my family up to a place that's warm and dry." She hoisted Mattie into her arms and finished the climb up the stairs, depositing her bundle of cold wet lover on the sofa, and helping Mattie out of her clothing. She grabbed a towel from where she had flung it over a chair, and vigorously dried her off before she dug through their drawers and located a warm flannel nightgown. "How's this?" She pulled it over Mattie's head. "Nice and soft."

"Perfect." Mattie sighed as some of the chill began to dissipate. "You, too." She gestured toward the bureau.

"I know." Rachel quickly shed her own clothing and dried off, then donned a flannel shirt and a pair of heavy work trousers and thick warm stockings. Her nose twitched and she looked around. "I smell food."

"Oh." Mattie suddenly perked up. "I forgot. I moved most of the food up here in that picnic basket, before you got home from the port." She started to get up, but a firm hand held her in place.

"Stay put and rest, sweetheart. I'll get you something." Rachel rummaged around in the wicker hamper, locating some bread and cheese, along with an orange. She quickly made up a sandwich and moved to Mattie's side and sat down.

"Thank you." Grateful hazel eyes shone with relief as Mattie bit into the hearty bread and the sharp cheddar cheese. She watched, chewing in pleasure, as Rachel began to peel an orange for her. She watched the play of her fingers and frowned, noting a large spreading red spot on Rachel's sleeve. She swallowed. "What's wrong with your arm?"

Rachel glanced down and grimaced. "Oh, yeah. I cut myself. Something hit me out there. It's nothing much."

"Honey, that is a nasty gash on your arm." Mattie lifted the blood-encrusted material, gingerly pushing it up. "Let me take care of that for you."

"Always taking care of me, aren't you?" Rachel smiled and ruffled her head. "Finish your sandwich, and that orange, while I hunt down something to clean it with." She got up and went back down to the second floor, and found they still had some running water. She thought about that and gingerly tasted it, nodding in satisfaction that it was still fresh and sweet. She quickly cleaned out a large bucket, then filled it with water for them to drink. Then she filled another small basin and pocketed some clean rags and a roll of bandage material, and made her way back upstairs.

"Here's our drinking water — about five gallons, I think." She set it down near the door. "And here's something to clean my arm." She sat back down and placed the basin on the low table in front of the sofa.

Mattie wetted a rag and carefully washed her arm, then bound it in a fresh strip of clean cloth. Once she tied off the bandage, she lifted the arm, kissing it softly before she snuggled up to Rachel and closed her eyes, glad to be out of the storm, warm and dry. A particularly strong gust shook the house, and she could hear the rain pounding overhead. The wind reminded her of a train whistle, and she frowned. "Sounds bad out there. You think the house will hold?"

"It better." Rachel idly stroked her damp head while she talked. Her sight turned inward for a long moment, remembering the vision of Adam's head bobbing and disappearing into the bay. "Lot's happened since this morning. You must be plumb tuckered out. Maybe you can try to take a nap."

"Too loud," Mattie commented. Outside, the wind picked up even more, and they could hear water pouring in on the first floor, even from where they sat on the third. "I'm glad you thought of drinking water. I seem to get thirsty more often with the baby."

Rachel patted her belly and kissed the top of her head. She looked across the room as sheets of rain lashed the windows. As she watched, a few small pellets of hail pecked at the glass. "Worse came to worse, I probably could have just stuck the bucket out the door downstairs for a few minutes."

Mattie laughed lightly. "True, but I'm glad you don't have to go back out there."

"Me, too." Her fingers caught in a snarl in Mattie's hair and she gently removed them. "How about we comb each other's hair out before it dries like this?"

Mattie sat up and lifted a handful of thick chestnut tresses. "Might be a good idea. This would be tough to remedy, dry." She smiled affectionately.

"It does quite resemble a rat's nest, doesn't it?" Rachel retrieved a hairbrush and comb from the bureau, and sat down.

"Let me do yours first." Mattie took the comb and began working at the severely tangled mass.

Rachel closed her eyes, partly from exhaustion, and partly in reflex at the comforting touch to her head. "I remember the first time you did this for me."

"Mmm." Mattie carefully worked at a particularly nasty knot. "When I brought your shirt to your room after I mended the elbows. Yes, I remember it too."

"I-I was already very attracted to you, and had been trying real hard to make those feelings go away." Rachel reached down, lightly patting Mattie's leg, which was pressed up against her hip. "When I felt your touch, I thought I was going to melt into a puddle. I remember I could feel your breath against my neck, and smell your toilet water. Then when you asked me to braid yours, I thought I might pass out. Your hair is so soft and beautiful. It was the sweetest torture."

"I had no idea," Mattie commented softly, as she finished braiding Rachel's hair. She tied a length of soft leather around it to secure it.

"Well, you had kissed me on the cheek already, when I'd gone by the shop." Rachel reached up and touched her face in memory of the sweet gesture. "I knew it was just gratitude, but I don't think I had a clear head for the rest of the day afterward."

"You were so kind to me." Mattie leaned in and kissed her neck. "Do mine?" She smiled as Rachel turned and pecked her on the lips, before she turned, offering Rachel her back. "That feels nice," she murmured as Rachel began working on her hair, causing pleasant chills to dance across her scalp.

"Don't know if just doing the right thing should be considered kindness," Rachel picked up the conversation again. "I saw your wrist that day, and I remembered seeing that faded bruise around your eye when we first met. When I figured out what was going on, I was so angry, and I felt so helpless."

"I had a bruise that morning? I don't remember that." She looked down, folding her hands in her lap. "Happened so often, though, I'm not surprised," she whispered. She felt Rachel pause in her combing, and long arms wrapped around her from behind, as Rachel pulled her close. "He's really gone for good this time, isn't he?"

"Yes." Rachel kissed her head and sat back, continuing to comb out her hair. She was afraid to say much more. Adam was dead and she couldn't bring herself to feel badly about that at all, but she had to wonder how Mattie felt about it. He had been a monster, but he was her husband. It must have been at least a little upsetting to watch him drown before her very eyes. "Do you need to talk about it — him?"

"I'm too tired to think about him very much right now. Maybe later." She sighed, realizing just how weary she was both physically and emotionally. "When you're finished combing, you can just leave mine loose until it dries."

"In that case, I'm just about finished." She set the comb aside and sat back, as Mattie turned and burrowed against her. She heard a few sniffles and rubbed Mattie's back in light circles. "We're home now. Everything is going to be fine."

The sniffles subsided, and she curled up even tighter against Rachel's side, and despite the chaos outside, felt her eyelids growing heavy. She blinked in a valiant effort to stay awake, but gave up as a gentle hand pushed her head down into Rachel's lap. That same hand stroked her head and gave a friendly scratch to her back, and soon she was fast asleep.

Rachel watched her for a moment, glad that Mattie could escape for a little while. Truth be told, she had no idea how the house would hold up. She heard tree limbs and other objects constantly hitting the walls outside, and wondered if the storm would scour right through the roof.

It was dusk-like out the window, although it was only mid-afternoon. Rachel stared idly outside, watching the rain sheeting down the thick glass. The wind whistled beneath the eaves and at times she felt the entire house shake as swift gusts buffeted the island, snapping tree trunks and effortlessly pulling tiles and boards from buildings. From time to time hail pelted the window and she thought she heard a window break on the floor below them.

Rachel absently stroked Mattie's hair, lifting it and letting it sift slowly through her fingers. She lay on her side, one hand tucked under her chin, the other curled around Rachel's knee. Her long red hair fanned out over Rachel's lap and part of the sofa, the clean silky waves shining in the lantern light.

Mattie's brow furrowed and she mumbled restlessly in her sleep, her tone distressed and forlorn. Rachel grazed her fingertips across her lover's forehead and around the curve of a soft, downy cheek, willing away the bad dreams. She studied the sprinkle of freckles on Mattie's nose, and the bow of her upper lip, and found herself falling in love all over again.

She was worried about Mattie. No one should go through the stress they had suffered in one short morning, much less a pregnant woman. That Mattie was able to sleep through the roar of the storm was testament to just how exhausted she was. She jumped as Mattie cried out in distress. She almost woke her, thinking she was in some sort of pain, but then Mattie settled down and she realized it must have been dreams torturing her lover. "Shhh." She rubbed Mattie's back and bent over, brushing her lips against the too-pale cheek.

Rachel sat back up, shivering as the wind howled like a raging, furious beast. Her eyes widened as she watched the walls sucking in and out, almost as if they were breathing. She recalled another, much smaller cyclone a few years back. That one she had weathered at the saloon, a much sturdier building than the boarding house. She remembered Mr. Bullock breaking windows and knocking holes in the floor to even out the pressure of both wind and floodwaters.

She studied the walls some more, and to her eye, the pressure seemed to be greater than it had been only a few moments before. She thought she could hear the house actually groaning, although it was difficult to separate all the sounds assaulting her ears. Almost like a plea for help, the wall next to her bowed out considerably, creaking loudly as it slowly settled back inward. "All right," she muttered. "Guess I need to go knock holes in the floors and windows. Better start with the first floor before the flooding gets too bad. Maybe that will relieve some of the pressure on the house."

Rachel carefully eased out from under Mattie, replacing her lap with an embroidered pillow. As an afterthought, she spread a knitted afghan over her lover, tucking it in under her chin. Mattie fretted in her sleep, and Rachel knelt down next to the sofa, watching her for a long moment. "I'll be back quick as I can, sweetheart." She softly kissed Mattie's lips, then rose and made her way out of the door and down the stairs.

She felt the house shaking in the wind as she traversed the first staircase, and she heard the steady flow of water from the first floor. She rounded the banister and stopped at the top of the second staircase, gasping at the water, which was halfway up the stairs. She sat down at the top, thinking. Near as she could tell, the water was only about a foot from the top of the ceiling on the first floor. Knocking holes in the floor was going to be difficult at best. "Guess I can dive under there and break some more windows."

She stood and trotted back through the second floor of the house, intent on finding something suitable for breaking glass. She wasn't all that familiar with the second floor, other than the water closet. Most of her tenure in the house had been spent in the kitchen, sitting room, and the third floor loft. She quickly scanned Angel and Betsy's bedroom, stopping to study some small framed photos on a bedside table. They were black and white shots of the women from much younger days, and two fresh-faced girls looked back at her from one photograph, peering stoically at the camera, standing ramrod straight and a polite distance from each other. Another photo was of Betsy sitting by herself, dressed in her Sunday best. She was smiling coyly and Rachel could only guess that Angel had been behind the camera. She smiled back at the photos. "Be safe, my friends, wherever you are."

She slipped out of the room, and stepped across the hallway into the guest room. A fireplace graced one wall, and over the mantel two civil-war era swords were mounted and crossed, hanging from shiny brass pegs. "One of those will do." She carefully removed one of the swords, hefting it in her hand and noting the comfortable fit of the hilt as her fingers curled around it. The blade was a polished silver curve and the hilt was a combination of brass, wood, and mother of pearl inlay. She flashed the sword in a forward arc, then swept it backward, testing her ability to shatter glass with the hilt. "Might be a little tougher to do underwater."

She nodded her head once and trotted back to the top of the stairs, where she stopped again, considering her options. Without further thought, she shucked all her clothing and descended the stairs, gritting her teeth as the icy water slowly covered her body. It was dark and she paused just as she reached the point where only her head was above water. "Here goes." She tentatively paddled across the sitting room, her head grazing the ceiling.

It was numbing and she tried to think of something, anything warm, to take her mind off the chill. She thought of Mattie, and the big featherbed on the third floor, and the soft old blankets that covered it. She thought of Mattie's flannel nightgown, which led to thoughts of warm, soft skin. She suddenly realized just how tired she was, and how much she wanted to go back upstairs and join Mattie in her nap, and pretend there was no deadly cyclone outside.

She reached the wall and took a deep breath, plunging below the surface. It was murky and salt burned her eyes as she opened them. She spied the two chairs that sat near the front windows, and dove down, pushing past them and holding onto one to keep herself from floating to the top. Her muscle mass was doing a fair job of keeping her below the surface, but the soft layer of feminine padding that covered the muscle was just enough to make her buoyant.

Grasping the sword hilt, she pushed the limp curtains aside and swung back hard, slamming it into the glass, which promptly broke, the pieces slowly floating down to the floor below her. Careful not to step in it, she moved to the other window and repeated her actions, then surfaced for air, gasping as her head broke the surface with a splash of water.

Drawing in great lungfuls of air, she glided over to the kitchen area and dove under again. She could see the window that was already broken, and swam over toward one across from it, quickly breaking it. She shoved backward in surprise as a fairly large grouper swam past the window outside, tiny bubbles following behind it. It studied her with a large questioning eye, then moved on. *That's not a good sign.* She broke the surface again.

She paddled over and stopped short of going up the stairs when she realized she hadn't thought to bring a towel with her. Her teeth chattered as she rose out of the water, walking up the stairs and laying the sword down on the top step before padding toward the water closet, leaving a puddle trailing behind her. She dried off vigorously with a thick towel, and quickly put her clothes back on, grateful for the warmth of the cotton as it hugged her chilled skin. She heard a whimper from the loft and took off, realizing that Mattie was awake.

"Mattie?" She entered the room, catching her breath from running upstairs. "Are you all right?"

"I woke up and you were gone. I got confused for a minute, thinking about earlier today, when you got washed under pulling the boat." She nibbled her lower lip. "It was a bit like having a nightmare."

"I'm sorry, sweetheart." Rachel sat down on the edge of the sofa and slipped her arms around Mattie in a comforting hug. "I went down to the first floor to knock some holes in the walls—keep the pressure from the flood and the wind from collapsing the house. I think we might ought to knock some holes in the second floor. Won't be long before the water's up here at the rate it's moving."

"I wish Billy were here to help you." Mattie clung to her. "I don't like the idea of you doing all that by yourself." She paused, her eyes widening in outrage. "You went to the first floor? Rachel, it must be underwater by now."

"Yes, but I'm fine." She decided to spare Mattie the details, given her reaction to merely being left alone. "What a mess it is, though. It'll take weeks to clean up after this is over. I wish Billy were here, too, and..." She trailed off, not wanting to upset Mattie with thoughts of their absent friends.

Sad hazel eyes met blue, as Mattie read her thoughts anyway. "I said a prayer for them earlier. All four of them." Mattie spoke quietly. "Prayed for their safety, and that they're together, Angel with Betsy and Billy with Lillie, wherever they are." Her eyes teared up and she closed them, sending moisture trickling down her cheeks. She felt Rachel brush it away and sniffled, burrowing into another warm hug.

"I know. I know," Rachel repeated. And she did. The conversation Mattie had relayed to her, it mirrored her own feelings exactly. *What Betsy did...* She knew she would have done the same thing in a heartbeat. Now that she knew what love was, she couldn't imagine life without Mattie in it. So yes, she would have picked up and hiked through whatever nature had to offer, if it meant going through it with Mattie, rather than being apart from her. She felt the tears gradually subside, and continued to hold Mattie close. "You've had a hard day, sweetheart. Let's move over to the bed. You need to get some more rest."

"So do you," Mattie mumbled against her chest. She sniffled and shifted in Rachel's arms as Rachel lifted her and carried her to the much more comfortable bed.

"You've been through too much today, Mattie." Rachel lifted her legs, placing a pillow under Mattie's knees and pulling the covers over her. "You need to take it easy for a while, get some rest for you and the baby."

"Was kind of hard to do out there," Mattie feebly protested. "I was good as soon as we got home, wasn't I?"

"Yes, you were." Rachel sat down on the edge of the bed, holding her hand and twining their fingers.

"I was so afraid earlier." Mattie began to cry again. Rachel reached across, smoothing the hair from her eyes. "Today, when you fell out there and went under, I thought I'd lost you. Then when I woke up and you weren't in here..."

"Hey." She felt helpless, torn between staying to comfort her lover and going to do what she sensed must be done. "Don't cry. We're here and we're together. Everything is going to be just fine, you hear?"

"Be careful when you go back down there. I don't want to lose you." She hiccupped, her body trembling as the wind roared loudly outside, and something large bumped against the house. "Rachel, I'm afraid."

"Hey, I'll be back before you know it." She smiled, trying to project every ounce of confidence she held. "I'll be right downstairs. You might even be able to hear me."

"Hurry." Mattie squeezed her hand and released it, watching fearfully as she left the room. She closed her eyes, listening as hard as she could, but all she could hear was the horrid cyclone, the wind and the rain beating against the house, trying to reach through the walls and snatch them up. After a bit she heard a faint, steady chopping sound and smiled. "You were right. I can hear you." She strained her ears, focusing in on that one sound above all the others. "We're lucky to have you, Rachel." She patted her stomach. "You take such good care of us."

The chopping sound stopped, but before she had time to worry, she heard Rachel's heavy boot steps, and the beloved face appeared in the doorway. "How about that nap now?" She flexed her sore hands as she moved to Mattie's side. She'd ended up using the butt of an unloaded rifle to knock out the wooden floors, and her arms ached from the jar of pounding against boards that were much thicker than she'd realized.

"A nap sounds wonderful." Mattie was already fighting to keep her eyes open. She sighed with relief as Rachel crawled under the covers with her. Mattie scooted up next to her, rolling to her side and draping an arm across Rachel's body, laying her head on a sturdy shoulder. "Do you love my baby?" she asked sleepily.

"Our baby," Rachel corrected her. "And yes, I love the baby almost as much as I love you." She kissed Mattie's head. "All of this has made me realize just how much I'm looking forward to having a family." Rachel rested one hand against Mattie's stomach. "I was so damned angry when I thought we might not make it home this afternoon, and miss out on that." She looked out the window. "And this..." She gestured toward the blowing storm. "I'll be damned if this is going to win. We've been through too much. Worked too had to be together to have it all just—swept away."

"You might not be able to give me a child." Mattie covered Rachel's hand against her stomach. "But the reverse of that was true as well. If things hadn't turned out the way they did, I wouldn't have been able to give you a child, either."

"I never realized how much it meant to me, until I began to visualize this baby." Rachel's chin quivered as she fought back tears. "I-I would have been so happy to be with you, even without children. If I could take back one bit of the pain you suffered..."

A gentle finger covered her lips. "That pain is what drew us together." She stroked Rachel's face, watching the blue eyes water up. "I'd not change a thing, if it would have changed the way things have turned out. It was all worth it, to end up here with you. I love you, more than I can ever adequately express."

"Love you too, Mattie," Rachel whispered as the tears spilled over, and Mattie kissed them away one by one. She closed her eyes, willing them to stop. At last they subsided, and she began a constant soothing stroking of Mattie's back, feeling her slump bonelessly against her. "Sleep now. The baby needs you to rest." She stared up at the ceiling, hearing her breathing as it slowed, warm breaths tickling her neck as Mattie fell asleep. She thought about her mother, and her baby sister, and a wave of fear gripped her briefly, before she pushed it aside. "Don't you go leaving me, Mattie," she whispered again.

She shook a fist at the window and forced herself to stay awake, keeping watch over her family.

WICKED WINDS WHISTLED around the orphanage walls while rushing water battered at its foundation, causing the entire building to slowly lean to one side. Once on a secluded section of beach, it was now a small, worn island in the middle of a raging flood. They were too remote from the main part of town to hope for any rescue, and it was far too late to try to leave and go to higher ground.

Sister Francis had untied herself from the children, and walked among them, doing her best to comfort the terrified, and tucking blankets around the ones who were cold. Half the roof was gone, though thankfully the room they were sheltered in was still mostly covered. She passed out slices of bread and orange halves, the only food she had been able to salvage from the flooded kitchen on the first floor. She had no idea what time it was, but her rumbling stomach told her it was near suppertime. The children nibbled listlessly at the scant meal, most of them having neither interest nor appetite.

Sister Francis cocked her head to one side, listening to the fury outside. It was as if Hell itself had descended upon them, and the devil was laughing in the undertones of the storm. The wind rose and fell, sounding like a booming off-key symphony mixed with a burlap bag full of angry fighting cats. She moved closer to the window and gasped as an entire palm tree flew past, roots first, smashing into the room next to them with a loud crack of wood and glass.

All the children screamed, trying to scramble away from the wall that separated them from the next room. Despite the barrier, they could hear the wind and rain beating inside the building now, pounding at the thin wall with a deafening thunder. They watched in horror as the wall began to buckle and crack, then the entire room began to cave in, as the wall fell inward toward them with a mournful creak, and the ceiling started to sink down toward the floor.

Chaos reigned as the children and nuns became hopelessly tangled together in their frenzied crawl away from the falling roof. A loud whipping gust blasted inside, ripping the roof from above their heads, carrying it away effortlessly, as the freezing rain poured in. Most of the children were crying uncontrollably as they were quickly soaked to the skin, and yelps of pain rang out as debris whirled into the room, pelting them with sand, shells, wood splinters, glass shards, and larger bits of roof tiles.

"Children!" Sister Francis yelled over the din, trying to bring order to the scene. Her voice was carried away and she watched as the outer wall began to bend outward under the strain of the circling wind inside. She realized, too late, that tying the children together had been a mistake. There was no way they could move *en masse* to the other side of the building. Some were frantically trying to untie themselves, but the wet ropes were almost impossible to work with.

The outer wall slowly collapsed with a great groaning sound, leaving them sitting on a rain-slicked floor with only one inner wall left. It was a useless bit of shelter. Now they felt the true fury of the storm, as one-hundred-mile-per-hour winds pummeled them, tearing at their clothing, whipping through their hair, and pushing impossibly high waves up and into the room with a thundering crash of water against wood. The children continued to cry as they were slowly sucked out into the cyclone and the rising flood.

"Albert!" Frank cried, clutching at his friend as his feet gave way and he fell down, sliding across the floor.

"Hang on, Frank!" Albert took William's hand. "Stop blubbering!" He smacked William across the face, which fortunately had its intended effect. William gasped in anger, but clarity returned to his features. "All for one and one for all!" Albert cried out. "Hang on to each other."

A whirlpool of water washed into the room, swirling around and sweeping the three boys away from the building and out into the vast expanse of churning waves. Albert snagged a large piece of wood, holding on with all his might with one arm, while he managed to haul his companions around so they could also grab hold. They were quickly swept away from the orphanage and toward the center of the island.

Albert looked up through the lashing rain and saw a frantic Sister Francis cry out after them. He watched helplessly as she dove into the water. "Shouldn't 'ave done that, lady," he mumbled under his breath. He quickly lost sight of her bobbing gray head, her head-covering long since blown away. Behind her he could see the children and the rest of the nuns, clambering to stay on the demolished second floor of the building. He closed his eyes, realizing that they were losing their battle. One by one, they fell away into the sea surrounding the building. The ropes acted as a chain, pulling one after the other toward what would surely be their death. As they tried to swim, the building itself was caving in, claimed by the sea and the storm.

"Albert?" Frank clung to the board with both arms, blinking as the wind and rain pounded at his face. "Are we gonna die?"

Albert slowly opened his eyes, determination and something akin to anger written across his face. "No." He pronounced the word loudly, but succinctly. "We are not." He looked forward, in the direction the waves carried them. Already, what was left of the orphanage was a small speck behind them. There was nothing he could do to help the others. They were most likely already dead. But the two with him... His eyes blazed with the challenge.

It was hard to make out anything through the heavy, choking rain. Odd shadows loomed in the distance, possibly buildings, or maybe just more of the tall waves that dipped up and down all around them. Albert gritted his teeth. "Look for something we can kick toward."

"Like what?" William found his voice. He imagined his face still stung from the slap, and he tried to maintain an indignant air. "I can't see a thing, and I can't hardly feel my fingers." He carefully tightened his grip on the splintered wood.

"A building." Albert scanned the horizon, squinting into the torrent. "Or a tree." His voice rose as he spied a tall thick trunk several yards ahead of them. "Like that." He gestured toward the tree with a tilt of his head. "Come on. Kick!"

The other two wiggled around until they were all on the same side of the board. Salt burned their skin and their stomachs heaved from the constant rise and fall of the waves, but now they had something to focus on. With deep frowns and powerful kicks of their young legs, they forced their small life preserver ever closer toward the large tree. They could see it now, its thick sturdy branches hanging proudly out over the floodwaters, defying the wind and rain to make it budge so much as an inch.

"That will do," Albert mumbled. "Kick harder!" He turned toward Frank, who was crying but kicking mightily, sniffling as he tried not to think about the friends they'd left behind.

The wind served as master for a brief span of time, helping to propel them toward their goal. At last they reached the tree, almost kicking past it as a large swell carried them to one side. Both Albert and Frank reached out, grabbing hold of the thick trunk as they held on to William with their other hands. Amid groans and grumbles, they scrambled into the thick sheltering branches, climbing up a safe distance from the whitecaps below.

The rain still pounded at them, and the wind threatened to blow them away if they dared let go, but there, sitting on wide rough-barked limbs, all three boys gasped for air, feeling their heartbeats slowly return to normal. Speeding winds rattled the branches, and they swayed back and forth, but the trunk itself held firm, standing tall and unbending. It was still cold, and there was no fresh water or food to be found, but for the time being, they had a safe harbor. Albert looked up, nodding with satisfaction at the plethora of sturdy branches over their heads. If the water rose, they could climb.

"Now what do we do?" William carefully inched into hearing range, wrapping his legs around both sides of his chosen branch as he clung to the center trunk with both arms. Frank imitated him on a branch across from him, inclining his head so he could hear his friends talk.

Albert leaned in until all three boys were touching foreheads. "We hang on, that's what." Three pairs of wide eyes peered at each other from very close range. The storm pounded at their backs, but suddenly, within their small circle, a tiny, warm spark of hope ignited.

IT WAS FULL dark and the storm could barely be seen. Rachel lay quietly in bed, gazing solemnly at the window. She could see the rain still streaming down the glass panes, but beyond that was an ominous inkiness. She could hear the constant howl of the wind battering at the wall behind the bed, and the rattling of rain and hail against the roof over her head. The house shook continually, tiny shivers as the storm beat down upon it. At times the wind rose to a fevered pitch, the roar unlike anything she had ever heard.

A lone lantern burned on the table next to the sofa. They had doused all other candles and lanterns, for fear that any extra-strong jolts to the house might knock them to the floor and start a fire. She rolled her eyes. It was absurd that they were in a flooding house and had to worry about it burning down.

She glanced over at Mattie's thick red waves of hair. Despite the deafening wail of the storm, Mattie had slept soundly, for the most part, save a bit of normal tossing and turning. Now she lay with her head on the pillow, curled on her side, one hand resting flat against Rachel's stomach. It was Mattie's left hand, and Rachel took a moment to study the ring she had given her. It fit Mattie, beautiful and dainty, yet sturdy.

Mattie's flannel gown draped fluidly over her lithe body, making her appear even smaller than she was. There was no sign yet of the life growing within her, at least none that anyone had seen, except Rachel and Mattie. Her bosoms were definitely fuller and the nipples darker, and if Rachel cupped her stomach, she could feel the beginnings of a roundness that would soon be much more pronounced.

She thought about her mother some more. It seemed like her mother had been pregnant more often than not during Rachel's childhood. She was all too familiar with babies, and used to caring for them, although this one, she acknowledged, would be different. It was Mattie's baby. And hers, too. Her responsibility to make a living for all three of them. That weighed on her, just a little.

Her job at the port provided steady income, enough for one person to live on, even two if they were careful. But a family... She nibbled her lower lip and her brow furrowed as she considered her options. Then she caught herself, just before she almost burst out in ironic laughter. There were no options. The port was gone, along with most of the boats, she suspected. All the warehouses and the mill were surely underwater, along with most of the rest of the island.

So.

There she was, taking shelter in a house that was flooded, on a submerged island, in a town that was most likely destroyed. She knew, logically, that a lot of work lay ahead of all of them once the storm was over. Just cleaning up the house would take weeks, if it was salvageable at all. She'd seen floods before, but nothing like this one. She'd even watched part of the island burn a few years before, but the town had risen to the challenge, rebuilding until it seemed as if there had been no fire at all.

Galvestonians were sturdy folk. A few would pack and leave after this, no doubt. But many, she knew, would stay and tough it out, rebuilding homes and businesses, and helping their neighbors as best they could. Still, the question of how she would earn a living was a real concern, at least for the foreseeable future. She had a wad of cash in the carpetbag under the bed, and another sizeable stash was tucked under the mattress.

They had enough to leave and start over somewhere else. It was something they had made provision for all along, just in case. But would they want to leave? The wind picked up even more and she heard something crash against the house outside. She grimaced. Would they have a choice?

Mattie turned and stretched at the noise, and patted Rachel's belly, as her eyes fluttered open. She glanced at the checkered flannel material and absently tugged at one of the buttons. Her hand was captured between large, scarred knuckles, and she looked over and smiled.

"How are you feeling?" Rachel's hand wandered down, resting against Mattie's lower abdomen.

"Much better, although I think I could eat again, and you should as well." Mattie took a deep breath and released it slowly, cocking her head to one side, listening. "Storm is worse."

"Yes, it is." Rachel rose up, resting on her elbows. "Why don't you stay put while I go make us up something to eat." Rachel leaned over and kissed her briefly, then swung her legs over the side of the bed and sat up, flipping her long braid back over her shoulder. She grinned as it was gently pulled, and she turned back around to find hazel eyes shining warmly back up at her as Mattie reached out, pulling her in for a much longer kiss. "Mmm." Rachel licked her lips. "You are feeling better."

"I am." Mattie patted her cheek, then pushed at her shoulder. "Go on. We need to take care of this baby."

"What do you think it is?" Rachel slipped around the end of the bed, making her way to the picnic hamper. "Boy or girl?"

"No way to tell, just yet." Mattie smiled at her. "I think this baby is a girl, though."

Their eyes met as they thought again of their friends. "Rebecca Evangeline," Rachel spoke softly. "We can call her 'Becky' for short, give her an identity of her own."

"Becky." Mattie tested the name. "Becky Travis." She smiled at Rachel's shocked reaction. "I like it."

"We can't call her that," Rachel protested. "It would be an outrage."

"I don't care." Mattie poked out her lower lip defiantly. "I'm not giving her his name. I don't care if he is dead. I don't even want his name." She peered shyly at her lover. "I like 'Travis'. Madeleine Travis. Has a nice sound, don't you agree?"

"Here." Rachel sat back down next to her, handing her another sandwich.

"Never thought cheese and bread could taste so good." She eyed Rachel's own hearty sandwich with approval.

"Do you truly want to call yourself by my name?" Rachel questioned gently. She took a healthy bite, realizing just how hungry she was. "I don't know that folks in town are going to cotton to it, Mattie. You've been Mrs. Crockett to them ever since you moved here, and the implications could cause trouble for us."

"Can I please be 'Mattie Travis' when it is just the two of us together?" Mattie's eyes misted over. "And our baby. I truly want her to be a Travis, not a Crockett."

"All right." Rachel leaned over and kissed her forehead. "I'm not so certain, though, sweetheart, that the law is going to allow us to put that name on a birth certificate."

"I could start calling myself 'Mattie Burnet' again." Mattie twisted her ring around on her finger as she spoke. "But I suppose putting 'Burnet' on a birth certificate might bastardize her, and I don't want that. I so wish that we could all have the same name." She looked wistfully up at Rachel, who studied her with wide, sad blue eyes.

"We could legally change your name, if it means that much to you." She covered Mattie's hand with her own. "One of the lawyers in town will draw up the papers for you. We can always say it is for the baby's protection. That since your husband is dead, you want me to take care of her if anything ever happens to you." Her voice faltered as she realized what she had said. "That is, if you would want that." She looked down uncertainly, plucking nervously at a lace flounce on the hem of Mattie's nightgown.

Mattie sat partway up, cupping Rachel's face with both hands.

"Of course that is what I would want." She stroked Rachel's cheek, catching a tear as it tracked downward. "This is our child. Ours. This ring, it means forever to me, Rachel. I know we have to put on airs out in public, but in our home," she looked around warily, "wherever our home may be, we are a family."

Too overcome with emotion to speak, Rachel simply pulled her into a hug, careful not to squeeze too hard. "I love you," she whispered softly into Mattie's ear.

"And I want to be Madeleine Travis." Mattie pecked her on the cheek before releasing her. "I want to quit living nightmares, and start sharing a life with you." Mattie shifted, rolling to her side and curling an arm across Rachel's legs. "Me, you, and our baby."

"Very well, then. When this is over, and we find a place to live, we'll go play on the beach as often as we can, Mattie, I promise. Me, you, and little Becky."

"Sounds lovely." Mattie kissed her lover's knee through her canvas work trousers. At that moment, a great roaring rushing sound grew, overtaking the howls of the wind and the constant lash of the rain. It increased in volume, and Rachel automatically stood, leaping across the floor to the window in a couple of steps, pressing her nose against it, trying to see outside. "What on earth?"

"Rachel, be careful." Mattie sat up all the way, intent on trying to join her. "Whoa!"

Something hit the house with great force and Rachel lost her balance, teetering until she landed on the sofa. A rushing, swirling, watery sound surrounded them on all sides, and the house shook as if it were coming off its foundation. It passed by them quickly, followed by a trickling sound from downstairs that gradually became a steady flow.

"That doesn't sound good." Rachel stood and made her way to the door. "I'll go see what happened."

"No!" The force of Mattie's voice stopped her. "It's black as pitch out there, and you can't see a thing. No telling what happened, but the house is still standing. Stay," Mattie pleaded. "Otherwise I'm going to have to go with you."

"But..." Rachel stopped, reading the fear in her lover's eyes. She reluctantly joined Mattie, and perched on the edge of the bed, her body twitching with the need to see what was happening outside the room. "I'll only go to the top of the stairs. Is that all right?"

Mattie thought about that and nodded, watching as she stepped outside the door. "Sweet mother of..." Her voice trailed after her, and Mattie sat up as her head appeared in the doorway. "Second floor is flooding fast, bottom step between here and there is already covered. I figure it's coming in those windows we left open. Good thing we did. The force of whatever hit us, I think it might've torn the house down with the pressure, otherwise. Near as I can tell, it must've been a storm surge."

"Anything we can do?" Mattie stood in alarm, hearing the rushing water below them.

"Far as I can tell, no." Rachel sat down in the doorway and patted the space between her legs as Mattie joined her. "We can see the stairs from here. Water's still rising."

They watched the narrow staircase, hearing the water pouring in from below them. It slowly crept up the steps, one at a time, threatening their last dry floor.

"Think we can get to the roof if we have to?" Mattie eyed the ceiling, looking for panels.

"We'd be blown away in that wind," Rachel answered. They watched for a while, until the water reached halfway up the stairs.

A low rumble reached Rachel's ears and she edged away from Mattie and crept down a few steps, bracing herself between the walls. "Something else is happening out there."

"Rachel, get back up here!" Mattie called after her as the rumble grew, shaking the house.

Rachel waited it out, sticking to her spot as she felt the stairs vibrating under her feet.

The rumble went on for what seemed like forever, growing closer and closer. Then it was right outside, a great splintering cracking sound coming in the window below, along with the constant flow of water. A sound like firecrackers rang out, then suddenly the rumble stilled, and the water quit flowing. They could still hear the wind howling, and the rain falling, but it seemed as if the flooding had ended. Rachel held her breath, pulling out a pocket watch. It was seven-thirty o'clock. She watched the hands for ten minutes, with no change in the water level on the staircase.

"I think the water's quit rising." She pocketed the watch. "Let's get back inside the room where it's warmer."

"Rachel, what was all of that?" Mattie tucked a hand in the crook of her elbow as they sat down on the sofa.

"I haven't the slightest idea." She eyed the picnic hamper hopefully and got up, digging around and finding a leftover apple turnover. She nibbled at it and swallowed. "Well, I do have an idea, but no way to tell until morning," she amended. "Sounds like the house next door took a beating." She dragged the hamper across the room and rejoined her lover.

Outside, the wind rose even higher, becoming a constant loud roar. Rachel listened for a moment, feeling the house shake harder. She turned and rooted around in the basket for a moment, coming up with another turnover. "Might as well have dessert while we ride this thing out. No way to see what's happened until sunrise."

Mattie took the sweet offering and nibbled at it, hoping fervently they would have a sunrise.

Chapter
Fourteen

THE WALLS OF St. Peters shook continually and the hail pounding the tile roof sounded as if it was slowly scouring it away. A few tiles had been torn away and in those spots the rain poured in, forcing those nearby to move away, slowly crowding everyone in the church closer together. No one was asleep, but almost everyone talked in low voices, if they talked at all. Many simply huddled with their loved ones, staring, terrified, into the darkness. There were only a scattering of lanterns in the large room, and their light did little to chase away the gloomy shadows that permeated the sanctuary.

Betsy was awake again, still resting in Angel's arms. Mostly, they were silent, listening to the deafening roar outside, and the occasional cry of babies inside, along with a few screams from frightened children any time a roof tile was blown away. Betsy felt a kiss to the top of her head and looked up, barely able to see Angel in the darkness. There were no lanterns in the balcony.

"Penny for your thoughts." Betsy patted her stomach, making comforting circles against the denim shirt Angel had been given by the nuns.

"I was just thinking about the first time I saw you." Angel chuckled. "You came waltzing into our little makeshift hospital, over in the schoolhouse, remember?"

"Yes." Betsy smiled. "I had a basket of socks for the soldiers. Lord, we had been knitting those things for a week. My fingertips were dry and cracked from the new-dyed yarn, and I was grateful the next day was Sunday."

"I thought you were the prettiest girl I'd ever seen." Angel stroked her hair. "Lucky for the feller I was working on, I'd just finished up his stitches, 'cause I dropped my needle and thread on the floor, and almost forgot to finish trimming off the ends of the thread on his arm. I don't remember much else after that. I think I floated through the rest of that afternoon."

"Oh, you." Betsy lightly slapped her on the leg. "I must've been a sight. It was hotter than all get-out if I recall, and I'd been working all day at the church. It was packed with ladies' aid women and we were almost shoulder-to-shoulder. I remember being glad of the chance to go outside and see if a bit of breeze would cool me off."

"You were a sight, you were." Angel kissed her forehead again. "More like a vision from Heaven. I went to church the next day real early and stood over to the side of the meeting house under a tree, waiting for you to show up."

"You never told me that." Betsy's eyes grew wide and she looked up at Angel, picturing twinkling mischievous eyes looking back at her, although she could not actually see Angel's face, hidden in the shadows of their corner. "You sly devil, you. You slid into that pew next to me, smooth as silk, all polite, helping me find my place in the hymnal, and asking if you could share my prayer book."

"I had to meet you, and I figured church was a safe place, and a safe bet of where you'd turn up." Angel took her hand, twining their fingers. She felt the wall behind her rattling and she shifted a bit, getting more comfortable. "I remember your Pa. He didn't take much of a shine to me. I think he saw what was between us before we did."

"He didn't like you one bit, that's certain." Betsy snuggled closer. "I didn't understand why until that day in the barn." She smiled shyly, despite the darkness. "You were absolutely petrified, when you decided to talk to me."

"My palms were sweating, my scalp was prickling, and my tongue felt twice its usual size. I remember thinking my heart was going to beat right out of my chest." Angel laughed quietly. "Did you honestly think I needed help saddling a horse?"

"No." Betsy joined in the laughter. "I knew you wanted to be alone with me. I wanted to be alone with you, too. I just didn't understand why until you asked if you could kiss me."

"What possessed you to just up and kiss me instead of answering the question?"

"You looked like you were about to keel over, sweetheart. I figured I'd best grab hold of you. Your lips were so soft." She reached up, touching the body part in question. " 'Course I didn't get much chance to sample them, since you keeled over anyway."

"But we made up for it when I came to, didn't we?" Angel leaned over, quickly stealing a kiss, careful to look for prying eyes first, finding none.

They broke apart and were silent for a long while. The wind grew louder, picking up velocity, and Betsy shivered.

"Do you regret any of it?" Angel's lips were very close to her ear.

"Not a minute. You made me feel loved, every day we've been together." Betsy shivered again, for a different reason. "I can't imagine a happier life than the one I've lived with you."

Warm lips nibbled at her neck and she closed her eyes, listening as those lips moved back to her ear. "You are my happiness, Betsy. I was born again the day we met, and my life was complete the first time I held you."

Betsy was crying softly and turned, burying her face into Angel's shoulder. She sniffled, feeling a warm hand gently rubbing her back as Angel held her, knowing her fear and feeling it echoed in her own gut. She could hear the water coming in through the gaping holes in the ceiling, pattering in a growing flood on the first floor of the church. Most of the people sheltering below them had taken to the pews, or moved into any remaining space in the balcony.

"Shhh." Angel stroked Betsy's hair, which was still flowing loose down her back. "No matter what happens, I'll be right here with you." She felt Betsy's shoulders, shaking as she cried silently, and felt the tears well up in her own eyes. "Did you think we'd ever meet two other women like us?" She tried to change the subject.

"No." Betsy smiled through her tears and took a deep shaky breath. "They're so sweet together, aren't they?"

"Yes, they are. I think they'll have an easier time than we did. They seem more comfortable than we were starting out."

"They had our example to follow, sweetheart." Betsy had quit crying, finding a strange peace growing in her heart despite the severity of the ever-louder storm.

"We've done well, though, haven't we?" Angel waited, knowing Betsy would look up at her. As she did, she reached out, catching a few remaining tears by feel, and brushing them away.

"We've done more than well. We lived our life as freely as we could, and not get arrested, I believe." Betsy leaned into Angel's hand, as it cupped her face, her eyes fluttering closed as Angel stroked her cheek with her thumb. "Maybe a day will come when people like us won't have to hide how we feel."

"I don't think we've done so good a job at that, my love." Angel traced the sun-worn wrinkles of Betsy's face, re-memorizing every line. "Anyone with eyes could see how we feel about each other. It's plain as day on our faces."

Betsy laughed softly. "That's true. I guess folks see what they want to see."

"Come here." Angel pulled Betsy back into a warm embrace. "Let's try to get some rest."

"Are you tired?" Betsy curled an arm around Angel's middle, resting her head against her shoulder.

"I'm always tired at the end of a workday, but this one has been especially trying." Angel closed her eyes, hearing Betsy's breathing close by, and further away, sounds of distress from a few of the people below them, as the floodwaters rose. The balcony was growing crowded as more and more people tried to move up higher, away from the water. Several people had taken up space on the stairs as well.

"This balcony won't hold all of them, will it?" Betsy read her thoughts, and felt a slight tremble in the warm body that held her.

"No." Angel spoke slowly. "I keep thinking about that family down there on the pew near the bottom of the stairs."

"The one with the three little girls?" Betsy could picture them down there now, terrified, most likely. The little girls all looked alike, with curly thick brown hair and large matching brown eyes. Their mother looked barely old enough to have borne all three of them, the father not much older.

"Yes. I keep thinking how their father must feel—helpless, I'd wager. Nothing he can do to protect them and there's no room left up here, leastwise not much."

"Our space on this blanket is big enough for all of them, isn't it?" Betsy spoke the unthinkable, eyeing the edge of their quilt. A few people had scooted closer to them, enough that they had whispered the more private aspects of their conversation. Their neighbors had been incredibly polite, however, most of them not paying much attention to two older women huddled together in the dark.

"No." Angel's response was measured. A part of her was willing to give up her life for another, but not at the risk of Betsy giving up hers as well. "Well, I guess it is. But still. No."

"We don't know how things will turn out here." Now Betsy moved closer. "We might survive this night, and we might not. But I don't know that I could survive the cries of those children down there if things get much worse."

"And I couldn't bear your cries if we give up this space." Angel held Betsy even closer, almost too tightly, only letting go a little when Betsy squirmed in her embrace. "Sorry. I didn't mean to squeeze too hard."

"I won't cry." Betsy's voice was very low and gentle. "And even if the water rises, you and I both know how to swim and float. Those little girls, if they've been raised like most girls on this island, they don't. I'm not even sure they're old enough to swim."

"But the water is so cold," Angel protested. "I don't want you becoming ill."

"I'll have you to keep me warm." Betsy took her hand, forcing her to sit up with her. "It's the right thing to do. You know it is."

Angel didn't answer, but held her ground, literally digging her heels in and keeping Betsy from standing. Betsy rose to her knees, taking Angel's face in both hands. "We've had a good life together, my love. My greatest fear of late has been facing the day when death might part us. I don't know how I'd go on without you. At the same time, I don't want to go first and leave you behind."

"If I go first, I'll wait for you at Heaven's gate." Angel's voice trembled and she swallowed, choking back unexpected tears. "And if you go first, I fear I might try to follow you before my time."

"I've thought the same thing." Betsy raked her fingers back through Angel's hair. "We can do a good thing here. We can give that family a fighting chance. And if we die, we die together. If by the grace of God we survive, we survive together. Come with me." She lowered her hands, taking Angel's and pulling her to her feet.

As if in a dream, they picked their way through the horrified and sometimes fitfully resting bodies that populated the balcony, and carefully navigated the stairs, reaching the bottom few steps that were already underwater. They waded the short distance to the last pew in the church, finding three very solemn little girls clinging to their parents, who had all three of the children tucked between them for protection and warmth.

"Excuse me." Betsy leaned over so the couple could hear them over the rushing wind outside. "We have a perfectly lovely spot in the corner of the balcony up there. We'd like for you and your family to take it."

"We couldn't." The woman's face showed hope, despite her automatic polite response.

"You must." Betsy felt Angel at her back, both hands resting on her hips from behind. "You see, we can't in good conscience sit by while your little girls are in danger."

"Go on," the man urged his wife. "Take the girls with you."

"You, too." Angel stepped in, moving to Betsy' side, and eyeing him sternly. "If your family lives through this night, they're going to need you."

"But I..."

"The offer is only good if all of you go." Angel held firm, feeling Betsy take her hand and squeeze it tightly. "Go on now, before we change our minds."

"Mama?" One of the little girls looked hopefully up at her mother's face. "Mama, I'm afraid."

"Thank you." The woman was already standing, picking up her youngest, barely out of diapers. Her husband followed suit, hoisting up the other two girls and balancing one on each side. "God bless you."

"Is there no room up there for all of us?" The man insisted.

"No. I fear there isn't. If there were, I'd find another family to take that space." Betsy clasped the woman's arm. "Can I ask one favor?"

"Anything." The woman's eyes shone with tears in the lantern light.

"If something happens to us, get word to some friends of ours, if they're still on the island. We pray to God they got off, but if not..." She carefully gave the couple their address, listening and nodding affirmatively as the man repeated it.

"Go." Angel could hear a rising roar outside, and grabbed Betsy, pulling her toward the pew and settling down. The water was almost up to the seat, and they stretched out lengthwise on the hard wooden bench, despite the fact that their feet were once again soaking wet.

The family scurried toward the stairs, reaching the top just as a wall of water came crashing through the front of the church, shattering what remained of some stained glass windows. Pandemonium broke out. The people nearest the front screamed as angry cold waves came rushing down on top of them, burying them instantly in a watery grave.

"Betsy?" Angel's voice was high-pitched, and they clung to each other, watching the water as it swirled toward them. She felt Betsy's hold tighten on her as the water quickly rose, lapping at the edge of the pew.

Betsy held tightly to her, finding her ear again, feeling oddly calm, given the circumstances. "Whither thou goest, I will go."

Angel felt the peace too, now, even as the water began to cover them. "Where thou diest, will I die," she answered, repeating their vows from so long ago.

Another great wave followed the first, breaking down the entire front wall, and filling the church to balcony level in a matter of minutes. Screams resounded throughout the room. Behind the water, the wind rose and burst into the room like a freight train, gusting to one hundred forty miles per hour, removing a good section of the cathedral roof in its fury.

In the corner of the balcony, a young family huddled together, crying silently in gratitude to two good Samaritans who had surely saved their children's lives, at least for the time being.

THE ROAR OF the storm was wearing on the occupants of the third-floor loft. Even talking was difficult over the shriek of the wind outside, and they sat in silence, listening to the storm and watching the low flicker of the lantern and the large shadows it cast on the walls around them. Mattie and Rachel sat propped up on the bed against a pile of pillows. They had pulled the sofa away from the window after a large hailstone cracked it.

Mattie sighed heavily and buried her face into Rachel's shoulder, covering her one exposed ear with her arm. She could almost, almost, block out the noise that way. With her eyes covered, and one ear pressed against Rachel's body, if she concentrated really hard, she could hear Rachel's heartbeat and her breathing, and if she inhaled deeply, she was rewarded with Rachel's own clean scent, tainted slightly by a salty smell which clung to her skin from their long trek home from the bridge. Soft cotton flannel caressed her face, and she could feel Rachel's fingers combing through her hair.

"Mattie?" Rachel leaned down close so she could be heard. "Are you all right?" She felt Mattie snuggle in closer, wrapping one arm tightly around Rachel's side, her fingers absently stroking Rachel, running up and down the small of her back. "Mattie?"

When she got no answer, she simply circled her lover with both arms, kissing the top of her head and nuzzling her hair. "It won't last forever, I promise you." She felt a shiver run through Mattie's body, and heard a quiet sniffle, and thought again about all they had been through in less than a day's time. "No storm can last forever. The sun has to come out again sometime."

From her dark, warm nest, Mattie pondered that, and her life, and how she had spent nearly all of it doing what other people told her to do, trying to be what they wanted her to be, and all the beatings she had suffered at Adam's hands when she failed at being what he wanted. She looked up, tears glistening on her eyelashes, which fluttered as a very concerned Rachel gently kissed the moisture away. She knew she was frightening Rachel, and she drew in a deep breath, trying to order her thoughts. "My whole life was a storm." She heard her own voice catch and stopped, swallowing.

"I'm sorry." Steel eyes lowered, as Rachel realized she could never truly understand everything Mattie had been through. She felt soft fingers trace her jaw line, tilting her head back up. "I wish I could..."

"You did." Mattie cupped her face. "You're right. No storm can last forever. Mine ended when I met you. You were the sun that came out, for me."

"I don't know that I deserve that. I wish I could have done something a lot earlier than I did." Rachel felt Mattie's thumb against her lips and she closed her mouth, waiting patiently as hazel eyes focused on her.

"You saved me, Rachel. Before you, I never knew I had a choice. You showed me what life was meant to be like. And convinced me I didn't have to stay with someone who hurt me." Another tear escaped, and Mattie sniffled, feeling Rachel's hand against her face, brushing it away. "So don't you ever feel like you haven't done enough for me. I meant it. To me, you are the sunshine that drove away the storm."

Rachel hugged her close, swallowing several times to clear her suddenly-constricted throat. "I think we saved each other." She finally found her voice. One hand wandered down, landing softly against Mattie's stomach, imagining the baby there, and wondering if it was sleeping through the turmoil outside. "How are you feeling?"

"Fine, now that I've eaten and napped." Mattie covered her hand with her own. "I'm a little bit afraid, Rachel."

"Of having a baby?" Long fingers danced against Mattie's nightgown before her hand rested flat again.

"Yes." Smaller fingers twined with longer ones, and she studied Rachel's hands. They were large, the backs covered liberally with scars. Her palms bore the calluses that were a testament to her work on the docks, and the skin on the back was a dark, rich tanned brown, in stark contrast to the pink and white tones of the palms. They were strong and capable, the muscles and bones plainly visible as they flexed, wrapping around her own hand and swallowing it. She'd seen Rachel heft two-hundred-pound bales of cotton with seeming ease, and watched those fingers nimbly work on the tiny clasps and catches on the horses' harnesses out in the barn. Her guts clenched as she thought about those same hands, which held her with infinite care, and caressed her with the gentlest of touches, bringing her pleasure she had never imagined possible.

She lifted Rachel's hand and reverently kissed it. She could already picture a tiny baby cradled in Rachel's arms, supported by those warm strong hands. She had no doubt that both she and the baby could never hope for a greater protector than the one holding on to her at that moment. "I never thought I'd have a baby. And I've not been around anyone much who was pregnant. I barely remember when Carrie was born. I've never seen anyone give birth."

"I have." Rachel's eyes took on a faraway look. She shuddered, thinking of her mother's last painful battle, and her father's stoic sorrow as he was presented with his seventh child, even as his wife lay dying in the next room. She remembered clearly her own grief and confusion as she was thrust into the position of mother to her six younger siblings. What she had never grasped was what her father must have gone through in those dark days, and what it must have been like to lose the wife he had been married to for almost twenty years. She had known Mattie for less than a year, and couldn't conceive of how she would carry on if anything were to ever happen to her. *No. I'm not going to think about that right now.* She shook off the morose thoughts. "Helped deliver a couple, actually. You will be fine. I have faith in you."

"You'll be with me when the time comes, won't you?" She looked down at their joined hands, resting against her body. "I think I can face anything if you're there by my side."

"I wouldn't miss it." Rachel lifted their hands, kissing Mattie's knuckles. "You can even hold my hand and call me names if you need to."

A red head cocked in puzzlement. "Why on earth would I want to do that?"

Rachel merely chuckled and snuggled up closer. "My mother usually had a few choice words for my father while in the throes of childbirth. And I suspect he heard them, even if he was all the way out in the barn at the time she was yelling at him."

"Such as?" Mattie poked her in the ribs, giggling when Rachel jumped.

"Ouch!" She smiled. "Wouldn't be polite for me to repeat them to a lady."

"But your mother was a..." Mattie stopped, listening intently. "Is the wind dying down?"

"I do believe it is." Rachel untangled herself from her lover and the covers and swung long legs over the side of the bed, ambling to the window and cautiously pressing her nose to the glass, trying to see outside. Then noise was indeed lessening, and the house no longer shook. "We should go check out the flooding."

"It's still dark outside. I don't think we'll be able to see much." Mattie joined her at the window, placing a hand at her back.

"No, the flooding downstairs." Rachel picked up the lantern, making the shadows on the wall dance and take on lurid shapes.

"Is it truly over?" The heavy, sheeting rain was gone, and the glass no longer rippled with the forceful winds that had battered it for half the night, but beyond that, there was little to see. "What time is it?" She hugged herself, rubbing away the chill in her arms.

"Little past midnight." Rachel checked her watch and placed it carefully back in its small, tabbed pocket at her waistline. She started toward the door, and felt her lover hook a finger through one of her suspenders. "You shouldn't get up, sweetheart."

"Rachel, I have to see. Please." She tugged harder to emphasize her words.

Rachel frowned but nodded her approval, and they crept toward the staircase. The stairs were once again all visible, though puddles of water were liberally scattered across the now warped and ruined wood.

"Stay put," Rachel cautioned. "Don't want you taking a tumble on these slick steps."

"You be careful." Mattie released her and watched as Rachel cautiously took the steps, one slow step at a time, swinging the lantern around to see ahead of her. She reached the bottom and peered into the second-floor hallway.

"Well, what do you know? No flooding down here, just a lot of very wet wood floorboards." Rachel shuffled to the next staircase. "This one's mostly clear, too," she called back up so Mattie could hear her. "I'm going on down and check out outside."

"Rachel, no!" Mattie scrambled down the stairs, grabbing her by the shirttail and giving her a forceful tug.

"But I want to see what's happening." She gently tried to pry Mattie's fingers loose.

"No!" Mattie pulled harder, digging in with her heels. "It's completely dark out there. It's still raining, and we don't know what that loud noise was earlier. Something might fall on you, or you might fall into the water."

"I'll be careful, I promise." She swung the lantern a little. "I have light to see by."

"And what if you drop it, huh? What if you get hurt and don't come back in here? What if I can't find you out there?" Mattie began to cry, great sobs wracking her body. "Please, Rachel. Wait for dawn."

"Sweetheart." Rachel carefully set the lantern down on a hallway table near the staircase, and took Mattie into her arms.

"Don't you dare leave me alone! I couldn't bear it." Mattie pounded at her chest, then grabbed handfuls of her shirt and buried her face into the soft cotton. "We don't know what happened to our friends. Adam is dead, and while I didn't love him, he was my husband. I watched him drown. In a way, he's given us a gift—a child and peace of mind to live without fear of him."

"Yes, he has." Rachel rubbed her back, but the sobbing continued. "Do you feel guilty about all of that?"

"A little, yes." Mattie's legs gave out, and they both sunk to the floor, Rachel against the wall with Mattie in a nest of her legs and arms. "I—just—my God, Rachel. I'm glad he's gone, but I shouldn't be. I have so much to look forward to. But if you go out there—if you get hurt or—or worse, what was it all for? Please. I can't lose everyone. I just can't. I couldn't live with myself if all I had left was a baby from a dead husband, and you and everyone I care about were gone."

"Shhh." Rachel kissed her head. "I'll stay inside until we can see." She hugged Mattie and frowned, as she continued to cry, with no let-up. "Mattie, he hurt you. Beat on you and beat you down with his words for years, correct?"

"Yes." Mattie sniffled, still buried against Rachel's chest.

"Even after you left him, you were practically in prison in this house, weren't you?"

"Yes, but I had you. I was happy."

"But you were always afraid he'd find you and hurt you again, weren't you?" Rachel rubbed her back, wondering just how many tears one person could cry.

"Every moment," Mattie choked out. "Every moment that I thought about him, I was afraid. He—he..." She began to cry harder, and Rachel rocked her a little bit, smoothing her hand over her head to comfort her. "He violated me in every way possible," she whispered. "I felt like nothing, Rachel. Like filth. He made me feel worthless and dirty every minute I was with him. He hurt me almost every day we were together. I never stopped hurting. I—I—hated him. I still hate him, and I'm glad he's dead. But it's wrong."

"No, it's not." Rachel kissed her head again, and tilted her chin up, wiping away the tears as they continued to fall. "I hate him, too, for what he did to you, and *I'm* glad he's dead. You have all the more right. He was an evil, evil man, Mattie. I've wondered how you kept your bright sunny side, considering how hard he tried to stamp that out."

"I had to keep smiling for the world, or I would have been crying all the time. I thought about killing myself, more than once," Mattie confessed softly. "When we met that day, when I was drawing your picture, he'd beaten me the day before, and then he forced me to..." She swallowed. "His way of apologizing, almost every time. Anyway, I was hurting all over, and I knew the only way I'd get away from him was to die. If I hadn't met you when I did..."

Rachel began to shake, keeping her thoughts quiet with great effort. She hugged Mattie close, and her own tears began to fall. "I thought I understood how bad it was, but I never did until just now." She sniffled, and nuzzled Mattie's hair, drawing in her scent. "What I think, is, he was a monster. And it's perfectly normal to wish a monster dead. And if they do die, perfectly normal to be relieved, because you don't have to be afraid of them anymore. You—and me—being glad he's gone, it would be more strange if we weren't glad."

"You truly believe that?" Mattie looked up hopefully, her tears finally beginning to subside.

"I know it." She ducked her head, briefly kissing Mattie's lips. "He took almost everything from you that he could, and you lived in constant fear. Me—he could have taken you from me. Maybe before we met, or maybe after, but I love you. You've changed my life completely, and given me joy I never knew possible. That anyone could hurt you the way he did, yes, I'm glad he's dead. And a little part of me is glad I didn't have to kill him, because I think I would have, eventually."

"Is that hard to live with?" Mattie touched her face, stroking her cheek.

"Yes, some. But I think all we can do is move forward from here, and try not to second-guess over what might have happened, but didn't." She returned the gentle touches, wiping more tears from Mattie's face. "Do you understand just how much our lives are about to change?"

"I think so." Mattie frowned. "It's good, isn't it?"

"Beyond my wildest dreams." Rachel drew in a deep breath, releasing it slowly and closing her eyes, resting her cheek against Mattie's hair as they continued to comfort each other. "We're free, Mattie. No more fear. No more hiding from him. No more worry that he will find out about the baby and try to take it away from us. We get to be a family. I don't think we should waste time feeling guilty that Adam had to die for us to be free."

"We are, aren't we?" Mattie's voice was full of wonder.

"Yes, so right now, maybe we should go back upstairs and try to rest until sunrise." She helped Mattie up and they began to climb the stairs to the third floor. "And when we go outside in the morning, you can go with me, because you don't have to stay locked up inside anymore. She felt Mattie stiffen, and then heard her sniffle as fresh tears began to fall. They hugged each other close, and when they reached the bed, they fell into it together, exhausted.

RACHEL BLINKED AND stared at the window in amazement. A simple sunrise had never been so welcome. It was gray out still, but she could just see the edges of light streaked across the sky, far off toward the east. "Mattie." She shook her gently. "Mattie, sun's up."

"Oh." Mattie slowly opened her eyes. "What a beautiful sight." She turned in Rachel's arms, and studied her face for a long moment. "That, too." Their lips met for an even longer moment, reaffirming they were alive and together.

They surfaced for air, and Mattie sat up, and slipped over to the window. Rachel was content to simply watch her walk, a little smile tugging at her lips. "Oh, dear God." Mattie gasped as she pulled back the curtains. It was just light enough for her to see utter chaos outside. "Rachel. It's all gone."

"What do you mean?" She got up. In all truth, she'd almost forgotten her earlier desire to check out the outside world. "Jesus, Mary, and Joseph." Rachel crossed herself, something she hadn't done in years. "Looks like Hell has come to Earth."

Before them was a two-story-high pile of boards, and rubble for as far as they could see. The town was no more. Here and there, mixed in among the shambles, large pools of water stood, some of them appearing to be rather deep. There was no one to be seen; not a living thing, not even a bird. "Come on, let's go out there and see how the house has withstood this."

They quickly dressed, and began the climb down the two staircases. "Ugh. It's clear of water now, but not of mud." The first floor and the staircase leading up from it were no longer submerged, but they were covered in a layer of mud and seaweed, mixed with a gritty substance Rachel suspected consisted of sand and fine shell fragments from the ocean floor.

"Pee-yew. Stench is pretty thick down here, too." Mattie hung on behind Rachel, dancing from foot to foot as cold gooey sludge oozed around her shoes. "Oh, it is truly foul down here." Her nose wrinkled at the stench of dead fish that greeted her.

They carefully descended the stairs all the way down to the first floor, and Rachel grasped the doorknob. "You ready?" Mattie nodded uncertainly, and Rachel opened the door, to be greeted by a wall of debris and shattered wood, piled up almost as high as the second floor. The stepped out on the porch, only to find more debris completely surrounding the front part of the house. The sun was rising quickly, and there was a healthy scattering of clouds, edged with pale pink light.

"My sweet lord." Mattie sat limply down on a heavy iron and wood porch bench, which had miraculously survived the storm and sat exactly where they last remembered seeing it.

Rachel remained silent, her eyes flicking around taking in the destruction. Without a word, she began climbing the pile of boards, stopping and pausing to pluck out an ornate brass doorknob. She studied the ornament in rapt fascination. "I do believe I'm climbing up the remains of the house next door." She tossed the knob to the ground.

"Rachel." Mattie stood at the base of the pile of rubble. "Your feet. You might get nails stuck through your boots. Be careful, please?"

"I'm watching out, sweetheart." Rachel continued her climb, teetering a few times on unstable boards, until she was near the top of the pile. She heard an odd sloshing sound and peered over the last pile of wood to find herself looking into a pool of water.

"What do you see up there?" Mattie watched her climb, fearful Rachel would fall.

"My God. It's a twenty-foot-deep pool of water." The debris had formed a dam of sorts, protecting the house from even more flooding. Beyond that, as far as she could tell, everything had been destroyed. She leaned over, covering her nose at the smell. Dead fish floated on the surface, and as she bent closer, something odd floated just beneath. She reached down, poking it, and a body ascended to the surface. It rolled over and a garish, bloated face stared at her with one open eye. She barely recognized the man as the neighbor with whom Betsy had traded baked goods for milk and eggs.

She squelched a scream, which died in her throat, and felt the bile rising in its place. Quickly, she scrambled down, almost tripping on her way to the ground. She landed with a thwacking sound in the mud, and stumbled to the side of the house, leaning over and retching violently.

Mattie was at her side in an instant, patting her on the back. "What happened?"

"Dead man." Rachel choked out, spitting and swiping the back of her hand across her mouth. She stood, feeling her knees shaking like jelly. She grabbed hold of a porch column, seeing spots before her eyes for an instant, before her vision cleared. "Mr. Jameson, I think."

"Oh, no." Mattie steered Rachel to the porch where she practically pushed her down onto the bench. "Are you all right?" She patted a pale cheek.

"Yeah. I'm fine." Rachel's sight turned inward, picturing their neighbor's face again. "I think we might ought to get used to seeing things like that."

"Why do you say that?" Mattie touched Rachel's forehead pushing back sweat-slicked bangs.

"I think we're alone." The dark head dropped down, as Rachel covered her face with both hands, resting on upraised elbows against her knees. She massaged her own temples, and felt Mattie stroking the back of her head.

" I don't understand." Mattie patted her on the leg. "What do you mean by 'alone'?"

"There was nothing else out there," Rachel whispered. "Not a house left standing, far as I could tell. Maybe across town..."

"That can't be." Mattie looked around, and up, at the slanted porch roof overhead. "There have to be others that survived."

"Just listen." Rachel cocked her head. The sound of a gentle breeze rustled past them, stirring leaves on the ground that had been stripped from the trees. It rippled across the water surface from beyond the debris pile, the liquid sound reaching their ears. Otherwise it was silent.

"I don't hear anything." Mattie frowned in puzzlement.

"That's my point." Rachel stood, pacing to the end of the porch, feeling the wind lift her bangs off her face, the refreshing coolness going a long way in settling her stomach. "No trolley cars, no dogs barking, or cows mooing, nothing at all. You'd think, after what we've been through, if anyone else out there had survived, we'd hear them now, doing what we're doing, going outside to see what we can see."

Mattie closed her eyes, taking in the sounds of what passed for peace, if not for the destruction all around them. The silence practically roared in her ears, replacing the blasting sound of wind she had all but become numb to. She crossed her arms over her chest and stepped down off the porch, around to the side of the house, trying to ignore the dozen or so dead fish as she picked her way through the debris that littered the ground.

She looked up to the sky. Between the rolling clouds, she saw the morning star, belying the cyclone that had so recently passed over the island. Even the rain had stopped, though the smell of it was still strong in the air, mingling with all the other odd scents, both pleasant and putrid. "Rachel, will you come down here, please?" She turned, spotting the brooding figure leaning against a column, staring out at the destruction.

The tousled head lifted, the morning light catching faint glints from Rachel's eyes, which warmed at the sound of Mattie's voice. "Be right there." She hopped over the porch railing, landing solidly in the muck, and slopped over through the thick goop to Mattie's side. "I feel limp."

"Your voice is shaking," Mattie commented mildly.

"And I'm trying very hard to pretend it isn't." Rachel circled Mattie from behind, resting her chin on the top of her head. "Damn." She could still feel the tremors coursing through her blood, making her limbs feel like water.

"You are not alone." Mattie draped her own arms on top of Rachel's. "We are not alone. Look up there." She raised one hand, pointing toward the sky. "The sun rose, just like it does every morning. This..." She gestured toward the remains of their neighbor's house. "This is a nightmare. But we are going to get through it." She turned in Rachel's embrace. "We were spared, Rachel. We're alive. If I ever needed affirmation of the love of God, I have it. If he were in the business of punishing sinners, we should have been struck down in the first few hours of this mess, but we weren't. I believe there is a reason we're still here. Here." She placed Rachel's hand flat against her stomach, feeling the long fingers splay against her in a gesture that had become automatic. At the same time, she placed her own hand against Rachel's heart, feeling it flutter at her touch before it settled down into even, steady beats. "Every reason in the world I need to live is right here with me. How about you?"

"You are my life." Rachel kissed her forehead. Her knees were still weak, and her brain was still spinning at the devastation she suspected was out there. It made her feel off balance in more ways than one. She wasn't used to losing her composure or showing weakness, but as she searched Mattie's face, she found only compassion and gentleness looking back at her, mixed with a healthy dose of concern. She closed her eyes, shutting out the wreckage all around them, and focused in tightly on what had become her whole world. "Thank you." She folded Mattie into a warm hug, allowing the love to wash away some of the horror.

"Come on." Mattie squeezed her before stepping back, leading her by both hands. "Let's go for a little walk, and try to clear our heads." She gave her a gentle tug, and they began to walk in silence.

Rachel followed, realizing that she didn't always have to be the strong one, and sheepishly suspecting that many times, true strength was of the heart, and came in petite redheaded packages.

Most of the front of the house was blocked by the wreckage of their neighbor's home, so they silently picked their way around to the back, and found to their relief that the back yard, while totally destroyed, was navigable, with only a few odd pieces of lumber washed into what had once been be the garden. The barn was nothing but a pile of boards, and both women realized the horses they had left in the livery stable were probably a loss. "Can't believe we were in there — what — was it yesterday morning?" Mattie stared at the remains of the stable. "Unbelievable."

"And to think that this time yesterday, our biggest worry was getting caught in that barn." Rachel felt a squeeze to her forearm, where Mattie's hand was resting.

All the homes on their side, other than Angel and Betsy's, were destroyed, crumbled and falling into one another in a long line.

"Looks like they all went down in a row, one after the other," Rachel commented. "Must've been that very loud crashing we heard last night. And I thought it was just the one house." She looked to the other side of the alleyway. "Fared a little better over there, I see. A few are still standing."

"Maybe it isn't as bad as we thought it was." Mattie heard a rustle, and a woman approached them from out of the shadows beside one of the houses. As she drew closer, Mattie recognized her as one of the women who had sometimes visited with Betsy over the back fence while they worked in the garden. She'd seen them from her hidden place inside the house, and had longed to be able to go out and join them.

"Hello." The woman's face was pale, and her eyes registered shock. "I'm looking for food. My husband—he's inside. Won't come out. I think his mind's done gone and left him. We're hungry. Do you have anything at your place to spare?"

"Y—" Mattie felt an almost painful squeeze to her hand and she closed her mouth, turning indignantly to Rachel to chastise her. A warning flashed from steel eyes and she stopped, waiting as the taller woman stroked the inside of Mattie's palm with her thumb.

"No, ma'am. We're looking ourselves. Maybe you could try fishing down on the beach. Storm's bound to have driven more fish than usual close to shore." Her eyes swept the woman's yard. "You have a fishing pole?"

"Yes." The woman's face lit up. "Why, yes. Yes, we do. It's still resting in the entryway where my James left it yesterday when he came home. I'll do just that. Thank you. And God bless you." She turned and wandered back inside her house, which was collapsed on one side, the roof caved in and the porch hanging askew off the back.

"Rachel?" Mattie looked up expectantly, waiting for an explanation.

"We don't know how bad it is, Mattie, and in this I'm going to be selfish." Her hand dropped to Mattie's stomach. "We don't have much food left—maybe a few days' worth. I won't risk it. Not when it comes to you and the baby. I-I guess that sounds harsh, doesn't it?" Her voice wavered uncertainly.

"No." Mattie lifted her hand, kissing it. "It sounds like someone this baby is going to be lucky to have looking after it." She tucked her hand back into Rachel's. "And so am I."

"I did the right thing, then?" Rachel's feet began to move, picking their way through rubble, as they walked on toward the east.

"Yes. I think you did."

As they walked on, the destruction became more pronounced, with long stretches of buildings completely leveled or washed away. At times it was difficult to figure out what street they were on, or if they were on the street at all.

The sun was full, and in the unforgiving light of day, the devastation was beyond comprehension. Entire blocks were leveled with not a recognizable building left standing in some parts of town. Mattie cried quietly, trying to come to terms with the numerous dead bodies they encountered, not only of animals, but of people as well.

Rachel kept her arm tightly around her lover, frequently stopping to allow Mattie to simply turn and bury her face into Rachel's chest each time they saw another body. The first one had been a horror, as had the second, third, and fourth. After that it became a walking nightmare, devoid of much color other than the brown of waterlogged broken-up wood mixed with sand.

Mattie studied yet another body at length, her large questioning eyes looking to Rachel for guidance. "We can't do anything for them, sweetheart." Rachel stroked Mattie's long red hair, which was hanging loose, spilling over her shoulders and down her back to her waist. "Clean-up will begin soon enough." She disengaged herself from Mattie long enough to respectfully drag the person, an older gentleman, from beneath the small pile of rubble that covered the lower half of his body. She laid him out flat in front of what she could only assume had been his house. She shuffled through the debris, looking for others, but found nothing else, save a scattering of dead fish in a shallow pool of water.

The smell was already rank, as the late-summer sun peeked through the clouds, ripening the carcasses of man and beast alike at a rapid rate, the stench carried away on a stiff, cool breeze. They lost count of the number of dogs, cats, and even a few horses and cows they passed, as they turned back to go home. Two blocks from the house, a clear, sweet chiming noise rang out, piercing the morning air and shattering the deathly silence.

"Ursuline Convent, if I'm not mistaken." Rachel lifted her head in wonder, cocking one ear toward the sound. "It's Sunday, and almost time for worship." She turned to Mattie with renewed hope. "Mean's there's others besides us and our backyard neighbors."

"We should go," Mattie declared decisively. "If only to see who all else is there."

Rachel engulfed her in a side hug as they continued on their way, only to be met by a few other dazed wanderers who were also following the beckoning church bells like the lost sheep the church proclaimed them to be.

As they arrived at the mostly broken-down convent, Mattie and Rachel stopped short, hovering together near the back of the small crowd. Most were in some state of disarray—clothing torn, wet, or dirty, hair unkempt, and expressions ranging from fear, to anguish, to shock. A few nuns wandered through the group, speaking quietly to each person in turn.

Some of the women were crying openly, and Mattie caught bits of whispered conversation regarding missing or presumed-dead loved ones and friends. She solemnly nibbled her lower lip, clinging to Rachel, not caring what anyone thought of her actions at that moment.

"Bless you, children." A plump kindly sister approached them, reaching out and taking one of Mattie's hands. "Child, your hands are freezing." She vigorously rubbed the hand in question.

"I—I'm just tired, is all." She felt Rachel's scrutiny and swallowed, looking up, unable to avoid her penetrating gaze. Her eyes dropped. "And a little bit hungry."

"She's with child." Rachel unconsciously placed one hand over Mattie's stomach. "Her husband drowned yesterday morning."

"You poor dear." The sister shooed both of them to a bench next to the ruined building. "Come, sit down. We're about to pass out some fresh loaves of bread. We had just finished baking them when the storm hit, and the blessed saints must have granted a miracle, for all the bread made it through intact." She disappeared inside and Mattie elbowed Rachel affectionately.

"My husband drowned yesterday?" She frowned at Rachel. "We both know I'm not exactly the grieving widow."

"Tell me you're not about to faint from hunger." Rachel studied her gravely, getting a half-hearted nod in response. "Thought so. I'm not beyond a bit of harmless deception when it comes to your health, Mattie, so get used to it."

"I-I'm sorry." Mattie looked down at her hands, which were folded in her lap. Her hair framed her face, hiding her trembling lower lip from Rachel's view. She suddenly felt very small, and extremely disoriented, and quite afraid to look up past the group. The destruction was starting to sink in, making her feel vaguely as if she were observing the world from some point outside her body. "What are we going to do?" she finally whispered, a small whimper of genuine fear choking out behind her words.

"Hey." Rachel pulled her close, tilting her chin up with gentle fingers. "I'm sorry, too. I didn't mean to hurt your feelings."

"I'm afraid, Rachel. It's too much." She felt Rachel's thumb against her skin, swiping her tears away. "What kind of world is my baby going to be born into?"

"Any world you want." Rachel cupped her cheek. "This one, or as far away as you want to go."

"What do you want to do?" Mattie hiccupped.

"I want to be with you." Rachel quickly kissed her forehead.

"And I want to be with you. We're together. That's all that really matters, isn't it? Let's see what the day will bring." Mattie looked up as the nun approached them.

"That's my girl." Rachel's breath tickled near her ear. "One day at a time, Mattie. That's probably the best any of us can do for now."

"Child, how far along are you?" The nun pressed three loaves of bread into Mattie's lap.

"About two months." Mattie could smell the fresh wheat scent of the bread, and her mouth watered as her stomach twisted and growled in anticipation. "Thank you." She patted the sister's arm.

"Sister." Rachel idly accepted a chunk of bread that Mattie tore off and handed to her. "What have you heard of the town north of here? And what about the orphanage and the warehouse area?"

"Gone." The nun knelt down, placing one hand on Rachel's knee. "Have you kin that lived in that area?"

"Gone?" Rachel's voice choked, as a lump rose up in her throat. "All of it?"

"The warehouses took severe damage, and the orphanage is mostly a loss." The sister shook her head. "As far as we know, not a child or sister survived.

"Oh." It was a pitiful little sound, and it took Rachel a moment to realize it came from her own lips. "Are you certain? Did you find all of them?"

"Oh, my child, no." The nun smiled sadly. "The orphanage was empty. So close to the beach, we can only assume the children and our sisters were all lost to the sea." She stood. "Mass will begin in a little while, but please rest here for as long as you need to."

"Thank you, sister." Mattie shaded her eyes with one hand, looking up into the sun as the nun walked away.

"I have to go up there." Rachel turned to Mattie. "I have to."

"You want me to stay at the house, don't you?" Mattie knew it was for the best, despite her yearning to come along.

"You need to rest, Mattie. It wouldn't be good for the baby. It's a long way, and no telling what all I might have to climb over and around to get there. I—I can see what became of your old house, and look for Billy and Lillie, and Betsy and Angel, and I have to look for the boys." Her heart hurt, thinking of Albert and Frank. "So young." Her eyes blurred for a moment and she swiped her hand across her face.

"Fine." Mattie sighed. All she really wanted to do was go home and rest, and try to forget everything for a while, although she wanted Rachel to snuggle with while she rested. "Please don't take long, and please be careful."

"I will. I'll go to the orphanage, and the warehouses, and the boarding house. Whether I find them or not, I'll turn around after that, I promise." She pulled Mattie close and rested her chin on her head, closing her eyes to block out the leveled buildings all around them. As she opened her eyes, she blinked. "It can't be."

"What is it?" Mattie looked up, and a little joyous yelp escaped her throat. "Lillie! Billy!"

Two disheveled figures approached them, making their way from the back of the small crowd in the church yard. "Sugar, y'all are a sight for sore eyes." Lillie engulfed both of them in a big hug. "We were so worried about y'all." She looked around "Where are Betsy and Angel?"

Mattie looked down, taking Rachel's hand and listening to her talk. "We don't know. They didn't make it home before the storm."

"So y'all didn't make it across the bridge?" Lillie sat down with them, while Billy stood, leaning against a palm tree.

"No. We ended up back at the house. How about y'all?" Rachel continued to stroke the back of Mattie's hand.

"We had a terrible time getting here. When Billy found me at the boarding house, most everyone was in a panic. He had to help a few of the older ladies get down the fire escape. The main porch had washed away and the whole building was pretty near to collapsing. I imagine it's gone now. Tweren't ever very sturdy in the first place. Lord knows where all of 'em went off to. We told 'em to follow us but none of 'em did." She beamed up at Billy. "Not him. He found us a spot in the Tremont Hotel, and we rode the night out there along with a bunch of other folks. We heard about the bridges, but hoped y'all had made it across before they were flooded over."

"No such luck." Rachel shifted slightly, and looked over at Mattie. "Adam's dead." She watched Lillie's cornflower blue eyes grow wide. "He came after us. Tried to stop Mattie." She stopped again, both hearing and feeling the catch in her throat. "He was..." She swallowed. "Damned fool tried to cross that flooded bay bridge. Big ol' wave washed him off. We watched him go under."

"Saved me and you the trouble," Billy mumbled under his breath.

"Well." Lillie watched Mattie carefully. "He can't hurt you anymore, sugar."

"No," Mattie murmured softly. She looked up, her eyes shining with moisture. "I was so worried about y'all. We thought about y'all, and Angel and Betsy. And we just found out..."

A nun interrupted them, holding a basket out in front of Lillie. "Bread!" Lillie's eyes lit up, and she smiled gratefully, taking a loaf. "Thank you. My tummy's been gnawing on me something fierce."

"There's more," Rachel sighed.

She stopped, looking from Rachel to Mattie and back. "What's wrong? Other than the obvious?" she hastily amended.

"They think all the orphans drowned." Rachel felt Billy's hand drop to her shoulder, and she covered it with one of her own. "Will you go up there with me? I just have to see — maybe somehow..." her voice trailed off.

"Sure." He looked to Lillie, who nodded her silent approval. "Might as well see what's left of this island while we're at it. You want to head up there right after mass?"

"No." Rachel's voice was low and decisive. "I want to head up there now. Lillie, you know how to use a gun?"

"Why, sugar, of course I do. You forget so soon where I used to earn my keep." She frowned. "Why?"

"After mass, take Mattie back home. Load up her pistol and keep it handy. Take turns keeping a lookout. Don't let any strangers in. Maybe not even friends." She spoke quietly, as she studied the crowd standing nearby. "This island has no bridges, no railroads, and no electricity, which means no telephones or telegraph. I expect some folks are gonna get mighty desperate for food and shelter before we get anyone from the mainland over here to help." She plucked at the crease in her trousers as she talked. "I can't take any chances with that house or our food supply. Have to think about my baby."

"Your...?" Lillie stopped herself, noting that Rachel didn't realize she had referred to the baby as her own. Her eyes met Mattie's, which shone with warm pride and affection. It was a small spark of hope in the middle of the most hopeless of circumstances. Those hazel eyes turned full on Rachel, the adoration clearly visible as they looked the taller woman slowly up and down. Mattie leaned over and whispered something in Rachel's ear. Lillie couldn't hear it, but there was no missing the blush that rose from the edge of Rachel's shirt collar, slowly flooding her face and neck to a dark pink hue.

"Ladies and gentleman." A man called them to attention and they all turned, recognizing him as one of the town councilman. "At ten a.m. this morning, Mayor Jones will convene an emergency meeting of what city councilmen are able to attend. The newspaper will go to press as usual, and we will get what news and plans we can to the general population, as soon as is practical."

"What do you think?" Billy tilted his hat back. "Go to the meeting first, then up to the orphanage?"

"Most certainly." Rachel stood and turned, leaning down to speak quietly to Mattie for a moment before she kissed the top of her head. "Ladies, we'll be home as soon as we can. You take care of her, you hear?" She pulled Lillie aside, out of earshot of Billy and Mattie. "She's stubborn, and prone to try to do more than she should. She needs to get in bed and sleep, and eat as much of a regular meal as you can pull together."

"Yes, ma'am," Lillie teased. "What did she whisper to you a minute ago?"

"Oh." The blush renewed itself, dusting Rachel's cheeks bright pink. "Partly, she called me 'Papa'. The other part, I can't repeat."

"Oh, come now, sugar. I've heard just about everything since moving to Galveston. There's very little that could shock me." Lillie tucked a hand into the crook of Rachel's elbow, whispering conspiratorially.

Rachel scratched her ear, which was even redder than her face. "She—um—naw. I can't. Not word for word, other than it had to do with her firm belief that if I tried hard enough, I could probably provide that baby with a sibling."

"Well, aren't you the debonair one?" Lillie ribbed her. "Sugar, I'm just glad to see the two of you happy. No two people I know deserve it more, and it does my heart good to see y'all together—makes seeing all this horrible wreck around us a tad bit more palatable."

"I am happy." Rachel smiled, glancing back at Billy and Mattie, who were engaged in what appeared to be rather serious conversation. "You told me I could be someday, didn't you?"

"I never doubted it for a minute." Lillie squeezed her arm. "I'll take care of your Mattie, and you take care of my Billy. Don't let him go trying to lift entire buildings, you hear me?"

"Deal." Rachel steered them back to the bench, where she collected Billy, and they set out for the north side of the island.

TWO SILENT FIGURES walked slowly along the beach, approaching the orphanage, which even at a distance was in obvious shambles. "I don't know if I can take this." Rachel grasped his elbow, curling her fingers around it and stepping gingerly over a pile of seaweed-encased debris, which included a few purple, bloated jellyfish. "I don't understand how something so awful could happen to children."

"It rains on both the rich and the poor." Billy patted her hand.

"True." Rachel looked up toward the cloudy sky, trying to reconcile it with the black roiling mass it had been the day before. "But the rich usually don't have leaky roofs."

Billy chuckled listlessly. "What did you think about the Mayor's announcement? Do you think y'all will stay here?"

"I'll have to discuss that with Mattie. We're both quite fond of the island, but I dunno—seems a daunting task ahead of us." She brushed a lock of hair out of her face and turned, studying his strong profile, and the mass of unruly blond hair covering his head. "What about y'all?"

"Difficult to say. Part of me is a mind to take off for parts unknown. Another part—seems like there might be a lot of opportunity ahead for steady work, assuming they're paying good wages to the workers involved in rebuilding." He chewed thoughtfully on a reed he'd plucked along the way, and twirled the end between his fingertips.

"Think you'd miss fishing and the docks?" Rachel herself was debating. She'd hoped to make something more of her life than that of a laborer, but she also saw the vast field of opportunity—a small silver lining to the very black cloud of the storm's devastation. She also thought about the docks, and life on the sea, and the peace of fishing, along with the satisfaction she felt at the end of a good day of it. "We know Gentry's dead. The port is a wreck, but they'll repair that right off—too much of the island's livelihood depends on the freighters being able to get in and out of here. What if you and I start up a fishing business of our own?"

"Now that is tempting, Miz Travis." His eyes twinkled as he gazed out toward the Gulf. "We ran Gentry's boat for him as it is.

Only thing wrong is he got most of the profits of the catch. Times are changing. Folks are traveling by train and by automobile. I even read about some folks out east trying to build a flying machine. This place..." He swept his arm around in an arc. "Folks will be flocking to it in years to come, I reckon. Hotels — saloons — dining establishments. Might be a steady market for a couple of enterprising fishermen."

"My thoughts exactly. Whether we're involved in rebuilding or not, seems like Galveston might be a very good place to make a living." She thought about Mattie, and their walks on the beach when they'd first met, and their special evening out on the fishing boat. "My heart is here. I think Mattie's is too. Betsy and Angel said we could stay with them long as we need to."

He gently cut her off. "Is the mill area next on your agenda?"

"Yes." Her face clouded and she took a long shuddering breath, realizing that they'd reached the edge of what once was the orphanage yard. "Well I'll be." She stopped, turning back and looking down the shoreline. "We've done passed the area where Mattie's house was. Beach is so changed by the storm, I can't even make out any landmarks. It's gone." She squinted, shading her eyes as she studied the long stretch of beach they'd traversed. "I don't think she'll spend too much time grieving over it."

"I can't imagine she has many fond memories of that place." Billy's own face darkened with rage on his friend's behalf.

A tiny smile played at Rachel's lips. "She might have one or two." She glanced up at him just in time to catch a charming blush. "But overall, you're correct. Seems like she's made every effort to leave that part of her life behind."

A rustling noise caught their attention, and they made their way closer to the back area of what had been the girls' dormitory. They heard the noise again, coming through a shattered first-floor window. "Hey!" Billy shouted. "Anyone in there?"

Three small faces popped over the edge of the windowsill, as three pairs of eyes grew large. "Miss Rachel?" Albert's hoarse voice cracked, as his face lit up with a very tired smile. "Miss Rachel, have we all died and gone to Purgatory?"

Rachel yelped with joy and ran toward the window. "No. Not at all. Hold on." She took the steps up and leaped across the porch, flinging the remains of the front door open and bursting into the room to be met by an armful of wet, frightened little boys. They almost bowled her over, and she just managed to keep her balance as she knelt down at boys-eye level. "Where were you earlier? Folks have already been by here and thought all y'all were..." she trailed off. "Anyone else in here?"

"No'm." Frank's voice was equally hoarse, and his small forlorn eyes looked down. "We's the only ones, Miss Rachel. The sisters, and all the other children — they done gone and drowned." He sniffled and swiped a hand across his eyes.

"We spent the night in a tree." William eyed the woman curiously. He'd seen her before, but was not as well acquainted with her as his two survivor friends. "We climbed down after the sun come up and the storm was gone, and come back here to look for breakfast."

"A tree?" Rachel laughed through happy tears. "How'd you end up in a tree?"

"We wasn't tied to the others." Albert unconsciously played with her long braid, tugging it as he talked.

"Tied?" Her face fell. "Oh, of all the ignorant things." In her mind's eye she could see a chain of children and nuns all pulled into the storm, one after the other. "The sisters did that? Tied the children all together?"

"Yes'm," Frank answered. He had fallen back on an old habit, and had to remove his thumb from his mouth to speak. "But Albert told me and Willie not to tie up, so we didn't."

"Smart boy," Billy's voice sounded from the doorway. "You boys want to go for a walk with us?"

"You gots any food?" Albert looked up hopefully, his stomach growling at the thought.

"I imagine we can rustle up something." He looked around the muddy and lopsided room. "Though probably not here. We're walking on into town a ways, then back to the house we're staying in." He looked at Rachel's face for clues and she smiled, nodding her head. "You boys can come stay with us until we figure out what to do with you. How'd you like to sleep in a nice warm house tonight?"

"Not sleepy." William yawned, despite his answer, and quickly clamped a hand over his mouth. "Leastwise not much."

"Willie—is that your name?" Rachel tousled his dark head as he nodded affirmatively, shy eyes blinking behind long lashes. "Willie, even I am sleepy, and I'm an adult. I imagine three boys who spent the night in a tree shouldn't be ashamed of needing a good night's sleep, or even a nap. After we get your bellies full, that is."

"Well." He kicked at the floor with the toe of a well-worn and soggy boot. "Guess I might could sleep some later, after breakfast."

"So could I." She stood, crossing her arms over her chest and looking out the window. A chill ran through her, as if a ghost had walked over a grave, and her heart felt heavy in her chest. Her back was to the room, but she could feel four pairs of eyes watching her. She heard Billy's feet as he moved toward her, and she turned, her jaw clenched tightly. With a toss of her head, she stood up taller, holding out a hand to Albert, as Frank slid in next to her on the other side. "Well, then. Let's go see what we can find at the mills, shall we?"

"Rachel. We don't know..."

"Don't." She cut him off, as gently as possible, trying to keep her voice from breaking. "Just—don't."

"Don't what, Miss Rachel?" Albert could feel the tremor in her hand, and he squeezed it, smiling when she squeezed back.

"Billy, maybe you should take them back to the house with you. Might not be fitting for them to see."

"And leave you to go looking alone?" Billy tipped his hat back, rocking back on his heels. "Mattie would not be happy with me if I turn back up without you."

"She'll understand, especially when she sees the boys. Tell her..." She pursed her lips inward. She could feel the doom ahead. There were some things a person just knew. "Tell her I'll be home before nightfall."

"Nightfall?" Billy frowned at her. "I don't understand. Surely it won't take you that long to find out..."

"No." She released the hands of her two charges, giving them a slight push in his direction. "Go on. Go with Billy here. He's my friend, and he's going to take you to my house and get you some breakfast. How does that sound?"

"Breakfast!" Frank's voice cracked with happiness. All three boys had sore throats from being out in the elements, and their cheeks were chapped and red from the night of lashing by wind and rain.

"You gots flapjacks at your house?" Albert tugged at Billy's trousers leg.

"Well, probably nothing quite that fancy, but we'll make sure you get fed. You three, go out on the porch for a minute, and let me talk to Rachel here. I'll be along shortly." He waited as three small pairs of feet shuffled out the door. They could see them through the window, and being boys, they quickly moved beyond the porch, down to the battered shoreline. Billy studied Rachel for several minutes. Her jaw clenched and she swallowed hard a few times. He'd seen the hardness there before, knowing it for what it was. Rachel was not going to let anyone watch her break down. "Rachel." He moved toward her, placing a cautious hand on her back, waiting until he was certain it wouldn't be shrugged away. "You don't have to do this alone. I can flag down someone to take the boys back to the house."

"I have to go, Billy." She turned to face him. "I can't remember how much I've told you. My mother—she was a good woman, but there were too many of us at home. I was the oldest, and sometimes there just wasn't enough mothering in her to go around. So I sometimes took that place with my brothers and sisters—filled in the places that she just didn't have time for. She meant well, but she never understood me. Saw nothing wrong with keeping me out of school to help out at home, and there was this sort of twisted logic—instead of letting me go when it was my turn, they figured best to let the ones already in school keep going—just have one ignorant child instead of a bunch of them."

"You're by no means ignorant." Billy rubbed her back in

comforting circles.

"Took me a long time to figure out that there was more to intelligence than just book smarts, but anyway," she ran her fingers through her bangs, fluffing them out of her eyes, "my mother, she loved me in her own way—and in her mind, I was going to do what she did, grow up, get married, and have babies, so the schooling, it weren't so terribly important in her mind. That's a long way of saying that I loved my mother, but she wasn't always much of a mother to me. Betsy and Angel—at times they showed me more mothering and concern than I ever got growing up, so, yes, I have to go do this alone. If it's bad, I need some time to put the pieces back together before I go back to Mattie. And I never was good at pulling myself together if there was someone else around I felt like I had to be strong in front of. Do you understand?"

"You don't have to be strong for me." Billy stepped back. "But I do understand, and respect what you want. Just—get home as quick as you can. Otherwise you might be having to put Mattie back together twice today. Once over you not being there and again if —if your news is bad."

"Good point." She cuffed him on the arm. "Go on, take those little fellows home and feed them, and see if there's any dry beds to be had besides the one in the loft."

She looked back out the window. "Albert! You boys get out of that water right now!" Three figures scrambled back to the beach. "My lord." She shook her head. "You'd think they'd had enough of being in the water to last them a lifetime. There's something to be said for how young they are, though. I imagine they saw some pretty terrible things last night, but they'll be fine a lot quicker than any of us will be."

"True." Billy draped an arm across her shoulders, giving her a quick hug before he moved to the door. "Come home, Rachel. Soon," he admonished her. "There are those among the living who are counting on you. Don't forget that."

"I won't." She flashed him a trembling smile, then waited, watching, until he and the boys were well on their way, before she finally began the long walk to the mill.

Chapter
Fifteen

MORNING SLOWLY SEGUED into afternoon as Rachel searched the mill and factory area, looking for the two older women who had come to mean so much in a very short period of time. Each place she looked brought more heartbreak and shock, and she was constantly drawn away from her task to help in one way or another. Makeshift shelters were being set up along the beach, and a temporary clinic for the injured, and there were many — broken bones from falls, cuts from flying debris, and some more gruesome ones — severed limbs and those who were so addled by the storm that they didn't seem to have full use of their minds.

Then there were the dead.

There were so many that those who had taken it upon themselves to take care of the dead were finding it difficult to keep the task organized. It seemed horrid to think that some of them might not be properly identified or mourned or even get a funeral before being disposed of, but disposal was paramount. On a humid subtropical island, in the summer, with pools of stagnant water everywhere, the stench was nigh unbearable, and there was fear of disease.

As she made her way from the mills into the more central part of the remains of town, she found places where the dead were being reverently gathered for transport to a giant barge that would serve to carry the bodies to a somewhat dignified burial at sea. She was heartsick as she carefully looked at each one, trying to determine if any of them might be Betsy or Angel, or anyone else she knew, for that matter. Most were strangers. A few, she recognized by face but not by name. The children were the worst, although the children she knew best of all were, thankfully, alive and well, and hopefully eating dinner back at the house.

She thought about the house, and the deed Betsy had entrusted Mattie with before she left in search of Angel. It was a good, sturdy house, obviously, having weathered the storm better than most, although it did have some leaks and missing roof tiles. It also needed some serious clean-up inside, especially the first floor, which was liberally covered in seaweed and sandy mud.

During the dark hours of the storm, it had hit home to Rachel just how much the baby had come to mean to her. She barely thought of it as Adam's, only Mattie's. And, she admitted with a wry smile, she had come to think of it as hers, too. Hers to provide for and with Mattie's blessing, to love as it if were here own. She chuckled quietly, thinking of taking the little tyke out on a boat and teaching him or her to fish, or out in the water to give swimming lessons. Maybe she would even learn to read well enough to help the child in that area as well.

"Take care of that baby, my love," she whispered. "And take care of yourself, too." The urge to go home was becoming almost unbearable, but the suffering all around her kept her moving, as did the need to go home with some sort of news of their friends, be it good or bad. While searching for Angel and Betsy, she found herself helping to move debris, and escorting folks to the clinic area, and giving advice on fishing to some of the ones without food. Everyone seemed lost, wandering about a place that no longer resembled home.

A few of the churches were organizing food and clothing drives, and those who had lost their houses were beginning to flock to them for both meals and shelter. Rachel politely accepted a cup of thick chowder, which was pressed into her hands by a nun, along with a square of cornbread. She didn't realize how hungry she was until she smelled the tomato broth and the steaming chunks of vegetables and fish floating there. She tore into the bread first, dipping a corner of it into the soup and chewing and swallowing it with pleasure. All she'd eaten was a few bites of bread at the convent that morning, and now she tried not to gobble down her meal.

The food gave her renewed energy and she pressed on, methodically checking every standing building, every pile of bodies, and every group of the living, looking for and inquiring of Betsy and Angel. Finally, she came upon a group gathered outside the remains of St. Peter's Cathedral. Families and couples sat around, sharing a noon meal in the shelter of whatever shade could be found.

She quietly went from group to group, describing her friends and asking if anyone had seen them. A few people seemed to recognize the women by her description, and thought they had seen them in the church. Unfortunately, none of them could tell her what had become of them, only that they thought they had taken refuge there.

As she walked away, a woman approached her and timidly tugged on her shirt sleeve. Rachel turned to see large, weary brown eyes framed by long thick dark hair. The woman had a young tot balanced on one hip, and two more little girls clutching at her skirts. "Excuse me, did you say your name is 'Rachel'?" The woman's face was bleak and tear-stained, not unlike many faces Rachel had seen that day. "I'm Gracie, and I think I know where your friends are."

"Are they...?" Rachel's voice trailed off, seeing the answer to her question written plainly in the woman's eyes. "Where are they?" Her shoulders slumped.

"I had them leave them on one of the pews inside, away from the others. They asked us to find you if—if anything happened to them." She led a numb Rachel inside the dark, damp-smelling building. It was cool in there, the strong scent of salt water still clinging to the walls and floors. The lower floor was in shambles, save for a few pews pulled together in one corner.

"Oh." Rachel choked off a sob, kneeling down next to Betsy's still form. She was resting on a long bench, head to head with Angel, who was also laid out, her arms crossed over her chest. They looked peaceful, as if they were asleep. She stroked Betsy's long gray hair, her vision blurred by tears. Gracie stood a polite distance away. She'd left her three little ones just outside the door, to spare them the sight of yet more death. "How—how did it end—for them?" She looked up, sniffling and dragging her shirt cuff across her eyes. "Do you know?"

"They gave up their lives for me and my family." The woman's voice also quivered as fresh tears tracked down her cheeks. "My husband, he's gone down to the beachfront to secure us some shelter. Our house is gone. But thanks to your friends, we have our lives."

"What happened?" Rachel gently kissed first Angel's forehead, and then Betsy's, then stood, deliberately turning her back to the gut-wrenching scene. Her heart felt as if it were about to squeeze out of her chest, and she found it difficult to breathe.

"The storm was beating down on us something fierce." Gracie took Rachel's arm, guiding her back out into the sunlight and away from the two women. "The waters were rising inside and my family, we were down on the first floor, trying to stay up on our pew and out of the water all around us. Your friends—they had a spot in the balcony and came down and insisted we take it."

"Why didn't they stay up there too?" Rachel's eyes were dark with anger.

"There was positively no room." Gracie closed her eyes, remembering the horror of the drowning people below them—the shrieks of those who were about to die, and the cries of children. "My husband—Jack—was going to stay below and let them take his space, but your friends would have none of it. They said we would need him, and we do. He's feeling less a man today for listening to them. I think it will be a long time before he comes to terms with the gift they gave us."

Rachel was weeping now, silent tears, as her body convulsed in her grief. "Damned old fools." She wrapped her arms around herself and looked down. "No offense intended, ma'am. I just wish they could've found a place, too."

"They died heroes." Gracie drew a handkerchief out of her skirt pocket, handing it over to Rachel, who accepted it with a gracious nod, and wiped her face. "My family and I—my girls—we wouldn't be here if not for them. No one else was giving up their spots up there. Just your friends. They died together. Would that be what they wanted?" She had somehow known the older women shared a special bond.

Rachel looked up, her eyes full of sorrow. A sad smile briefly appeared on her face, and she took a deep, resigned breath. "Yes." Her voice was solidly adamant. "It's exactly what they would have wanted. What I would want..." She trailed off.

"Excuse me?" The woman frowned in confusion.

"Nothing." Rachel reached out and clasped the woman's shoulder. The little girls had carefully moved back behind their mother, and all three of them peeked out from behind her, wide eyes studying the strange crying woman who was dressed like their Pa. Rachel crouched down, crooking one finger to the girls, who looked up at their mother in question.

"Go on." Gracie nodded and stood back.

The girls shuffled forward, the oldest one keeping herself between her sisters and Rachel's commanding presence. "You girls grow up to make your parents proud, you hear me?" Three solemn pairs of eyes looked back at her, as the girls all nodded in agreement. She briefly ran her hand across each small head, then stood back up. "Ma'am, if you'll keep watch, I'll go hire a cart to take them home. They deserve a proper funeral by folks who loved them, not a group one at sea."

"My husband and I would very much like to be there, if you can wait a day or so." Gracie glanced back over her shoulder at the open church door. "I know there's a rush to take care of the dead, but..."

"Tomorrow evening, at sunset." Rachel was already fishing for a stub of pencil to give the woman directions.

"No need." Gracie finally reached out, touching Rachel's hand. "They told me where you live. We'll be there."

"Until tomorrow, then. I—I'd like to meet your husband." Rachel tipped her hat and turned, forcing her feet away from the church and turning toward home at last.

IT WAS NEAR dusk when a lone figure trudged slowly through a break in the large pile of rubble in front of the house. She'd invited both Billy and Lillie to live there for as long as they needed to, and it was obvious they'd taken her invitation to heart. Progress had been made, both on clean-up and repair of the structure, as evidenced by a new collection of trash that sat on the ground toward one end of the long porch. The porch itself was in remarkably better condition than it had been that morning. A support pillar that was hanging askew had been put back in place, and the slats on the porch's surface had been scrubbed clean of its earlier coat of mud and seaweed.

Rachel sniffed, her nose detecting the scent of something cooking—bread, and possibly some sort of fish. She stumbled up the steps and quietly opened the door, stopping and standing, leaning against the sturdy door frame for a long moment, as she observed the now somewhat-clean entryway and parlor to the old home. Back in the kitchen, through the parlor doorway, she could hear a rattle of pans and Lillie's voice talking to someone.

"Hands off that leftover bread, now. I warmed it up, and it's still piping hot. You'll burn your tongues." A young voice answered her in indiscernible protest and Rachel smiled wearily. She'd almost forgotten the boys were there. It was nice to remember that through all the death she'd seen that day, those three very young ones had been spared, and handed a second chance at growing up.

There was no sign of Mattie, and Rachel finally pushed off the door frame, noting that it had also been cleaned of grubby fingerprints. She moved through the parlor, which had been stripped of the large rug that normally occupied the hard wooden floor. The floor was freshly scrubbed, and all the furniture was pushed back against the walls.

With leaden feet, she paused at the kitchen entry, now seeing three tousled dark heads sitting around the kitchen table, where a pan covered with a yellow and white checkered cloth sat cooling. "Howdy." She cleared her throat as four heads quickly turned at the sound of her voice.

"Rachel." Lillie's eyes lit up. "Did you...?" She saw the pain in the steel blue eyes and stopped, glancing at her three charges. "Oh." Lillie wiped her hands on her apron and shuffled around the table, debating on hugging her friend or keeping her distance. As she closed the distance, she compromised, wrapping an arm around Rachel's waist and giving her a quick squeeze. "They're gone, aren't they?"

Rachel nodded, looking down at the floor and studying her scuffed-up boots. "Where is everybody?"

"Billy is upstairs, making up some pallets for these young'uns, and your Mattie is up in the loft, resting, just like you told her to." She clicked her tongue. "Stubborn one, that one is."

"Tell me about it." Rachel found a true smile, her eyes clearing of some of the sorrow she felt in her heart. "Please tell me she didn't help with any of this." Rachel gestured around the room behind them. "Not that I'm not grateful that y'all have been working so hard."

"She didn't do anything too strenuous." Lillie patted Rachel's side and let go of her. "Once we got the stove lighted, I delegated cooking to her. She started in on some chowder, after Billy went down to the shore and caught a few fish for us. But I didn't let her scrub floors, no."

"Thank you." Rachel's eyes trailed toward the staircase. "I think I'll—oh." She grinned as Lillie gave her a shove toward the first step.

"Go on," Lillie urged. "She's been asking about you most every hour since mass was over. I only got her to stay up there when I promised to send you up to wake her as soon as you got home. So wake her. She's been out for a couple hours."

"All right." Rachel hurried, her boots stomping on the stairs, and she grabbed the banister, practically swinging herself up to the second floor and doubling her speed toward the next set of steps. She almost collided with Billy, who came out of one of the bedrooms just as she passed it.

"Whoa, Nellie." Billy reached out, grabbing her shoulders before she smashed full-on into him. "So?" He searched her eyes warily, watching them water up. "I'm sorry, Rachel." He hugged her, hearing a slight sniffle.

"Some men are bringing them here for burial tomorrow." She took a deep breath and regained her composure. "Gotta go tell Mattie. Not looking forward to that."

"I think Mattie knows." He shrugged at her puzzled expression. "She just seems to. Kept muttering all day about how much she wanted to be with you to comfort you."

"Despite her size, I do believe that woman is truly the stronger of the two of us," Rachel marveled, shaking her head and smiling sadly.

"Make that three." Billy wiped a tear from her cheek and stepped back. "Boys have beds on the floor in there, when they're done with their supper. This floor still needs work, but we at least got downstairs a little cleaned up today. Lillie and I will bunk downstairs until this floor is cleaned up, if that's all right."

"Billy, thank you so much for yall's hard work today. I can't say how much it means. I feel like I've been a sloth in my duties, out gallivanting around while y'all did all the work." She lowered her eyes, then looked back up as he touched her arm.

"No, my friend, we merely labored today. You've done the hardest work of all." He gave her arm a little rub. "This floor can wait until tomorrow, as can the back porch. I think we all need a warm meal in our bellies and a solid night's sleep before we do anything further."

"Agreed." She smiled. "I'll carry my share of the load tomorrow, maybe finish patching up the holes I knocked in the floor." She glanced at the gaping opening a few feet behind Billy, then wrinkled her nose. "Glad we can leave the windows open up here. Place still smells of fish and damp wood."

"True." Billy also sniffed the air. "Get up there, Rachel. She's been waiting all day."

Rachel nodded then scooted on up the next staircase, slowing at the landing and peering through the open doorway. Just as she spied the bed, Mattie rolled toward her and opened her eyes.

"Oh. You're home." She sat up, holding out both arms. "Come here, my love."

Rachel suddenly felt weary, and stumbled across the floor, sitting roughly down next to her lover, as slender but sturdy arms engulfed her. As Mattie rubbed her back, Rachel simply buried her face into her neck, feeling soft skin and silken hair against her cheek. She closed her eyes, surprised as the tears rose up and she heard a sob, before she realized it was her own.

"Shhh." Mattie crooned softly into her ear, feeling Rachel shake as the emotion of the day finally came crashing down on her. "I know." Mattie kissed her cheek and continued with a slight rocking motion meant to soothe her lover. "They're gone, aren't they?"

"Yes," Rachel choked out. "Damned old fools."

"You mustn't talk about them like that." Mattie's words were gentle, with no hint of true admonition. "They're together now, and we both know this day would be even harder if Betsy hadn't gone to her. It's time to honor them, love, not curse them."

"I know." Rachel's voice was muffled against the soft cotton of Mattie's simple house dress. "I just wish I could've done something to make things turn out different. Maybe if..."

"No." Mattie gripped her arm for a moment to emphasize her words. "Don't you go second-guessing yourself. You came back here and took care of me, and they wouldn't have had you do anything different. This was not your fault."

They clung together in silence, absorbing the comforting warmth of their joined bodies, as they each felt the other's breathing and heartbeat, further soothing frazzled nerves. Mattie felt as if she could fall asleep there, sitting up, propped against Rachel's solid warmth, with only the sound of her breathing to lull her into slumber. She felt a hand come to rest against her stomach, caressing it, and she smiled, tilting her head back up and quickly kissing Rachel's lips.

"I love you," Rachel breathed against her skin.

Mattie laid her head on Rachel's shoulder. "I missed you so much today."

"And I thought a hundred times of turning around before I found them." She cupped Mattie's face with both hands, cradling it as she looked into warm hazel eyes. "You are what kept me going today. Every time I saw more death and destruction, I said a prayer of thanksgiving that you were spared, that we were given the chance to go on and live. We have a lot to talk about."

"Billy filled me in on the plans for rebuilding the town." Mattie placed her hands over Rachel's, brushing them with her thumbs. "Where you go, I go too. Oh, I almost forgot. I have a surprise for you." She slowly stood, drawing Rachel up with her. "Come outside, in the back."

Intrigued, Rachel allowed herself to be led downstairs, and out the back door. It was full dark now, and she blinked, as her eyes adjusted to the blue-black evening. A tarp was stretched between two tall trees, and under it, two large shadows loomed, moving in the darkness. "Is that...?"

"The horses, yes." Mattie was quivering with happiness at the delighted awe in Rachel's voice. It was one small gift she could give back to her lover in the face of all she knew she had seen that day. "They came wandering up mid-day, dirty as all get-out but none the worse for wear. No telling where they were holed up during the cyclone, but here they are. Billy said he'll help build a better shelter for them tomorrow."

"What a miracle." Rachel wandered down the steps, leaving Mattie standing happily under the porch roof. She gave the horses a cursory examination, whistling under her breath at their remarkable good health. They were munching on hay, and one of them nickered in welcome, lipping her hand as she held it out to stroke a velvet nose. "We'll be needing horses in the days to come. Lots of hauling to be done around here."

She finally turned back, joining Mattie on the porch, sitting down on the top step. Mattie snuggled up and pressed something into her hand. She rolled it in her fingers, then drew it under her nose, sniffing. "Cigar!" She laughed. "Where on earth did you find a dry one?"

"Had a few stowed in my carpetbag for a while now." She produced a match, striking it against the wooden porch support and holding it up as Rachel cupped her hand around the cigar, sucking at it and drawing in air as it lit up. Fragrant smoke curled up around them, and Rachel sat back, draping an arm across Mattie's shoulders and smiling with satisfaction as Mattie leaned against her.

"You are an angel." She drew heavily on the cigar, releasing a smoke ring, pleased when Mattie smiled. The smile gave way to giggles as Rachel's stomach growled.

"Oh." Mattie patted her belly. "I think we can remedy that. I believe supper should be just about ready for us, judging from the smell coming through that window there. You interested in some corn bread and chowder? I believe the boys have been fed. I heard Lillie shooing them up to bed while you were checking on the horses, so we should have some peace and quiet while we eat."

Rachel smoked in silence a minute more, then dropped the stub to the ground, rubbing it out with the toe of her boot. "Seems strange to be doing something so normal as eating a meal cooked in that kitchen, when last night I was swimming in it."

"Let's be thankful for the little bits of normal we get. I have a feeling they may be few and far between for a while." Mattie rubbed Rachel's leg, feeling the muscles flex under her fingers as the taller woman stood, holding out her hand to help Mattie up.

They drew together in another long hug, before leaving the darkness of the porch for the cheery lantern-lit kitchen.

A LIGHT BREEZE fluttered through the few palm trees that remained standing in the back yard after the storm. A solemn figure sat on the edge of the steps, hazel eyes gazing out at two mounds of relatively fresh soil at the back edge of the yard. They had buried Angel and Betsy in temporary graves two weeks before. The cemetery was decimated and in the chaos of disposing of the dead from the storm, they had decided it best to lay their friends to rest nearby until order could be restored to the rest of the island. They would be moved to proper graves with proper headstones once everything settled down.

Trolley cars were once again running, as were the trains, bringing much-needed food stores and building supplies to the industrious town-folk. All day long hammering and sawing could be heard across the island, especially in the downtown area, as merchants worked from dawn until dark to rebuild what they had lost.

Mr. and Mrs. Vaughan had miraculously survived the storm, and Mattie quietly went calling on them, filling them in on most of the details since her 'disappearance' from their employ over two months prior. She didn't tell of her relationship with Rachel, but did share of her impending motherhood, a little of her abuse at Adam's hands, and his demise. They quickly asked her to come back to work for them, as many people had lost all their clothing, and several had put in large orders at the tailor's shop for replacement wardrobe pieces.

It had been a difficult two weeks, fraught with heartsick emotion and bone-tiring work. One by one, they learned of the fate of many they knew, while many others were still unaccounted for. It was estimated that between six and ten thousand people had perished in a twenty-four-hour period.

Their house was fairly back in order inside, and Billy and Rachel had taken care of all necessary exterior repairs. There was still a fair amount of cosmetic work to be done on the house—repainting, most of all, but both Billy and Rachel needed to get back to the business of earning real wages. Many of the dockworkers had drowned in the storm, some on the very boats they owned and worked on. Mr. Avery, Rachel's boss, was gone, along with several of her and Billy's comrades.

Mattie drew her knees up closer to her body and wrapped her arms around her lower legs, resting her chin on one kneecap. Her belly was full of a tasty supper, and Rachel was inside taking her turn at scrubbing the dishes. Mattie was home from her first day at the tailor's shop, and was pleasantly tired, her fingers dry from work to which they were unaccustomed. She had a few needle pricks to show for her efforts, but overall, it had been a good day. Good to see life going on around her, and people managing to persevere despite loss and depression, and in some cases, sudden homelessness and poverty.

"Seems unreal, doesn't it?" A warm voice burred at her back as strong hands came to rest on her shoulders. Rachel leaned over and kissed her on the cheek, before sliding in next to her and sitting down. "You going to sit out here all night, or come back in and keep me company?"

"It does seem unreal." Mattie turned, gazing thoughtfully at her lover. "Sometimes I can't believe they're gone, just like that. It must have been horrible." Her forehead wrinkled. "That man and his family that came for the funeral — Jack — he made me a bit angry."

"How so?" Rachel reached across, smoothing away the frown.

"He seemed aloof, maybe ungrateful — almost like their sacrifice was nothing to him." She peered earnestly at Rachel. "It didn't anger you? He just stood off over to the side, and hardly said anything. Seemed like he just wanted to get away."

"Sweetheart." Rachel clasped Mattie's knee, squeezing it. "He was very conflicted, because he acted as a husband during that storm, but I think he feels he didn't act as a man."

"I don't understand."

"I think he probably feels that he should have died and let Angel and Betsy have his spot in that balcony."

"No one blames him, Rachel. Gracie said Angel and Betsy told him to go with his family." Her voice rose slightly, her ire still piqued. "Least he could've done was mourn them with the rest of us."

"Oh, Mattie." Rachel kissed her cheek again. "I think he was mourning them, and will most likely mourn them for the rest of his life. They gave him a second chance at being with his wife, and at seeing his girls grow up. He wasn't being disrespectful, he was simply ashamed. He saw our pain at losing them, and knew if not for him, they would maybe still be with us."

"Oh." Mattie thought about that. "I guess I can forgive him, then. It's just that they gave so much to us, you know?"

"Yes, they did, more than we could ever have repaid." Rachel draped an arm around Mattie's waist, hooking a thumb inside the waistband of her skirt. "They began their life together in the middle of a tragedy, and ended it together in the middle of another. In between they squeezed in a whole lot of happiness. Think we can follow their example?"

"I'd like to think we can." Mattie snuggled up closer, inhaling the scent of salt water and bay rum. She decided it was a scent she would like to end every day with. "How was your day?"

"More bodies washed ashore today." Rachel's voice was distant, her nose crinkling up in memory of the smell. "We should've thought twice about dumping them at sea. Mother ocean doesn't seem to want all our dead. She keeps sending them back."

"So you had to burn more?" Mattie's heart hurt for the families who still had not accounted for their missing loved ones. To the horror of the islanders, after the dead were given a massive funeral on the beach and burial at sea, bodies began washing back ashore, and the decision was made to burn them at large funeral pyres. It was the only solution, given the number of bodies to deal with and the limited amount of cemetery space.

"I am learning to loathe the smell of burning flesh, yes." Rachel grimaced. "But it has to be done if we are going to keep the dock area clear for rebuilding, and for boat traffic."

"I'm sorry, my love," Mattie crooned softly. "I can't imagine dealing with that. I'll be glad when you can concentrate on work you enjoy." She sniffed reflectively, twirling a finger in a lock of Rachel's hair. "Speaking of work that you love, how was your talk today with the bank? Did you have time to go see them?"

Rachel's eyes remained fixed forward, her throat working as she swallowed. Her eyes twinkled in the low dusky light, but a slight twitch in her jaw gave away her uncertainty. "They said if I want a loan to build or buy a boat, I can have it, on the condition I open an account with them. Government is offering subsidies to help folks get back on their feet, so I might not have to pay all of it back, or any of it back, depending on what they offer."

"And Billy?" Mattie dropped one arm from around her own legs, squeezing Rachel's thigh.

"He's talking to Lillie right now." She swallowed again, watching as two seagulls flew past over the newly-built barn and out toward the Gulf. A few stars were starting to appear in the night sky, and she heard crickets chirping in the grass that had begun to grow back in the ill-tended garden. They had lost their vegetable plants, and it was late in the year to try to replace them, so they had chosen to let it go until spring.

"And what about you?" Mattie nudged her lover.

"I'm talking to you right now." A smile played at Rachel's lips. "Billy or no Billy, I'm in this if you are, Mattie. If you're not, I'm just as much of a mind to do something else or go somewhere else."

"I think I would like to be a fisherman's wife." She sighed happily, feeling Rachel's cheek come to rest against the top of her head.

"What about that little house on the beach?" Rachel nuzzled her hair, enjoying a clean washed fragrance with just a hint of lilac.

"I think I'd like that, too, eventually, but this one is good for now. There's so much to think about, with the baby on the way, and the boys, and Lillie and Billy have been such a help to us. I think we should think of them, too, and see what their plans are." She closed her eyes as Rachel's exploration moved lower, giving an experimental lick to her earlobe and a tickling nibble to her neck.

"I think our loft is a very good place right now." Rachel's voice was right in her ear, sending a thrill through her body.

"Our loft would be a very good place right now. Oh..." she laughed as Rachel somehow got her arms beneath her, lifting her and walking back up the steps. "Please, Rachel. If Billy and Lillie see us."

"Went for a walk." Rachel kissed her soundly. "Wished me a good evening before they left."

"The boys?" Her body was quickly losing interest in anything but Rachel's kisses and the teasing fingers tickling the back of her thigh where Rachel held her.

"Already tucked in for the night." She kicked the screen door open, holding it with her toe as she backed in, then eased it closed so that it wouldn't slam and wake the boys.

It was amazing how easy it suddenly was to navigate the two flights of stairs after a hard day's work, despite Mattie's added weight, although she was lighter than a bail of cotton or some of the larger fish they'd caught. Rachel laughingly bounced Mattie in her arms as she crossed the bedroom threshold. She dropped her bundle on the bed, pulling her own clothing off before she crawled up, hovering over Mattie, her eyes shining as she delicately worked at the buttons on Mattie's shirtwaist.

Mattie sat up as Rachel slid the ruffled blouse off her shoulders, and pushed down her chemise underneath. As Rachel worked her way down, removing the rest of Mattie's clothing, she paused, kissing all around her belly, which was just starting to show a rounding fullness. Just as slowly, she worked her way back up, until she hovered over Mattie, her weight braced on her forearms.

Mattie could feel the power over her, Rachel's entire being vibrating with life. She reached up, squeezing both bulging biceps. She loved Rachel's body — its puzzle of almost-masculine muscles covered in a layer of smooth soft very feminine skin. She traced a line with her fingertip, brushing over a broad, tanned shoulder and down to a creamy white cleavage, then teasingly circled Rachel's breast, smiling as large blue eyes slammed shut and Rachel trembled slightly at her touch.

The steel blue eyes fluttered open, and Rachel smiled at her, then bit her own lower lip as Mattie continued to explore. This time she kept her eyes open, conveying wordless emotions to Mattie as the younger woman's fingertips danced over sensitive spots while her other hand came up, cupping Rachel's face. Rachel was wide open to her, her love for Mattie clearly visible in her eyes, and her desire unmistakable in her touch.

"You're beautiful," Mattie whispered, feeling the heat in her own flushed cheeks, and the rising craving in her body — a need to merge with her lover and celebrate the simple joy of survival.

Rachel turned her head, nibbling at Mattie's palm. Delicate fingers traced her lips and she kissed each finger in turn, feeling the delicious sensation as Mattie's touch seemed to reach her everywhere.

"I need you so much." She spoke softly, her eyes alight with desire.

Slowly, Mattie pulled Rachel down on top of her, hearing the hiss of pleasure as their bodies came into contact. Rachel ducked her head, finding Mattie's lips and kissing her slowly and thoroughly, as she lifted up just enough to brush her own skin full against Mattie's, groaning as Mattie slipped a knee between her legs. She felt Mattie's hands come to rest on her hips, guiding her as they moved together. "Show me life, Mattie."

Mattie reached up with one hand, grasping the back of her neck and pulling her face back down. "This is life, Rachel. Being with you like this." She kissed her passionately. "I love you."

"I love you too," Rachel gasped out, then abandoned herself to Mattie's gentle touch.

Much later, Mattie lay propped up slightly against two pillows, with Rachel resting in her embrace, a departure from their usual sleeping arrangement. Her head rested just above Mattie's stomach, where she was idly tracing circles with her fingertips. Her other arm was beneath Mattie's leg, her hand curled up and around an inner thigh, resting softly against warm soft skin. She felt Mattie's fingers, combing through her hair, which she had slowly unbraided while they made love.

It was comforting there, with her face so close to their unborn child, her hand so close to the source of Mattie's passion, and feeling Mattie's hands, the one playing with her hair and the other rubbing her back. "I want to stay right here forever."

"Oh, most certainly, right up until you smell cookies coming out of the oven downstairs, or you hear the fish are biting out in the Gulf," Mattie teased. She felt Rachel laughing silently, and she lightly trailed her fingernails along the back of Rachel's neck, watching in fascination as goose bumps rose up in her wake, all across the broad, tanned shoulders. "Does that feel nice?" She bent over, kissing a path behind her fingers, and heard a quiet mewling sound.

"Much more of that and I'm going to roll you over and ravish you again." Rachel rolled over onto her back, her head pillowed in Mattie's lap. She looked up, smiling as Mattie's hand dropped to her stomach, tracing the same random circles on Rachel's stomach she had just been tracing on Mattie's. "Every time you touch me, it feels nice." Long dark lashes blinked slowly over large vulnerable eyes. "More than nice."

"Truly?" Mattie was pleased, given away by a slight lilt in her voice. "I'm ever so glad, because I don't have words for how your touch makes me feel. I only know I could get lost in it and never wish to be found."

"All during that storm, two things kept me going — you and this little one you're carrying. All I could think about is that I wanted us to live — wanted to see this baby be born, and grow up, and then I want to sit on the porch swing with you somewhere when we're old, and rock and sip our tea while we watch the sun rise."

"And where do you want that swing to be?"

Rachel read her thoughts. "You want to come live with me in that little house on the beach?"

"I'd live with you in a boxcar on the railroad tracks, if you asked me to." Mattie smiled.

"Nah. I've lived in one of those for a while on the way down here. Too drafty." Rachel sat up, leaning in nose to nose with her lover, her weight braced on one arm. "What do you say, Mattie? I'll buy that fishing boat and we'll build us a house down on the Gulf side. I'll come home every night and we'll eat supper, and then me and you and this little one can go for a walk on the beach. Then we'll put her to bed and we'll sit on our porch and spoon until the moon rises."

"It sounds like a dream." Mattie kissed her lightly. It was too tempting, with Rachel's lips so close.

"I'll make it come true for you, Mattie. As best I can, I'll try to make all your dreams come true." She cradled the back of Mattie's neck, slipping her other arm around her waist and across her back.

"You already have." The room suddenly tilted, and Mattie found herself on her back as Rachel's hands began to wander over her skin. "What are you doing?"

Rachel smiled at her, her touch becoming much more insistent. "Helping you get lost."

"RACHEL," MATTIE WHISPERED softly into her lover's ear. "Rachel." She placed a light kiss on full lips, watching as relaxed features took on tone and expression. "Come with me, please."

"What?" Rachel blinked and looked toward the window, spying the dark blue sky of pre-dawn. "Come where?" She rolled over, resting her head on an upraised hand, and reaching out in instinct, tracing the curves of Mattie's face, which was mostly in shadow.

"Go for a walk with me? Just the two of us, please?"

"Walk?" Rachel frowned. "Before breakfast? Where are we going?"

Mattie sat up. "Please. We have to go down to the beach. Not real far."

Curiosity got the best of her, and Rachel rolled up, locating her boots. She tugged at the rawhide laces, pulling them tight and double-knotting them. "No telling what we might see, sweetheart. Bodies are still washing up every day. I don't want anything upsetting you."

"Rachel." Mattie knelt down, placing her hands on her lover's knees. "There won't be any sheltering me from this. Don't even try. Please, come with me, because I have to go down there and I want you there with me."

"I'm dressing as fast as I can." Rachel covered both of Mattie's hands, chafing them once before she stood, helping Mattie up with her. "Hey. You're already dressed." Now fully awake, she noted the trousers and man's shirt. "And ready for the road, I see." She found a smile.

Mattie tucked a hand in the crook of her elbow, dragging her toward the door. Rachel shook her head, but her lips twitched in amusement, nonetheless, in anticipation of whatever it was Mattie had in store.

They carefully descended the stairs all the way down to the first floor. It was still mostly dark, and they paused on the porch, looking up to see a navy blue sky and just a few remaining stars. All around them, most of the houses were still in shambles.

"This whole thing is surreal, isn't it? I don't feel quite myself, almost as if I'm standing outside looking over some strange dream." Mattie shook her head, her shoulders slumping in sadness. "I need to find a place that feels normal. That's why I needed to go for this walk. Come on." She led on, out of the yard and down a path that roughly followed what used to be an alley between houses.

Mattie's eyes were thoughtful, catching the first rays of dawn. "I know you must think I'm crazy, but I just have to see the beach. We haven't been down there since before the storm." She drew in a breath of fresh salt-tinged air as her first view of the Gulf came into sight.

"I don't think you're crazy, I think you're beautiful, and carrying a baby I can't wait to meet. Speaking of carrying..." Rachel suddenly scooped her up, carrying her the last block of their walk, as Mattie giggled, pretending to struggle for a few steps before she finally settled into Rachel's arms, enjoying the ride. "Still light as a feather. Any place on this here beach you want to go in particular?"

They reached the sand, which was packed flat, the sand dunes washed away in the flooding. "No landmarks, are there?" Mattie looked around as pale gold light began to paint the sand at their feet. "They're all gone."

"Afraid so." Rachel spied the remains of an overturned boat several yards down, and began walking toward it. "Is this a good spot for what you had in mind?"

"It'll do." Mattie felt herself deposited on the sand, her booted feet hitting it with a wet thunk. "Sit with me, please?"

They rested against the boat's hull, as Mattie settled into the curve of the arm Rachel offered her. "You want to tell me why we're here?"

"Shhh." Mattie touched a finger to Rachel's lips. "Close your eyes and listen. And smell."

Rachel complied, blocking out the rolling waves and cloudy sky. The roar of water filled her senses, waves crashing ashore near them. She could just make out the sizzling foamy sound as they broke up and ran way up the sand, and the slight trickling suctiony sound as they washed back out to sea. A gentle steady wind sifted through her hair, and brushed the fine hairs on her arms, tickling across her skin.

She drew fresh, salty air into her lungs, tainted by the scent of leftover rain. The wooden scent of the boat drifted up around her, along with a hint of soap from Mattie's freshly-washed face. With her eyes still closed, she buried her face into Mattie's hair, allowing just that scent alone to completely overtake everything else. She felt Mattie relax against her, her head against Rachel's shoulder, and she laughed quietly as Mattie found a bare spot of skin just below her ear to nibble at. "Mmm." She inhaled. "You smell good. And that feels very nice."

The nibbles traveled up as Mattie explored further, nipping at an earlobe. "What do you hear?"

"The ocean, mostly." Rachel tried to focus her concentration outward. "And your breathing. Otherwise, it sounds just like it always has. Am I listening for anything in particular?"

"No." Mattie ceased her nibbles and simply rested against Rachel's body, feeling the rise and fall of her lungs as Rachel breathed. She placed one hand against her left ribcage, smiling as she found the steady heartbeat there. "Now, open your eyes."

The steel blue orbs fluttered open and Rachel blinked, feeling the warmth of the sun begin to hit her face. Out to sea, it was mostly cloudy, though the rays of the sun fought valiantly, breaking through in an arc of light out over the water, fanning across the horizon in alternating stripes of pink and gray below billowing white and dark clouds. Way up above the clouds, clear blue sky began to peek through, promising a new day, just like every other morning. "It's beautiful," Rachel whispered.

"You were correct, that night of the storm. I just had to come out here and see it for myself." Mattie rubbed Rachel's belly, then squeezed her thigh. "The sun will surely rise, and life is going to go on. Our whole world may be upside down, Rachel, and people we care about are dead, but out here, we can still see a part of our world that stayed the same." She turned, taking both of Rachel's hands in her own. "There are so many things I'm not sure of. What kind of mother I'll be. Where we're going to be living—how we'll earn our keep in the days to come. But three things I'm certain of are right here with me on this beach."

"Yeah?" Rachel was getting lost in earnest hazel eyes, feeling the warmth and the connection between them. She shook her head, focusing in on her lover. "And what are those three things?"

"That ocean out there is going to keep rolling ashore, come rain or come shine. And that sun up there, it will eventually rise, just like you said it would. And this." She placed her hand over Rachel's heart, feeling Rachel's larger hand curl around it. "What we share between us. Everything else might be swept away, but the one thing I know is this love we share—it can withstand any storm."

There would be more tragedy to face in the months ahead, as the death tolls mounted, and hours of bone-weary work lay ahead, but it couldn't touch this one golden moment, sitting there on the beach as the sun rose and a few brave sea gulls flew overhead. There were no more words for what they were feeling, as Rachel drew Mattie to her in a warm solid hug. She kissed the top of Mattie's head tangling her fingers in thick red waves as they rocked back and forth slightly. "I love you," she whispered, finding Mattie's lips as they gratefully welcomed a brand new day.

Epilogue

April 1901

A SHINY BLACK bicycle sped around the corner onto Broadway, and down a low-grade hill, dodging pedestrians and buggies, and bumping precariously over clumps of sandy soil in the middle of the packed dirt street. Rachel was glad she'd chosen the bicycle over the wagon that morning, as it would have taken extra time to go to the livery stables and hitch up the horses. As her legs worked furiously, her mind ran even faster ahead of her, wondering how Mattie was doing and what she might be able to do to help out in the coming hours. She blinked as a spattering of rain hit her face.

The fat, heavy drops fell slowly for a few minutes, then picked up speed, and suddenly the sky split open with a loud crack of thunder and the heavens poured down on her, quickly soaking the streets and forming puddles she dodged between as she made her way ever closer to the house. The rain was refreshing at first, washing away the last traces of fish from her skin and clothing, but soon she was shivering, her teeth chattering as the temperature dropped ten degrees in rapid time. She was grateful when she finally turned the corner and made her way to a small house on stilts on the beach.

She smiled at the cheery cottage, which had been built a few months after the cyclone, along with several other similar small homes that dotted the beach, all of them perched on thick, heavy columns that were pounded deep into the ground. Billy and Lillie had gotten married, and their new house was a short buggy-ride away, where they lived with the three boys. The friendship between the two couples continued to flourish. Rachel and Mattie bought the house and moved into it only a few months before, after selling Angel and Betsy's house for a tidy sum that left them with money in the bank, even after purchasing the new home.

Neither woman had realized the old house was making them glum until they left it. Although their life together had started there, the ghosts of friends were around every corner, and the memories were sometimes too painful to bear. Besides, both women felt it was much too big a house to take care of. In the new house, on the beach and away from the ongoing saga of rebuilding in town, a measure of good humor had returned to both women, and Mattie's last few months of pregnancy had been marked by contentment, as she happily prepared the nursery next to their bedroom.

Rachel jumped off the bicycle and stowed it under the house. She made a quick run back to the barn to check on the horses, then trotted toward the house, taking the long set of stairs up to the front deck two at a time. She flung the door open, and heard two female voices drifting in from the cozy back bedroom.

"Mattie?" She poked her head around the doorframe, spotting her lover propped up against a pile of pillows on the bed. A sheen of sweat shone on her forehead, and her hair was plastered back off her face. Lillie sat in a chair next to the bed, sponging up cool water she dabbed about Mattie's face and neck.

"Come on in, sugar, and take over here, while I go get Dr. Mills." Lillie stood, only to be stopped by a hard tug at her skirt.

"No Dr. Mills." Mattie's voice was hoarse, and she grimaced as another contraction rolled through her body. "Ouch." Her eyes scrunched closed for a moment before she opened them and drew in a deep breath. "That one was bad."

"Sugar, I thought you wanted the doctor here." Lillie placed her hands on her hips, fretting as she moved aside to allow Rachel to sit down.

"Hello, sweetheart." She took Mattie's hand, squeezing it gently. "I have a feeling you were already in labor when I left for the boat this morning, weren't you?"

"Yes." Mattie smiled sheepishly. "Figured there was no sense in worrying you when it might be hours. The pains actually started up right after we went to bed last night."

"That long?" Rachel frowned. "That's been over twelve hours, Mattie. You must be getting pretty close to having this baby."

"She is," Lillie interjected. "That's why we need to go get Dr. Mills now, before it's too late."

"No," Mattie reiterated. "You've both delivered babies. You told me so. I don't want him here. You two can do this. I know you can. Oh," she hissed, as another contraction made her rise up from the pillows a bit, her body contorting from the pain.

"Why?" Rachel waited for the pain to pass, then bent over, kissing a damp forehead.

"I don't want to have to hide how I feel about you, when this baby gets here." Mattie's eyes glistened with tears. "I want to share this with you as your wife, not as your friend."

"Oh." Rachel felt warm all over, as her lover's words soaked in. She glanced at Lillie. "What do you think?"

"I think I'd best go boil some water, and make sure we have a sharp knife for the cord." She winked at Rachel. "I'm willing to do this together, if you are."

"I am." Rachel smiled at Mattie. "What can I do?"

"Get some towels under her." Lillie tossed a pile of them in her direction. "And get her out of all her clothing, except her nightgown. That skirt and petticoat have got to go. I'll be back." She disappeared from the room, and Rachel heard the sound of water running into a metal pan.

"Mattie, let's get you settled here, shall we, sweetheart?" She bit her lower lip as Mattie gripped a handful of blanket, while she rode out another contraction.

"I think it's pretty close." She watched as Rachel pulled the covers back and carefully tucked the towels under her, moved further up, and began unbuttoning Mattie's blouse. "You're all wet." Mattie smiled. "I heard the rain when it started. Sounds pretty heavy now." She looked at the window, where sheets of rain lashed at the glass, driven by a whistling wind.

"It is." Rachel helped her sit up enough to wriggle out of her blouse and skirt, along with her petticoat and chemise. Her drawers were already off, as she had removed them when her water broke. "Wish you would've said something this morning, Mattie. I would have stayed here and not gone out today."

"Was it a good morning of fishing?" Mattie's jaw clamped down as pain gripped at her body.

"Yes, it was." Rachel found a large, comfy nightgown in a dresser drawer and moved toward the bed, intent on helping Mattie put it on.

"No." Mattie almost growled. "I'm hot. The air feels good on my skin. Just pull the sheet over me, please. I don't think I could bear clothing right now."

"Whatever makes you comfortable, sweetheart." Rachel complied, pulling the soft white cotton over Mattie's flushed body, before she sat down on the chair, unconsciously swiping wet bangs off her face.

"I'm glad you had a good day of fishing, and weren't here worrying all morning." Mattie reached across, tracing a rather sensitive spot, smiling as Rachel jumped at the unexpected touch. "Besides, seeing you all wet in that see-through undershirt takes my mind off the pain."

"Oh." Rachel blushed and looked down, finally noticing the translucent cotton plastered against her chest. Goose bumps danced across her skin and Mattie's fingers traced a pattern up her forearm.

"You're cold, though. Maybe you should change." She lifted Rachel's hand and brought it to her lips, kissing it. "I'm glad you're here now."

"Me, too." Rachel stood. "You sure about changing? Wouldn't want to take away your entertainment." She flashed a cheeky grin.

"I'll live," Mattie grunted, trying to ignore another shot of pain through her lower back and legs.

Rachel quickly located dry clothing, and made her way back to the bedside. "Mattie, I need to check you, see how things are going down there. I remember that much from my mother all those times. Is it all right if I..."

"Go on." Mattie lifted the sheet. "I seem to have lost all modesty in the past few hours."

Rachel kissed her forehead again, then gingerly pulled the sheet the rest of the way down, studying Mattie's condition in the light of the lamp on the bedside table. "Oh." Her eyes grew wide. "I think I see the top of its head here, just a little bit." She glanced up at Mattie's incredulous face. "You're hiding some of the pain, aren't you?"

"Best I can." Mattie gritted her teeth and then gasped. "Getting difficult, though."

"Let it out. Scream if you need to. It's just me and Lil, and lord knows we've heard women give birth before. You're one of the most cheerful women I've ever been around in your condition." She put the sheet back down. "Let me just go tell Lil about seeing the head, and I'll be right back."

Mattie nodded, her face contorted in pain. Rachel frowned and slipped out of the bedroom, ducking around the corner into a small but functional kitchen.

Rachel glanced over her shoulder. "Lil, I can see the head."

"Oh my goodness." Lillie put down a large knife. "Check to make sure it's face down. You know what you have to do, don't you?"

Rachel nodded. "She's pretty close, I think."

"She is," Lillie agreed. "If the baby's face down, you go ahead and call me in there after it gets here."

"But..." Rachel's mouth flew open in protest.

"Rachel," Lillie patted her on the arm, "this time is for you and Mattie. She's been fine so far. Go on in there and deliver your child. I'll be right here if you need me."

The rain beat down overhead and time stood still for a long moment. Rachel looked up at the ceiling and pursed her lips, gathering her courage. She thought about her mother and her youngest sister, and her mother's cries of agony as the baby ripped through her body. She shivered, then pushed the fear aside as a low groan from the bedroom brought her back to the present. Mattie was in pain, but showed no signs of the extreme distress her mother had suffered. "All right." She nodded meekly. "Have that water and knife ready, Lil."

"Rachel!" Mattie's voice called out from the bedroom. "When are you coming back in here?"

"Oh, Lil. Stay close by. I need to get back in there." Rachel slipped around the corner and back into the bedroom, where Mattie had flung off the sheet and had her heels dug into the mattress, her breathing coming in short puffs of air as she suffered the largest contraction yet. "Hurts," she cried out, as she dropped back against the pillows. "It hurts, Rachel."

"I know," Rachel cooed at her. "I need to do something that is going to make it hurt a little bit more for a minute."

"What?" Mattie's eyes snapped in painful anger, and she dug her nails into Rachel's arm. "I had no idea you were a sadist."

Rachel suppressed a smile. "I'm not. I need to make sure this baby is in the right direction."

"It's coming out. There is no other direction." Mattie moaned as she saw stars from yet more pain.

This time a chuckle escaped, though Rachel managed to turn it into a cough. "It has to be face down, just let me..." She sat down, warily approaching Mattie's female parts. She slipped a finger inside and underneath the baby's head, carefully sliding in until she located what felt to be a nose.

"*Oooh.* Rachel. Please." Mattie sobbed. "Nothing else can fit in there right now. Trust me."

"I know." Rachel withdrew her finger. "This baby is in perfect position. All you have to do now is push down each time you feel the pains, Mattie."

"Easy for you to say." She drew her knees up and arched upward, pushing hard as the next contraction hit. "Oh. It's tearing me up. I can feel it."

"Shhh." Rachel looked carefully at Mattie's body and smiled. "No tearing, sweetheart. But we do have most of the top of a head. Come on, push hard. It will be over soon."

"*Ohhh!*" Mattie's voice rang out across the room, as she pushed again. "Rachel. It hurts so much."

Rachel sat on the edge of the bed now, next to Mattie, where she could see what was happening and still make eye contact with her lover. "Oh." She smiled. "We have the head. Just a few more pushes. Come on." She placed a supportive hand under the baby's head, while she felt Mattie grab her other one, squeezing it with all her might. She squeezed back, watching in fascination as Mattie's body came almost all the way off the bed.

"*Rachel!*" Mattie screamed, as thunder rolled across the island, rattling the roof overhead. Lightning crashed out over the water, and the rain poured down. She felt a great ripping and tearing, and she pushed with all her might, screaming again as the baby slipped out of her, landing in Rachel's arms.

"Oh!" Rachel cradled the small body, peering in wonder at its red face. Two tiny fists curled up, and a small mouth opened, releasing a wail so loud, it startled her. "Whoa." Her eyebrows shot up. "Healthy lungs, most certainly."

"Rachel?" Mattie's voice was weak but insistent. "What is it?"

Rachel looked carefully at the small bundle of warm, wet,

wriggling baby, and smiled, leaning over and placing the baby on Mattie's chest. "She's a girl, just like you said she would be."

"A girl?" Mattie smiled through her tears. "We have a girl. Oh." She gasped in pain as the afterbirth left her. "Oh, that felt queer. I forgot about that part." She focused on the baby, counting ten fingers and ten tiny toes. "Happy birthday, Rebecca Evangeline Travis."

"Ladies, may I cut that cord now?" Lillie tiptoed into the room and made quick work of her task. "May I?" She gently picked up the baby, wiping her down with some warm wet towels, then wrapped her up in a small fluffy blanket before handing her over to Rachel. "Here's your daughter, Rachel Travis."

Rachel studied the baby in wonder, noting a cap of bright red hair on its head. "She's got your hair," she smiled, sitting down on the bed next to Mattie, who had hitched herself up to a halfway sitting position. Lillie quietly removed the soiled towels and helped Mattie get cleaned up. "No tearing, Mattie. You did real good, sugar, especially for your first baby." She helped Mattie put on a nightgown, leaving the laces undone. "You might want to see if she's hungry. I'll leave you two be, for a while, and go clean up the kitchen."

"Thank you, Lillie," Mattie called after her. She pulled her nightgown aside and eased the baby over, offering it one of her breasts. With a bit of prompting, Rebecca latched onto a nipple and suckled for a few moments, her little cheeks visibly moving as it took in Mattie's nourishment. "Oh." Mattie winced. "That is going to take some getting used to."

One small eye blinked open, and then the other, as Rebecca took in her first sight of the world. She released Mattie's breast, blinking in the low light of the weather-darkened room. "How about that?" Rachel had joined her lover, sitting next to her as Rebecca seemed to look up at her. "She's got nice dark blue eyes, doesn't she?"

"Yes, she does." Mattie swallowed. She looked up, cupping Rachel's face with her free hand. "Just like yours."

Rachel looked down, saying nothing. She felt gentle fingertips trace her cheeks. "No one in my family or Adam's has blue eyes, Rachel. My family is all browns and hazels, and his was all dark brown, almost black." She felt Rachel quit breathing for a moment, before the steel eyes hesitantly looked back at her. "It's a gift, Rachel. She has your eyes."

"Mine?" Rachel watched as those small eyes tried to focus on her. "Hello there, Rebecca." She smiled. "I'm your other mother." She held out her hand, as a small fist curled around her finger. "What a grip you have, little one." Fresh tears tracked down her cheeks, and her lips quivered as Mattie's fingers swiped the wetness away.

"How are you, my love?" She stroked Mattie's still-damp head. "You did such a good job."

"I feel fine." Mattie patted the space next to her. "Tired and very sore, but fine. I think I need a little nap. Rest here, with us?"

Rachel shucked her trousers, crawling under the cover clad in her undershirt and drawers. She stretched out next to Mattie, smiling as Mattie curled up against her, with the baby resting between them. "She's perfect, isn't she?"

"Yes, she is." Rebecca hiccupped a few bubbles as she fussed, until Mattie turned her over and rubbed her back until she let out a tiny burp. "That's our girl." Mattie shifted until Rebecca was once again resting against their joined bodies. Mattie's eyes blinked sleepily, matched by small blue ones, and soon both mother and baby were sound asleep, wrapped in Rachel's protective embrace.

Rachel looked down, gently kissing Rebecca's cheek, and then Mattie's, feeling both of them stir slightly at her touch. Mattie's lips curled into a sleepy smile and she nestled closer to Rachel. Steel eyes looked up overhead, then out at the rain, which was no longer raging, but had trickled down to a light sprinkle. "Seems we'll always be facing storms," she mused. "But out of the storms, we're always given a blessing." She settled back to rest, but not to sleep. Life was much too exciting at present to miss a single minute. "My family." She held Mattie and Rebecca close, feeling both warm bodies breathing against her. "A year ago I could never have conceived of so great a gift."

Outside, the sun broke through the clouds, and a full rainbow arched across the sky out over the Gulf. The bright colors dazzled Rachel's eyes, as she looked out the window for a long while. With a smile, she turned away from it, gazing back down, keeping watch over her family as they slept.

THE END

Bibliography

Bettmann, Otto L. *The Good Old Days -- They Were Terrible!*
    New York: Random House, Inc., 1974.

Cartwright, Gary. *Galveston A History of the Island.*
    Fort Worth: TCU Press, 1998.

Drago, Gail. *Galveston.*
    Houston: Lone Star Books, a division of Gulf Publishing
Company, 1999.

Galveston County Daily News website. *The 1900 Storm.*
    http://www.1900storm.com

The History Channel. *Isaac's Storm.*
    Docudrama based on the book by Erik Larson, 2004.

Israel, Fred L., ed. *1897 Sears, Roebuck & Co. Catalogue.*
    Philadelphia: Chelsea House Publishers, 1993

McCutcheon, Marc. *Everyday Life in the 1800's.*
    Cincinnati: Writer's Digest Books, 1993.

National Oceanic and Atmospheric Administration website.
    http://www.noaa.gov.

Timeandate.com website.
    http://www.timeanddate.com

The Weather Channel. Various televised storm-related
productions.
    http://www.weather.com

FORTHCOMING TITLES

published by
Yellow Rose Books

Dark Dreamer
(Heartstoppers Series)

by Jennifer Fulton

"Jennifer Fulton has rescued the romance from formulaic complacency by asking universal questions about friendship and love, intimacy and lust."
The Lesbian Review of Books

Best-selling horror author, Rowe Devlin has had two flops in a row and keeps falling in love with straight women. Seeking inspiration and a fresh start, she abandons life in Manhattan for an old Victorian house in Maine. But Dark Harbor Cottage is a far cry from the tranquil writing environment she envisioned. For a start, the place is haunted and the ghost is none too friendly. To make life even more difficult, her neighbors are a huge distraction. The Temple twins, Phoebe and Cara, are identical and profoundly alluring, and Rowe is soon under their spell, unable to decide which of the two she is more in love with. Just when it seems things can't get any worse, she finds herself embroiled in a mystery more bizarre and frightening than anything she's ever written.

Intrigue, passion and suspense combine in this taut paranormal thriller/romance, the first in Jennifer Fulton's new *Heartstoppers* series.

INFINITE LOOP
by Meghan O'Brien

When shy software developer, Regan O'Riley is dragged into a straight bar by her workmates, the last person she expects to meet is the woman of her dreams. Off-duty cop, Mel Raines is tall, dark and gorgeous but has no plans to enter a committed relationship any time soon. Despite their differing agendas, Mel and Regan can't deny an instant, overwhelming attraction. Both their lives are about to change drastically, when a tragedy forces Mel to rethink her emotional isolation and face inner demons rooted in her past. She cannot make this journey alone, and Regan's decision to share it with her has consequences neither woman expects. More than an erotic road novel, *Infinite Loop* explores the choices we make, the families we build, and the power of love to transform lives.

CURVE
by Carrie Brennan

A lawyer and a cop? Not the most likely pair, but then isn't that what makes life — and love — interesting? Anne Doyle is a successful lawyer who has it made, just as long as she doesn't think too much about her past. Maggie Monahan is a tough-talking bike patrol cop who can face down a criminal...but not her family. When these two run into one another, more than their world views collide. Will the roadblocks of Anne's past and Maggie's future prove too much for them, or will they find a way to take life's journey together?

Other YELLOW ROSE Publications

Georgia Beers	Turning The Page	1-930928-51-3	$ 16.99
Georgia Beers	Thy Neighbor's Wife	1-932300-15-5	$ 13.95
Carrie Brennan	Curve	1-932300-41-4	$ 16.95
Carrie Carr	Destiny's Bridge	1-932300-11-2	$ 13.95
Carrie Carr	Faith's Crossing	1-932300-12-0	$ 13.95
Carrie Carr	Hope's Path	1-932300-40-6	$ 17.95
Carrie Carr	Love's Journey	1-930928-67-X	$ 18.99
Carrie Carr	Strength of the Heart	1-930928-75-0	$17.95
Jessica Casavant	Twist of Fate	1-932300-07-4	$ 12.95
Jessica Casavant	Walking Wounded	1-932300-20-1	$ 13.95
Jessica Casavant	Imperfect Past	1-932300-34-1	$ 16.95
Jennifer Fulton	Passion Bay	1-932300-25-2	$ 14.95
Jennifer Fulton	Saving Grace	1-932300-26-0	$ 15.95
Jennifer Fulton	The Sacred Shore	1-932300-35-X	$ 15.95
Jennifer Fulton	A Guarded Heart	1-932300-37-6	$ 16.95
Anna Furtado	The Heart's Desire	1-932300-32-5	$ 15.95
Gabrielle Goldsby	The Caretaker's Daughter	1-932300-18-X	$ 15.95
Maya Indigal	Until Soon	1-932300-31-7	$ 19.95
Lori L. Lake	Different Dress	1-932300-08-2	$ 19.95
Lori L. Lake	Ricochet In Time	1-932300-17-1	$ 18.95
Meghan O'Brien	Infinite Loop	1-932300-42-2	$ 18.95
Sharon Smith	Into The Dark	1-932300-38-4	$ 17.95
Cate Swannell	Heart's Passage	1-932300-09-0	$ 17.95
Cate Swannell	No Ocean Deep	1-932300-36-8	$ 18.95
L. A. Tucker	The Light Fantastic	1-932300-14-7	$ 24.95

Linda Crist was born and raised in Dallas, Texas, has also lived in Nacogdoches, Port Aransas, and Austin, and is back in Dallas, where she lives with two spoiled rotten cats. She has been a Paralegal for over 15 years, and prior to that was an editor at the *Dallas Times Herald*. Her previously-published novel, *The Bluest Eyes in Texas*, made the Open Book's top ten best-selling list for 2002, and spent several months on the top twenty list at Libertas in the U.K. She has also published short stories in two charity anthologies, *At First Blush*, and *Telltale Kisses*, and has won numerous on-line writing awards.

Linda has a Journalism degree from the University of Texas at Austin, where she was awarded a scholarship position working with the Lady Longhorns sports information office. She began writing while in preschool, drawing picture stories on the bulletin during church. She is on the Orlando BardCon staff, and has written two episodes for the Xena Subtext Virtual Season. When she's not working her day job or writing, she enjoys scuba diving, hiking, camping, golf, sailing, snow skiing, biking, traveling, reading, sketching, photography, and making music videos.